Sophocles and the Language of Tragedy

Onassis Series in Hellenic Culture

The Age of Titans: The Rise and Fall of the Great Hellenistic Navies
  William M. Murray

Sophocles and the Language of Tragedy
  Simon Goldhill

Onassis
Foundation (USA)

Sophocles and the Language of Tragedy

Simon Goldhill

OXFORD
UNIVERSITY PRESS

OXFORD
UNIVERSITY PRESS

Oxford University Press, Inc., publishes works that further
Oxford University's objective of excellence
in research, scholarship, and education.

Oxford   New York
Auckland   Cape Town   Dar es Salaam   Hong Kong   Karachi
Kuala Lumpur   Madrid   Melbourne   Mexico City   Nairobi
New Delhi   Shanghai   Taipei   Toronto

With offices in
Argentina   Austria   Brazil   Chile   Czech Republic   France   Greece
Guatemala   Hungary   Italy   Japan   Poland   Portugal   Singapore
South Korea   Switzerland   Thailand   Turkey   Ukraine   Vietnam

Copyright © 2012 by Oxford University Press, Inc.

Published by Oxford University Press, Inc.
198 Madison Avenue, New York, New York 10016

www.oup.com

Oxford is a registered trademark of Oxford University Press

Library of Congress Cataloging-in-Publication Data
Goldhill, Simon.
Sophocles and the language of tragedy / Simon Goldhill.
p. cm. — (The Onassis series in Hellenic culture)
Includes bibliographical references.
ISBN 978-0-19-979627-4
1. Sophocles—Language. 2. Sophocles—Appreciation.
3. Sophocles—Criticism and interpretation—History.
4. Tragedy. 5. Tragic, The. I. Title.
PA4417.G65   2012
882'.01—dc23   2011023273

1 3 5 7 9 8 6 4 2

Printed in the United States of America
on acid-free paper

CONTENTS

Sophocles and the Language of Tragedy

Introduction

You could describe this book both as profoundly conservative and as rashly revolutionary – or as rashly conservative and profoundly revolutionary . . .

It is conservative in that it takes one of the grandest of all dead white males, Sophocles, and investigates the most canonical of works from the most canonical of genres, Greek tragedy – and does so by looking at some of the most time-honoured categories of analysis, which I am happy to call formalist. Under the general rubric of Sophocles' language, its chapters treat the use of irony, the use of silent characters on stage, the use of *stichomythia* (dialogue of single line exchanges), the use of lyric metre, and the role of the chorus. There is a history of criticism on each of these topics stretching back to antiquity. What's more, the second half of the book continues with some more grand figures – the mavens of German idealism, the celebrities of classical scholarship in the heyday of Victorian Britain, the luminaries of feminist criticism – to see how tragedy has become the canonical genre it is for modern criticism, how the chorus relates to the highest levels of philosophy as well as to the modern stage of opera and theatre – how, in short, tragedy became the most privileged genre of the privileged sphere of classical antiquity for the elite of the European empires of the nineteenth and twentieth centuries. Formalist literary criticism and the high classical tradition: what could be more familiar and more intimately embedded in the institutional and intellectual conservatism of scholarship?

How then can it claim to be revolutionary? It would be easy enough to point out that the return to form is right at the cutting edge of contemporary criticism in classics and elsewhere, and that the treatment of each of the topics – from irony to reception – is an attempt to take forward an already heated current debate into new territory (as we will see, shortly). But for me the revolutionary aspect of this book is in its structure, and the argument this structure embodies and speaks to. Let me try to explain.

There have been in recent years many fine books on Sophocles, from which I, like all scholars of ancient tragedy, have learnt profusely. These have generally treated the corpus, play by play, according to particular themes and interests: every modern bibliography worth its salt duly and correctly cites Bernard Knox, Reg Winnington-Ingram, Charlie Segal, Mary Whitlock Blundell (who is now Ruby Blondel), Pat Easterling; or, from a slightly earlier era, but still hugely influential, Karl Reinhardt, Cedric Whitman, Maurice Bowra. Behind these books – and one could, of course, add others to this inevitably invidious roll call – lies a vast agricultural territory of articles, commentaries and handbooks, supporting what has grown into the industry of criticism of tragedy.[1]

At the same time, however, particularly in the last twenty years, there has been a flourishing debate about reception theory and the classics – with a string of notable books especially on tragedy and modern performance or on how particular plays have had a lasting influence through their appropriation by modern Western culture. Both the theory of *Rezeptionsgeschichte* (the history of reception) and the historical work of uncovering the shape and meaning of particular stagings of ancient theatre have led us increasingly to view ancient drama through historical and historicizing lenses.[2]

Yet to a surprising and remarkably blinkered degree these two strands of work have continued without significant interaction. So – to take two seminal and, to my mind, outstanding studies as my examples – George Steiner's ground-breaking study of how *Antigone* has been read over time, especially in post-Enlightenment Europe, only very rarely actually engages with the Greek of Sophocles' play to see how his deep historical understanding might change our reading of the text, just as he resists engagement with contemporary critical understanding of the texts of tragedy.[3] From another angle, Charlie Segal's long and detailed investigation of the texts of Sophocles proved to be one of the most influential studies of what has become the dominant contemporary critical tradition; yet for all Segal's extensive and incisive critical reading, his book barely looks forward to see how his understanding relates to – or is informed by – the long history of criticism that Steiner outlines.[4] Both books are exceptional: but their projects proceed with barely a glance at each other. And in this they are exemplary.

This book sets out to do three things. First, it aims to make a contribution to the project of Sophoclean criticism by looking at Sophoclean language. I

---

[1] I have had my go at describing the state of play in the introduction to Goldhill and Hall (2009); see Knox (1964); Winnington-Ingram (1980); Segal (1981); Whitlock Blundell (1989); Easterling ed (1997); Reinhardt (1979); Bowra (1944); Whitman (1951).

[2] See, for example, Steiner (1984); Flashar (1991); Hall, Macintosh and Taplin eds (2000); Goldhill (2002); Hall, Macintosh and Wrigley eds (2004); Hall and Macintosh (2005); Ewans (2007); Brown and Ograjensek eds (2010); Foster (2010); Foley (forthcoming); and more generally Martindale (1993), (2005); Martindale and Thomas eds (2006); Zajko and Leonard eds (2006).

[3] Steiner (1984).

[4] Segal (1981).

have spent several decades reading Sophocles, but this book emerges now in part because of an intense period of five years teaching the plays to talented graduate classes, especially at Princeton, and to undergraduates at Cambridge. Trying to share my wonder at Sophoclean dramatic poetry led me to an even deeper pleasure in his language and a greater desire to explore it through its formal qualities.[5] Second, the book aims to contribute to the project of the reception of Sophoclean drama by looking at how the language of tragedy – the language by which we approach, describe, understand tragedy – has defined the genre for modernity in criticism and in performance. Again, my critical engagement with the tradition of the performance of Sophocles goes back a long way, most notably in the long chapter on Strauss' *Elektra* in my earlier book, *Who Needs Greek?*[6] But, as will be clear, this book is also the result of a five-year project funded by the Leverhulme Trust on Victorian culture, during which, as a director, I have learnt a huge amount from my colleagues.[7] I have become increasingly convinced of the importance of understanding our modern engagement with nineteenth-century criticism and its twentieth-century heirs to appreciate our twenty-first-century preoccupations. Third – and here's the rub – I want finally to see if the two projects can interrelate. Can we bring together a detailed appreciation of the dramatic poetry of Sophocles and a historical understanding of how Sophocles has been read in different times and places?

This has turned out to be far more difficult than I had originally hoped. The structure of this book, with its first half on Sophoclean language and its second on reception and its theoretical implications, is novel in itself, especially for ancient tragedy. (I can think of no other book that tries this extended balancing act, although there are, of course, a handful of volumes on tragedy which end with a brief section on reception.) The book's structure sets out – instantiates – the question of *how historical* an engagement with Sophocles is or must be. This structure is an attempt to lay out what I believe to be the most pressing question facing classics as a discipline today: the tension between historical self-consciousness and the values invested in classical texts. This is a question which goes to the heart of the status and authority of the field of classics itself in this era of post-colonial, post-imperial studies, world literature, and other modern polemics about the ideology of the canon. I wish I could say I had found a solution to this tension, some panacea for the anxieties of modernity. It may be, however, that by the end what we will have is no more than a clearer appreciation of the depth and complexity of the problem – and what

---

[5] This project is more in line with a work such as Budelmann (2000) than Long (1968).

[6] Goldhill (2002) 108–77.

[7] "Abandoning the Past: Past versus Present in Victorian Britain": my fellow directors are Mary Beard, Clare Pettitt, Jim Secord and Peter Mandler: see Goldhill (2011).

I hope is a good journey on the way to the final *aporia*. "*And yet* we do not know . . .", as Plato's *Lysis* concludes.

I am not going to offer detailed summaries of the chapters here (always a waste of the space of an introduction, I think), but I would like to stress how the topics have come to be chosen, and some of the ways in which the interconnections between the two sections of the book advance the argument overall.

The first five chapters constitute an account of what I think could not reasonably be left out of a description of Sophocles and the language of tragedy. So the first chapter takes on that hoariest of topics, irony and the reversals of narrative, to discuss how the audience reads the flickering instabilities of Sophoclean expression. Tragic irony has been a staple of the literary criticism of tragedy since the nineteenth century and, as the coda will show, *only* since the nineteenth century; this chapter hopes to take this debate forward by moving away from the model of irony that stresses the reader's or audience's superiority to the actors on stage, and to investigate rather how the security or stability of knowledge of the reader or audience is set at stake. The second chapter starts from the commonplace that Sophocles introduced the third actor, and looks at how an audience is constructed on stage, watching, listening, judging – and the implications of this for the audience in the theatre. If the first chapter is focused on over- and under-reading, the second looks at the role of silence on stage – how silent or reactive audiences on stage become a model for the audience in the theatre: reading between the lines, as it were. These first two chapters are linked thus around the question of how the language of Sophocles' drama engages his theatrical audience. The third chapter analyzes Sophocles' extraordinarily dense and intense *stichomythia* – the dialogues of single-line exchange between characters – to explore conflict and violence in and through the language of tragedy: what is the relation between the form of dialogue and the social and moral dissension enacted in and through it? Reading, line for line . . . The fourth and fifth chapters investigate the construction of the choral role, how the chorus functions, as a lyric voice and as an actor in the drama – again, this is a discussion with a long history going back not just to Aristotle's *Poetics* but also to the famous and much repeated detail from antiquity that Sophocles was said to have written a book on the chorus, encouraging us thus to think of his choral writing as especially self-conscious, theoretical, historically aware.[8] How does the dialogic interplay between chorus and actor work within the plot and soundscape of tragedy? How do the different metres of tragedy, its different voices, sung and spoken, interact? Each of these five formal elements has been long recognized as central to Sophoclean tragedy and to what makes Sophocles' tragic language specific

---

[8] Suda Σ 815.

and distinctive. This first section aims to make a contribution towards understanding and defining this specificity, this distinctiveness.

The phrase "the language of tragedy" applies in an obvious way to these five opening chapters, in their shared focus on how language is used, how communication itself becomes a dramatic theme, how the grammar of speech and song and silence is expressive – and in the interconnections of these areas of critical discussion. But there is a second and no less important sense of my title, to which the second half of the book is directed. This is the critical language through which the notions of tragedy and the tragic have come to be understood. When we say "tragedy", "tragic", "the chorus", "the tragic actor" – the language, that is, with which we approach the genre – with what meanings are these crucial terms invested, and how have they developed into a modern discourse? That is, what is the history of "the language of tragedy" – the critical language of tragedy? The following four chapters of the second section are not, needless to say, a full and comprehensive discussion of such a topic, which would be unmanageably huge and distinctly indigestible, but rather each is focused on a specific central element of this modern discourse with regard to Sophocles, and each is closely related to the thematics of the first section of the book.

So Chapter 6 starts this investigation by looking at the idea of "the tragic" itself as a generalizing term applied to the genre, and what is at stake in such an abstract aesthetic ideal. How does the generalizing language of "the tragic", particularly the vocabulary and concepts developed in the nineteenth century, set an agenda for the criticism of ancient Greek plays? In particular – picking up the themes of the democratic audience and rhetoric that have run through the first section – how has the abstract notion of "the tragic" affected modern understanding of the politics of tragedy, and how has it dealt with tragedy's own exploration of the language with which its heroes and heroines comprehend their tragic experience? Within this general framework, Chapter 7 goes on to pick up discussion of the choral voice in Sophocles (Chapters 4, and 5) to look in detail at how a generalizing notion of the chorus (not a chorus, or choruses, but *the* chorus) was developed through the nineteenth century and came to affect performance tradition as well as later critical writing. Can modern discussions of the chorus escape the intellectual map drawn by these largely German theorists? Turning from these very broad concepts to specific plays, Chapter 8 takes a start from one of the most frequently repeated critical judgements on Sophocles in the nineteenth century – that he was "pious" – and explores what this term might mean through a history of how his *Electra* has been read over the last two centuries, especially in Britain. This chapter reveals how Sophoclean drama has been evaluated and re-evaluated through the categories we explored in the first half of the book – how irony and reversal, judgement and doubt, actor and chorus interaction, become the battleground of critical interpretation and disagreement. Through *Electra*, we can see how generalizations about tragedy and generalizations about the chorus, the concerns of the first two chapters of the section, become instantiated in the treatment of a single play, and, above all, how broad religious and social thinking does not merely frame but actually informs and even constitutes judgements about Sophocles' tragic language. Chapter 9 takes on Antigone and some of her modern feminist readers, as they respond to Hegel in particular, in order to explore ideas of communality and conflict that provided the agenda for the earlier discussion of *stichomythia*. The evaluation of Electra through the nineteenth and twentieth centuries was in part dominated by changing stereotypes of femininity. In the latter decades of the twentieth century a more explicit theorizing of gender has repeatedly made *Antigone* a privileged test-case, not least because of Hegel's immensely influential discussion of the play. What – where – is the conflict of the *Antigone*? How does the language of conflict, community and gender contribute to the conceptualization of tragedy?

It will be clear from this brief prospectus that the second half of this book is concerned not just with the historical construction of readings of Sophocles but also and more particularly with the relation between nineteenth-century critical thinking and our contemporary discussions of the language of tragedy. Each chapter finds an essential critical foundation in German Idealist thinking about tragedy: the generalizations about the tragic which I discuss, repeatedly go back to Hegel, Schlegel, Schelling and Schiller, as do the conceptualizations of the chorus – where Schlegel's phrase "the ideal spectator" is perhaps the most quoted (and least understood) critical judgement on the chorus over the last 200 years. Even the performance tradition of Greek tragedy, it will be demonstrated, is fundamentally organized through German eyes. The evaluation of *Electra*, even when we trace it primarily through English schools and universities and theatres, uses models developed from German Idealist writings. The modern feminist discussions repeatedly take their start "since Hegel", and continue to argue with their German fathers. It must be emphasized here that there is, of course, a much longer critical history that could be written. German Idealist writers themselves engaged with their eighteenth-century predecessors; we could stretch back through Racine and others to the Renaissance. But it is striking that the influence of German Idealist thinking is so pervasive and dominant that after the 1820s it is as if the eighteenth century (and earlier eras) no longer existed for the vast majority of critics. There is a specific and pointed and instrumental relation between the development of nineteenth-century ideas and ideals of tragedy and our modern contemporary discourse, and this is what the second half of the book aims to uncover. As the first section of the book seeks to find what is distinctive about Sophocles' language, so the second aims to reveal how the critical language of tragedy has been distinctly organized into a regime of knowledge. Neither section is comprehensive – but together they are designed to open a new perspective on Sophocles and the language of tragedy.

The second half of the book designedly poses a challenge to the first. How does a historical understanding of the language of tragedy – the changing institutions and discourses of the criticism of tragedy – affect the work of appreciating the language of Sophoclean tragedy – the philological work of reading the Greek of these plays? To what degree should we embark on the laboriously self-reflective process of attempting to locate our historically determined position as critics or readers? To what degree are critics capable of escaping from their historical locatedness, to what degree are they authorized by it? Self-consciousness about one's own place in the history of criticism is necessary to critical maturity, and yet . . . and yet . . . brings its own potentially crippling hesitations. Classics as a subject, with its connections with elite institutional authority as well as idealistic political progress, the ideology of Empire as well as sexual transgression, artistic idealism as well as the dead hand of tradition – caught, that is, between the profound and rash forces of conservatism and the revolutionary – knows this tension perhaps more than any other field.[9] The book ends with a brief coda – a coda with which to wag the dog – that opens up these questions. As with the first chapter, which enacts its own narrative of irony and reversal by constructing and then undoing its analysis of the language of *lusis*, so the book as a whole uses the ambiguity of the phrase "the language of tragedy" to create a double and potentially unsettling movement between its two parts, between the work of philology and the work of historical criticism. The coda will not resolve this tension, I should probably warn now, but will set out, like Odysseus at the end of the *Odyssey*, on its travels again, looking for the elusive place where history and philology rhyme.

* * *

It is a pleasure to be able to thank here those friends and colleagues who have helped me in the gestation and completion of this book. Pat Easterling, a wonderful reader and teacher, has been prodding me with her expert and nuanced knowledge of Sophoclean language for three decades now, and she read and improved several of these chapters as they developed. Miriam Leonard and I have been debating these issues intensely for many years, and the second half of the book in particular has been written in conversation, real and conceptual, with her. I can't imagine a more generous or committed reader and friend. Felix Budelmann, too, has been a vivid correspondent and conversationalist. John Henderson helped hugely with the second half of the book, and with the nagging anxieties of composition. James Diggle, Richard Rutherford, Patrick Finglass, Jim Porter, Joshua Billings, Erika Swales, and Edith Hall in seminars, correspondence, and chatting, have assisted the

---

[9] For varied responses to this see Goldhill (2011); DuBois (2001), (2010); Goff ed (2005); Goff and Simpson eds (2007); Hardwick and Gillespie eds (2007); Vasunia (forthcoming).

honing of the case. Sarah Nooter, former student, now colleague, has shown me her work in progress, from which I have benefited. Pete de Bolla and Charles Martindale have both been long-term disputants about matters Kantian. Many other seminar participants and chums have had their impact: especially in Virginia with Rita Felski; in Chicago and Cambridge with Renaud Gagné; in Princeton with Froma Zeitlin, Constanze Guthenke, Brooke Holmes, and Andrew Ford; in Berkeley with Mark Griffith and Donald Mastronarde. Thanks for all these invitations to speak and share the discussion. I have tried throughout to keep footnoting to a decent minimum, even and especially in areas where a huge bibliography could be given. Parts of the book have been published in different forms elsewhere, but the volume has been conceived as a whole, and each chapter has been rewritten to this agenda.

{ SECTION I }

Tragic Language

{ 1 }

Undoing

LUSIS AND THE ANALYSIS OF IRONY

"Words often understand themselves better than do those who are
using them".

—SCHLEGEL

I Sophocles' Drama of Undoing

In the third episode of the *Oedipus Tyrannus*, Jocasta leaves the highly disturbed Oedipus inside the palace and comes out to pray to Apollo, the god whose absent presence is everywhere in the play. She asks the divinity specifically to provide (921), *lusin euagê* "holy release", "an undefiled solution".[1] Her prayer receives what appears to be an instant answer with the immediate arrival of the messenger. His news seems to give Jocasta exactly what she has hoped for: the death of Polybus means that Oedipus cannot kill his father as he currently fears. Of course, the messenger will provide further information which will lead to the full unravelling of the plot.[2] The answer to the prayer will turn out to be ironically fulfilled in a way Jocasta could not predict. *Lusis* is the term Aristotle uses for the dénouement of a plot (and dénouement means "untying" – *lusis*), and it is the messenger's news which leads to the violent end of the tragedy.

We are well prepared for this irony. When the messenger enters, his standard request to learn where he is and where the recipient of his message is to

---

[1] Jebb's "some riddance from uncleanness" has far too biblical a ring, though it does capture the proleptic force of the adjective. Each future citation of Jebb is to Jebb's seven volume commentary and to his note on the line in question, unless otherwise indicated. Bollack (1991) 602–3 discusses the sense of εὐαγῆ and its proleptic force at length.

[2] As discussed by Knox (1957) 172–184; Kitto (1961) 132–44; Winnington-Ingram (1980) 180ff – who writes "every prayer in the play is ironical" 191 – and more generally Bushnell (1988).

be found is turned by the most extraordinary versification to echo with the name of Oedipus and to produce "violent puns"[3] on the king's name and the language of "know where" (924–6):

> ἆρ' ἂν παρ' ὑμῶν, ὦ ξένοι, μάθοιμ' ὅπου
> τὰ τοῦ τυράννου δώματ' ἐστὶν Οἰδίπου;
> μάλιστα δ' αὐτὸν εἴπατ' εἰ κάτισθ' ὅπου;

> May I learn from you, strangers, where
> The house of the king, Oedipus, is?
> Can you tell me in particular if you know where he is?

The jingling rhyme at the end of each line – *mathoim' hopou, Oidipou, katisth' hopou* – sounds out an etymology for Oedipus – "know where" – which the whole play shows to be a painful recognition of the king's ignorance, and which the scene to come will prove to be a turning point in revealing. The chorus in reply points out Jocasta as (928) γυνὴ δὲ μήτηρ ἥδε τῶν κείνου τέκνων, "This is his wife and mother of his children". In the tiniest gap between *hêde* and *tôn* we can hear the hint of "this is his wife and mother".[4] When the messenger announces his news may please and upset, Jocasta asks (938), "What is it? What sort of double power does it have like this?" It is precisely the double power of the message which will reveal her double status as wife and mother, and that Oedipus does not know what he thought he knew, most of all, where he is.[5]

Lusis is a marked term, then, a promise of release that turns out to be ironically and tragically fulfilled. The scene continues to play with the term, however. When Oedipus tells the messenger of his fear that he would kill his father, the messenger happily asks (1002–3), "Then why, since I have come here with kindly intent, have I not released you from this fear?" The verb here is *exelusamên*, and the irony again is palpable. This is not a moment of salutary release, but it does release the one piece of information which will lead to the horrible revelation of who Oedipus is.[6] What is more, the messenger reveals that he has "released" Oedipus once before (1034): "I released you when your ankles were pinioned together", *luô s'*. The chorus had exhorted the king when he argued with Teiresias that the best course was to find out how best to "solve" – *luein* – the oracles (440), after Oedipus accuses Teiresias of failing to say anything *eklutêrion*, "by way of release",

---

[3] The phrase is from Knox (1957) 184, who notes how commentators resist recognizing puns in Sophocles as intentional and significant. That trend, among literary critics at least, has certainly changed in the last thirty years.

[4] As noted already by the scholia, who call it "an ambivalence which gives pleasure to the listener", τὸ ἀμφίβολον ὃ τέρπει τὸν ἀκροατήν.

[5] For the role of language and names in the *Oedipus Tyrannus*, see Segal (1981) 207–48; Goldhill (1984b), and, more circumspectly, Goldhill (1986) 199–221.

[6] On the force of the middle here see Allen (2006) 116–18.

"by way of a solution", to the citizens during the crisis of the Sphinx (392). Oedipus himself had predicted that the only "release", *eklusin*, for their current sickness would be to find Laius' killers (306–7) – just as the Priest had recalled that Oedipus himself had "released", *exelusas*, the city of Thebes from the predations of the Sphinx (a process of release that had led Oedipus unknowingly into his current disastrous position). "Release" in the *Oedipus Tyrannus* is used repeatedly for a crucial juncture of the plot, and in each case what appears to be a solution to a problem, a positive salvation, turns out to be entwining the victims deeper and deeper into the meshes of the tragic plot.

This use of *lusis* goes to the heart of Sophocles' tragic perspective, where humans, in their pursuit of knowledge, their attempts to change things, their hope to escape from the narratives in which they find themselves enmeshed, are relentlessly and with grim irony drawn back into disaster at every turn. *Lusis* and its cognate vocabulary becomes a sign in Sophoclean theatre for the failures of human control, and ultimately for the only release that is inevitable and sure, that of death.

Heracles in the *Trachiniae*, with the clarity that traditionally comes to the dying hero in Greek literature, spells out the misprision that lies at the root of this idea of *lusis*. The old oracles and newer prophecies concur, he says (1169–72):

> ἥ μοι χρόνῳ τῷ ζῶντι καὶ πάροντι νῦν
> ἔφασκε μόχθων τῶν ἐφεστώτων ἐμοὶ
> λύσιν τελεῖσθαι· κἀδοκοῦν πράξειν καλῶς.
> τὸ δ'ἦν ἄρ' οὐδὲν ἄλλο πλὴν θανεῖν ἐμέ.

> The prophecy said that at the present and now living time
> Release from the toils laid upon me would be
> Fulfilled. I thought that meant a happy future.
> I now realise it meant nothing else than my death.

Heracles thought *lusis* must mean a prosperous future; he now knows it means death. But Sophocles layers even such a bleak recognition of the failure of hope with a more ambiguous look to the future also. The word *teleisthai* "will be fulfilled", "brought to pass" is the word repeatedly associated with the fulfilment of prophecy in this play (cf 79, 167, 170, 174, 824–5), but it also implies "consummation", "death" and also a ritual initiation into a new state. It is the word used, for example, for initiation into the mysteries. "Escape from labours" *apallagê ponôn* is the phrase used for the state of transformation through the mysteries, which may find an echo here in *mokhthôn . . . lusin*, "release from toils".[7] Heracles is about to demand that he be set on a pyre by his son. Although

---

[7] As in Aeschylus *Agamemnon* 1, as discussed by Thomson (1935) and Tierney (1937) (but not by Fraenkel (1950)).

Sophocles' play does not show it, one dominant traditional story is that from the pyre Heracles ascended to heaven, where he marries Hebe, and lives on Olympus with the gods, the only human to be deified because of his heroic exploits.[8] The strange language of "living time", together with the phrase *praxein kalôs* which I have translated "happy future" (literally, "I thought things would go well for me"), and the note of realization (*ara* and the imperfect) that this means "nothing else but death" – which sounds against the traditional future of the immortal Heracles – may all hint at the hero's transformation to come – a *lusis* of a different kind. As Heracles spells out the ironic misprision of his earlier understanding of *lusis*, he may be performing another misunderstanding of how his narrative is unfurling.[9]

As in the *Oedipus Tyrannus*, this climactic use of *lusis* has been prepared for earlier in the play. The messenger arrives in the first scene and proudly announces (180–1):

> δέσποινα Δηάνειρα, πρῶτος ἀγγέλων
> ὄκνου σε λύσω.

> Queen Deianeira, I will be the first of the messengers
> To release you from fear.

Deinaeira's fear is a key-note of the opening of the play.[10] As in the *Oedipus Tyrannus*, the messenger appears to bring good news, and hopes to get a reward for being the first to bring it. This *lusis* too will turn out to be grotesquely misplaced, and, indeed, as soon as the second messenger, Lichas, arrives, it is precisely this first messenger who will lead to the tragic fears of Deianeira being redoubled (with all their terrible consequences) by outing Lichas as a liar and thus informing the queen of the significance of the arrival of Iole, her rival for the affections of Heracles. It is another release that is no release.

Deianeira's response is to attempt to win back Heracles' desire for her with the drug of the centaur's blood, which turns out to be a poison rather than a love philtre. She announces her plan to the chorus as something *lutêrion*, "bringing release", "leading to a solution", "freeing" (554).[11] The ambiguity of *pharmaka* as cure and poison is very well known in tragedy, and is redoubled here by its interweaving with the narrative of misplaced hope for *lusis*. So, in language that looks back to Deianeira's hopes and forward to Heracles' despair, the chorus celebrate with desperately misplaced enthusiasm (653–4):

---

[8] See Easterling (1982) 17–19.

[9] See Heiden (1989) 144–8.

[10] See Heiden (1989) 22–30.

[11] The noun in this line with λυτήριον may be λύπημα, as the manuscripts have, and has been defended by Stinton and most recently Lloyd-Jones and Wilson; or λώφημα, as Jebb proposes, or νόημα, as Campbell suggests and Easterling prefers: in each case the emphasis is on the first word of the line – her desire for *lusis*. See Lloyd-Jones and Wilson (1990) 162; Stinton (1976) 138; Easterling (1982) 142–3 *ad* 553–4; Campbell (1881).

νῦν δ᾽ Ἄρης οἰστρηθεὶς,
ἐξέλυσεν ἐπιπόνων ἀμερᾶν.

Now Ares stung to madness
Has set free from the days of toil.

"Ares stung to madness" is a "lyrical condensation"[12] of the military narrative of the sack of Oechalia which we have just been told (359–65), but *oistrêtheis* implies not merely "roused to fury" [Jebb], but also "stung by the madness of sexual desire", a motive force which not only drives Heracles, but, it is suggested, also dangerously impels Deianeira. So, as Easterling notes, the object of the verb "has set free", "released", could be taken to be Heracles, whose *ponoi*, "labours", are now at an end, but it also indicates release for Deianeira and the chorus from their anxiety about Heracles.[13] It need hardly be emphasized that their delight here in such release will prove temporary and desperately misguided.

In the light of this language, Deianeira's first description of how she came to marry Heracles may turn out to ring with greater significance than she can appreciate. In her opening speech, she describes how Heracles won her by fighting off her horrific suitor Achelous. *Ekluetai me*, she says, "he set me free" (21). She herself immediately underlines the uncertainty of this narrative of salvation (25–6): τέλος δ᾽ ἔθηκε Ζεὺς ἀγώνιος καλῶς, εἰ δὴ καλῶς, "But, Zeus, who decides conflicts, brought an end in a good way, if in fact it was in a good way". The freedom which marriage to Heracles brings is also a constant round of fear, she explains. Yet even this doubt of hers will turn out to be inadequate. The word *telos*, as so often, marks the further irony.[14] We are progressing towards her killing of Heracles and her own tragic death – a *telos* she cannot here anticipate. (Both *telos* and *kalôs* anticipate Heracles' own recognition of the twists of his fortune [1169–72] with which I began.) Once again, the language of salvation in *ekluetai* (21) actually signals one step in a more complex, destructive narrative.

In *Electra*, we see a similar patterning of the language of *lusis* leading to a marvellous climactic moment. It begins with the chorus trying to control Electra's wild and constant outpouring of grief by pointing out that such wailing can provide no *analusis kakôn*, "dissolution of evils" (142). The language of *lusis* immediately looks towards a consummation, an end of trouble. Electra herself picks up this language first with Chrysothemis, as her sister prepares to take Clytemnestra's offerings to the grave of Agamemnon. Electra asks with great bitterness (after describing Agamemnon's mutilation) (446–8): "Do you think these offerings can bring release [*lutêria*] for her?! It is not possible". *Lutêrion*, "bringing release", "freeing" [from guilt], here sarcastically marks

---

[12] Campbell (1891) cited by Easterling (1982) 154 *ad* 653.

[13] Easterling (1982) 154 *ad* 164.

[14] See Zeitlin (1965); Lebeck (1971) 68–73; Goldhill (1984) – for the multiform language of *telos* in the *Oresteia*, which often seems to lurk behind Sophocles' tragic Greek.

Clytemnestra's necessarily failing attempts to extricate herself from the situation she has created for herself. Electra recognizes the impossibility of her mother getting *lusis*. We recall this when Clytemnestra prays her unpleasant, muffled prayer for the death of her own child (634–59). She calls her prayers *lutêrious*, bringing release, "freeing" (635). As with Jocasta's prayer for *lusis* in *Oedipus Tyrannus*, Clytemnestra's *luterious euchas* here receive an instant, ironic answer from Apollo in the form of the arrival of a messenger, whose news will bring downfall to the one who prays, though at first it seems to be the perfect answer to the prayer. In this case, the false tale of the death of Orestes, as told by the Paidagogus, also involves a story of unloosing, as the charioteers "loose" [*elusan* (755)] Orestes' bloody body from the reins of his chariot. As Electra has demanded, Clytemnestra's hopes for *lusis* prove all too false.

In her agon with Clytemnestra, however, Electra justifies her father's sacrifice of Iphigeneia (574–5): οὐ γὰρ ἦν λύσις ἄλλη στράτῳ πρὸς οἶκον οὐδ᾽ εἰς Ἴλιον, "For there was no other solution for the army either for home or for Troy". Electra's rhetoric in this scene is so aggressive and forceful that even the chorus who support her, comment that they are not sure of the justice of her case (610–11).[15] Here while it may be true that Agamemnon could find no *lusis* – his is the *locus classicus* of the tragic double bind – it scarcely simply exonerates him. Electra shows no hint of upset over the sacrifice of her sister. Chrysothemis, for her part, points out to Electra that there is no point in dying horribly, even if they get a noble name (1005–6): λύει γὰρ ἡμᾶς οὐδὲν οὐδ᾽ ἐπωφελεῖ βάξιν καλὴν λάβοντε δυσκλεῶς θανεῖν, "For it gives us no release or benefit to win a noble report and die infamously".[16] Both passages put pressure on the term *lusis*: what could bring "release"? What would be the right form of "release"? So Electra cries to the now recognized Orestes (who wishes she would restrain herself) (1246): "Aiaiai, you recall the nature of my evil, which cannot be veiled, cannot be released [*katalusimon*], cannot be forgotten". The question is mounting: what would release mean for Electra?

All this by way of preparation for the last stunning use of the vocabulary in the play. The children have led Aegisthus to uncovering the slaughtered body of their mother, his lover, and Orestes has taunted him. Aegisthus asks to be allowed to say a few last words, but Electra, who has been told to shut up by every character in the drama, now demands silence from her enemy: "Do not let

---

[15] Even Jebb notes that in Aeschylus' *Agamemnon* Agamemnon speaks as if it were possible, if shameful, to go home. No such scruples for Electra. Jebb (1894) 84 *ad* 573.

[16] Finglass (2007) *ad loc* against Jebb suggests the two verbs here must be parallel ("gives neither advantage nor benefit") and takes λύει in the sense of λυσιτελεῖ. It is better to see a more fluid semantic drift between the two verbs, λύει and ἐπωφελεῖ. Since λυσιτελεῖ takes the dative, the phrase λύει ἡμᾶς is hard to hear as λυσιτελεῖ. Hence Elmsley emended ἡμᾶς to ἡμῖν. The emendation is not necessary. The sentence first suggests "release", but ἐπωφελεῖ retrospectively encourages the sense of benefit to be heard: the whole question is whether release is really a benefit. In *O.T.* 316–7 τέλη λύῃ is used – uniquely, according to Jebb – for λυσιτελῇ, but for an extended reading of the continuing ambiguity of such usage see Guay (1995) especially 40–47.

him speak more!", she snarls (1483–4). He must be put to death as soon as possible, and given a humiliating burial. This, she says, is her only release (1489–90):

> ὡς ἐμοὶ τόδ᾽ ἂν κακῶν
> μόνον γένοιτο τῶν πάλαι λυτήριον.

> Know that this alone for me would prove
> To bring release [*lutêrion*] for the woes of the past.

These are the last words of Electra. Her very last word is to anticipate "release". We have read enough already in Sophocles and in this play to scent the grim irony in this word.[17]

The ending of the *Electra* play is a celebrated problem, as we will see in detail in Chapter 8.[18] The absence of the Furies, the absence of any moral judgement or even discussion of the matricide, the absence of any indication of what happens after Orestes leads Aegisthus back into the darkened house, have led to a debate since the nineteenth century which shows surprisingly little sign of dampening down. Few today would follow Jebb, the greatest Victorian British scholar of Sophocles, and the nineteenth-century Germans, and declare that Sophocles is simply looking back to the days of Homer in celebrating Orestes, who follows the god's command unproblematically to become the "happy matricide" (as Schlegel unhappily termed him). It is hard to repress the qualms of the *Oresteia*, especially when Sophocles' play echoes Aeschylus' great trilogy so often and so pointedly.[19] It is equally hard to imagine how an unproblematic matricide could be conceived within any moral system: it is significant that Orestes, who is held up as an example for Telemachus in the *Odyssey,* is never said to have killed his mother in Homer. And after the *Oresteia,* there are no examples of Orestes being promoted as a straightforwardly positive role model. For Winnington-Ingram (following Rohde, and thus creating another German genealogy), the Furies are to be seen as forces within the personalities of Orestes and Electra, allowing, encouraging, driving on the children's murderous intent. The play here displays the dangerous consequences of a passionate commitment to violent revenge: the Furies within. Even if one resists the psychological bent of Winnington-Ingram's reading of the Furies, the ending of the play must at least be seen to provoke a question of judgement from the audience, a worry about what happens next, about what to think of the matricide and its consequences for the murderers. Sophocles anticipates such concerns with the finely self-reflexive last word of the play, *teleôthen,*

---

[17] March (2001) writes on this line: "There is no trace of uncertainty in her words". This confuses the tone of Electra (whatever it is taken to be) with the audience's understanding of her words. Finglass (2007) surprisingly makes no comment on the irony of any example of *lusis* in the play.

[18] See, each with further bibliography, Winnington-Ingram (1980) 217–47; Segal (1981) 249–91; Batchelder (1995) 111–40; Ringer (1998); March (2001) – who goes against the modern trend wholly in her support for the unproblematic acceptability of the matricide.

[19] For the interplay between the final scene of the *Electra* and the *Oresteia,* see Goldhill (2003) 172–6.

"finished", "consummated", "fulfilled", against which the open-endedness of the play's final questions resounds.

The play has undoubtedly focused on the figure of Electra; it has raised the question of what release might mean; it has shown us the misplaced hopes of humans in release, and the despair of finding it. It has shown us Clytemnestra offering prayers of release that rebound against her. And it has shown us how like her mother Electra has become (and recognizes herself to have become [619ff]). In this last scene we have seen her acting out a role with false words and a false face to lead a man to his death – just like her mother. How then does the play end for Electra? It is not an issue of trying to divine how the silent Electra feels in the play's final moments: Segal darkly imagines "her spiritual and inward isolation"; March, more fluffily, sees her as "vibrantly alive and present on stage".[20] The point is rather that the hoped for release has become ironized by the play's treatment of the vocabulary of *lusis*. So what is the release that Electra can expect? It seems to me typical of Sophocles' searing and provocative drama-turgy to leave us with that question – and to provoke it by her last word.

The problem of Electra's end finds physical form whenever the play is per-formed. There are at least three possible things for Electra to do at the end of the play. One is to leave the stage with Orestes, to enter the house and thus take part in the murder directly (something Strauss and von Hofmannsthal refuse her in the most brutal and disturbing way by having her dance herself to death on stage as the murder takes place inside the house[21]). This exit makes her fully complicit with all the questions of what happens to the matricide(s) after the death of Aegisthus. Second, she can leave the stage with the chorus, being returned as it were to the world of the women, the collective of female support. This exit would offer a different image of her future. Aeschylus, of course, returns her to the house *before* the revenge, to separate her from Orestes – and to wait inside, inactive, according to the Greek normative model of a how a good girl should behave. Euripides takes a different route and marries her off – separating her from the farmer and setting her up with Pylades. Both Eurip-ides and Aeschylus allow straightforward narratives of a projected future for Electra (however upsetting the Euripidean solution has seemed to modern au-diences). Or, third, she could stay on stage. This is the route most modern productions take. This leaves her in the strange space she has inhabited throughout the play, just outside the house, a space crossed by others on their way to the palace or the tomb of Agamemnon, a liminal space – where she inevitably is, in terms of standard Greek models of female behaviour, out of place.[22] Leaving Electra on stage emphasizes most strongly the ironic uncertainty

---

[20] Segal (1981) 266–7; March (2001) 229.

[21] For a full discussion of Strauss' *Elektra* see Goldhill (2002) 108–77.

[22] The association of women with the inside, and the concomitant sense of transgression in coming outside, is a commonplace since at least Foley's (1982) corrective to Shaw (1975).

of what release she can hope for and where she can hope to find it. Staging the final moments of Electra in this play focuses precisely on what sort of release the director thinks Electra should have.[23]

The strongly marked pattern of misplaced hope for release and ironic fulfilment of such hopes in these three plays helps us read the full weight of two other examples of the vocabulary of *lusis*. In *Antigone*, Creon is finally persuaded by Teiresias' prophecies, the chorus' careful warnings and his own misgivings to try to save Antigone. As he rushes from the stage towards the cave, he declares (1112–4):

> αὐτός τ' ἔδησα καὶ παρὼν ἐκλύσομαι.
> δέδοικα γὰρ μὴ τοὺς καθεστῶτας νόμους
> ἄριστον ᾖ σῴζοντα τὸν βίον τελεῖν.

> I myself bound her, and I myself will be there to release her.
> I suspect that it is best to go through life
> Preserving the established laws.

This is a climactic moment, not least because it is so rare for a Sophoclean hero to change his mind. It is, of course, thoroughly Sophoclean that he has learnt too late, and his hope to alter what he has set in motion will prove vain. Antigone has been walled up in a cave: the language of binding and setting free therefore extends to a more metaphorical sense. He wants to "undo" what he has done – and will be quite incapable of so doing. Indeed, "being there" (*parôn*), he will be stabbed at by his son, Haimon, who then kills himself over the already dead body of Antigone (1231ff). The language of the final couplet here with which he indicates his change of mind, hints at the disasters to come. He suspects or fears (*dedoika*) that it is best to go through life preserving the established laws: the phrase *ton bion telein* can also be translated to "end one's life". He wants to undo what he has done, but his last words as he runs out anticipate the death he will not be able to prevent.[24]

There has been scant if striking anticipation of the language of *lusis* in the *Antigone*. The chorus in one grimly prophetic stanza (594–5) lament the long history of the Labdacid family and its constant round of god-sent miseries: *oud' ekhei lusin*, they conclude ringingly, the family "has no release". Ismene, a survivor like Chrysothemis in *Electra*, expresses her diffidence at the beginning of the play with

---

[23] We can only guess how the first performance or any other ancient production staged this last scene: all three closures discussed here are possible for the ancient theatre, too. For the record, Mantziou (1995) 194 suggests Electra stays on stage; Finglass (2007) *ad* 1510 (against Calder [2005]) prefers her to enter the palace with Orestes and Pylades. The characters leave with the chorus in e.g. *Philoctetes* (and possibly Creon in *Antigone*: ἄγοιτ' "lead me away" (1339) could be addressed to the chorus, rather than "attendants" as Griffith assumes). Most ancient plays end with an emphatic *exeunt*, but this does not mean that the option of Electra staying on stage is impossible.

[24] See Griffith (1999) 313 *ad* 1113–4.

a proverbial sounding phrase perhaps drawn from the sphere of music (39–40): "Poor sister, what more could I contribute by trying to loosen [*luous*'] or to tighten [*haptousa*]?". The expression is a familiar one and sees circumstances as a lyre string (or possibly a knot) which can be tightened or loosened.[25] It is a way of saying "whatever I do", and indicates Ismene's unwillingness to act in any direction (which leads to her survival as well as her failure to influence the course of action at all).[26] In the exodus, Creon picks up the language of *lusis* briefly again to lament the death of Eurydice his wife. Twice (1268, 1314) he uses the word *apoluesthai* to mean "die" ("be dismissed from life"): not only could he not undo what he had done, but it has led to further acts of "loosening" which add to his woes.

"Undoing" one's former wrongs is what Neoptolemus hopes to do at a key turning point of the *Philoctetes*. Neoptolemus has the bow of Philoctetes. Odysseus has arrived and taken the boy offstage towards the ship, leaving the chorus with the enraged and hopeless Philoctetes. Then, suddenly, Neoptolemus, pursued by Odysseus, hurries back on to the stage. Odysseus (and the audience) is desperate to know what he is intending to do. Neoptolemus declares (1224):

λύσων ὅσ' ἐξήμαρτον ἐν τῷ πρὶν χρόνῳ.

I intend to undo [*lusôn*] all the mistakes I made before.

This is a bold statement of intent. When he announces he has come with fresh words, Philoctetes is unimpressed: he has heard such deceit before (1268–70). When Neoptolemus promises that this time he is telling the truth, Philoctetes retorts that the boy had seemed convincing before (1271–2). It is harder than Neoptolemus imagined to undo what he has done: once trust has been lost by verbal deceit, how can words put it back together again? So he gives back the bow: a deed, an *ergon*, rather than a word.[27] But Philoctetes immediately wants to use the bow to kill Odysseus, Neoptolemus' leader, and the boy has to restrain the hero from murder. But even now, with this token of trust in hand, Philoctetes cannot be shifted from his hatred and his determination to return home. Neoptolemus cannot undo all his former mistakes, and keep the plot on track. As Neoptolemus is forced to recognize in the face of Philoctetes' angry rejection (1373), λέγεις μὲν εἰκότ', ἀλλ' ὅμως, "What you say is reasonable; but nonetheless . . .". It takes the arrival of Heracles to redirect Philoctetes towards Troy. The climactic use of *lusôn*, first word of the line, announces Neoptolemus' intention to "undo" his mistakes, but the unfurling of the plot shows just how difficult it is to achieve that aim. *Lusôn* marks not

---

[25] Useful note in Griffith (1999) 129–30 *ad* 39–40.

[26] This hesitation of Ismene is nuanced, but not contradicted, either by her willingness to take responsibility for Antigone's action after the event (536), which Antigone rejects; or by Creon's initial willingness to punish both girls (789), an option which he rejects shortly afterwards.

[27] For the contrast between words and deeds in this play see Segal (1981) 328–61, followed by many later critics; on the actions see Taplin (1971), also followed by many later critics.

just Neoptolemus' hope for release but also his continuing failure to determine and control the moral crises in which he is caught.

I said earlier that the only *lusis* which is inevitable and sure is the *lusis* of death, and we have come across more than one occasion where the vocabulary of *lusis* is brought into contact with the vocabulary of *telos*, which means both "end", "fulfilment" and "death". There are a surprising number of uses of the language of release or undoing in the context of death in Sophocles: we have already seen Heracles' death as his "undoing"/"release" (*Trach.* 1171); the "undoing" of the body of Orestes from the chariot (*Electra* 755); the dismissal from life of Eurydice (*Ant.* 1268, 1314). The background may be the familiar Homeric expression *luein gounata*, or *guia* "loosen the knees" or "the limbs" in the sense of killing (rather than desire); but (in the spirit of Jebb) it might be worth recalling the immense pathos of the simple words of Shakespeare's broken man, King Lear: "Come, unbutton me here". So Deianeira in the *Trachiniae* says farewell to her marriage bed and (923–4) τοσαῦτα φωνήσασα συντόνῳ χερὶ λύει τὸν αὐτῆς πέπλον, "She said such things, and with intent hand undoes [*luei*] her own dress . . .". Undoing the dress precedes stabbing herself in her side. Similarly, Oedipus, as he approaches his transcendent death in the *Oedipus Coloneus*, sits εἶτ' ἔλυσε δυσπινεῖς στολάς, "then he undid [*eluse*] his dirty robes" (1597). In *Antigone*, Eurydice before her death by suicide, also sits and (1302) λύει κελαινὰ βλέφαρα, "undoes [*luei*] her eyes into darkness" – a striking expression, where the distant echo of *luei gounata* anticipates her death. (With a different nuance of *luein*, Creon in *Oedipus Tyrannus* announces that the oracle has indicated that they must either exile the murderers of Laius or "requite slaughter with slaughter", φόνῳ φόνον πάλιν λύοντας (101): the addition of *palin* here "back" as well as the repetition of *phonos* helps the sense of requital: not just "undo" a wrong, but "atone for", "pay back".) *Luein* in Greek, as with "undoing" in English, can always imply either a "solution", or an "untying" or a "downfall" – or all three. Sophoclean language works with this potential ambiguity to explore the fragile control humans have over their narratives.

The language of *luein* and death which I have been discussing is synthesized strikingly in a wonderful phrase at the end of the *Oedipus Coloneus*. The chorus, encouraging the children to stop their lamenting at the death of Oedipus, sing (1720–1): ὀλβίως γ' ἔλυσεν τὸ τέλος, ὦ φίλαι, βίου, "In true blessedness, friends, he dissolved [*elusen*] the end of life". My translation struggles to get the full sense here. *Luein* together with *telos* might be thought to imply "profit" (as at *Oedipus Tyrannus* 316), but here rather seems to mean "put an end to", "dissolve". In which case, one might expect the object to be simply *bion*, as at Euripides' *Iphigeneia at Tauris* 692 *lusai bion*. So Jebb translates "he hath found a blessed end, friends", which gives an easy sense, but is forced to give *luein* an impossible sense. *Telos biou*, what's more, is a normal phrase for "death" (and *telos* can connote "the end of life", "death" on its own).

The strangely overladen phrase seems to be suggesting not simply that Oedipus has died, but that Oedipus has gone beyond the limits – as indeed he has with his god-driven transformation. He has transcended both life and death in his becoming a hero: he has "blessedly dissolved the end of life". The dense language of the chorus captures the mystery of Oedipus' end, his passing.[28]

My final example of a marked use of *luein* in Sophocles also comes from the *Oedipus Coloneus*, and it occurs in one of the most haunting and difficult expressions in this most difficult of plays.[29] The messenger tells us of Oedipus' final moments. Before his mysterious end comes, Oedipus bids farewell to his daughters, Antigone and Ismene. He recalls the sufferings they have experienced looking after him and comments (1615–9):

> ἀλλ᾽ ἓν γὰρ μόνον
> τὰ πάντα λύει ταῦτ᾽ ἔπος μοχθήματα.
> τὸ γὰρ φιλεῖν οὐκ ἔστιν ἐξ ὅτου πλέον
> ἢ τοῦδε τἀνδρὸς ἔσχεθ᾽, οὗ τητώμεναι
> τὸν λοιπὸν ἤδη τοῦ βίου διάξετον.

> But indeed only one word
> Undoes [*luei*] all these hardships.
> Love – you could not have more from any man
> Than from me, whom you will be without
> Now, as you pass the rest of your life.

Oedipus suggests that all the girls' difficulties are dissolved by the single, magic word *philein*: he is looking back over their life together and forward to the problems to come. Nineteenth-century Christian readers (and their modern humanist heirs) are keen to translate *philein* as "love" (as I have, unwillingly, above). *Philein* here, however, should not be assimilated simply to a transcendent modern Western theological notion. At the very least, *philein* implies mutual bonds of obligation and duty within a family and an extended range of kinsmen and friends, rather than a predominantly affective tie. But it should not be forgotten that in the previous scene Oedipus has re-iterated the curse on his son, Polyneices, which will take the murderous feud between *philoi* into the next generation. Ismene, who has arrived "not without difficulty" (328), has told Oedipus of the machinations of his *philoi* – and she will suffer from them, before being saved by Theseus. What is more, for an incestuous family such as Oedipus', to extol the values of "family ties" is always an ambivalent virtue. There is indeed no man who could be more *philos* to Antigone and Ismene than Oedipus, their

---

[28] This sense of mystery has, of course, been prepared for throughout the messenger scene cf e.g. 1585, 1601–5. On Oedipus' end, see Easterling (1997c).

[29] See Wilson (1997) 165; Markantonatos (2007) 224–30.

father/brother.[30] *Oedipus Coloneus* was produced at the end of Sophocles' life, well after the *Antigone*: the future of Antigone, τὸν λοιπὸν τοῦ βίου, "the rest of your life", where in Sophocles' play at least the one word, *philein*, plays such a destructive motivating role, has already been written. The *Oedipus Coloneus* draws also on the power of its great tragic predecessor, to layer Antigone's imagined future with her own bleak intensity. When Antigone exits (1168–72) towards Thebes to try to stop the intrafamilial slaughter – sent on her way to her own death graciously by Theseus (1173–77) – the sense of further impending disaster is emphatic.

This is a deeply moving scene, and the daughters and Oedipus embrace in a tearful farewell. But should we not hear yet again a worrying note in the promise of "release"?

The language of *lusis* and its cognates is a repeated concern in Sophocles, and its dense signification and layered ironies are typical of Sophocles' language of tragedy. In *Oedipus Tyrannus*, *Trachiniae*, and *Electra* there is an extended semantic network where release is hoped for and promised and sought after, but which turns out to be impossible to find, misplaced as a hope, or ironically and destructively fulfilled. In *Antigone* and *Philoctetes* single, marked uses of the term are also replete with the ironies of reversal and misguided expectations. Release becomes associated with death through the language of "undoing". Even in the *Oedipus Coloneus*, where Oedipus' heroization gives a potentially less despairing conclusion to a tragic narrative, the language of *lusis* weaves an ambivalent thread through the text. In Sophoclean theatre, humans struggle to escape from the tragic circumstances in which they find themselves, and struggle to exert control over their own narratives. The language of *lusis* in Sophocles reveals the self-deceptions within such struggles, and the constantly failing attempt to find the solution to the *aporia* of human action. The drama of undoing.

II The Analysis of Sophoclean Irony

Now, since the nineteenth century there is no more familiar topic in Sophoclean criticism than dramatic irony.[31] Integral to the critical treatment of this foundational trope is the rhetoric – the performance – of superior knowledge. We – the audience in the theatre or its surrogate, the critic – watch a man whom we know to be the killer of Laius try to find out who the killer of Laius

---

[30] Note Ismene's opening address (324): ὦ δισσὰ πατρὸς καὶ κασιγνήτης ἐμοὶ ἥδιστα φωνήματα . . ., "O most sweet double names of father and sibling". *Dissa*, "double", "ambiguous", is tellingly left out of Jebb's translation ("Father and sister, names most sweet to me . . . "). Ismene reminds us – to Jebb's distaste, apparently – of the doubled and confused genealogy of the family, as she brings the news of yet another intrafamilial disagreement.

[31] We shall return to the history of this discussion in the coda, below p252–6.

is; we watch the man whom we know to be married to his mother, gradually discover the miserable secrets of his identity. The audience is placed in a position of superiority to the characters on stage and responds to the action through this knowledge: irony lets an audience see itself as *le sujet qui sait*, "the subject who knows".[32] So, paradigmatically, the critic who outlines irony for the reader reveals what is unknown (to the characters on stage, to the reader who did not previously perceive such an irony, or even to the author, who may not have recognized the fissures in his own text). My discussion of Sophoclean *lusis* has followed precisely such a strategy. It has opened up the density of Sophoclean language by critical *analusis* [undoing/analysis] to reveal the implications in characters' language that they do not appear to realise, to show to an audience how words come to mean more than has been recognized. But I also want now to build back into this discussion something of the dark undertow, the sense of necessary failing, which Sophocles' repeated recognition of the misplaced certainties of the human rhetoric of *lusis* should encourage in the critic.[33]

There are two interwoven strands in this undoing. On the one hand, I will be looking at how Sophocles ironizes irony: that is, he encourages an uncertain and destabilized comprehension of the terms integral to the standard model of dramatic irony, such as "we", "know", "learn", "again". On the other, I will be expanding on the dangerous ordinariness of the language of Sophoclean irony. *Luô* and *lusis* are common, unexceptional words, frequent in the poetic and prose record from Homer through the classical era and beyond.[34] In what follows, my four (carefully chosen) examples will be of apparently casual or functional comments, clichés, standard phrases – all forms of expression that seem to resist too close an attention. Everyday words.[35] Sophocles, however, has an uncanny ability to suggest the horror lurking in mundane language, its predictive or even causal force. But I use the word "suggest" advisedly. The question that emerges from these readings is not simply "is there irony here?", so much as "how far should we see irony here?", "how sure can we be of the boundary between the casual and the causal?" In this way, Sophocles turns back against the reader (critic, audience) the fiction of superiority and controlled knowledge. These

---

[32] This modern dictionary understanding of dramatic irony runs through into modernist criticism as much as in more traditional readings: "What is in plain sight of the audience is hidden from the participants", Segal (1995) 162; "It is only for the spectator that the language of the text can be transparent at every level in all its polyvalence and with all its ambiguities", Vernant and Vidal-Naquet (1981) 18. The origin of the vocabulary of dramatic/tragic irony will be further discussed in the coda p252–6.

[33] Romantic irony has its own configurations – see Dane (1991); Muecke (1970); Booth (1974); Handwerk (1984); Simpson (1979) – and de Man (1996) who has been particularly influential in contemporary discussions of irony. I regret that I feel that I should emphasize gently the performativity of my argument here, in undoing the analysis of irony.

[34] And *luô* is the commonest modern paradigm with which to learn Greek verbs, of course: one could say that the orderliness of undoing is basic to our learning Greek.

[35] See Easterling (1999) for the complexity of "plain words" in Sophocles.

examples of flickering irony leave the reader in a far more uncomfortable position than the strong model of dramatic irony supposes. Each of my four test-cases will be concerned, then, with the *limits* of our reading of Sophoclean irony.

My first example will prove to be the most extreme limit case and concerns the word *hopou*, "where", in the *Oedipus Tyrannus*. The *Oedipus Tyrannus* is the *locus classicus* for the most developed sense of what is meant by dramatic irony in Sophocles, and this play has been extensively analysed in terms of the audience's superior gaze, aimed at the knowledge claims of the central character as he seeks after knowledge. The central term *oida*, "I know", introduces a theme of vision on the one hand – it means etymologically "I have seen" – which is fully played out with the blind prophet Teiresias who knows, and the final blinding of Oedipus, when he learns the truth of his identity; on the other hand, *oida* echoes in the many puns on Oedipus' own name, showing how "knowing [where]" is at the heart of his narrative. The play constantly suggests that it is the moment that you have a superior feeling of knowledge about yourself that you are most vulnerable to self-deception and to self-destructive decisions. "Seeing" is associated with false knowledge (as we look on at Oedipus' tragedy); the play shows Oedipus, the seeker after knowledge and control, failing in the most basic knowledge of himself, and offers a paradigm for all readers in their pursuit of knowledge; Oedipus shows us a man who thought he knew where he was at the cross-roads, and challenges everyone to recognize an uncertainty about the road of life, about where we are going.[36]

Within this familiar general reading of *Oedipus Tyrannus*, I want to return briefly to the entrance of the messenger, who arrives apparently in response to Jocasta's prayer (924–6 above p14). His questions take the simplest form of expected introduction – where is the palace, where is the ruler for whom I have a message? – and fill them with unexpected meaning, partly by the versification, which allows two lines to end with the word *hopou*, "where", partly by the jingling rhymes of *hopou* with *Oidipou*, partly by the play on words of knowing *mathoim'/katisth'* and the word "Oedipus", which emphasizes the role of knowing encoded in the etymology of the king's name. The arrival of the messenger is already and immediately ironized by the timing which makes it the answer to Jocasta's prayer, but Sophocles makes his language, also apparently simple questions, into a richly ironic, thematically dense, and shockingly programmatic utterance. These lines powerfully encourage us to hear a profound, dislocating irony in the word *hopou* and to hear it even in the name of the king. For Oedipus, "to know where", as much as "to know who", is the fundamental riddle of his life.

But does this mean we should hear *hopou* with ironic overtones when it occurs later in the play? Does "where" become a sign of irony? When the

---

[36] See Segal (1981) 207–48; Goldhill (1986) 199–221.

exangelos narrates Oedipus' screaming rampage through the house, he describes the king seeking (1256–7):

μητρῴαν δ' ὅπου
κίχοι διπλῆν ἄρουραν οὖ τε καὶ τέκνων.

where he might find
The double, motherly furrow of both himself and his children.

This description is certainly richly layered. "Double" (*diplên*) reminds us of Jocasta's worry about what words have "double" power, now with the added sexual frisson of her double role as wife/mother, already hinted at in the messenger's earlier questions (see above p14). The "furrow" (*arouran*) recalls the language of the wedding ceremony, here at its greatest transgression. Even *te kai* "both and" echoes with the surrounding repetitions of *teknôn* and *tekoi* "children", "give birth" (1250). What, then, of *hopou*? Is Oedipus just looking for Jocasta, or does his word echo with the puns of the messenger? Now as he knows and struggles to articulate the position of the "wife no wife", does the word "where" recall all the anxieties of place in the play? How marked a term can "where" become?

So, Oedipus begs Creon to expel him (1436–7):

ῥῖψόν με γῆς ἐκ τῆσδ' ὅσον τάχισθ', ὅπου
θνητῶν φανοῦμαι μηδενὸς προσήγορος.

Throw me out of this land as quickly as possible, where
I may enter into conversation with no human.

As in the messenger's opening speech (924/926) and in the *exangelos'* narrative (1256), *hopou* appears in the last foot of the iambic line, a rather odd position, especially with so strong an enjambment, though less odd for Sophocles than the other tragedians.[37] Oedipus wants to find a place for himself, a place beyond language, beyond address (*prosêgoros*). Here too, then, we might ask what echoes

---

[37] At *Ant.* 318 and *Ajax* 103 it is the final word of a line, in sharp *stichomythia*. See also *Trach.* 40, *Phil.* 443. Sophocles is much more free than Aeschylus or Euripides in ending a iambic line with a conjunction, especially ὅτι. There are at least fifty examples in the seven extant texts. The enjambments at *Phil.* 263 or 312 (or *OC* 14, 17, 495) are especially striking. By contrast, in the six extant plays of Aeschylus, there are only two examples: *Aga.* 1371, where the dramatic effect of the distorted expression in the mouth of the confused chorus is clear, and *Cho.* 98 (ὅτι). In the seventeen plays of Euripides, there are only eleven examples of such conjunctions in the final foot of a non-lyric line, and never used with the boldness of Sophocles. ὅπως *Med.* 322; *Her.* 420; *Tro.* 1008; *Phoen.* 1318; *IA* 56; ὅταν *Her.* 77; *Tro.* 880, 1236; ὅτι *Med.* 560; *Phoen.* 1617. The single example of ὅπου comes in the phrase οὐ γὰρ ἔσθ' ὅπου (*Her.* 186) which makes for a less jarring usage than the examples in Sophocles. Other strong enjambments are also much rarer in Euripides. The fact that the *PV* alone has eleven examples (61, 259, 322, 328, 377, 384, 463, 725, 793, 839, 951), including six cases of ἵνα, I take to be further evidence that the play was finished after the death of Aeschylus. See Griffith (1977) 96, for discussion and bibliography. For enjambment in Sophocles see the fine discussion of Dik (2007) 168–224. Sophocles' versification, as with his scene construction, is often far more novel and experimental than that of his contemporaries, though this rarely enters the discussion of "radical tragedy".

are to be heard in *hopou*. It seems to me that it is reasonable on the one hand to say that the *Oedipus* (of all plays) encourages an intensely paranoid attention to language, and, further, to recognize that "whereness" is a major theme of the play; but it is also reasonable, on the other hand, to say that *hopou*, "where", can slide back into being an unmarked term: *hopou* with the negative *mê* and the future is, after all, an extremely familiar idiom in Sophocles, as elsewhere, for the wish to be removed from human contact. That is, even if we agree that *locus* is a thematic focus of the *Oedipus*, we might disagree whether therefore every use of spatial vocabulary becomes charged with such thematic weight. Or, better, we might disagree *how* charged each use of spatial vocabulary seems. How ordinary is Oedipus' use of *hopou*? The judgement of a reader is a judgement not of grammar but of how ironic you think the plea to be elsewhere must be, and how precisely evoked by the simplest of words, "where". Or: how ordinary can language be in the *Oedipus*?

The *Oedipus Tyrannus*, then, not only dramatizes an uncertainty of knowing but also requires its audience to perform such uncertainty by making the most mundane of words a site of instability. We don't quite know where we are in this *locus classicus* . . .

As with knowing, so with learning. My second example concerns *didaskein* in the *Trachiniae*. I have already mentioned the entrance of the messenger (above p16). His simple opening utterance, "Queen Deianeira, I will be the first to release you from fear" (180–1), turns out to say far more than might be expected, partly because of the thematically significant false promise of "release from fear", where both *luein* and fear become thematically significant terms in this tragedy, and partly because his self-description as "first of messengers" anticipates the arrival of more. There are indeed several more messengers in this tragedy.[38] Lichas arrives from Heracles; Hyllus brings back to his mother the news of Heracles' death; the nurse brings on the story of Deianeira's death. The lies of Lichas (together with their exposure) lead us to beware the force and motivation of messages. Hyllus' tale, addressed to Deianeira, drives her to commit suicide. Deianeira's suicide is narrated by the victim's companion and carer, deeply moved. The power and significance of words play a major role in this play and necessarily frame this discussion.

When Hyllus enters, his first line seems as anodyne and functional as is possible. His mother tells him that the nurse, a slave, has uttered a good piece of advice, like a freeborn woman, and he replies (64):

ποῖον; δίδαξον, μῆτερ, εἰ διδακτά μοι.

What is it? Teach me, mother, if it may be taught to me.

The phrase *didaxon ei didakta* is a very familiar formula ("tell me if it may be told"), and it is precisely echoed later in the play by the chorus: *didaxon ei*

---

[38] See Kraus (1991).

didakton, "teach if it may be taught" (671). The imperative *didaxon* also occurs in the play elsewhere (233, 394), when Deianeira asks for information about Heracles from Lichas, and when Lichas asks Deianeira for instructions as to what he should say to Heracles from her. But the word *didaskein*, in its intensive form *ekdidaskein*, "to teach fully", or more commonly in the passive form, "to know fully", "really to know", will also become a specific marker of the difficult narrative of the young Hyllus. Hyllus' words drive his mother to suicide, but the boy then learns the truth of the centaur's involvement in the plot and lies bitterly weeping on his mother's corpse: *ops' ekdidakhtheis* (934), "he had learnt fully all too late". This phrase seems to capture not only Hyllus' fate but also that of Heracles and Deianeira: "'Finding out' is a key theme in this play",[39] as the very first lines of the play (ironically) announce. "Every report signals a too late".[40] Indeed, this is the problem of many Sophoclean characters: the destructiveness of partial knowledge and the lateness of full understanding.

Hyllus' education continues with his encounter with his father, who makes him swear to obey him, and then instructs him first to set fire to him on the pyre on Oeta (though Hyllus begs off setting the torch himself [1210–16]), and then to marry his concubine, Iole. Hyllus is deeply shocked. His father demands obedience and reminds him that it is just to do what a father asks (1244). Hyllus retorts with passion (1245):

ἀλλ᾽ ἐκδιδαχθῶ δῆτα δυσσεβεῖν, πάτερ;

Am I then to be really taught [*ekdidakhthô*] to commit impiety, father?

What Hyllus is to learn from his experience in this play remains a searching question.

His first request, then, "Teach me . . . if it may be taught" may come to seem to be less simply functional than it may at first have appeared; it may cue the most pressing problem of Hyllus' narrative. So, at what point does an audience begin to hear a heightened significance in the standard vocabulary? When the chorus uses the same phrase, is it inured from the perils of Hyllus' narrative? Hyllus' desperate question to his father about impiety (1245: *ekdidachthô dêta*) may powerfully echo the nurse's summation of his folly (934: *ops' ekdidachtheis*), but does this retrospectively colour the *chorus'* politeness (671)? With the example of *hopou* in the *Oedipus Tyrannus* the question was whether or how much the messenger's ironic language infected the later uses of the term; with *didaskein* in the *Trachiniae* the question rather is whether or how much the earliest uses of the term become marked as anticipatory by their later ironic use. It seems to me that Sophocles' play opens the possibility of hearing a grim irony as Hyllus enters; but the degree to which such apparently unmarked usage can flair into significance retrospectively

---

is extremely hard to determine. Hence the audience's uncertainty – provoked, as it were, by a half-heard irony in the mundane exchange of son and mother, echoed by the chorus' formulaic language. Perhaps.

From the half heard to the unsaid. My third example concerns the lack of the first-person plural in Antigone's language. *Antigone* dramatizes the tensions between differing perceptions of the collective and between different claims of duty. This invests the language of "the common", *to koinon*, with a particular force, as we will see in detail in Chapter 9, as an expression that captures the overlapping ties between family members and citizens in the city. The central question which joins and separates Creon and Antigone is whether the shared blood of the family outweighs the hostile intent of a brother towards the political community.[41] It has also been noted by several critics that there is, particularly at the beginning of the play, "a dense cluster of duals ... describing natural but frustrated *pairings* – murderous brothers, disunited sisters, sister and dead brother, dying bride and groom".[42] What is common becomes a question of what two share, should share or cannot share. This is conjoined with a repetitive use of the numbers two and one. So, for example, Ismene describes how δυοῖν ἀδελφοῖν ἐστερήθημεν δύο, μιᾷ θανόντοιν ἡμέρᾳ διπλῇ χερί "we two together were deprived of two siblings together, both dying together on one day with a double hand" (13–14). The dual nouns and verbs, together with the number "two" and the adjective "double" overlay different images of doubleness to contrast with the "single day" of their conjoining. She picks up the same terms shortly later where her "two brothers together on one day destroying one another, wretched together, in a common doom with hands against one another" (55). Again, the dual nouns, verbs and adjectives, together with the numbers and words of commonality and mutuality construct a language of multiple doubling. Even Creon talks of the brothers dying "by a double fate on a single day" (170–1).

This sense of pairing and separation, doubleness and singleness is worked out in a surprising linguistic way with Antigone and Ismene, which has not been noticed by the critics. As Antigone and Ismene disagree, the progressive separation of the sisters is anticipated in a fascinating habit of Antigone's language. She never uses a first-person plural verb to refer to herself and another person (and indeed only uses the form once altogether, to refer to herself, in her last iambic sentence), and she never uses the word, *hêmeis*, "we/us" in any case. When she first refers to the sufferings of Ismene and herself, she says τῶν σῶν τε κἀμῶν ... κακῶν, "yours and my evils", with a first-person singular verb. Creon's announcement has been σοὶ κἀμοὶ, λέγω γὰρ ἐμέ, "for you and for me – I mean *me*". Polyneices is τὸν γοῦν ἐμὸν καὶ τὸν σόν,

---

[41] For the modern political and critical implications of this, see Goldhill (2006). On the general issue of communality and Sophocles' language see the excellent Budelmann (2000).

[42] Griffith (1999) 121 *ad* 2–3. See Segal (1981) 185–6.

"actually mine and yours" (45). This three-fold repetition of "mine and yours" instead of "ours" is part of her rhetoric of persuasion, but also constantly anticipates the separation of the sisters away from a "we" into a contrasting "you" and "I".[43] Twice, in not especially emphatic places, Antigone uses the dual of *egô* in oblique cases (νῷν), once in her first address to Ismene (3), and once referring to the brothers of "the two of us" (21), the barest hint in the opening lines of Antigone trying to bring the sisters together. But her general unwillingness to align herself linguistically with her sister – or anyone else – as a pair or as a group plays a role in the increasing isolation of Antigone through the play, and in the expression of her extreme commitment to self. When she describes herself as a metic with no home among the alive or the dead (850–852), she is expressing the *egô*, who can form a "we" neither with her family on earth nor with her family in Hades.

Antigone famously claims to have been born to *sumphilein* rather than to *sunekhthein* (523), "to join together in mutual bonds of duty and obligation" rather than to "join together in hatred". Yet joining together with others, ironically enough, is exactly what she finds hardest to do. The lack of the word "we" in her vocabulary may seem to mark this. But how confident can a reader be in such an argument from silence? When does an *absence* of a word become recognized as an ironic lack? As with my first two examples, the temporality of reading is an integral factor in the fragile and uncertain recognition of irony.

Much of what I have been discussing with these three examples concerns re-reading: turning back from the end of a play to realise the full significance of what had appeared simple. How, then, does Sophocles treat the act of turning back? My final example of the precarious boundaries of irony is a single word from the *Philoctetes*, which indicates the act of "turning back". Odysseus accompanies Neoptolemus as he rushes back on stage "to undo all the mistakes I made before" (1224; see above p22). Odysseus asks (1222–3):

οὐκ ἂν φράσειας ἥντιν' αὖ παλίντροπος
κέλευθον ἕρπεις ὧδε σὺν σπουδῇ ταχύς;

Will you not indicate on what journey you are again
Returning in this way with such keenness and haste?

This is a superb example of the density of functional language in Sophocles' dramaturgy. First, the form of the question with its rather polite use of *an* and the optative indicates Odysseus' control: worried, polite, keen to persuade, he does not yet threaten or bully Neoptolemus. Second, the lines indicate for the

---

[43] In *Ajax* (1008), Teucer is horrified at the thought of returning to his grim father Telamon without his brother Ajax, and expresses his alienation and separation in a similar phrase: σὸς πατὴρ ἐμὸς θ' ἅμα, "your father, and mine too".

audience (and the actors) that Neoptolemus is not doubtfully re-treading his route towards Philoctetes, but is doing so with intent (*spoudê*) and speed (*takhus*). This is in contrast with his hesitations about what to do in the previous long scene. Third, the question itself indicates that Odysseus does not know what Neoptolemus is doing, which both cues the discussion to come, and marks the breakdown in their relationship, its shifting dynamics as now Odysseus is made to follow the boy. *Au*, "again", often occurs with *palin*, but here also specifically marks the repetition and difference of the path taken: here they are again travelling between ship and cave, but this time, Odysseus fears, it is different in intent.

But the word on which I wish to focus is *palintropos*, which I translated with *herpeis* as "returning", but which means "turning again", "turning back". Unlike the previous three test-cases of the irony of the ordinary, this is a rare word, and its use here is distinctive. First of all, it shows a similar ambiguity to *polutropos*, the first adjective applied to Odysseus in the *Odyssey* and a term closely associated with the hero (as well as the trickster god, Hermes, the only other figure in the Homeric poems to be called *polutropos*).[44] As was noted at least from Plato onwards, *polutropos* in the first line of the *Odyssey*, implies both "of many turns" in the sense of "many journeys", and "of many turns" in the sense of "very wily". That is, *-tropos* can connote both an idea of physical journey and an idea of mental attitude. *Keleuthon*, "path", *herpeis*, "you go", and *takhus*, "quickly", all suggest the element of journeying. *Spoudê*, "keenness", which is also picked up by much of the dialogue to come, indicates here a change of mind, a change of attitude. The ambiguity is, of course, significant (as in *Odyssey* I.1): the change of heart is demonstrated by the change of path.

By the fifth century, *tropos* has also come to mean a "style" or "manner" of rhetoric. In this play, with its emphasis on different types of speech performances from lies to shrieks, from oracles to false messages, what Odysseus is also announcing is a change of verbal performance from Neoptolemus – no longer deceptive and plotting but now sincere and exposing. This anticipation will be fulfilled (1267ff) as Neoptolemus tries (and fails) to persuade Philoctetes that he now is speaking the truth. *Palintropos* expresses Neoptolemus' backing away from *dolos*, "trickery" – and how hard it will be to put back together trust through words alone. *Palintropos* conceals a question as well as a narrative to come: can one "turn back" the clock once trust has been destroyed?

My reference to the Homeric use of *polutropos* was not merely for the semantics of *-tropos*. When the character of Odysseus uses a word which sounds so similar to such a particular and significant epithet of the character

---

[44] On *polutropos*, see Pucci (1982); Ellmann (1982); Goldhill (1991) 3–5 (with further bibliography).

of Odysseus in Homer, it sets up a potential intertextual reading.[45] Of course, each time Odysseus or any other Homeric character appears on the fifth-century stage, their figuration is worked through their Homeric inheritance. Odysseus in the *Philoctetes* has to be understood through his Homeric paradigm. The echo of the Homeric *polutropos* is here telling, however. We are watching the first collapse of Odysseus' powers of persuasion over Neoptolemus; in this play, which revolves around the return of a hero from an island far from any human inhabitation, this is a turning point, as Neoptolemus returns to Philoctetes to re-negotiate his return, though Philoctetes will insist on a *nostos* to his own island and refuse to go to Troy. The programmatic use of *polutropos* in Homer announces the return of Odysseus from his wanderings thanks to his powers of guile. The use of *palintropos* here, the re-writing of *polutropos*, signals the failure of Odysseus' guile and a new crisis in the narrative of return.

Palintropos is also picked up in the dialogue that follows. Odysseus asks Neoptolemus (1231) "What action are you going to take? Know that a certain fear is creeping over me". Neoptolemus replies (1232):

$$\pi\alpha\rho' \ o\hat{\upsilon}\pi\epsilon\rho \ \check{\epsilon}\lambda\alpha\beta ov \ \tau\acute{\alpha}\delta\epsilon \ \tau\grave{\alpha} \ \tau\acute{o}\xi\alpha, \ \alpha\hat{\upsilon}\theta\iota\varsigma \ \pi\acute{\alpha}\lambda\iota\nu \dots$$

From whom I took this bow, back again . . .

Odysseus immediately interrupts with "O Zeus, what are you going to say?" in order to stop the finality of Neoptolemus' pronouncement that would confirm Odysseus' fears. This leaves *authis palin* hanging in the air. It points out that underneath the phrase *au palintropos* is not just a return journey but a giving back, a paying back, a reversal of a (corrupted) exchange. So Odysseus asks (1247–8) "How exactly can it be just to give up again (*palin metheinai*) the things you actually got by my plan?": the word *palin*, recalling *palintropos* and *authis palin*, again stresses the physical act of "returning" the bow which underlies the "returning" of Neoptolemus to the cave.

Finally, the return of Neoptolemus and Odysseus also encourages the audience to return to the previous scene, where they watched Neoptolemus stand in silence in the face of Philoctetes' rant, confess an onset of pity for the outraged hero, but then leave with Odysseus and the bow. What may have appeared as a hardening of the young man's intent, now appears as a struggle of conscience; where we might have wondered how sincere Neoptolemus' expressions of sympathy for Philoctetes were, now his rejection of Odysseus retrospectively validates the honesty of his expressed feelings. The return,

---

[45] Many critics have argued for an influence of Heraclitus on the language of Sophocles in this play (where a bow is life). I have wondered whether one might just hear an echo of *palintonos*, that key Heraclitean term, here in *palintropos* as Neoptolemus carries the bow back. One may also hear an echo of Parmenides fr 6, itself possibly an echo of Heraclitus: πάντων δὲ παλίντροπός ἐστι κάλευθος, "Of all things, the path is backwards turning" – from a passage on the confusion of humans. Parmenides' recognition of human confusion as a "backwards turning path" would suit Neoptolemus' return here.

Neoptolemus' change of heart, leads the audience to re-evaluate his earlier responses. *Palintropos*, and the repetitions of *palin, au, authis*, also cue the audience's re-consideration of Neoptolemus' *tropos*: a sign to re-read.

Odysseus' words, as he enters with Neoptolemus, can be shown, then, to resonate with a semantic density to match their functional complexity: there is an ironic excess of signification in Odysseus' language, echoing beyond his apparent immediate expression. But to what degree does the depth of reading offered here stand in tension with the functional role of the line? This difficulty can be made vivid by looking at how David Grene renders the line in his best-selling translation of the play: "You have turned back, there is hurry in your step. Will you not tell me why?".[46] It is, of course, hard to hear the semantic range of *palintropos* in the resolutely ordinary "you have turned back", and consequently hard to see the line as anything other than functional, indeed totally mundane. So we might ask: how much of the ironic excess of signification is to be appreciated in the rushed entrance? How expansive a moment of irony is this? Here, too, the temporality of reading is integral to the uncertain recognition of the irony: how much irony is recognized here depends on how much of the buried life of the word is accessed in the moment – the process – of reading, how much attention is paid to the passing word, as the men cross the stage.

Each of these four test-cases has focused on particularly everyday language – "know", "where", "teach", "we", "back" – and on apparently functional expressions, whose role in the drama appears to be primarily to progress the action. In each example, we have tried to trace the ironic horror that Sophocles lets emerge from the ordinary. In contrast with the great heroes and grand actions that dominate tragic theatre, apparently trivial, unnoticed, and mundane words turn out to conceal a buried life of dangerous, excessive meaning, over which the characters have little control. The word in passing, as Oedipus found at the feast, is never just passing. It is always all too late that we learn fully the significance of the language we use and hear.

But these four examples were also chosen because each reflects on the dominant model of tragic irony as establishing the audience in a position of secure and superior knowledge. "Knowing" and "teaching" become terms of tragic misprision rather than comfortable recognition; the sense of place of an audience, a sense of collectivity are set at stake. The very act of re-reading, integral to irony, becomes invested with excessive and provocative significance. What is more – and this is most important for my argument – each of these test-cases raised a deeply problematic question about the very recognition of irony. I wrote above "*we have tried to trace* the ironic horror . . ." because in the process of exploring Sophoclean irony at work, in each case our attempt to

---

[46] Grene and Lattimore (1954).

trace irony came up against the uncertainty of how far to press Sophocles' language, to what degree to perceive irony in the language of the unfolding tragedy. In contrast to the dominant model of tragic irony, in these examples the audience cannot see itself simply as *le sujet qui sait*, but finds itself implicated in the doubts, uncertainties and fissures of tragic language. "We dwell within", as Rilke writes.[47] Like a Sophoclean character, each reader is faced with the question of how far to go.[48]

The hardest question, however, remains how we should bring together the systematic picture of the failure of human attempts to control narrative with this more edgy, flickering uncertainty. How should we reconcile the knowing recognition of irony and the uncertain recognition of possible irony; the audience as *le sujet qui sait* and the audience conscious of the *glissement*, the slipping and sliding, of its knowing? Does the slipperiness or instability traced through the limit cases of potential irony frame and undercut the systematic understanding of *lusis*? Or should the examples of limit cases be treated as exceptions, which do not significantly affect the thematics of undoing?

In contemporary critical discussion of tragedy, there is a fierce though not always intelligently articulated debate about the openness of meaning, about how much ambivalence there is in tragedy. Irony (inevitably) introduces instability into discourse – since what is said is always a mask for other meanings – and critical reading involves negotiating this instability. Such a negotiation can have very different emphases – stressing, for example, coherence, or, by contrast, stressing the stress-fractures in such coherence. But a critical reading that sees only instability, indeterminacy, doubt, is unlikely to take adequate account of the political, normative power of the plays, just as a critical reading that sees only the expression of ideology or the declaration of a message is unlikely to take adequate account of the slipperiness of tragic discourse and the response to it. What I have tried to show in this chapter is first that Sophocles is much concerned with humans' lack of control over narrative and language, and with the structures of self-deception which inform the misplaced attempts to achieve such certainty. But, second, that the instability introduced by the ironies in Sophocles' texts is itself a condition of possibility of critical disagreement – critical disagreement for which resolution will only ever be temporary: *oud' ekhei lusin.*

---

[47] Rilke (1948) II, 308.

[48] The scholia on *OT* 264 seem to allude to the awkward boundaries of irony: αἱ τοιαῦται ἔννοιαι οὐχ ἔχονται μὲν τοῦ σεμνοῦ, κινητικαὶ δέ εἰσι τοῦ θεάτρου. αἷς καὶ πλεονάζει Εὐριπίδης, ὁ δὲ Σοφοκλῆς πρὸς βράχυ μόνον ἅπτεται πρὸς τὸ κινῆσαι τὸ θέατρον. There are several comments in the scholia which note what we term tragic irony (with various forms of expression) – *ad OT* 34, 132, 137, 141, 372, 928, 1183 – but this seems to go further in its recognition of discomfort – the potential lack of solemnity in irony, which is none the less moving – and in its recognition that Euripides, in contrast to Sophocles, goes too far with it.

Both the lack of control figured in the language of *lusis* and the challenge to the audience's secure sense of understanding need to be seen within a political dimension, however. The audience is a central and integral element in Athenian democracy – privileged as the voting, sovereign body of citizens.[49] Democracy depends on its citizens listening, evaluating and judging arguments put in front of them; discussing and predicting the flow of events in their decision-making. Tragedy is the institution where the reliability of these processes is held up to most consistent scrutiny. The audiences on stage make error after error of understanding, decision-making is repeatedly flawed, and, the final twist, the audience in the theatre is not only awed, emotionally overcome by what is staged before them, but also finds itself implicated by the drama in its own narrative of uncertainty. How tragedy is political has become one of the most heated debates of the contemporary academy. The most profound questioning of democracy, I would suggest, is not to be found by searching through the tragic texts for any direct engagement with specific political policies or concrete issues of foreign or domestic strategy. Tragedy's politics is to be found rather in the searing exploration of the basic elements of democratic principle: responsibility, duty, masculinity, decision-making, self-control and so on. In the case of the Sophoclean ironies I have been discussing, the shaky ability of characters to predict and understand their own narratives, and the shaky ability of the audience fully to understand the ironies of the language articulated in front of them, holds up a mirror to the audience in the theatre – a mirror which gives an uncomfortable view of the audience's political role as judging, evaluating citizens. Tragedy asks questions of the self. And Sophocles' ironic tragedy asks a painful question of the confident self of fifth-century democracy. Where so much of the fifth-century enlightenment, especially in the decision-hungry democracy, is concerned with producing answers, Sophocles reminds his audience again and again that in the human world secure solutions are harder to find: *oud' ekhei lusin.*

---

[49] On the audience of democracy, see below ch 2, and e.g. Ober (1989); Lanni (1997) (with the added background in Lanni [2006]); Sinclair (1988); Hansen (1991); Boegehold and Scafuro eds (1994); Finley (1983); Ober and Hedrick eds (1996); Cartledge, Millett and Todd eds (1990); Meier (1990); Loraux (1981), Hesk (2000) – each with further bibliography; on theatre audiences see McGlew (2002), Henderson (1991), Goldhill (1994), (1997), and (2000), which has been critically discussed in Nightingale (2004), who offers a different context for ideas of *theoria.* See most recently Revermann (2006). A very long bibliography could be given for audiences for tragedy: for two exemplary versions of the potential of audience studies see Orgel (1975) and Thomas (2002).

2

The Audience on Stage

RHETORIC, EMOTION, AND JUDGEMENT

Democracy – and its malcontents – requires a theory of the audience.[1]

In ancient Athenian participatory democracy, the audience, in its different forms, can be seen as a privileged arena in which citizenship is enacted. The citizen performs his civic duty as a juror in the law court, as a voter in the assembly, as a spectator in the theatre, and even as a *theoros* [official attendee] in the *agônes* [contests] of festivals. In each case, as we noted in Chapter 1, the role of audience member is to listen, to judge, to vote (or in the case of theatre at least to observe his representative, selected by lot, voting). By fulfilling one's role as a listening, voting member of a collective audience, a citizen engages in *ta politika*, the political life of the city.[2] Consequently, in the classical era the discussion of persuasion spreads far beyond the formal rhetorical techniques for speakers as enshrined in the rhetorical handbooks, in order to scrutinize the intellectual and emotional practise of being in an audience – both from the

---

[1] This chapter was first written with huge affection and respect in honour of Pat Easterling. My subject was chosen partly to revisit tragic audiences, which I discussed under her inspirational editorship in the *Cambridge Companion to Greek Tragedy*, and partly because Pat is someone I always listen to carefully, though, like many a Sophoclean character, I may not realise the full wisdom of what I am told till much later.

I have had a further go at thinking about audiences in Goldhill (1994), (1997), and (2000), which has been critically discussed in Nightingale (2004), who offers a different context for ideas of *theoria*. See most recently Revermann (2006). A very long bibliography could be given for audiences for tragedy: for two exemplary versions of the potential of audience studies see Orgel (1975) and Thomas (2002). I should probably say from the outset that the phrase "theory of the audience" does not imply at all that an audience is to be thought of as a single, undifferentiated body, as Heath seems to think (*G&R* 2010).

[2] A huge bibliography could be given for this: see in particular Lanni (1997) (with the added background in Lanni [2006]); Sinclair (1988); Hansen (1991); Boegehold and Scafuro eds (1994); Finley (1983); Ober and Hedrick eds (1996); Cartledge, Millett and Todd eds (1990); Ober (1989); Meier (1990); Loraux (1981) – each with further bibliography.

point of view of the speaker (double guessing his audience) and from the point of view of being the listener (critically responding to a speaker), and, most importantly, as a dynamic exchange, a battle of wills, between the two.[3] Rhetoric works, which is why it is taught, practised and feared. If words have power, if the weaker argument can be made the stronger, if to be persuaded is to lose authority or self-determination to another, how can one listen and not be a victim of words? How can one properly perform one's role as a judging, responsible citizen, faced by the swirl of competing arguments which make up the political discourse of Athens?

These questions were explored in different genres with differing degrees of theoretical explicitation. The fifth-century sophist and rhetorician, Gorgias, for example, is fascinated by the psychology of the passive audience – thrilled, manipulated, led, and yet still resistant: he brilliantly imagines the total passivity of a listener to his *logos* in order to explore the power of speech.[4] Thucydides' Cleon mocks, cajoles and bullies the citizens in the assembly through an explicit discussion of their passivity, their capacity for pleasured inaction: and Thucydides is fully aware of the self-reflexive irony of this rhetoric of inaction in action.[5] Demosthenes too teases and twists the Athenians with their own awareness of their reputation for a love of words and an inability to follow up plans with action: complicity as pressure towards collective action.[6] Yet in sharp contrast to Gorgias' image of the *logos* as a powerful master (*dunastês*), Demosthenes – with no less slyness and rhetorical adeptness – claims "I see that for the most part the audience is in control of the power (*dunamis*) of the speakers".[7] Plato's snarling image of the crowd in democracy as a beast titillated and fed by the politicians, who are themselves slaves to the mood of the beast, articulates a philosophical disdain for the dynamic of speaker and audience in public political life, which is matched by the comic scalpel of Aristophanes' theatre, where the character Demos – the People – allows his slaves license to flatter and steal before he finally comes to his (self-interested) senses, led as he is by an even more outrageous demagogue.[8] Aristotle theorizes persuasion fully in terms of the collective expectations of a mass audience, and laments

---

[3] See for discussion in particular Hesk (2000); also Ober (1989); Buxton (1982); Ford (2002); Jarratt (1991); Wardy (1996).

[4] See Wardy (1996), with further bibliography.

[5] Thucydides III. 38; the rhetoric of Thucydides, in comparison with, say, Herodotus or Tacitus, is not as thoroughly discussed as one might expect. See for the types of discussion available e.g. Cogan (1981); Crane (1996), and more recently and more congenially Price (2001); Rood (2004) and Morrison (2006).

[6] I am thinking, for example, of *Olynthiac* II 12: but see more generally Ober (1989) and Hesk (2000).

[7] Dem. 18.277: καίτοι ἔγωγ᾽ ὁρῶ τῆς τῶν λεγόντων δυνάμεως τοὺς ἀκούοντας τὸ πλεῖστον κυρίους.

[8] See Aristophanes' *Knights* with the not wholly satisfactory McGlew (2002).

the philosopher's inability to get it quite right, where a man of the street can sway a crowd.[9]

Plato's clever and fearful arguments against what he calls democracy's *theatrocracy* have become so fully incorporated into modern Western political thinking that it seems still a quite remarkable theoretical assertion that a vote by a large group of citizens will be better founded than a decision by the single most informed or most authoritative or most intelligent individual. Yet this is a theory of the audience repeatedly promoted and projected by democracy – and required by the direct democracy of ancient Athens. What is more, modern political discussion has become obsessed, it seems, with the perils of media manipulation – spin; that is, with the ability of politicians to manipulate, persuade and use the necessary tools of democratic debate to their own advantage (a concern already hugely familiar from ancient Athens).[10] Without a more developed theory of the audience (the collective of citizens) and its role in decision making, it is hard to see how such a debate can progress beyond politicians' self-serving and mutually undermining claims and counterclaims of "our truth" versus "their manipulation". Democracy requires a theory of the audience both in the sense that its institutional processes are predicated on such a theory, and in the sense that it does not yet possess such a theory in a fully worked out form.

We will see in Chapters 6 and 7 how the role of the audience becomes absolutely integral in German Idealist thinking about tragedy, both as an aesthetic frame and as a political entity. In this chapter, however, I shall suggest that Sophoclean theatre is an excellent place to think about the audience of democracy. In the first chapter we saw how Sophocles' flickering irony engaged and destabilized the knowing audience of the theatre – the knowing audience precisely as a key figure of democracy. Now we will turn to look at how this audience finds itself represented in Sophoclean drama. My main concern is not with the constitution and reactions of the fifth-century Athenian audience as such (nor with its heirs in the many and continuing modern responses to Sophocles' plays).[11] Nor is it to question the trivial rhetoric with which so many critics have continued to use the imagined audience as a bastion for their own opinions ("surely no audience would . . .", "the audience would instantly recognize . . ."). The multiform make-up of a theatre audience (on the one hand) and its drive towards a collective response (on the other), especially coupled with an audience's ability to develop its views in discussion *after* a play as much as in the performance time of the play, create complex and temporally extended tensions which will only be oversimplified by such naïve and

---

[9] Aristotle *Rhetoric* II 22. See Wardy (1996) 108–38; and more generally Furley and Nehemas eds (1994). The category of the enthymeme is central to Aristotle's discussion.

[10] See Hesk (1990) and from a different angle Ober (1989).

[11] See Goldhill (1997); Goldhill (1994); Henderson (1991); Podlecki (1990).

univocal idealization of the audience as a single and instant body. Rather, I want here to look at how Sophocles dramatizes the process of being (in) an audience: how does Sophocles put the audience on stage?

I

Now, tragedy as a genre of staged dialogue is obviously full of audiences: every speech is addressed to someone who could be said to be its audience; even monologues are spoken before a chorus (with the exception of Ajax's suicide speech in the *Ajax* [815–65], and even that is full of vocatives addressed to the gods and the unfeeling earth and sun). What's more, tragedy is also a genre of misunderstanding or of multiple and conflicting understandings. Characters use the same words in different ways, as Vernant influentially expressed it, and the clash between these tensions and ambiguities is a motive force of the plotting of tragedy: tragic language displays the difficulties of the city's developing political language to the audience of the city through the failure of the actors on stage to avoid the violent outcome of their own misunderstandings.[12] All of this is fundamental to tragedy's functioning in the city as a political genre. But I want to focus in this chapter on a specific dramatic device of creating an audience on stage beyond the omnipresent chorus, and beyond the addressee of any particular speech. It is a device which Sophocles uses often and with insistent interest; it is made possible largely by the use of the third actor, an innovation which Sophocles is said to have introduced; and it demonstrates, I believe, a sustained engagement with the widest implications of democracy's audience. It is a dramatic structure from which in turn Bertolt Brecht, for example, learnt much.

This dramatic strategy is best introduced by a simple and very well-known example. The opening scene of the *Ajax* brings on stage Odysseus, sniffing around the tent of Ajax. Athene – who may or may not be seen by the audience[13] – lets Odysseus (and the audience) into the plot so far, and announces she will bring the mad Ajax out from the tent – much to Odysseus' discomfort, which the goddess teases him about, in the bantering style she usually adopts with her hero. This sets up the discussion between the still enraged and maddened Ajax and the goddess – which is overheard by Odysseus. He is an audience on stage, who is silent and concealed from the protagonist, and who acts as a focalizer for the audience in the theatre. When Ajax leaves, Athene turns towards Odysseus and asks (*Ajax* 118–120): "Do you see, Odysseus, how great the power of

---

[12] Vernant and Vidal-Naquet (1981); in general see Goldhill (1986) especially ch 3.

[13] See Taplin (1978) 185 n.12, who insists she is visible to all, including Odysseus. Segal (1995) 19 thinks she is invisible to Odysseus (as does Jebb). Hesk (2003) 43–4, most recently, hedges his bets. See also Heath (1987) 165–6; Garvie (1998) 124.

the gods is. Who could have been found more sensible than this man? Who better at doing what time required?" But Odysseus sees something else (121–6): "I do not know of any one. But I pity the wretched man nonetheless, even though he is my enemy, because he has been harnessed to a dire disaster. I do not look to his case more than my own. For I see that we who live are nothing more than images or a vain shadow." Odysseus takes Athene's generalization about the gods and makes it a generalization about mortals. Where she offered him the objectification of a judgement on a once great man, now laid low ("Who [was] more sensible than this man?"), Odysseus takes his own position (*egô*, "I", *oid'*, "I know", *horô*, "I see") and puts it together with such potential objectification (*nin* "him"), and through a gesture of pity or compassion discovers from the "his" (*to toutou*) and the "my" (*toumon*) the "we" (*hêmas*) in the example. Not only does Odysseus recognize the weakness of humans where Athene declared the strength of the gods, but also this perspective allows him to bypass the aggression of human hates and violence ("even though he is my enemy"). This shift of perspective is marked in the repeated words of seeing: "do you see?" [*horâis*] asks Athene; "I see", [*horô*] replies Odysseus – but what he sees is indeed his own shadow, his own likeness: not just the emptiness of human achievement, but how each human is an image of each other in their weakness and suffering.

As several critics have argued, this short dialogue looks forward to the closing scene of the play, where Odysseus effects a closure by persuading the Greek leaders to control their antipathy to Ajax.[14] It also anticipates the debate about the figure of Ajax, which takes up the second half of the play, and which sets in motion strikingly opposed judgements on the worth of the hero. But the scene depends on constructing Odysseus as an audience on stage. The emphasis on what he has seen and understood of the scene, stage-managed in front of him by Athene, creates an image of the critical observer – an observer who does not simply follow the stage directions of the goddess, but takes his own view of what has happened. This image of the critical observer offers a model for the audience in the theatre, faced as they will be by Ajax's deception speech and the chorus' delighted reaction to it, and by the violent row over the worth of Ajax between Teucer, Menelaus and Agamemnon. The difference between Athene's view of the scene and Odysseus' creates a space for the audience to discover its own critical distance from the violent and extreme words on stage.

The *Philoctetes* is deeply concerned with persuasion, trust, and with staged scenes.[15] The audience in the theatre not only watches the extended twists and turns of the characters' interactions, but also watches their reactions to staged

---

[14] See e.g. Winnington-Ingram (1980) 66–72; and in most detail, Whitlock Blundell (1989) especially 60–8 and 95–105.

[15] See, of course, Easterling (1978); also especially Segal (1981) 328–61; also Roberts (1989); Ringer (1998) 101–26.

scenes. So the False Merchant's message prompts different responses from all the characters on stage, as we watch Philoctetes being gulled, Neoptolemus responding both to the offstage prompting of Odysseus and to the fresh material released by the False Merchant; and the chorus responding both to their master, Neoptolemus, and to the object of their pursuit, Philoctetes, as well as to the False Merchant himself. The play is filled with such complex layers of dramatic cross-currents.

But I wish to focus here on the end of the great central episode, where Odysseus returns on stage for the first time since the opening moments of the play. From the beginning of the play, we have watched Neoptolemus respond to Philoctetes, though it is often hard to tell precisely how much of his emotional response is genuine, and how much required by the plot against the hero. When Philoctetes first starts to show the painful physical symptoms of his wound, Neoptolemus seems powerfully moved (759–61):

> ἰὼ ἰὼ δύστηνε σύ,
> δύστηνε δῆτα διὰ πόνων πάντων φανείς.
> βούλῃ λάβωμαι δῆτα καὶ θίγω τί σου.

> Oh, oh, wretched you,
> Really wretched, it's revealed, in all your sufferings.
> Do you want me really to hold you and touch you somehow?

The repetitions, especially of *dêta*, indicate strongly emotional expressivity. (It would be more idiomatic to translate the second *dêta* as "then", as it normally has a consequential force with questions: I have translated both occurrences as "really" only to keep the force of the repetition.) Are we to see this as part of Neoptolemus' plotting, playing his role to perfection? Or is it his true emotions of pity boiling to the surface? It is very rare to see the particle *dêta* repeated in the same couplet like this (and it is also in his previous question, *ti dêta drasô*, "What really [then] should I do?"): is this the sign of real grief? Or an over-the-top attempt to convey how really, really upset he is? What is being "revealed" here?[16]

Shortly after this, when Philoctetes collapses into agony, Neoptolemus goes quiet (805): Philoctetes in desperate pain cries out: "What are you saying? Why are you silent? Where on earth are you, child?". Neoptolemus replies (806): "For a long time in fact [*palai dê*] I have been upset, grieving over your misfortune". As Neoptolemus watches Philoctetes in agony, we watch and evaluate his reaction. It seems powerfully felt, yet thirty-five lines later he is celebrating the success of the first part of the plot as Philoctetes sleeps: no remorse or regret is evident (839–842).

---

[16] Segal (1981) 335–6 followed by Pucci (2003) *ad loc* notes the extraordinary delicacy of τι in this line: "shall I touch you *in some way/ in some place*" – the hesitancy and intimacy conveyed by this small word is indeed remarkable. Kosak (1999) 124 undertranslates the line but has a good discussion of the reasons for Philoctetes refusing Neoptolemus' touch.

Neoptolemus' silence, highlighted in these earlier scenes, becomes an even more powerful dramatic resource as Odysseus' entrance is approached.[17] Neoptolemus, now with Philoctetes' bow in his possession, has revealed to Philoctetes the plot against him – but has refused to give back the bow since "justice and expediency constrain me to listen to those in authority" (925–6). Philoctetes bitterly laments, and desperately pleads for recognition and the return of his bow (927–62). His speech returns three times to Neoptolemus' silence and its possible significance: "But he will not even address me. He looks away again, as if he will never release the bow" (934–5); "Please now be yourself still. What do you say? You are silent. I am nothing, a wretched man." (950–51); "May you not yet perish, until I know if you will change your judgement" (961–2), a plea that receives no answer. (Looking away, looking down, breaking visual contact becomes a trope in rhetoric as much as in poetry, and in art too, a recognized somatics of disengagement.[18]) This extended attempt at persuasion – at breaking through Neoptolemus' silence – prompts the chorus to ask their master what they should do, and Neoptolemus confesses that a strange sense of pity has come over him, not just now but for some time since (963–6), lines that recall his response to the physical symptoms of Philoctetes earlier. *oimoi ti drasô*, "Alas what am I to do?", (969) asks Neoptolemus – the archetypal tragic question – and *ti drômen, andres*, "What are we to do, men?" (974). It is at this moment of hesitation – a half line – that Odysseus enters to take control of the scene.

He enters into a strident row with Philoctetes; Philoctetes has to be held down as he threatens to kill himself; by the end of the scene, Philoctetes is left quite humiliated and isolated, as the Greeks prepare to sail off with the bow. What is striking about the dramaturgy of this scene is that Neoptolemus is silent from the entrance of Odysseus to the final moment of the action. He is an audience to the row between Philoctetes and Odysseus.[19] His silence prompts two questions (at least). First, especially after Philoctetes has drawn attention to the significance of silence, and Neoptolemus has indicated his own growing feelings of pity, what are the emotions with which Neoptolemus watches these two older men fight? Second, especially after Neoptolemus has twice asked what to do, what *is* he going to do?

These questions are made insistent by the staging of the end of the scene. Philoctetes turns to Neoptolemus at last (1066–7): "Child of Achilles, will I be not addressed by even your voice? Will you go away like this?" – a question which draws attention both to his silence and to his actions – and which acts as a moving plea once again (*prosphônêi'* 934; *phones . . . prosphthegktos* 1066–7).

---

[17] See, with useful general background, Montiglio (2000) 247–8.

[18] On art see Frontisi-Ducroux (1995); on rhetoric and audience noise see Bers (1985) and Hall (2006) 363–6, and in general Boegehold (1999).

[19] Seale (1982) 29: the scene "invites the audience to watch Neoptolemus' action, to observe him observe".

But Odysseus replies by addressing Neoptolemus (1068–9): "Go! Don't look at him, noble though you are, lest you mar our fortunes". Odysseus does not let him speak, ushers him out – and is clearly worried that his character will lead him to damage their venture. The audience is again encouraged to wonder about Neoptolemus' potential responses, as his silence is drawn attention to. So Philoctetes tries the chorus (1070–1): "Will I really be actually left in this way deserted by you, friends? Will you not pity me?". These questions recall Neoptolemus' growing pity as well as the chorus' earlier feelings. But their answer recalls their own diffident questions earlier, addressed to Neoptolemus, of what they should do (1072–3): "This boy is our commander. Whatever he says to you, we too must say." They cannot act critically or with any form of self-determination because of their role in the hierarchy. But notice their expression "whatever he *says* to you, we too must *say*" – after 100 lines of silence, there is mounting and conflicting pressure on Neoptolemus to say something (and mounting expectation for the audience in the theatre). Will he express pity again? Will he bow to those in authority? Will he answer?

His response is perhaps something of a surprise. Neoptolemus does not address Philoctetes (though no doubt he intends Philoctetes once again to be an unacknowledged audience to his words). He replies to his crew. He does allude to his feelings, but only in passing as he indicates that he will follow his commanding officer's instructions (1074–80):

> I will get a reputation for fulsome pity from him [Odysseus].
> But, stay, if it seems good to him [Philoctetes],
> For as much time as the sailors need
> To prepare the boat and we to pray to the gods.
> Perhaps in the meanwhile he [Philoctetes] will find some
> Better thinking with regard to us. We two are departing, then.
> When we summon you, come quickly.

This is a markedly unemotional speech after his turmoil before. He does not express pity, but notes he will get a reputation for it. He does not address a word to Philoctetes, who begged to hear him speak to him, but merely hopes – in the third person – that he will change his attitude. He is clearly bonded with Odysseus ("we two" – the dual in Greek), and, after his apparently anguished questions about what to do, now he has no doubt: he is following those in command, and leaving, and instructs the crew to join them promptly. The speech seems functional and clear. It is as if Neoptolemus in his role as audience has moved from his confusion and wavering emotion now to a certain distance from his own earlier feelings, and a clarity about what he is to do.

Yet when he returns on stage in the next scene pursued by the extremely worried Odysseus, it is, as he puts it, "to undo all the wrongs I have done previously" (1224). They face off against each other as each threatens to draw a sword (1254–5), a reworking of the famous scene of *Iliad* I where Achilles,

Neoptolemus' father, makes to draw his sword against Agamemnon, Odysseus' chief. Even here, though, action is deferred, and it is, initially, words (*logous*) that Neoptolemus announces he is bringing to Philoctetes (1267). There is much we could say about this scene as the culmination of the thematics of persuasion, action versus words, and trust, all focused on the possession of the bow. But, above all, Neoptolemus' change of heart requires a re-reading of the previous scene, his apparent hardening of spirit. Now we are encouraged to see more tension beneath his performance, more doubt within him than was expressed to Odysseus. His role as audience develops as a fully active process, part of the questions of character, truthfulness, deception, questions which the figure of Neoptolemus raises throughout the drama.

The silence of Neoptolemus in his role as audience becomes a sign to be read and re-read by the audience in the theatre (and by the characters on stage): it becomes a hermeneutic crux – part of the play's fascination with speech acts (from screams, to tricks, to messages, to oracles). However the silence was read first time (hardening? deception? self-deception? desperate attempt to toe the line?), the return of Neoptolemus (which repeats again and again the language of change, reversal: *au, palintropos, en tôi prin, neon, neon, authis palin*, "again", "turning back", "before", "afresh", "afresh", "back again" [1222–32]) demands a re-evaluation of his earlier performance. Who is Neoptolemus deceiving as he leaves the stage with Odysseus? Philoctetes – either because he is still fully engaged with the plot against him or because he is denying his strong feelings towards him by maintaining his silence? Odysseus – because he no longer will be able to uphold his position within the plot, but acts as if he can? Himself – because in his rejection of Philoctetes, he is either pretending he can repress the feelings that will erupt in the next scene or because he still thinks that "obeying those in command" is an adequate criterion for ethical action? Or all of these . . .? The complexity of ethical judgement here is created for us, the audience, by watching Neoptolemus watching – that is, by the audience on stage.

There has been an extensive discussion of "character" in Greek tragedy, and, specifically, the issue of inwardness: how the language of tragedy reveals the inner life of a person on stage.[20] Here we can see how Sophocles brilliantly creates a question of character for the audience, not only by Neoptolemus' change of mind (which happens offstage) but also by giving him no words to say through a crucial scene. The contrast with, say, Medea's celebrated monologue before the murder of her children is striking. Medea expresses herself volubly, as she shifts position, hardens her heart, and comes to a decision. Her articulated complexity of feelings became a standard topic for poetry and art. Neoptolemus' silence becomes a screen on which the audience projects its interpretation of what he is thinking or feeling. The device of the audience on

---

[20] Easterling (1973); Easterling (1977); Easterling (1990); see also Gould (1978); Goldhill (1990).

stage becomes a way here of engaging the audience in the theatre in the processes of moral choice and doubt – wondering about character and action. The audience on stage becomes the lynchpin of the play's provocation of the audience in the theatre.

II

A wonderful example of the emotional side of this technique occurs in the *Oedipus Tyrannus*. The arrival of the messenger, apparently in answer to Jocasta's prayer for *lusis*, is, as we have seen, a scene of deep narrative and linguistic ironies. Jocasta is delighted with his message; she calls out Oedipus to hear it. The messenger, keen to help Oedipus recover from his traumatic fear, reveals the shocking fact that Polybus is not his real father (1016). Oedipus cross-examines him. The discussion between the messenger and Oedipus stretches from 988 to 1059 (one of the longer stretches of single line stichomythia in Sophocles). As the new information is revealed about his origin in the palace of Laius, Oedipus turns finally to Jocasta, who has been listening silently, and asks her if indeed the man who gave the baby to the messenger is the same one as the herdsman she has already summoned (1054–5). Jocasta replies with a despairing appeal to him to look no further into the matter (1056–7), and continues to try to stop Oedipus searching any more for his identity. At 1071 – less than 20 lines on – she flees the stage to commit suicide with her final words: ἰοὺ ἰού, δύστηνε· τοῦτο γὰρ σ᾽ ἐγὼ μόνον προσειπεῖν, ἄλλο δ᾽ οὔποθ᾽ ὕστερον, "Aaah, aaah, wretched man. This is all I can call you. Nothing else ever more." No more words and names, not only because she is going to kill herself, but also because whatever she might call him – husband, son – is horrifically mixed in the morass of incest.[21] Jocasta has realised the truth of Oedipus' identity, and the recognition has taken place during her silent observation as audience to the discussion of Oedipus and the messenger. The audience in the theatre watches not just Oedipus cross-examining the herdsman with increasing fervour and drawing the wrong conclusion of his lowly birth, but also the dawning, silent horror of the queen. Again the invitation to project the internal moral and emotional turmoil of the queen seems clear.

Electra uses the device of the audience on stage in the most striking way three times, and constructs through this an extraordinary self-reflexive commentary on tragic emotion.[22] Clytemnestra's prayer to Apollo, which closes her agon with Electra, is highly conscious of its audience. She describes her prayer

---

[21] See Goldhill (1986) 206.
[22] See Batchelder (1995); Ringer (1998).

as *kekrummenên baxin*, "concealed, shrouded speech" (638), necessary because "My speech is not among friends, and it is not fitting to open all to the light when *she* is standing near" (639–40). A muffled prayer is a grotesque speech act. But it receives ironic and instant response with the arrival of the Paidagogus with the false news of Orestes' death. The irony is strongly underlined when Clytemnestra responds to the announcement of good news with *edexamên to rhêthen*, "I have received your utterance [as an omen]" (668), the standard recognition of a cledonomantic moment, that is, when a listener turns a speaker's words into a prophecy of the future.[23] As Clytemnestra turns the words into an omen, she is quite unaware of what sort of an omen she is ratifying – and for the audience, recognizing the frisson of such a twist on the power of words, the irony produces a self-conscious awareness of the doubleness of language, an awareness which is a defining characteristic of an audience. The Paidagogus' news, and especially his long speech that describes Orestes' fatal chariot crash, set up in this way, is delivered to three audiences: Clytemnestra, the chorus and Electra (as well, of course, as the fourth audience in the theatre). The difference in response is drawn attention to immediately: Electra cries out (674), and the queen bursts out with "What do you say, stranger? What do you say? Don't listen to her!". Electra is to be the excluded audience. So Clytemnestra requests the whole story with "You [Electra] do your own stuff! But for me, stranger, you tell me the truth, how he died." (678–9).

The speech is a celebrated, riveting narrative. The response is three-fold. The chorus lament the destruction of the family, the loss of the child who offers the hope of generational continuity (764–5). But Clytemnestra is less univocal: "O Zeus, what is this? Should I call it good fortune, or terrible [*deina*] but profitable news? It is bitter, when my own disasters save my life" (766–8). This surprises the Paidagogus, who had thought his news an unmixed pleasure for her. She explains with the memorable line δεινὸν τό τίκτειν ἐστίν, "it is a strange thing [*deinon*] to give birth" (770), where the nuanced and hard to translate *deinon* ("awesome", "terrible", "amazing", "strange") picks up her previous line "terrible" (*deina*), and gives the word a different spin, indicating her difficulty of finding the expression for her confused feelings. She finally turns towards her daughter. Electra has not spoken for 110 lines. She has been the audience both to the speech and to the reactions to it. Her reaction is . . . what?

There are two general points I want to make on Electra's response. First, she takes up the role (like Odysseus in the *Ajax*) of a focalizer for the audience, and, in particular the audience on stage, the chorus (804–7):

ἆρ᾽ ὑμὶν ὡς ἀλγοῦσα κὠδυνωμένη
δεινῶς δακρῦσαι κἀπικωκῦσαι δοκεῖ

---

[23] See Fraenkel (1950) *ad* 1653; Peradotto (1969).

τὸν υἱὸν ἡ δύστηνος ὧδ' ὀλωλότα;
ἀλλ' ἐγγελῶσα φροῦδος.

So did she seem to you to weep and wail
Terribly, like one grieving, in pain,
The wretched woman for her son, perished like that?
No, she went out laughing.

Electra has been an audience to the queen's response, and now tries to direct her audience's response to what she has been watching. *Deinôs*, "terribly", seems to echo the queen's search for a response (*deina* 767, *deinon* 770), now with a bitter and sarcastic tone.[24] It should seem (*dokei*) like an act to them, she asserts: "*like* [*hôs*] one grieving". The queen was laughing, declares her daughter. There was nothing in the Paidagogus' response to indicate the queen was anything but moved, nor was there anything in her exit line to indicate that she was (literally) laughing. How good an audience is Electra? Is she accurately describing her mother's arrant and finely performed hypocrisy? Or is she quick to find an emotionally overwrought and aggressive slant on her hated mother's more complex feelings? The tension between Electra's reaction to her mother, and the mother's reaction to the news, throws up a question about each. Should we really read the queen's *deinon to tiktein estin*, "it is a strange thing to give birth", as a *kekrummenên baxin*, a "concealed utterance"? Should we really read Electra's declaration of her mother's hypocrisy as a distorted exaggeration? Electra's role as (problematic) audience on stage raises for the audience in the theatre a self-reflexive concern about its own role in evaluating the emotions and words in front of them. What to see in Clytemnestra's or Electra's reactions?

This leads to my second point about Electra's response, a point which will return more insistently in the second scene of an audience on stage in this play. We watch Electra responding to a speech with her customary strength of feeling: the scene is written so that we watch not only the Paidagogus' masterful performance, but also the three audiences to it, and perhaps especially the pain of Electra as a contrast to the feelings of Clytemnestra. (The multiple audience response on stage to a speech should worry the critics who assume audience response to be homogenous in the theatre.) Yet we also know that the speech is a fiction. As an audience to a fiction, we are watching audiences to a fiction.[25]

This self-reflexivity becomes most pointed when the urn arrives (the second scene of an audience on stage). The speech that Electra delivers over it is one of the most moving in Greek tragedy, as she – along with the metre and sentence

---

[24] As Reinhardt (1979) 142 comments brilliantly (with regard to the more obvious example of 287ff), "to make known what she has suffered, Electra must start to imitate the voice she hates".

[25] See Segal (1981) 278–91; Ringer (1998) 127–212.

structure – breaks down in grief. This outpouring is watched by Orestes, the
audience on stage, who in turn becomes overwhelmed by his feelings, and
reveals himself in such a way that threatens the security of the venture of revenge
(as the Paidagogus points out [1326ff]). As Electra weeps, we know she is grieving
over an empty urn: passionate grief over a fiction – the paradox of tragic emotion, where audiences cry over what they know to be staged action. Yet Orestes,
who also knows that the urn does not contain his ashes, is also so moved by his
sister's grief that he cannot control his tongue (1174–5), a reaction more powerfully felt than the chorus' conventional consolation "remember you are a mortal
and do not grieve too much" (1171–3). Critics have made much of the metatheatricality of the urn here. The urn, writes Segal paradigmatically, "functions as a
symbol of the deception of the theatrical situation per se. . . . The urn embodies
the paradoxical status of truth in dramatic fiction. It is a work of elaborate arti-
fice . . . which gathers around itself the power of language to deceive or to establish truth. It functions, then, as a symbol of the play itself, a work whose falsehood
(fiction) embodies truth".[26] This is a strong reading of how the play's interests in
logos and *ergon*, on deception, and on staged scenes, come together to provoke a
question about tragedy's status (which Segal goes on to link to Gorgias' paradoxical pronouncement that it is better to be deceived, to give in, that is, to the en-
chantment of *logos* in the theatre). But the grief over the empty urn also asks
what I think is a more insistent and troubling question about the audience.

Electra's emotions have the ability to sway Orestes even when he knows
they are based on a falsehood, even when it threatens his own plot. As an audience in the theatre too, it is hard to watch the outpouring of her grief without
being affected. Electra, in turn, has been wholly swayed by the false speech of
the Paidagogus, so that she dismisses her sister's correct and overjoyed announcement of the return of Orestes. The difficulty of resisting the lure of
logos, the difficulty of resisting the persuasion of another's emotions, reveal the
fragility of the self-control of the audience on stage, and – this is where the
self-reflexivity hits home – the audience in the theatre, the audience of democracy. The image of the responsible, judging, critical citizen – the bedrock of
democratic decision making – is thrown hard up against the emotional distortions and self-deceptions of our watching Orestes watching Electra. We could
put the question starkly for the audience watching these audiences on stage:
how like Electra and Orestes are you (prepared to be)?

The final scene of the play is the most stage-managed scene of all. Orestes
brings on stage – probably via the *ekkuklema*, the trolley could wheel a tableau
out from the inside of the house – the dead body of Clytemnestra, shrouded,
concealed. In the *Oresteia*, Orestes appeared over the dead bodies of Aegisthus
and Clytemnestra to display to the citizens of Argos the end of the double

---

[26] Segal (1981) 128. See also Ringer (1998); Batchelder (1995).

tyranny (before fleeing the onset of the Furies). Here instead we have an exqui-
site scene of staged nastiness. Electra has greeted Aegisthus with a finely acted
show of stoic grief—exactly what she had accused her mother of. It is one of
the grim ironies of this play how Electra fulfils her own heated remarks to
Clytemnestra (619–21): "Hatred from you and your actions compel me by force
to do these things: shameful deeds are taught by shameful deeds". Electra
shows what she has inherited and been taught as she leads a man to his death
by her deceptive words. Aegisthus instructs Orestes to uncover the body.
Orestes fends this off: "It is yours to see this and to address in a loving/familial
[*philôs*] way" (1470–1). Aegisthus calls for Clytemnestra, and, with studied
irony, Orestes declares "She is near; don't look anywhere else" (1474). As Aegisthus unveils the body, he is observed by both Orestes and Electra, an actor in
their drama. Aegisthus will be taken into the house finally to be slaughtered.

Here the very brief moment of the audience on stage is constructed as a
fantasy of control. The two avengers, for so long the victims, set up the scene
and direct it with precision. At last they have Aegisthus in their power, and
they revel in their position by their play-acting and heavy irony. Yet the ending
of the play, in typically Sophoclean style, while it may have a strong sense of
formal closure, also opens up more problematic vistas. This question is usually
discussed by critics in terms of the absence of Furies or the lack of moral
response to the act of matricide within the play. Where Aeschylus had taken a
further play to resolve the tensions set in motion by the god-ordered matricide
and had brought a trial on stage to find a resolution, Sophocles' aggressive
silence leaves the question for the audience in the theatre (making them the
jury of the trial as it were). The future is alluded to in a way which encourages
the audience to reflect on what is to happen next: Aegisthus and Orestes talk
pointedly of prophecy and who can know what the future will bring (1481,
1499, 1500). Aegisthus wonders if the house of the Pelopids will always suffer
(1497–8). But what interests me most is the way in which the control of the
avengers, and in particular Electra, is undercut.

Electra's role in this last scene is fascinating. She concludes her brief dialogue with Aegisthus in this way (1464–5):

καὶ δὴ τελεῖται τἀπ᾽ ἐμοῦ· τῷ γὰρ χρόνῳ
νοῦν ἔσχον, ὥστε συμφέρειν τοῖς κρείσσοσιν.

See! My part is being fulfilled. In time
I have gained wisdom, so that I accede to those more powerful.

Kai dê, her first words, indicate that she is actually doing what she says she is
doing – a deictic particle drawing attention to her own performance. *Teleitai* is,
as ever, difficult to translate with one English word. It implies fulfillment as well
as closure; an end that can be death; a paying (back). At one level she is indicating
to Aegisthus that her old life is finished, and that she will fulfil his commands.

At another, as Jebb notes, she is underlining her own role in the fulfillment of the vengeance. (One could almost translate: "Look! My part is being acted out . . .") Her irony is continued in her expressed willingness to accede to those more powerful – a double-edged irony since it is not clear exactly what the more powerful forces at work in Electra's narrative here might be; and this irony marks her own sense of growing power, her sense of control. The last word of the play, however, is *teleôthen*, "finished", "consummated", "ended". Self-reflexive, of course, and a superb way of highlighting the tension between the end of the play and the open-endedness of the action: how ended is this end? It also re-frames Electra's use of *teleitai*. How much in control of her narrative is she? How certain can she be of the end she is pursuing? The ironic ambiguity of the word *teleisthai*, which Electra manipulates, is, by the end of the play, turned against her.

Her own last word has a similar doubleness, as we saw in chapter 1. Aegisthus asks to say a few last remarks, and Electra interrupts demanding his silence. She requires his instant death. "Only this", she declares, "could provide release for my ills of old" (1489–90). Her final word is *lutêrion* "release". All the characters who think they have found *lusis*, "release", are mistaken, and usually find that what they thought was release is bringing them into deeper disaster. As we asked before, what happens to Electra at the end of the play? What release can she hope for once the hatred that has dominated her life no longer has an object? How much self-deception is there in this hope for release? Where Electra had expressed her control over Aegisthus through irony, here she is the victim of the irony in her own words.

Electra and Orestes set up a little staging to enact the slaughter of Aegisthus. Their superiority and control are performed in their irony and their stage-management as much as in the physical act of revenge. Yet the superiority and control of each are fragile. Neither Orestes as seer of the future, nor Electra in her belief in release can throw off the pall of self-deception. Of being locked into a tragic, overdetermined narrative, which is beyond their control. Electra and Orestes, as audience to their own staged drama of the tricking of Aegisthus, reveal the illusions of control which power gives to an audience.

Electra gives us multiple audiences on stage. It shows us multiple responses and multiple interpretations of audiences. It shows us the audience losing control to overwhelming emotions. It shows the illusion of control in an audience in charge. The *Electra* is a highly provocative play in many ways, but it is provocative specifically for the audience of democracy in that its images of an audience are so hard to reconcile with the ideal of the critical, controlled, authoritative citizen doing his duty in the institutions of the city. It is here that the *Electra's* self-reflexivity or metatheatricality has a political bite.[27]

---

[27] I am here tacitly disagreeing with Griffin's opinion that Sophocles' *Electra* is fundamentally unpolitical: Griffin (1999). The discussion of metatheatricality in Segal (1981) and Ringer (1998) do not broach the political adequately.

My final example is Antigone's *kommos* in the *Antigone*, her lament as she leaves to her death in the cave. She sings in counterpoint with the chorus, and eventually Creon interrupts to hurry her offstage. We cannot be certain that Creon is on stage throughout the scene: but Griffith considers it likely that he is (his entrance is otherwise unannounced and unmotivated), and the lyrics continue after his entrance. I would like to consider the implications if he is on stage from 780 or from 806 onwards.

Antigone enters processing as in a funeral march, but singing her own funeral dirge (a bizarre ritual performance allowed by her strange circumstances). The traditional *kommos* is antiphonal, and involves consolation from the group to the individual mourner as well as shared, often incantatory expressions of grief.[28] The exchanges between the chorus and Antigone in this scene, as we will see in detail in chapter 5, construct a dynamic and transforming interaction, as she mourns and they switch between consolation and condemnation, and she asks for sympathy by her laments but also successively alienates herself from her surroundings. The *kommos* enacts a developing relationship between the judgemental chorus and the increasingly isolated young girl. But as the *kommos* ends, Creon speaks in terms that echo what we have seen (883–90). "No-one would stop wailing before death", he expostulates, "if it were necessary" (that is, if it would put off the moment). So, he upbraids the attendants, get a move on. Take her and leave her "alone (*monên*) and deserted (*erêmon*)" in the cave. "Any way (*d'oun*)", he concludes, "She will be deprived of her residency (*metoikias*) on the earth above". The strange description of life as an "(alien) residency" – as a metic – echoes Antigone's own description (851), and his use of *monê*, "alone", "isolated", echoes both the chorus' and her own fears and laments. So what is the effect of having Creon watch the *kommos* and then respond as he does?

In contrast to the *kommos*, where the chorus struggles to find an adequate judgement for Antigone's actions and attitude, where praise, dismissal, consolation and hesitancy rub together, and where Antigone now laments her life, a life which she apparently willingly gave up (and even declared herself long dead [559–60]), Creon is brusque, aggressive, certain and even, as Griffith puts it, "crass". Where Odysseus as audience on stage in the *Ajax* attempted to offer a differently nuanced and more sympathetic response to the scene staged before him, Creon reacts in a far *less* nuanced and wholly unsympathetic manner to the scene he watches. When Antigone laments that she has no *philos* to cry for her, her *philos* Creon is watching unmoved. And we are watching him watching. This not only affects an audience's view of the king, but also works to isolate him from the action, an isolation which will increase throughout the rest of the play as his *philoi* are stripped from him one by one, until he ends up, like Antigone, alive but "no more existing than a nothing" (1325).

---

[28] On mourning, see in general Alexiou (2002); Dué (2003); and, best of all, Foley (2001) especially 19–56, 145–71.

One of the great contrasts in the *Antigone* has been regularly ignored by critics since Hegel. This is the contrast between the ideologues or extremists who see the world according to fixed and exclusive principles, even when these principles lead to self-contradiction and even self-destruction – Creon and Antigone, say – and the characters who try to muddle along in a more complex and less extremely coloured world: the guard who can change his mind, burble for self-preservation, and resist the polarizing certainties of political rhetoric; or Ismene, who can care, and fight and wonder, but without the all-embracing extremism of her sister. It is they who survive, perhaps unremembered, but still alive. What we watch when we watch Creon observing the *kommos* is the increasing isolation and stubbornness of the ideologue. His distance from the action gives us the distance to observe him.

The first play Brecht worked on after the Second World War was his *Antigone*, based on Hölderlin's translation of Sophocles (and first produced in Switzerland in 1948). During the early years of the war he was drafting what became published eventually as *The Messingkauf Dialogues*. The *Messingkauf Dialogues* contains one of the longest discussions of Brecht's theories of alienation in the theatre, his desire to break the audience away from their emotional absorption in the narrative world of the theatre towards a more reflective, distanced and intellectual appreciation of what was being staged in front of them. I think one could make a case for Brecht having learnt a good deal from Sophocles, and in particular from the device of dramatizing an audience on stage. The effect of putting an audience on stage is to provide a mirror to the audience of its own processes of reaction. It works to distance the audience from a direct emotional absorption and to see itself watching. It has become a standard response to literature in recent years to uncover literature's self-reflexivity, its talking of itself as art, its reflection on the status of fiction, or the materiality of form. Yet it is never likely to be enough of a conclusion to discover that literature is (again) self-reflexive. What Sophocles shows rather is that such self-reflexivity, such dramatization of the audience on stage, speaks significantly to the social context of democracy in which Athenian drama was written and performed. As Pat Easterling writes, "What is important . . . is that the ironic play with the dramatic medium is intimately related to the central issues" of the play and of democracy: "the collusion in which the spectators are invited to participate has nothing in the least frivolous or trivial about it".[29] Theatrical self-reflexivity is a demand for the audience to be (more) self-reflective.

The role of the audience in the Assembly or Law Courts was not merely of theoretical interest in democracy but also a matter of life and death – state

---

[29] Easterling (1997a) 172–3.

policy, individual careers, the future of families and the city, depended on the decisions of a large group of citizens, listening to arguments and making moral, practical and policy decisions. When Thucydides comments that it was *eros*, "passionate desire" that led the youth of Athens to vote for the disastrous Sicilian expedition, when Aristophanes sneers that all an orator needed to say was "gleaming Athens" and the citizens sat on the tips of their buttocks, puffed up with pride, or when Plato describes the Assembly as a collection of cobblers making decisions about high politics, they are all expressing concern (or a harsher antipathy) for democracy's cherished principle of a collective of citizens debating and deciding, as it worked in practice in Athens. One of the great dramatic scenes of Thucydides' account of democracy is the Mytilenian debate, which turns on a highly emotional audience's changing its mind overnight – and debating its change of mind as a principle. Sophocles' drama does not have such explicit political posturing. Rather, setting an audience on stage is a specific dramatic way of opening to question the role of rhetoric, judgement, and the emotions for the audience of citizens in the theatre, and in the other institutions of the city. It is an encouragement to see oneself watching, and, through such self-reflection, to explore what responsible citizenship might involve – and how difficult it might be to avoid being what Thucydides' Cleon attacks (III.38) as mere "spectators of speeches" (*theatai tôn logôn*), "victims of pleasure in listening, more like spectators of media super-stars (*sophistôn*) than citizens engaged in the political business of the city".

3

Line for Line

Stichomythia, the formal exchange of usually single lines between two characters on stage, is an instantly recognisable element of Greek tragedy. Instantly recognisable, but conceptualized in profoundly different ways by modern theatre. In Peter Hall's production of Tony Harrison's *Oresteia*, each line of verse was delivered in a style which was indeed highly formal, each marked off by a crash of music, as if the words were ritual objects exchanged in a ceremony of public spectacle: masked characters declaiming from either side of the large stage. In Deborah Warner's production of Sophocles' *Electra*, Fiona Shaw and John Lynch, locked in grief and pain, edged towards a mutual recognition and the physical contact of an embrace in a realistic, halting, intimate conversation. A.E. Housman's famous parody of *stichomythia* captures cleverly the alienating effect that the formality of exchange can have on readers nourished by the conventions of novelistic realism (let alone the panache of Stoppard's wit or Beckett's barbed and shattered fragments, or the very different formalism of Pinter's aggressive dialogues):

> CHORUS: To learn your name would not displease me much.
> ALCMAEON: Not all that men desire do they obtain.
> CHORUS: Might I then hear at what thy presence shoots?
> ALCMAEON: A shepherd's questioned mouth informed me that—
> CHORUS: What? For I know not yet what you will say.
> ALCMAEON: Nor will you ever, if you interrupt.
> CHORUS: Proceed, and I will hold my speechless tongue.
> ALCMAEON: This house was Eriphyle's, no one else's.

Housman captures not just the horror of naïvely literal translations, labouring with the cultural difference of a foreign idiom, but also, and with wicked precision, the sense that *stichomythia* is weighed down by its own formality of diction ("Might I then learn at what thy presence shoots?"), made pompous and cumbersome by the requirement of always filling a whole line ("a shepherd's questioned mouth", "I will hold my speechless tongue"), and, above all, that the very rules of encounter result in distracting contributions that seem no more than "fillers": "What? For I do not yet know what you will say." There are modern performances, too, which seem unwittingly indebted to Housman's parody . . .

This chapter is about *stichomythia*.[1] Its first aim is to look at this form of exchange, as a dramatic, narrative resource – the embodiment of manipulation, persuasion, violence, intimacy, self-assertion, care . . . an integral element of Greek tragic drama. The exploration of the flexibility, expressiveness and power of *stichomythia* in Sophocles' plays, however, will also lead to a discussion of how *stichomythia as a form* plays a role in tragedy's dissection of the politics of language and the power-plays of self-representation. At one level, then, my concern is to investigate the relation between *stichomythia* and what might be called in French *publicité*, a sense of public life and public discourse, never far from the heart of the event of Greek tragedy: language put *es meson*, as it could be expressed in Greek, "into the public domain to be contested", words "up front and in your face".

At another level, while this discussion continues my focus on the language of tragedy and, in particular, the role of *form* in criticism, this chapter also emphasizes the value and practice of close reading – the political, intellectual, social *value* of patient, critical, extended attention to words in action. The clash of languages that *stichomythia* repeatedly stages, dramatizes the dangerous power of words to mislead, misrepresent, lead to destruction, as they have the potential to reveal, instruct, inform, sympathize. In chapter 1, we saw how Sophoclean irony performed a sort of deferred close reading, showing in retrospect how words' flickering depths of meaning, not read fully before, thus eluded control. In chapter 2, we analyzed how the device of the audience on stage, listening, observing in silence, required the audience in the theatre to watch an audience on stage, and thus stimulated a heightened attention to the process of listening, watching, comprehending: insisting on the close reading of the performance. In this chapter, I shall be trying to read closely how *stichomythia* throws a spotlight on the *failure* of close reading, where patience and critical attention are overwhelmed by aggression, manipulation, and distortion. As an academic and a teacher, I am committed – addicted – to cherishing the nuance and weft of language; but this is not, I think, just a professional or personal formation: there is a political value to listening more carefully, more critically, to the slogan's claim, the ideologue's insistence, the rhetorician's winningness, the headline's stridency, the emotional blindness of militarism (a value which is

---

[1] The study of *stichomythia* as a form has been largely limited to a very conservative tradition of German scholarship: Gross (1905) and Jens (1955) are less useful than Schwinge (1968), Seidensticker (1971), and Pfeiffer-Petersen (1996). See also Hancock (1917), Myres (1949) and for a list of the nineteenth-century German dissertations Schwinge (1968) 11–32, especially 12n4.

worth insisting on, however crushed it can appear in the Realpolitik of modern media-led politics). In the context of contemporary literary theory, it might seem perverse or simply out of date to emphasize "close reading", a phrase redolent of I.A. Richards' work in Cambridge between the World Wars; but thinking hard about the work of words, how meaning is produced, remains a pressing task, and one which the language of tragedy especially demands.

Let me begin with an example, and an example where political self-definition is at stake. In *Antigone*, Haimon comes to his father Creon to try to persuade him not to punish Antigone with death. Creon welcomes him with a long, reasoned speech about social and familial order, and the need for obedience within the state. Haimon replies with a long, reasoned speech about how flexibility is a crucial skill in government. "There is something to be said on both sides", says the chorus in strained diplomacy. At this point, father and son explode into a violent argument that belies their reasoned speeches about control and flexibility.[2] The *stichomythia* will enact their growing separation and disagreement till it reaches mutual accusations of "madness", "witlessness", "emptiness" (753–4), and mutually enraging threats (750–1). In a bare forty lines, Creon's commitment to the proper order of the state is stretched into wild self-assertion of personal authority, just as Haimon's principle of flexibility turns into a strident threat which will be instantiated in his suicide. Sophocles, as ever, brilliantly captures the twists of reason into extremism, and brings out in excoriating detail the emotion seething in articulate, self-confident political stances. One small word is repeated nine times in the first twenty lines of the exchange: *gar*. There is no other passage of tragedy that has this density of repetition of the term.[3] The particle *gar*, which usually occurs as the second word in the sentence, is standardly translated "for", and marks the logical connection of the sentence with the preceding utterance. In what follows, it will sometimes be translated by a shift in tone or word order rather than the more clunky repetition of "for". In *stichomythia*, where the previous sentence is the other speaker's, *gar* marks the picking up of an idea in agreement or disagreement ("no, because . . .", "yes, because . . ."). It is the node of distortion. It indicates the moment where the speaker takes up the assumption of the other and aggressively wraps it into his own world-view. *Gar* traces the transformation of reason into hostile disagreement. Let us trace this process of violent transformation in the opening twenty lines of the dialogue.

---

[2] For representative discussions of the whole scene, see Reinhardt (1979) 84–6; Knox (1964) 70–73; Segal (1981) 186–90; Whitlock Blundell (1989) 121–8; Goldhill (1986) 99–102.

[3] Except (nearly) *Ajax* 1120–39, where Menelaus and Teucer argue violently and *gar* occurs eight times. Different, but worth comparing are the first four connections in Thucydides, all of which are *gar* – an emphatic statement of the necessary logic of historical argumentation. Different, too, but instructive is the extremely chary use of *gar* in the Gospel of Mark, where faith makes a different claim on reason (and where *gar* bizarrely is the last word of the [uninterpolated] text). For the general point about repetition in this *stichomythic* exchange see Pfeiffer-Petersen (1996) 65.

Creon's opening response is addressed to the chorus, but is an emotional rejoinder to the didactic tone of the young man's speech as well as the chorus' hope that each man might learn from the other (726–7):

> οἱ τηλικοίδε καὶ διδαξόμεσθα δὴ
> φρονεῖν πρὸς ἀνδρὸς τηλικοῦδε τὴν φύσιν;

Are men of my age actually to be schooled, then,
In wisdom by men of his age and nature?[4]

The word "schooled" (*didaxomestha*) is heatedly emphasised by *kai*, "actually", and *dê*, "then": it is the power relation of teaching that Creon resists, expressed in terms of the age (and nature) of Haimon with regard to himself, as the repetition of *têlikosde*, "of such an age" underlines.[5] Not just teaching, but being taught how to be wise (*phronein*) – a term the play has repeatedly set at stake.[6] Haimon's appeal to flexibility leads Creon angrily, inflexibly, to dismiss him, in the third person – "*his* age" – to the chorus, as if he is appealing to his counsellors to support him against the upstart.

Haimon replies with a sensible come back (728–9): "In nothing that is not just. If I am young, look not to my years but my deeds [τἄργα],", a reply which prompts the first use of *gar* from Creon, as the initial exchange of couplets sharpens into a line for line dispute (730):

> ἔργον γάρ ἐστι τοὺς ἀκοσμοῦντας σεβεῖν;

Is it a 'deed' to honour the disruptive?

Gar (which I have translated by the inverted commas around the word "deed") specifies that Creon is picking up Haimon's expression: "I see, so I suppose that . . .", just as *ergon*, "deed" picks up *targa*, "deeds" from Haimon's own words. Haimon has used the word *erga* in a general way: judge me by "my actions". Creon is adding an edge to the term, as if "deed" means something of which one is especially proud, a "worthy task" (as Jebb suggests): "is it your job to . . .?". As *gar* stresses, the king takes up Haimon's language, and, with an aggressive twist of re-definition, appropriates it to his own view of things.

Haimon again responds reasonably, adding weight to Creon's use of the verb *sebein*, "honour" (731): "I wouldn't demand proper honour [*eusebein*][7] for bad people", but again Creon – with *gar* – snaps back (732)

---

[4] I have translated τὴν φύσιν perhaps too strongly: Jebb would have it mean solely "in birth" i.e. strengthening the point about age. But *phusis* more commonly means "nature", and the "nature" of the young is a familiar slur, formalized by Aristotle *Nich. Eth.* I iii 5–7; VI viii 5; VII xiv 6.

[5] On the background here see Strauss (1993).

[6] See Goldhill (1986) 175–80; Whitlock-Blundell (1989) 136–48; Griffith (1999) 41–3; and more generally Nussbaum (1986) 51–82; Foley (1996).

[7] Both uses of *eu/sebein* echo Antigone's statement of principle (511) that she "honours (*sebein*) kin" (*homosplankhnous*), on which see Segal (1981) 183–6.

οὐχ ἥδε γὰρ τοιᾷδ᾽ ἐπείληπται νόσῳ;

Isn't that woman afflicted by such a disease?

The *gar* indicates a thought process once more: "He says that he doesn't hon-our the evil: is he suggesting she . . .". Like Haimon, Antigone appears objectified as a third person, unconnected: not "my niece", "your fiancée", but "that woman". Haimon, with a classic rhetorical move – equally objectively, it seems – appeals to what everyone knows, expressed as a political, collective decision (733): "The assembled people [*leôs*] of this our Thebes denies it".[8] Creon (734):

πόλις γὰρ ἡμῖν ἁμὲ χρὴ τάσσειν ἐρεῖ;

Is the city going to tell me what orders I must give?

The *gar* here marks the king's attempt to draw out the political implications of Haimon's full-blown rhetoric: is a ruler to take commands from the people? If Creon's remark would make sense in a military situation, or in Homeric epic, it is anathema in democracy where the people are indeed sovereign – as Haimon im-mediately points out, neatly turning back Creon's anger about age (735): "Do you see how you have spoken in this like a man too young" – too young for power, the stereotype of a tyrant not yet ready for office. This is a deeply insulting remark for a son to make to his father, but Creon replies still in the political vein (736):

ἄλλῳ γὰρ ἢ ᾽μοὶ χρή με τῆσδ᾽ ἄρχειν χθονός;

By whose view but mine ought I to rule this land?

The connective *gar* continues his resistance to Haimon's argument. To be a ruler is to make judgements: how can he suggest that any other understanding is possible? A ruler, alone, rules. Haimon dismisses this argument ringingly (737):

πόλις γὰρ οὐκ ἔσθ᾽ ἥτις ἀνδρὸς ἐσθ᾽ ἑνός.

No city exists which is one man's.

Here *gar* both expresses his reasoned denial of his father's claim ("no, because") and helps give the sentence a sententious tone. But the genitive *andros henos* "one man's", "of a single man" opens the way to Creon's reply (738): "Isn't a city considered its ruler's?". "Do we not say "Blair's Britain?", "Obama's America"? This is seen by Haimon as missing the point, mere wordplay (739): "On a desert island you would be a great ruler on your own". His sarcasm – and his comment about Creon's isolation – pushes Creon

---

[8] On the political overtones of *leôs*, see Haubold (2000). On the rhetoric of "what everyone knows" see Hesk (2000) 242–91. Especially in view of the chorus' support of Creon, it would be unwise to take Haimon's words at face value, as many critics have.

towards the chorus. None of Creon's remarks in this *stichomythia* so far have been directly addressed to Haimon: all are general remarks in the third person, as if he is talking to Haimon through the chorus, but now he is explicitly dismissive (740): "This fellow, it seems, is fighting alongside the woman". Like a good advocate, he is attempting to align the audience with his own position, excluding the opponent from the embrace of sympathy (and as with many a lawyer, then and now, the misogynistic sneer is a blatant element in his strategy). Haimon in the face of this third person language – objectified by the king's discourse – reaches out directly to his father, an appeal for contact (741):

εἴπερ γυνὴ σύ· σοῦ γὰρ οὖν προκήδομαι.

If you are the woman. For it is you in fact I care for.

Reaches out? Or deliberately antagonizes? The juxtaposition of *su* and *sou*, ["you"/ "you"] is certainly emphatic, especially in reply to Creon's *hode*, "this fellow" – a face to face address rather than Creon's objectification – but the suggestion that Creon is a woman, however delivered, in a play where gender has been a motive force, is unlikely to be a winning remark, and seems redolent of his growing sarcasm. Indeed, Creon is moved to react with his first direct response in the second person to Haimon and his first use of any familial language (742):

ὦ παγκάκιστε, διὰ δίκης ἰὼν πατρί.

You shameless wretch, taking your father to task!

The insult *pankakiste*, "shameless wretch", is a strong term, and the combination of the phrase *dia dikês* with its legal tones of *dikê* (justice, court case, courtroom) with *patri*, father, implies a moral outrage as if a son could prosecute a father in the courts (a case now well known from Plato's *Euthyphro*). Now when Creon turns to Haimon directly, it is in anger and distaste. The emotional ground Creon has staked out has just shifted: politics has exploded into explicit personal rancour. Haimon's response, however, continues his style of pleading (743)

οὐ γὰρ δίκαιά σ᾽ ἐξαμαρτάνονθ᾽ ὁρῶ.

Actually, I see you making an unjust mistake.

The sentence is hard to get into good English. *Gar* ["actually"="yes, because . . ."] seems to imply "I am disagreeing with you (but not taking you to task), because I see that . . .". The close connection with Creon's outburst is reinforced by *ou dikaia* "unjust" which echoes *dikês*. Creon, however, seems to hear only the word "mistake" (744):

ἁμαρτάνω γὰρ τὰς ἐμὰς ἀρχὰς σέβων;

A mistake? Do I make a mistake in respecting my authority?

Gar – along with the repetition of *hamartanô*, "make a mistake" – signals how Creon is picking up and attempting to crush Haimon's critical language, with also a further reminder of the need for respect, *sebein* – a process reversed immediately by Haimon himself (755):

οὐ γὰρ σέβεις, τιμάς γε τὰς τῶν θεῶν πατῶν.

Respect? There's no respect if you trample on the honour of the gods.

What has been at stake in the dialogue is precisely respect and trampling. The formal parallel between Creon's *hamartanô gar*, "A mistake?!" and Haimon's *ou sebeis gar*, "Respect?!", where each man picks up the verb of the other and questions its assumption (*gar*), indicates the shift in the dialogue where both men are now face to face in opposition and hostility. In a bare twenty lines a dramatic narrative has been followed (and for a director or actor the lines have a marvellous patterning of implicit stage directions): Creon is at first turned towards the chorus, objectifying Haimon, arguing from a position of authority about authority, but he has now faced his son directly, and been goaded into personal insult (ô *pankakiste* (742), ô *miaron êthos* (746), "filthy character!"), and slurs about the masculinity of his son: no more theory. Haimon's reasonableness in turn has been pushed into sarcasm and sneering – and will end with barely coherent threats. Creon has taken the lead, the dominant position, throughout; all Haimon's remarks are responses – caps – to his father's. This leads Griffith to comment "Thus Haimon emerges as the clear moral and verbal victor in the debate".[9] I am less sure that Haimon escapes quite so untainted from the debate, not least as he wholly fails to persuade Creon and ends up threatening and insulting him. His final lines turn out to be bitterly misplaced. He screams (762–4): "No! Not by me! Don't ever think it! She won't die by my side; and you will never see me with your own eyes; so live and rave with any family and friends who will have you!" The syntax of these lines is fragmented, emphatic, with "furious pleonasm"[10], and a passionate reversal of his opening line: "Father, I am yours" (635) were his first words; his last are a repudiation of his familial ties. It is not merely that this outburst is so far from his principle of bending with the wind, but also that it proves to be wrong in every detail, just as Achilles' enraged taunt to the dying Hector in the *Iliad* will turn out to have been precisely wrong[11]: Antigone's dead body *will* lie

---

[9] Griffith (1999) 247 *ad* 726–65.
[10] Griffith (1999) 252 *ad* 762–5.
[11] *Iliad* 22. 345–54.

next to him; Creon *will* see him again with his own eyes (in terrible circum-stances); and Creon *will* be left far from raving but crushed by grief, because he is without his *philoi*, his friends and family. In chapter 1 we saw how often the opening and closing lines of scenes in Sophocles were veined with ironies of misrecognition, and here Haimon's violent words ironically foreshadow his own violent death. Haimon's victory is hollow at best. It is typical of the nuance and complexity of Sophocles' representation of conflict that even if Haimon may seem, as Griffith suggests, to have the moral high-ground, his position is also veined with a self-destructive and self-defeating extremism.

This piece of *stichomythia* stages a familial breakdown; it allows destruc-tive feelings and aggressive personal language, laced with gender-based insults about masculinity, to drown the apparently principled discussion of politics. The language articulates an intricate and precise pattern of physical and mental contact and discontinuity, as the chorus plays a silent jury both to Creon's manipulative objectifying rhetoric and (then) to his intense, enraged dismissal of his son. The repetition of *gar* structures the interchange as a process of appropriation and rejection. In fearsomely dramatic fashion, it sets before an audience the process of the failure of dialogue to do more than widen the gaps of understanding and care between the men on the path towards destruction.

Not all *stichomythia* is as disturbingly disruptive as this – though there are certainly other scenes of intrafamilial hostility in Sophocles which match it for power and passion. But my second example shows a quieter, more sinuous and sly debate between an older man and a younger, rather than the hostility of father and son. In *Philoctetes*, a play much obsessed with language's power to manipulate, distort and curse, the opening exchanges between Odysseus and Neoptolemus display for the audience in the theatre a spectacle of persuasive rhetoric at work.[12] Again, in a mere twenty lines, we see an extraordinarily complex dance of shifting positions acted out. Neoptolemus has declared to Odysseus his willingness to fail nobly rather than to succeed ignobly, and Odysseus has gently suggested that a goodly way with words is a better route to success than heroic bravery alone. Neoptolemus is Achilles' son, and from Homer onwards the opposition of Odysseus, the man of manipulative decep-tion, and Achilles, man of straightforward and direct honesty, has been a staple of the stereotyping of character through heroic models (however much more complex the representations of the two figures are in Homer himself) – and this opposition haunts the interactions of Odysseus and Neoptolemus in this play. So, Neoptolemus, his father's son, immediately asks (100): "What are you ordering me to do except tell lies [*legein pseudê*]?". His father had famously said

---

[12] On the *Philoctetes* and language see Segal (1981) 328–61; Winnington-Ingram (1980) 280–303; Roberts (1989); Worman (2002) 139–48.

to Odysseus "I hate like the gates of hell a man who says one thing and hides
another in his heart" (*Il.* 9. 312–3), and Neoptolemus' noble nature here – like
father, like son – wants to refuse the shameful practice of telling lies. Odysseus
retorts (101):

λέγω σ' ἐγὼ δόλῳ Φιλοκτήτην λαβεῖν.

I am telling you to get Philoctetes with a trick.

This simple line is a beautiful demonstration of the extraordinary depths of
Sophoclean simplicity. First, *legô*, "I am telling . . .",[13] picks up Neoptolemus'
verb from the previous line, *legein* "tell [lies]". "You say . . . but *I* say" – and *legein*
also means "to mean": it is not just a question of giving orders or telling lies but
a question of meaning – and meanings are more shifty than young Neoptolemus might assume.[14] So the plan is, Odysseus says, as he sees it, [*egô*, emphatic:
"*I*"] rather a *dolos*, a trick. In the *Odyssey*, guile is Odysseus' watchword.[15] He
announces himself to the Phaeacians as "a concern among men for all sorts of
tricks [*doloisi*], famed to heaven" (*Od.* 9. 19–20). His standard epithet is *polume-
tis*, "of many wiles". Odysseus is offering a positive gloss on his plan, privileged
by Homeric association, his literary and epic past: not the corruption of lies but
the necessary and famous flexibility of guile. The final phrase, *Philoktêtên
labein*, both personalizes Neoptolemus' general qualm – this is not about lying
per se but a specific case: as Odysseus has said, in support of bowing to contingency (83–5): "In current circumstances, give yourself, I ask, to shamelessness
for the brief part of a day, and then for all the future be called the most righteous
of humans"; but it also reminds Neoptolemus of the aim – to *get* [*labein*]
Philoctetes.[16] Is the image wrestling – take him down? Or military – capture?
Or more blandly open "get"? What sort of – masculine – activity is proposed?
This word *labein* recurs throughout the play and is a perfect example of how
everyday words in Sophocles become invested with heightened meaning.[17] The
question of what it is to "get", "capture", hold", "touch", "take" – these are all
familiar senses of *labein* – either Philoctetes or his bow is one of the most
pressing questions of the drama. Philoctetes will beg to be taken on board ship
(*labein* 675); he does not want anyone to get his bow (*labein* 652); Neoptolemus
asks to get (*labein* 656) a look at it; asks Philoctetes what he wants to take (*labein*
651) with him onto the ship; Neoptolemus has got (*labôn* 671) Philoctetes as a
friend; Neoptolemus has taken (*elabon* 1231) the bow; Odysseus declares that
you couldn't get (*laboio*) anyone more pious than he (1051), Philoctetes despairs
that Odysseus has "taken" (*labôn*) the boy as his screen (1007) – and so forth.

---

[13] See Pucci (2003) 172 *ad* 101.
[14] See also Pfeiffer-Pedersen (1996) 126–7.
[15] See Pucci (1987) – with further bibliography.
[16] See Budelmann (2000) 112.
[17] See Easterling (1999).

The verb *labein* structures the physical plot of the play as the bow is taken and given, as Philoctetes becomes the object of a plan of taking, as the characters touch, hold, support and restrain each other – and the ethical drive of the drama as characters "take" each other in friendship and deception. Here, as so often in Sophocles, a thematic marker is introduced almost inaudibly.

Neoptolemus – lured immediately into the Odyssean world of shifting meanings – asks "Why must it be by guile and not by persuasion?" Persuasion, *peithô*, is often opposed to force [*bia*] as a means of gaining one's aim, and formulates *dolos*, "guile" as a corruption of its own openness.[18] Neoptolemus re-glosses in a negative guise Odysseus' own gloss in the name of direct and open exchange. But "He will never be persuaded", predicts Odysseus with some accuracy (103) – "and you could not get [*labois*] him by force [*bia*]". Force, *bia*, picks up the implied opposition in *peithô*, persuasion – but notice that Odysseus also repeats the verb *labein*, reinforcing the aim of the enterprise: to get him. Neoptolemus asks why force couldn't work (104) and Odysseus explains that he has the ineluctable and lethal arrows of Heracles (105). "Isn't it rash, then, even to have contact with a man like that?", asks Neoptolemus, to which Odysseus replies (107):

οὔ, μὴ δόλῳ λαβόντα γ᾽, ὡς ἐγὼ λέγω.

Yes! Unless you have *got* him by a trick, as I am telling you.

The third use of *labein* in four lines by Odysseus, emphasized here by *ge*, "at any rate" (which I have translated just by italicising *got*), maintains his focus on the end of the operation (as well as increasing the thematic focus on the term *labein*). "As I am telling you" [*egô legô*] recalls the "I am telling you" [*legô egô*] of the first time he had introduced the idea of a trick (101): the repetition marks the re-emphasis of what Odysseus is doing: telling the boy what's what. It is a conclusive rejoinder.

So Neoptolemus tries another tack, and returns to the status of lying (108):

οὐκ αἰσχρὸν ἡγῇ δῆτα τὰ ψευδῆ λέγειν ;

Do you really not think it is disgraceful to tell lies?

The emphasis [*dêta* "really"] is on the verb "think". Neoptolemus is avoiding the specificities Odysseus has raised, and nags away at what is for him the central issue. How could one conceive that telling a lie is not a disgrace? Odysseus' reply draws on a long and venerated Homeric tradition, as well as some blunt pragmatism (109): "No! Not if safety is what the lie brings." Odysseus in the Cyclops' cave lied about his name to save his life and the life of his men: it is part of his heroic fame.[19] Faced with the direct question whether it is morally acceptable to tell a lie, Odysseus, accepting the description "lie", puts his words under the category of

---

[18] See Buxton (1982) especially 121.
[19] For the links between *Philoctetes* and *Odyssey* 9, see e.g. Levine (2003).

self-preservation: a necessary falsehood. Neoptolemus, wavering, is still unsure (110): "How could one have the face to talk like that?". A question that is perhaps all too easy for Odysseus to answer, famous as he is for his powers of deceptive disguise, verbal and physical: Odysseus is celebrated for sitting stony-faced and unmoving as his wife, whom he has not spoken to for twenty years, cries before him. Putting on a face is what Odysseus does (or: in the tradition of Homeric epic, how you look is crucial to heroic identity but manipulated most effectively by Odysseus). "When you do something for profit", replies Odysseus (111), "it is unfitting to shrink back". This is a telling moment: lying for self-preservation has here become an expression of a more contemporary sophistic agenda. It is "profit" rather than survival that is the express motive – a different economics of truth-telling. Self-advancement at any cost is a charge often thrown at the sophists – as making the weaker case the stronger, or allowing the ends to justify the means, are self-advancing claims of expertise for the sophists. "Profit" is a buzz-word in fifth-century ethics and politics that focalizes the issue of the boundaries of acceptable behaviour – exactly the matter at hand in this scene. Odysseus' reply does not merely cue sophistic argument, however, it also performs it. With knowing paradox, he dismissed Neoptolemus' ethical scruples with the assertion that, when lies bring profit, it is actually *improper* to hesitate – as if not lying were a form of cowardice, a failure of proper manhood. The impropriety of lying is twisted into the impropriety of fearful hesitation in the sight of the enemy (or profit). Odysseus will indeed increasingly emphasize Neoptolemus' moral duty to obey his military commanders and to act according to the army's requirements rather than his personal feelings. For Odysseus, the ends certainly justify the means.

When Neoptolemus then asks (112) "What profit is it for me that he should go to Troy?", he is won over. In a handful of lines he concludes (120), "Let it be! I will give up all scruple and do it!". It takes little now for Odysseus to get Neoptolemus to the tipping point. "Only these weapons are destined to take Troy" (113), explains the older man. "Am *I*, then, not the one to destroy it, as you said? (114), asks the boy: Sophocles, with brilliant concision, opens a vista onto the back-story of persuasion that has led to this moment – a history of manipulative and enticing stories leading Neoptolemus from home to Troy on an epic mission in which he [emphatic *egô*, "*I*"] is the conquering hero. "You could not do it without them, nor they without you", specifies Odysseus – one version of the oracle which has prompted the mission, an oracle which will be further explained and glossed in different ways as the play proceeds: do the Greeks need the bow, or Philoctetes and the bow? Do they need to come willingly? The true and determining message from the gods becomes a shifting and variably emphasized control once it enters human language, and it cannot be formulated by humans without human language.[20] So, concludes Neoptolemus (116):

---

[20] See Hinds (1967); Easterling (1978) 31–4; Gill (1980); and in particular Budelmann (2000) 109–132; and in general Bushnell (1988).

θηρατέ οὖν γίγνοιτ᾽ ἄν, εἴπερ οὕτως ἔχει.

It would appear, then, that they must be hunted, if this is the situation.

The boy's grammar embodies the trace of his hesitation as he accepts (with what grammarians call a "mixed conditional"). The optative *gignoit' an*, "they would be" ["it would appear"], expressing potential, is combined with the gerundive expressing compulsion, *thêratea*, "must be hunted", and made dependent on the conditional, *eiper*, "if", where the indicative "is" expresses the state of things not as potential but as fact. It is precisely the connection between the certainty of facts, the sense of compulsion and the potential of action with which the boy is struggling. It is in the gap between what is and what might be where ethical action takes place (we inhabit mixed conditionals, as Rilke or Anne Carson might put it). The recognition that he must, then, hunt down his prey is already and ironically veined with the back-tracking the boy's narrative will painfully enact.

This short dialogue, as one might expect from the opening moments of a play, establishes the scene, with a density that is remarkable for its brief scope. It does this in part, as all openings do, by seeping necessary information: Philoctetes is not for persuading; the abandoned hero has lethal weapons. It also opens vistas onto the past (the stories Odysseus has already told Neoptolemus), and, through the carefully vague allusion to the oracle, hints at a divinely determined broader plot line – though the very vagueness of the allusion itself becomes part of the thematic concern with language and truth that structures the play. The characterization of both figures is under way, as Odysseus manipulatively leads the boy along, not able to see his way through to resistance.[21] The dialogue, however, is also vertiginously self-reflexive: it is about the potential of persuasion and force as it performs a scene of forceful persuasion. The discussion about persuading Philoctetes enacts the persuasion of Neoptolemus: the language of *peithô, dolos, bia, legein, labein*, as they are debated as the means of engaging with the absent Philoctetes, are doing their work on Neoptolemus: he is being "taken", "got" by words. The *stichomythia* is in this way programmatic for the action to come, not only because the play is replete with scenes of persuasion, and not only because the language of taking, persuading, tricking continues to provide the moral focus of the drama; it is programmatic also because the self-conscious performance of Odyssean rhetoric by Neoptolemus, as both master and victim of persuasion, will underlie the ethical and dramatic crises of the narrative as it unfurls. The form of this *stichomythia* encapsulates a structuring of the drama to come.

There is for a theatre audience a lurid fascination with watching a scene of seduction in action, as Shakespeare knew as well as anyone, with his Iago and

---

[21] See Worman (2002) 139–48.

Richard II, even and especially where the motives are mean and the ends immoral. Aeschylus' Clytemnestra, leading Agamemnon across the crimson tapestries to his death in the house, is the most spectacular icon of this lure of persuasion
in Greek tragedy. But here the double perspective of Sophoclean self-reflexivity
also sets up a puzzling dynamic for an audience – which can be expressed most
simply by asking how Odysseus' language should be applied to Odysseus' performance. Is he tricking Neoptolemus? Persuading him? Lying to him? It is hard to
predict with certainty to what degree any audience will see Odysseus as a corrupting rogue, a manipulative pragmatist, a heroic figure adopting his traditional route
to success – but, as with the device of constructing an audience on stage which we
discussed in chapter 2, the self-reflexivity of the scene works to engage the audience in the complexities of judgement that are being played out and debated in
front of them. The scene anticipates *in nuce* the uncertainties the audience will feel
faced with Neoptolemus' journey of doubt and sincerity.

Take the extraordinary scene where Philoctetes collapses in the anguish of
his disease into a brief, feverish unconsciousness. In chapter 2, I mentioned
how Neoptolemus' apparent sympathy for Philoctetes here needs to be read
both with regard to his willing continuation of the deception – that is, as false,
feigned feeling – *and* as a precursor of his change of heart – that is, as a sign of
sincere emotion – and the clash of these two trajectories produces a tension for
the audience. We can now see how this scene plays out in the *stichomythia*,
which in turn is then developed in later scenes in the play.

Philoctetes, as his illness racks his body, refuses Neoptolemus' delicate offer
of a therapeutic touch (as we saw in chapter 2) and has given Neoptolemus the
bow instead – one aim of the plot completed – and now, as he mentions the bow
again to the boy (803), he waits for an answer (804): "What do you say, boy?".
These words are *extra metrum*, and allow for – demand – a pause afterwards.
The next line (805) emphasizes the break in the exchange: "What do you say?
Why are you silent? Where on earth are you, child?". Silence is marked,[22] and
the answer screwed out of Neoptolemus' silence seems significant (806): "For a
long, long time [*palai dê*] I have been in pain, in anguish at your troubles". *Palai*,
as with *palin* which we discussed in chapter 1, is a simple, ordinary, word which
becomes invested with great weight in the *Philoctetes*. The thematic significance
is cued in the False Merchant scene: the Merchant with the intensity signalled
by the first antilabic exchange in the play (*antilabe*, where two or more characters share a single metrical line, usually indicates especially intense dialogue),
insists (589): "Look what you are doing, boy!", to which Neoptolemus retorts "I
too for a long time [*palai*] have been looking". Critics have argued whether this
exchange is the swapping of some private code between the two plotters, or
whether it is a piece of "acting . . . to impress Philoctetes"[23], or whether it is a

---

[22] See in general Montiglio (2000).
[23] Jebb (1890) 100 *ad* 589.

first telling indication of Neoptolemus' pained self-analysis. I wish merely to emphasize that *palai* opens a potential narrative of the past, Neoptolemus' past and ongoing reflection [*skopô*], that will become more and more important as he travels towards his change of heart. So, as he steels himself to reveal the plot, he declares (906): "This is what has been grieving me for a long time [*palai*]", a half-line he repeats word for word in anguish shortly later (913). So later he sums up his own story of transforming emotion (965–6): "In my case at least, a strange pity for this man has been coming over me not now for the first time but also for a long while since [*palai*]". *Palai* in Neoptolemus' mouth marks his growing awareness that over time he is changing – and provokes a question for the audience of when they think this transformation has started. In Philoctetes' mouth, time has no such transformative power, locked as he is into the extremism of his own certainties: "I am nothing", he laments (1030), "and I have been dead for you for a long time [*palai*]". The word *palai* at crucial junctures of the drama evokes the young man's narrative of change over time set against the *longue durée* of Philoctetes' pain, the struggle for consistent, continuous ethical character against the inflexibility of the hero's commitment. Like *palin*, it invites an audience to think back over time and re-play Neoptolemus' reactions.[24]

Philoctetes – taking Neoptolemus to be sincere – pleads with him (807–9): "Please, child, be strong too. Know this thing comes on me sharply and departs swiftly. Please, I beg you, don't leave me alone". The hero's pathetic need is clear and insistent, and the dialogue matches this insistence as it breaks the next line into three short speeches (810): *Ne.* "Do not worry. We will remain." *Phil.* "Will you really stay?". *Ne.* "Know it for sure!". But Philoctetes is still desperate (811): "But I do not think it right, child, to place you under an oath, at least". The particles again carry the precise force of the sentence: *ou mên* is adversative ("but"), but implies something like, "I would prefer an oath, but I don't think it right to ask"; *enorkon* "under oath" is qualified by *ge*, "at least" which delimits the term: "anything so strong as an oath". Neoptolemus avoids the formality of promising (812): "Know that it is not right anyway [*ge*] for me to leave without you". "Right" [*themis*] is also qualified by *ge*: oath or no oath, and whatever I want, it isn't lawful to desert you. But Philoctetes presses on (813): "Give me your hand as a pledge!"; Neoptolemus: "I give it – to stay". Again the half lines mark the intense symbolic, physical moment: the two men grasp hands in what Philoctetes calls "trust" [*pistis*], exactly as he is being deceived.[25] But as if dramatizing the internal tension in that asymmetrical moment, the dialogue immediately collapses into a broken pattern of half and third lines, and incoherent miscomprehension and demand (814–8):

---

[24] A rare moment of insensitivity in Dik (2007) 223 when she says *palai* is a "filler".

[25] See Taplin (1971); Segal (1981) 331–3; Kaimio (1988) 22–4; Kosak (1999); and in general van Erp Taalman Kip (2006) 46–50.

Φι. ἐκεῖσε νῦν μ' ἐκεῖσε **Νε.** ποῖ λέγεις ; **Φι.** ἄνω
Νε. τί παραφρονεῖς αὖ ; τί τὸν ἄνω λεύσσεις κύκλον ;
Φι. μέθες μέθες με. **Νε.** ποῖ μεθῶ ; **Φι.** μέθες ποτέ
Νε. οὔ φημ' ἐάσειν. **Φι.** ἀπό μ' ὀλεῖς, ἢν προσθίγῃς.
Νε. καὶ δὴ μεθίημ' εἴ τι δὴ πλέον φρονεῖς.

Phil. To there, now, to there, me . . . *Ne.* Where do you mean? *Phil.* Up.
Ne. Why are you mad again? Why are you looking up above at the sky?
Phil. Let me go, let me go! *Ne.* Where should I let you go to? *Phil.* Let me go.
Ne. I declare I will not let you. *Phil.* You will kill me if you touch me!
Ne. There, see, I let you go, as you are in some degree more sensible.

Philoctetes seems to want to go "there", though it is unclear to Neoptolemus
where "there" is – "up" (which Jebb takes to mean back to the cave) is still baffling
to Neoptolemus, especially as Philoctetes is staring crazily up at the sky, as far as
the boy can tell. Philoctetes desperately demands not to be touched – after demanding Neoptolemus' hand – and Neoptolemus again fails to follow, and thinks
he wants to be allowed to go somewhere, and, as Philoctetes demands again even
more desperately to be let go, the boy declares that he will *not* let him go, which is
what Philoctetes had previously seemed to want. The hero explains "You will kill
me if you touch me" – the verb *apo m' oleis*, "you will kill me", is itself split in two
around the elided personal pronoun in archaic *tmesis* (and anguish). As he refused
the touch of Neoptolemus before, now a touch will kill him. Neoptolemus promptly
lets him down (*kai dê*, "there, see!"), and he slips to the floor in unconsciousness.

This passage continues the extraordinary variety of verse form in this scene –
extra metrum outburst, half lines, third lines, three line speeches responded to
by single lines. The breakdown of the formal pattern of the verse is matched by
the breakdown of the language: Philoctetes' sentences are unfinished, just prep-
ositions and pronouns, imperatives. Neoptolemus cannot follow and struggles
to comprehend what Philoctetes is struggling to communicate. If we take the
dialogue as implicit stage directions too, as I have no doubt we should, there is
a physical drama here too: the boy has just grasped the hero's hand when the
older man breaks into an attempt to move away; he looks up and away from the
boy; he is desperate to break contact; the boy won't release contact; then finally
he does, and Philoctetes slips from his upright, supported, restrained position
onto the ground. It is almost as if the touch of the boy – hypocritical, laden with
false promise – brings on the final stage of the disease. The broken verse form
and broken language enact the breakdown of reciprocity, the collapse of the
basic physical exchange of care. The scene is like an extended dramatization of
the tension within the idea of *labein*, of *getting hold* of Philoctetes.

When Philoctetes recovers, however, Neoptolemus is moved to reveal the
plot against him: and the *stichomythia* replays the conversation we have just
seen except in reverse, as it were. "Help me up", asks Philoctetes (as he had at

879), and, "Stand up", says Neoptolemus, helping (893), "And support yourself" –
perhaps implying "on me" (the suggestion that the chorus might help (887) is
implicitly rejected, emphasizing the connection and obligation of the two lead
characters). The hero who has been let down, is raised to his feet. "Do not
worry", replies Philoctetes (894), with the same term, *tharsei*, Neoptolemus had
addressed to him (810), "My accustomed practice will get me to my feet".[26] The
physical contact and simple struggle of the hero now seems too much for Neoptolemus: *papai*, he cries out – the exclamation Philoctetes had screamed in *his*
pain (785, 786, 792) – "What on earth could I do from this point on?". Now it is
Neoptolemus' language that falters, and Philoctetes who cannot understand
what Neoptolemus means. And as the scene develops – as we saw in chapter 2
– there is a complete disjunction between the men, as Neoptolemus refuses to
give back the bow, turns away from Philoctetes in silence, and three times refuses to answer his pleas (934–5; 951; 961–2). The dialogue enacts a different type
of breakdown, a different collapse of reciprocity, as the deception is made patent,
and dialogue falls into a monologue of exclamations and unanswered pleas.

In their earlier exchange (468–506), Philoctetes had movingly supplicated
Neoptolemus, a scene which surely recalls the celebrated supplication of
Achilles, Neoptolemus' father, by Priam at the close of the *Iliad*, pitiful older
man to young warrior – a recollection that bitterly underlines Neoptolemus'
uncomfortable complicity with the morality of deception.[27] Priam, in some of
the most memorable and moving lines of the epic, concludes his supplication
(*Il.* 24. 505–6): "I have dared [*etlên*] to do what no man before has done: I have
kissed the hand of the man who killed my child".[28] After crying, Achilles
reaches over and raises the old man to his feet. Here, as Neoptolemus raises
the older and broken man to his feet, the question of how he will play out his
father's role is insistent in the physical echoes of the epic. The emphasis on the
physical support, on the raising of the older man to his feet, after the replay of
the supplication, layer the physical action with a memory of epic morality, as
the behaviour of Neoptolemus is placed in question. Neoptolemus' rejection
of Philoctetes, the collapse of exchange into monologue, echoes against his
father's embrace of his enemy.

The holding of Philoctetes is recalled when Odysseus reveals himself to his
weaponless enemy. As we saw in chapter 2, Philoctetes threatens to throw himself
onto the rocks in suicide and is grabbed by the sailors on Odysseus' command
(1003). A gesture of restraint barely masked as care – and then turned into hostility by the cruelly manipulative Odysseus (1054–6): "Let him go; don't touch
him any more. Allow him to stay. We do not even need you, since we have these
weapons". Grabbing Philoctetes, and then letting him go is a way of emphasizing

---

[26] On the language and significance of care in this scene see Kosak (1999).

[27] This strong parallel is surprisingly not adequately discussed by critics, e.g. Kosak (1999).

[28] A line which may be distantly echoed at 536–7 when Philoctetes says "no other man but I could
bear [*tlênai*] this".

his helpless isolation, his lack of heroic worth to the Greeks. The physical gesture of embrace and release is part of Odysseus' rhetorical persuasiveness. The act of restraint – saving Philoctetes from suicide – reverts into dismissive humiliation. Again, physical contact between Philoctetes and others is the scene of violent breakdown and crossed purposes.

A fourth physical connection with Philoctetes takes place when Neoptolemus finally does return the bow. "The deed will be clear," declares Neoptolemus (1291–2), "Stretch out your right hand, and take control of your weapons". As Philoctetes had demanded Neoptolemus' hand in trust, only to be deceived, now Neoptolemus demands Philoctetes' hand to receive the bow again, "an object of special *trust*".[29] This will be a deed, and it will be clear, unlike the twisting obscurity of language. At this highly symbolic and dramatic moment, Odysseus emerges, as before, in an attempt to prevent the gesture of return, but this time Philoctetes now has the bow and is about to let off an arrow, when he is grabbed and held down by Neoptolemus (1300): "Ah! Never, no, don't, by the gods, shoot! [*methês belos*]". Philoctetes (1301):

> μέθες με, πρὸς θεῶν, χεῖρα, φίλτατον τέκνον.

> Let me go, by the gods, my hand, dearest child!

With the same phrase he had cried out in his anguish of disease – let me go! *methes me* – Philoctetes again tries to break from the grasp of the boy. Again – under these very different circumstances – Neoptolemus refuses (1302): οὐκ ἂν μεθείην, "I could not let you go" – another intensely dramatic half-line. The drama of the relationship of young man and older hero, a drama not just of deception and revelation, but of contact and breakdown, finds physical embodiment in these mirrored scenes where the younger man grasps the older, who pleads to be let go: in the first, the care is both feigned and yet suggests the stirrings of pity; the physical embrace part of a tormented exchange that can only stress the disjunction between the men; in the second, the act of helping Philoctetes to his feet leads to the revelation of the deception; in the third, Neoptolemus prevents Philoctetes from killing Odysseus, from enacting his hatred in the violence of revenge. When Neoptolemus does finally agree to lead Philoctetes to his ship, the two men probably support each other (1402): *Ne.* "Lean against me." *Phil.* "As best I can anyway".[30] Taplin pointed out long ago that this exit mirrors the earlier false exit, but now the two men are helping each other in friendship not deceit.[31] The lines here are trochaic

---

[29] Taplin (1978) 90. See also Kosak (1999).

[30] The Greek here is not entirely clear. Jebb and Dawe (1978) 61 both argue against physical contact on the grounds that if Neoptolemus says "lean thy steps on mine", the response, "With as much strength as I can" would be a foolish reply. Dawe deletes the lines. Lloyd-Jones and Wilson (1990) 211–2, and Robinson (1969) 42 argue that "Lean on me as you walk" is a good translation of Neoptolemus' request, and the reply is quite coherent. Webster (1970), Taplin, Kosak and Kaimio line up with Lloyd-Jones and Wilson.

[31] Taplin (1971).

tetrameters, split between the characters as in the previous crises of interaction. But it is not a moment destined to last. Heracles' epiphany which immediately follows, redirects the heroes to Troy, and hints at the very different fates they will experience there. This mutually caring exit is equally a false exit, a self-deception, as both men are returned to the mythic narrative of destruction.

It is rare enough in Greek tragedy for the scripts to specify physical contact between characters, and Taplin must be right that any such moment is charged with a special symbolic force.[32] Yet in this play Philoctetes is held four and probably five times. In each case, until the final exit, the act of embrace or support or restraint enacts a breakdown of reciprocity, or simple care, in deception, hostility, confusion: each act of holding on marks a crisis in exchange. Each time Neoptolemus gets hold of Philoctetes, the broken pattern of exchange is embodied in the verse: half lines, third lines; or silences. But it is also the case that the *sequence* of *stichomythic* exchanges together thus creates a significant narrative of mirroring scenes.[33] In their form the exchanges echo each other, and pattern the relationship of Neoptolemus and Philoctetes as a score of contact and disjunction, holding and breakdown. The patterning of the dialogue form across the play is part of how the play develops its meaning.

Philoctetes is a late play in Sophocles' career, and is one of the most formally experimental of all extant Greek tragedies. The date of the *Electra* remains uncertain (and fiercely contested), but it also uses the patterning of *stichomythic* exchanges as an expressive framework. In chapters 4 and 5 we will look in detail at the opening of the play, and the *kommos* [mourning song] and the recognition scene between Orestes and Electra. Here I want to look at the central scene of the play, the argument between mother and daughter, and how one very short passage of *stichomythia* is framed.[34] The architecture of the play here is strikingly bold. Electra has two long, painful discussions with her sister, Chrysothemis, which clearly mirror each other. In the first (328–471), Electra interrupts Chrysothemis on her way to their father's tomb, and in the course of a heated display of their different responses to their current condition in the palace, persuades her not to make their mother's offerings at the graveside but to supplicate their father for help in revenge. In the second (871–1057), Chrysothemis returns from the tomb, exulting in the signs of Orestes' return she has seen at the grave, only to be persuaded by the distraught Electra that Orestes is dead. But Electra is unable to convince Chrysothemis to join her in a plan to murder their mother and her lover. Both scenes are powerful discussions between sisters (a matter we will return to in chapter 9), which articulate the very different characterizations of the two figures. In between these two scenes,

---

[32] Taplin (1971).

[33] See Pfeiffer-Petersen (1999) 154–6, and Schwinge (1968) 11–32 on the history of looking at symmetry between scenes.

[34] On this scene, see for representative approaches Winnington-Ingram (1980) 217–25; Whitlock Blundell (1989) 149–72; Ringer (1998) 152–85.

formally separated from them by a choral ode and a strophic *kommos* between the chorus and Electra, stands the huge central scene of the play, the row between Electra and Clytemnestra, and the deceptive speech of the Tutor, delivered to both women and the chorus. The first and most simple point, then, is that the clash of mother and daughter is thus framed by scenes of clashes between sister and sister: Electra's extreme self-expression – and her familial anguish – is formulated in conflict and contrast with her sister and her mother.

The argument between Clytemnestra and Electra is unique in extant Greek tragedy in that it is explicitly a screaming match that the participants have repeatedly acted out. Both women's positions are well mapped out and anticipate each other's rejoinders. This is not merely a gesture of realism, a recognisable representation of the compulsions and tensions within a traumatized and violent family. Rather, the issue of repetition is fully interwoven into the thematic texture of the play. On the one hand, Electra's constantly repeated lamentations, beyond the measures and control of the rituals of mourning, define her behaviour and her excessive action in the eyes of all the other characters. All ritual requires repetition: but when does repetition become excess, obsession? What is the effect of such repetition on the figure who mourns in such a way? On the other hand, the issue of repetition goes to the heart of the ethics of the play, both in the repetition of revenge – is it always right? at what cost? – and in the repetition of character: can a daughter not reproduce the traits of her mother? How like Clytemnestra has Electra become when she deceptively receives the returning Aegisthus and leads him towards his death? The repetition of the *agon* is part of a pathology of repetition in this play.

It is in this context that I wish to look at the short exchange that concludes the *agon* of mother and daughter. At one level, the dialogue has the familiar structure we saw with Creon and Haimon in *Antigone*, father and son. After the two women lay out their positions in extended speeches, the dialogue articulates a breakdown into more bitter and personal conflict. That is an expected form of the *agon*. Despite the aggression on show, Clytemnestra and Electra, unlike Creon and Haimon, end in inconclusive stasis (as befits the repetitive nature of their disagreements). But the connections between the *stichomythia* and the problems of repetition are developed with extraordinary density and focus.

Clytemnestra responds to Electra's speech, as Creon did to Haimon's, by stressing to the chorus her sense of outrage (*hubrisen*) at being given such a lesson, especially from someone so much younger (*têlikoutos* cf *Ant.* 726–7). Is she – the objectifying third person – "without shame" [*aischunê*]? But Electra surprisingly accepts the charge (616–8): "You should understand that I do have shame [*aischunê*] for these deeds, even if it doesn't seem so. I know that my behaviour is excessive, and not befitting for me". Electra recognizes that her actions go beyond the normal limits of acceptable female behaviour, especially for a daughter towards her mother. But this disarming self-knowledge is only a foil to an insult (619–21):

ἀλλ' ἡ γὰρ ἐκ σοῦ δυσμένεια καὶ τὰ σὰ
ἔργ' ἐξαναγκάζει με ταῦτα δρᾶν βίᾳ·
αἰσχροῖς γὰρ αἰσχρὰ πράγματ' ἐκδιδάσκεται.

But my reason is that hatred from you, and your deeds
Compel me completely by force to do this.
For disgraceful actions are completely taught by disgraceful actions.

Electra represents herself bitterly as a victim – "compelled" [*exananka-zei*], "by force" [*bia*]. Her mother's hatred and her deeds [*erga*] make her "do" [*drân*] what she does. Disgrace teaches disgrace. Her aggressive tone is emphasized by the repeated prefix *ex*– which I have emphatically translated with "completely": the compulsion, the teaching, is total. The logic – notice the repeated *gar* ("my reason . . .", "for") – for her is inescapable. Electra proclaims an overwhelming reciprocity: her mother's actions have caused her actions.

Clytemnestra is outraged, and immediately rounds on her daughter (622–3):

ὦ θρέμμ' ἀναιδές, ἦ σ' ἐγὼ καὶ τἄμ' ἔπη
καὶ τἄργα τἀμὰ πόλλ' ἄγαν λέγειν ποιεῖ.

You disrespectful creature! Is it really the case that I and my words
And my deeds give you cause to speak too much!

Clytemnestra's first word as she entered – *aneimenê*, "on the loose" (516) – described Electra as if she were an animal (always an option in denigrating a female), and here Electra is insulted as a "creature" – less than human – and as "disrespectful" – a very human transgression. The queen's repetition of *tama*, "my", after *egô*, "I", is emphatic: is it *my* words, *my* behaviour that causes your excesses – and Electra's excessiveness is specifically verbal: Electra – as every character in the play notes – talks too much. Electra's response twists each of the queen's terms (624–5):

σύ τοι λέγεις νιν, οὐκ ἐγώ. σὺ γὰρ ποιεῖς
τοὔργον· τὰ δ' ἔργα τοὺς λόγους εὑρίσκεται.

You say it; not I. For you do
The deed. The deeds discover the words.

Electra accepts the queen's sarcasm as truth, and affirms that, yes, her mother is right; she is responsible; she did do the deed – the murder, the adultery – and her actions find for themselves (*heurisketai*) the speeches Electra delivers. This is close reading with a vengeance: close as the intimate twisting of family hatred, close but catachrestic, – that is, deliberately misrepresenting and distorting, in line with her aggressive rhetorical intent. Line for line here – the battle-lines –

mark the mutual intertwining of two figures, sharing a language, pulling in opposite directions, unable to stop the intertwining or the hostility. As Reinhardt brilliantly put it, "Electra must start to imitate the voice she hates".[35] The simplicity of Electra's grammar ("you say it", "you do the deed") works to assert the simple self-evidence – the truth – of her aggressive assertions. Words and deeds, *logoi* and *erga*, are standardly opposed in fifth-century rhetoric, expressing a polarization of reality and argument, truth and excuse, fact and explanation. Here, Electra tries to construct a causal relation: deeds cause language, as if her verbal outpourings are inevitable consequences of her mother's actions.[36] Yet for Electra, words are her weapons. And immediately Clytemnestra turns to threat (626–7), "You will regret this boldness when Aegisthus gets home", and after another taunt from Electra, demands a propitious silence for her prayer to Apollo ("Do your sacrifice!", replies Electra, "Don't blame my mouth; know that I won't keep speaking out"[37]). Words are also performative: threats, silence, prayers, have an effect, especially in the world of tragic language. We will shortly see Electra reduced to heartfelt tears by the words of a man, as the Tutor enters with the false tale of Orestes' death in response to Clytemnestra's prayer. Words do things. Electra's logic is undermined as she proclaims its self-evidence.

The exchange of words is about the power of words; the exchange of words enacts a power struggle. In this sense, the dialogue is intensely self-reflexive. But there is more: the very exchange, the pattern of word for word, line for line insult and retort, is enacting the process of repetition and inheritance that structures the relationship of mother and daughter. The *stichomythia*, which has each repeat each other's words (about words), dramatizes the question of how alike mother and daughter are. The form of the *stichomythia* informs the ethical drama of intrafamilial trauma. Watching this family argue about what words do prompts the question of what such words, such arguments, are doing to the family.

The *Electra*'s concern with words and deeds reaches a climax in one of the most disturbing scenes of all tragedy, which uses the form of *stichomythia* to brilliant effect. After Orestes, Pylades and Electra enter the palace with the urn, the chorus sing a very short ode, and Electra returns surprisingly to the stage. She is there, she says, to watch for Aegisthus' arrival. In the next chapter, I will look briefly at the patterning of iambic and lyric language in this scene. Here I want to look just at the climactic moment of Clytemnestra's death. From offstage, inside the palace, Clytemnestra screams out (1410–11): "Child, child, pity the woman who bore you!" In Aeschylus' *Oresteia*, Clytemnestra bared her breast and asked for respect as his mother. It caused Orestes to hesitate in the

---

[35] Reinhardt (1979) 142: "language becomes imitative . . . imitative in a way that stems from the inner movement of the words".

[36] See Pfeiffer-Petersen (1999) 107; Winnington-Ingram (1980) 202.

[37] *Ouk an pera lexaim' eti* is translated by Jebb simply as "I shall say no more", but I think one should also hear the sense of "excessively" in *pera*. It is not just speaking that is the issue but speaking unpropitiously (as she has been).

archetypal moment of tragic doubt. Pity and respect are combined repeatedly in Homer at moments of supplication. Here, Clytemnestra brings together the weight of Homeric moral restraint and Aeschylean dramatic authority, as well as her maternal ties, to appeal to her son. The only answer we get, however, is from Electra (1411–12): "But neither he nor the father who sired him was pitied by you". Pity is swiped aside in the logic of revenge. In the *Oresteia*, not only does Orestes hesitate before his mother's appeal, and ask Pylades what to do, but also Pylades, in a *coup de théâtre*, answers with the only lines he speaks in the play, re-iterating the authority of the god's command, giving, as it were, divine imprimatur for the killing – and Electra is inside the house in silent absence. Here, however, Orestes does not answer; Orestes is not seen to hesitate; Pylades gives no divine authority; instead, Electra, from outside the house, on stage, gives a merciless commentary on the need for revenge. Even the chorus (1413–4), who have been so close to Electra and, indeed, talking intimately with her as the scene opens, significantly turn away and address the city and the race: "O city, O wretched race . . .". For many years, like other critics, I have worried why the chorus addresses the city here[38]: but what is crucial is that they do not speak to Electra or any other figure on stage. The surprising address to the city emphasizes that they are disconnected from Electra at this point: a stage direction of intense significance. Even the chorus speaks out to an absent addressee (and the city has been barely an express presence in this play, in sharp contradistinction to the *Oresteia*).[39] It is as if each character in this scene can find no response to their words, can make no verbal contact with each other.

So, too, even more shockingly, when Clytemnestra is stabbed and cries out (1415): *ômoi peplêgmai*, "alas, I am struck", Electra reacts (1415): παῖσον, εἰ σθένεις, διπλῆν, "Strike twice as hard, if you have the strength!". Clytemnestra's cry echoes the offstage cry heard in Aeschylus' *Agamemnon* when the king is killed by the queen (*Aga.* 1343 *ômoi peplêgmai*, "alas I am struck . . ."). It is as if Clytemnestra in *Electra* is paying back for her namesake's crime in the earlier tragedy. But in the *Agamemnon*, it is the chorus on stage who hear the cry – and wonder first who it is crying out, and then what they should do: they fragment into different voices in their uncertainty and hesitation. No hesitation, no uncertainty for Electra here: rather, a plea to redouble the violence. *ômoi mal' authis*, "alas, once again", cries out Clytemnestra (1416), just as Agamemnon in the *Agamemnon* also cried (*Aga.* 1345). "I would the same for Aegisthus", says Electra (1416) in grim satisfaction and anticipation. Again, the contrast with the choral response in the *Agamemnon* is insistent and telling.

It would be hard to imagine a scene which more vividly dramatizes the ethical crisis of violence as a breakdown of communication, or which more strikingly

---

[38] Segal (1981) 255; Kells (1973) 220; Lloyd-Jones and Wilson (1990) 74; Finglass (2007) 515–6.

[39] Griffin (1999) is right in this, though I would not draw his conclusions.

embodies it in the form of its verse exchange. Clytemnestra appeals to Orestes who does not reply. Electra responds to Clytemnestra and encourages Orestes, but from outside the house. Neither answers or acknowledges – or even hears? – her. Pylades is resolutely silent and unaddressed. The chorus is disengaged from the woman it has been so keen to support. There is a triangle of broken exchanges, where each character addresses a family member but is not responded to. Shouts and silence, mismatched, misfired. The violence within the family is expressed through a *stichomythic* exchange where characters do not inhabit the same space – offstage/on stage – do not engage with each other, do not affect each other with their words. The form of *stichomythia* is violently dislocated.

The representation of matricide in the *Electra* has become a familiar critical anxiety, which we will return to in chapter 8. But the ethical issues raised, it should be clear, cannot be separated from the disrupted, disjointed *stichomythic* form in which the death itself takes shape. The moral authority of Pylades, the expressed justifications of Orestes as well as his hesitation, the moral qualms of Electra about matricide – which are foundational to the discourse of the *Oresteia* – are all silenced or turned to absolute certainty and aggression in the *Electra*. The rewriting of the *Oresteia*, and the collapse of the *stichomythic* form, structure the representation of the matricide – and if the rewriting of Aeschylus poses the ethical question of how to evaluate the children's unhesitating behaviour, then the fragmentation of the scene of communication into multiple, misconnecting voices grounds and intensifies that question.

I have looked here at only a handful of paradigmatic passages of Sophoclean *stichomythia*, but enough has been said to indicate the extraordinary richness, variation, intricacy and precision of the form. We have seen how *stichomythia* dramatizes the turn from political debate into personal insult through the distorting and hostile rationality of appropriative rhetoric. We have investigated the manipulations of persuasion through the shiftiness of ethical language. We have considered how passages of *stichomythia* echo each other, become layered with Homeric reminiscences, and, as sequences of mirror scenes, develop intricate patterns of signification. We have argued that the very form of repetitive, line-for-line arguing, or the collapse of that form into fragmented miscommunication, become part of the ethical questions of tragedy.

Three general points run through the analyses I have pursued. First and most simply, the language of Sophoclean *stichomythia* is quite remarkable in its dense and incisive expressiveness. The line-for-line exchange involves each character giving a close but catachrestic reading of each other's words. That is, a line picks up precisely and even obsessively what has been said – in a productive and pointed misreading or redefinition. Such repetitions, coupled with the articulation of the particles, and the patterning of address, act as an internal set of stage directions, almost physical points of emphasis: *stichomythia* is a form in which dynamic shifts of power, changes of feeling, turns of nastiness or care, are developed in a very short space and with passionate intensity.[40] Under the pressure of such intensity, self-representation, the mapping of positions, becomes a self-exposure, a revelatory power-play. Whether *stichomythia* acts as the establishment of a scene or as the climax of conflict, it is dramatic dialogue of the most focused kind, and its own obsessive wording requires an especial attentiveness. Its close readings require our close reading.

Second, the form itself signifies. In recent years, critics have seen tragedy's exposure of the fissures of language, the multiple obscurities and tensions of civic discourse, as a defining aspect of the genre as a civic event, and, at the most general level, *stichomythia* may be said to be the dramatic exchanges in which these fissures, these tensions, become most evident.[41] But more pertinently, we have seen how half lines, silences, the fragmentation of exchange, repetition itself – the flexibility of the form of *stichomythia* – are integral not just to the drama of dialogue but also to the play of meaning in tragedy. Tragedy remains fascinated with forms of exchange, how language manipulates, hurts, twists, reveals its speakers and listeners: *stichomythia* displays what the form of arguments does to speakers and listeners.

Third – and this follows on from both of the first two general points – there is a striking self-reflexivity in the examples of *stichomythia* I have been considering. A debate about persuasion is used to persuade; an argument about whether another's deeds compel you to speak out is a demonstration of compulsive speaking out. That a literary form is self-reflexive is in itself a conclusion of limited import. But in each case of this *stichomythic* self-reflexivity, such self-consciousness about language is also a fundamental part of the play's ethical drive. Self-interested rhetoric and the breakdown of trust are integral themes in the *Philoctetes'* exploration of the politics of language, just as the self-commitment and self-destruction of Electra – her obsessive speaking out – ground the problem of the ethical evaluation of her figure in *Electra*. What is more, in each case these thematic concerns work to engage the audience in what could be called contemporary politics of the fifth-century city: the breakdown of trust and the destructiveness of long-term hatred speak directly to the *polis* after the fall of the oligarchic coup (the violent group of aristocrats who seized power in 411 and were in turn ousted violently by democrats); the psychological distortions of a desire for revenge has insistent purchase in the city of *stasis* (civil discord), even when the city is not the explicit focus of the play. The self-reflexivity of the *stichomythia* is part of how an audience becomes engaged

---

[40] "Dynamisch" is a key word for Seidensticker (1971) 206 and his sense of how Sophocles develops from Aeschylus.

[41] Following on from Vernant and Vidal-Naquet (1981), see Segal (1981); Goldhill (1986); Budelmann (2000) – and many others.

in the ethics of the drama, its questions. The exploration of *stichomythia* as a form of tragic language leads to a recognition of how tragedy explores language and its forms of exchange within the politics of the city.

Stichomythia, in short, as a form displays to the audience in the theatre a sharply instructive and disturbing image of dialogue – and in fifth-century Athens as today dialogue is a lauded principle of democratic society. Dialogue is often held up as an ideal for the political process and as a token of civilized life, and rightly so: but Sophocles' tragic *stichomythia*, with painful irony, uncovers the potential naïvety in such idealism. Line for line, Sophocles' *stichomythia* stages the full range of the nastiness of what people do to each other with words.

{4}

Choreography

THE LYRIC VOICE OF SOPHOCLEAN TRAGEDY

For Friedrich Hölderlin, struggling between the inevitable loss of the Greek past and his idealistic longing for it, the lyric voice of Greek tragedy embodied a paradigm of expressiveness towards which he yearned and reached.[1] Richard Wagner, a generation later, but also obsessed with the sublime of Hellenic art, re-conceptualized the orchestra of opera as the chorus of tragedy, an emotional and expressive counterpoint to the tragic action of the characters on stage.[2] For Matthew Arnold, a further generation on, it was particularly in the chorus of Sophocles where the master's steady and whole vision of things was in evidence, untrammelled by the messy specifics of politics, law, conflict. Throughout the long nineteenth century, the chorus and particularly the chorus of Sophocles, provides the transcendent poetry of the classical ideal. So, in a charming scene of Edwardian schooldays, David Blaize in E.F. Benson's novel *David Blaize* (1916), discovers himself – or at least beauty, friendship, art – through translating a chorus of the *Oedipus Coloneus* with his older friend and mentor, Maddox: "'Why, it's ripping!' he said to himself under his breath . . . then he lost himself again, diving into wonderful translucent depths. . . . This was the education of David . . .'". As they finish translating together, Maddox leads him into a discussion of the wonders of Greek civilization. "'Oh, David'", he concludes, "'let's save up and go to Athens'. 'Rather!'", said David.[3] The novel is a schoolboy book – though widely read by young men in the trenches of the First World War, nostalgic for the cakes and cricket desperately unavailable to them – but, however ridiculous Benson's prose may sound now, it too finds its sublime in the

---

[1] See Billings (forthcoming).
[2] See chapter 7 below.
[3] Benson (1989) [1916] 248–51.

Sophoclean chorus. And Fred Benson had a particularly sharp ear for the trends of the age.

For Hölderlin, Wagner, Arnold and Benson, Greek tragedy was fundamentally an exercise of the imagination. Although Benson may have seen a Cambridge Greek Play – his brother, Arthur, certainly noticed the devastatingly handsome Rupert Brooke in a non-speaking role in the *Oresteia* of 1906 – the number of performances of Greek tragedy across Europe was small, especially in the earlier part of the century, and, as performances, such productions were rarely celebrated as capturing the sublime – with a tiny handful of obvious exceptions such as Mounet-Sully's Oedipus in Paris.[4] The twentieth century, by contrast, saw an immense increase in productions, and there were – and continue to be – so many stagings of tragedy both in the professional theatre and in university settings, especially from the 1970s onwards, that the theatrical revival of Greek tragedy is a phenomenon that calls out for explanation. One consequence of this buoyant performance history is that the chorus has become a problem. The modern theatre has struggled to find adequate modes of representation for a collective on stage, let alone a collective that sings and dances. The solutions are often painful: a severe monotonal chanting; a Hollywood-tinged singing and dancing; the reduction of the chorus to a single figure or to a pair or three; abstract dancing with handbags; embarrassed bystanders to passionate grief – though the successes of a Mnouchkine, say, or Harrison/Hall, or, from the earlier years of the century, Reinhardt, also have each created an extended afterlife of influence.[5] The anxiety about the performance of the chorus is mapped by critical discussions in the academy, which have moved from the nineteenth-century notion of the "ideal spectator", inaugurated by Schlegel and Schelling, to anthropologically informed concepts of ritual bands, to recognitions of the chorus as a collective within the ideological understandings of community specific to democracy. If for Hölderlin, the loss of lyric sublimity underlies his pursuit of the choral voice, for modern production it is the otherness of a collectivity lost in modern alienation and social atomization that grounds the pursuit of choral experience.

This and the next chapter are about the language of the chorus in Sophocles, and my argument is located between the chorus as great poetry and the chorus as performance. The term "choreography" is chosen to indicate the way in which the chorus moves through a performance – not in the sense of its specific dance steps, which are almost entirely lost to us, but in the sense of the emotional, intellectual, and physical transitions enacted by the chorus through the course of the drama. The term "lyric voice" is added, however, because I also want to focus on how a specific mode of lyric utterance is integral to that

---

[4] See in general Hall and Macintosh (2005), and the discussion below in chapters 6, 7, and 8.
[5] See chapter 7 below for discussion and bibliography.

choreography. The dense, sung poetry of lyric is an elemental voice of tragedy, and its place in the soundscape of the genre and the soundscape of the city needs attention.

There are three initial areas of debate. First, I want to investigate the way in which the chorus, and especially the chorus in dialogue with the heroic actors, engages in the narrative of the play. As well as exchanges of intricate verbal texture, some of the finest poetry in the corpus, there are in these scenes dramatic narrative sequences of considerable sophistication – narratives of power relations, and emotional contacts and disruptions. One term I use for these exchanges is "score" or "scoring": this is to be taken primarily in a musical sense, treating the words and the metre as a notation to be activated in performance. But it also has a more extended sense to underline the emotional or intellectual passage of the chorus and actors through the scene.[6] This is an area of Sophoclean dramaturgy that is strikingly underappreciated by modern directors, in my experience, and by all who work from translations, which so often fail to note a move into lyric, let alone changes of metre within it. It is also an area where modern criticism is underdeveloped. This first concern could be summed up as an extended gloss on Aristotle's claim that Sophocles made a character of the chorus. How do the chorus become part of the *action* of drama?

Second, I want to demonstrate the extraordinary experimentation in *form* that we can see in Sophoclean handling of the chorus. Throughout this book I have been emphasizing the importance of the form of tragic drama – its flexibility, dramatic variation, and semantic richness – and the chorus is one of the most important areas for such a discussion.[7] We will end with *Philoctetes*, a play which is perhaps the most revolutionary in its use of the chorus of any Greek drama, but I am particularly concerned to read the specificity of choral writing in each particular play before reverting to generalizations about "the chorus": the specific form of the chorus in each play is integral to the drama. It is a striking fact that, as far as we can tell, it is only in drama that a chorus both speaks and sings (iambics and lyric): in other genres, epinician, say, or hymns, the lyric voice is uninterrupted. How do iambic verse and lyric verse interact in the choral voice? The speaking and singing chorus is a new element in the soundscape of the *polis*: and Sophocles plays a series of brilliant variations on its formal possibilities. How, too, does Sophocles adopt and adapt elements of choral writing from other genres, and use other voices for his choruses? So, the next chapter discusses in particular the role of the *kommos*, the ritual lament,

---

[6] An extended sense of "scoring" as a critical term goes back at least to Goodman (1968); see for critical discussion Worthen (2010) 8–12.

[7] This is surprisingly underdeveloped in both Gardiner (1987) and Burton (1980), and indeed, in Goward (1999).

in dramatic choral lyric. The second concern, then, is with how the formal elements of the language of the chorus are manipulated by Sophocles.

Third, I want to argue that my enquiry into choral performance and choral voice will together let us develop a more profitable route for understanding the political importance of Sophocles' writing for chorus. How the choral voice functions as a collective, with what authority, and in what relation to the individuals who lead it or threaten it, are questions that go to the heart of democratic process.[8] But to appreciate the political thrust of these questions, we need to move beyond the rather unnuanced generalizations that want to see the chorus as always the survivor, or as always the voice of the community or of tradition.

I The Construction of the Choral Voice

How, then, is the lyric voice constituted, and how should the institution of the chorus be understood? Although I declared above that my discussion will be led by the specifics of particular plays, as it will, there is a long-standing critical debate about the status of the chorus and its utterances, in and against which my arguments will find a place. I want first thus to express in lapidary form four assumptions, of increasing complexity and importance, that underpin the following discussion, and thereby give something of a view on the *status quaestionis*. Each of these four claims in barest expression is easy enough to agree with, and may even seem self-evident; but each also has far reaching and highly contentious implications once the business of reading Sophocles gets under way.

The first two assumptions have already been explicit in what I have written. First, to understand the tragic chorus, it is important to be aware of other choral forms in Athens and in other cities, not just by way of institutional or formal contrast, but also because tragic writing for the chorus picks up and manipulates elements from other genres of choral form (as Laura Swift has recently discussed at book length).[9] The dithyrambic competition, for example, although it involved more performers than the tragedies at the Great Dionysia Festival, and had a strong tribal basis in its institutional organization, has all too rarely been made part of the discussion even of the Great Dionysia.[10] My turn in the next chapter to the *kommos*, too, is not merely a formal, literary concern, but also recognizes that tragic choruses sound against performances elsewhere in *polis* life, and this is a crucial part of how

---

[8] A discussion begun in Gould (1996) and Goldhill (1996).

[9] Swift (2010).

[10] For the history of these sometimes wild choral songs, performed in competition by tribal choruses at the festival of the Great Dionysia see Zimmermann (1992).

the choral performance engages with or reflects or redeploys the social life of the city. As Vernant paradigmatically emphasized, we need to see "how tragedy assimilates into its own perspective the elements it borrows".[11]

Second, choral form adapts and changes over the course of time, and there is a history of the genre, for all that our lacunose sources make it hard to outline with absolute confidence. Aristotle's teleological declaration that in his day tragedy had introduced *embolima*, that is, inset odes between scenes, which could be sung for any play, and thus were not necessarily linked to the play's thematics in any significant way, and which were an integral aspect of the travelling repertory companies of actors in the fourth century who could perform thus with a local chorus, has had a profound effect on the history of criticism of choral *stasima* (lyric songs in stanza form). Recent scholars have made an industry of demonstrating that choral odes are "relevant" (although no one in the last fifty years has actually made a significant case for the irrelevance of any extant *stasimon*, and even in the nineteenth century, when an Aristotelian teleology was more dominant, there were fewer serious claims for the irrelevance of any particular ode than one might think, especially for Sophocles).[12] I will not be emphasizing how any particular ode "picks up", "echoes" or "anticipates" linguistically any particular earlier or later scene, except in so far as such a claim is necessary for my argument. I tend to believe that there are no wasted words in Sophocles, and the onus is on the critics who think they can prove irrelevance to do so. The focus on the thematic connections between *stasima* and the rest of the play has been integral to understanding the richness of tragic discourse, but has also had the effect of obscuring the formal experimentation of the use of the chorus in tragedy. If my first assumption requires us to look outside the genre of tragedy to see the relevant frames of comprehension, my second suggests that an internal history of the form of the chorus is still inadequately articulated within classical studies.

My third assumption is that whatever other terms we use to discuss the chorus, it is a grounding principle that the chorus, as an institution and as a performance, foregrounds a dynamic, or a tension (to use a Vernantian keyword), between a collective and an individual hero. This dynamic has been very differently evaluated. The collectivity of the chorus has been used to argue for their role as an idealized spectator, though few critics today would take this as a fundamental model for the tragic chorus. The chorus regularly is far from ideal, far from directive and even alienated from the audience in the theatre. More commonly, the chorus has been taken to represent the collective in the

---

[11] Vernant and Vidal-Naquet (1981) 8.

[12] Particularly relevant for this chapter is Kitzinger (2008) who has extensive bibliography; see also Segal (1981). As will also be clear, I regard the iambic interventions of the chorus as serious dramatic contributions, against e.g. Kirkwood (1954) 3: "The dramatic value of the iambic lines of the chorus in the episodes is slight"; or Norwood (1948) 79–80: "opportunities for the audience to applaud the speeches without missing any important remarks".

theatre, a figure for the *demos*. This model too has been roundly criticized: most choruses are marginal figures – women, slaves, slave-women – and even when they seem to speak as citizens, they are also markedly a subset of the citizenry. The Old Men of the *Antigone*, for example, are elderly advisors to the king, but the Guard and even Haimon offer different models of citizen political engagement at work in the play, and there are discussions in the play about the collective of the *polis* which bypass the chorus. What's more, the archaic or Homeric setting of almost every tragedy introduces a potential distantiation from the present, which must complicate any lines of identification between contemporary audiences and the action – nor can it be assumed that audiences identify only with figures like themselves, collective to collective, rather than with individual heroes.

The interrelation between the chorus as a group and the heroes on stage is also structured in very different ways, even at the most basic level of affiliation. So, Aeschylus can make the chorus a leading figure in the action and debate (as in *Supplices* or *Eumenides*), opposed quite aggressively to the individual actors. Euripides can construct a chorus which is apparently tangential to the actors, the action and the setting – the foreign virgins caught in transit in *Phoenissae*, say. So too he can create a chorus uncertainly drawn towards and alienated by the hero (*Medea*). In Sophocles' case, in six of the seven extant plays, the chorus is closely connected to the lead figure of the play (Ajax and Neoptolemus with their respective crews; Electra's and Deianeira's female supporters; the political advisors of Oedipus in the *Oedipus Tyrannus* and Creon in *Antigone*). Even in the apparent exception of the *Oedipus Coloneus*, the chorus of citizens are closely connected to Theseus as ruler, to the local environment in which the play takes place, and, gradually, to the figure of Oedipus. But whatever variations of relationship between chorus and actors any play develops – and the variety is evident even from these oversimplified comments – the chorus acts as a collective, and mobilizes ideas of communality. And since democracy, the political context for the institution of tragedy, makes such a noise, in theory and in practice, about the relation between the individual as such and the collective as such, few critics have resisted the temptation of seeing an analogy between the structuring dynamic of tragedy and the structuring principle of democracy – even if the politics of such an analogy are fiercely contested.

The concerns of this chapter are initially more closely focused. The relationship between a chorus speaking iambics and singing lyrics is partly a question of individual voice versus collective, especially if we agree, as most critics do, that some iambics at very least are spoken by the *koruphaios*, the leader of the chorus, an individual singled out from the collective. So too, the *kommos*, as a process of mourning, dramatizes the ritual whereby a group comforts an individual mourner, or mourners, and brings the individual(s) back into the social group from the isolation of their grief and loss. Both of these topics, that is, enact at a microcosmic level the detailed interaction of group and individual, and consequently the wager of this chapter is that through detailed analysis of such scenes a clearer view of at least the complexity of the question of community and hero will emerge.

The fourth assumption follows closely from the third. The tragic chorus' voice is constituted by a tension between its role as collective with the drive towards authority, and its role as a specific group, with a voice mired in the doubts, evasions and hopes of everyday communication. That is, the chorus can sing with the authority of a tradition, generalizing, mobilizing mythic narrative, the voice of the past, constructing the exemplarity of the present within a frame of the city's understanding. Yet a chorus can also perform the happenstance of a moment – being a character, as Aristotle would put it. When the chorus of the *Ajax* jump for joy after Ajax's so-called deception speech, it is markedly the utterance of a group of sailors, delighted that their leader has pulled back from the brink. In their previous ode, they have sung of how they are terrified on their own account by Ajax's disaster; later, their first response to his death is (900) *ômoi emôn nostôn* "Alas for my homecoming": their fear is that his death threatens their own safe return. Here (693) they believe he has changed his mind about suicide, and they are delighted with a personally motivated and explicable joy. The audience, far from the embrace of tradition, is distanced – to whatever degree – from the chorus' misunderstanding. When the sailors sing *ephrix' erôti*, "I am thrilled with passion" (693), it is the excitement of a moment, and not the reflection on the role of *eros* that the chorus of the *Antigone*, for example, construct: ἔρως, ἀνίκατε μάχαν, ἔρως ὅς ... desire, unconquered in battle, desire, which ..." (781–2). Now, even this choral ode in the *Ajax* turns to the comfort of generalization: πάνθ' ὁ μέγας χρόνος μαραίνει, they sing (714), "All things great time withers".[13] But not only is this a cliché which is related directly and immediately to their miscomprehension of Ajax ("since, at any rate, Ajax has unexpectedly [*ex aelptôn*] changed his mind from his rage and great rows with the Atreidai" [716–8]), but also it is marked as a cliché in contrast to Ajax's own powerful lines to which they are responding and which they echo as a trivialising mirror: ἅπανθ' ὁ μακρὸς κἀναρίθμητος χρόνος φύει τ' ἄδηλα καὶ φανέντα κρύπτεται κοὐκ ἔστ' ἄελπτον οὐδέν, "All things, long and countless time brings to birth in darkness, and hides after they have been revealed, nor is anything unexpected" (646–8). Their desire to locate Ajax within a generalizing discourse is itself placed as the specific failure of a particular group of sailors to appreciate the hero's tortured commitment, and the audience in the theatre responds to this *méconnaisance*.

When, by way of contrast, the chorus of *Antigone* sing the so-called and much celebrated "Ode to Man" (*Ant.* 332–75), alone on stage, there is no direct

---

[13] My point here is not affected by the textual problem: the Ms adds τε καὶ φλέγει, which as Jebb notes is almost certainly an interpolation.

reference to the action that has preceded it, nor to the other characters of the drama (for all its extensively discussed thematic relevance to the play). It takes the widest framework, the very nature of man as a social and intellectual being, and universalizes through reference to the oceans and sky and the city as an abstract entity. It could be extracted from the play as a self-standing ode – and so indeed it turns up unannounced but apparently at home in the script of *The Gospel at Colonus*, Lee Brewer's and Bob Telson's superb black gospel-music version of *Oedipus at Colonus*. The ode on *eros*, by contrast, although it too generalizes at the widest level about love's power over the whole natural and physical world, at least puns on the name of Haimon in its reference to τόδε νεῖκος ἀνδρῶν ξύναιμον, "this family [*xunaimon*] argument of men", as it links its generalizing discourse to the preceding scene by the deictic, "this". As scholars have carefully traced, the generalizing language of the "Ode to Man" echoes previous literary tradition, especially the central ode of the central play of Aeschylus' *Oresteia*, stanzas on the dangers of female desire (*Cho.* 585–651), as well as Homer, Hesiod and the moralizing tradition of wisdom literature, and places such ideas in a new context of contemporary political thinking. What is more, the chorus alone on stage, expressing such broad ideas, is easy to place in an institutional tradition of choral performance connected to the education of the young, and to the circulation of the normative repertoire of mythic narratives as charters of traditional thought, or rather as the continuing performance of traditional thought. Here the authoritative, collective voice of the chorus as institution and as performance is privileged.

The sailors' joy in the *Ajax* and the Old Men's reflections in the *Antigone* stand at opposite poles of a continuum of happenstance and universalization; but most *stasima* are more intricately poised *between* authority and insecurity, as the choral voice shifts and slides between authoritative generalization and character-led specificity. And this has led to much critical disagreement, as different aspects of the choral voice are emphasized by different readings. The shift between lyric and iambic voices is one place where this tension is most obviously insistent. In their iambic utterances the chorus or the *koruphaios* act most directly as engaged participants in a scene, even and especially when they tend towards ameliorizing commentary in the face of the more heated conflicts of the heroic actors. The shift in and out of lyric towards iambics is partly a move towards and away from the role of the chorus as embodiment of traditional, mythic wisdom: so in the scene that follows the "Ode To Man", the chorus first announce in anapaestic metre and in emotional, judgemental language the arrival of the apprehended Antigone, "captured in folly" (376–83), then comment to Creon in iambics on Antigone (471–2), "It's clear that this girl is the wild off-spring of a wild father; she does not know how to yield before trouble" – a personal judgement on Antigone's temper and her father's character, a judgement with which many critics have been quick to disagree, perhaps rashly. A *kommos* offers a different version of the general problem. For it is part of the expectations of a *kommos* that comforters and mourners will refer to mythic examples of death and mourning ("like Niobe . . ."), will universalize the issue ("all men must die"), and, as participants in a ritual, will play the role of comforter and mourner. The question with mourning therefore is: how individualized and specific can the scene of mourning become within the frame of ritual? As we will see in the next chapter, tragedy's *kommoi* manipulate the conventions of mourning in very striking ways.

These four assumptions – that tragic choruses need to be heard against other choral lyric forms; that the genre of tragedy experiments with choral form; that the tragic chorus is integrally bound up with concerns about the relation of individual and community or collective; that the chorus can reach towards both the authoritative voice of tradition, education, the group, and towards the specific utterance of a character in a situation – will be more fully explored in what follows, and represent in a general form what I believe the majority of contemporary critics would agree to be suitable starting points for the study of the chorus.

My treatment of the interrelation of the form of the chorus and the tragic narrative will, I hope, take forward current debates on the role of the chorus. But it is also an argument developed out of what I regard as the most telling recent criticism on Sophocles. In particular, the relation between ideas of collectivity and the language of Sophocles have been excellently analyzed by Felix Budelmann's study of communality and communication: my argument shares many concerns with his, and, although it moves on a different trajectory, we end up with similar general questions about the politics of tragic language.[14] The relation of lyric voice and the actors has been beautifully analyzed by Sarah Nooter's recent volume on the singing voice of actors.[15] Her concern is fundamentally with the moment when heroes burst into song; mine with the role of the chorus. But there are evident overlaps, where our questions and analysis of the lyric voice of tragedy are complementary. Edith Hall is one of very few critics to look seriously at metre in tragedy from a political angle. She has tried both to link specific metres and singing itself to characters defined through class and gender, and, more recently, to investigate the politics of genre through metre.[16] My interest is located rather in terms of metre and dramatic story-telling, and how this might be related to a political thrust of tragedy. But we share the conviction that modern scholarship has underappreciated the semantic power of metre. There are, of course, many scattered

---

[14] See Budelmann (2000).

[15] Nooter (forthcoming).

[16] Hall (1999b) redrafted in Hall (2006) 288–320. Scott (1996) following on from the more impressive Scott (1984) made a full-blown attempt to link metre and sense, but I find his readings of the play (e.g. "cheerfulness . . . in the final scene" (152) of the *Electra*) and his focus solely on the *stasima* unsatisfactory.

comments and arguments from which I have learned and which will appear in my footnotes and my discussion. But it is worth stressing from the outset that my argument is to be placed within these current issues of how the collective choral voice speaks to the audience in the theatre and to the other characters on stage; of how the shift of voice in Greek tragedy between spoken and sung forms is explored by Sophocles; of how metre itself, thus, becomes part of the signifying repertoire of tragedy.

II The Voice of the Chorus: Metre and the Slippages of Song

It is fully familiar that the chorus both sings lyric *stasima* and also utters a set of iambic lines in the scenes, which are often dismissed as fillers, a sniffiness which, as we have already seen in previous chapters and will see again here, is profoundly misplaced in the case of the scripts of Sophocles. It is usually assumed that iambic lines attributed to the chorus are spoken by the *koruphaios*, the leader of the chorus, and lyrics are sung ensemble, and it is also generally thought that anapaests, particularly so-called marching anapaests, may have been chanted in recitative, as it were – a third voice. The evidence for these near universally asserted assumptions is both surprisingly late and regrettably exiguous. The term *koruphaios* barely occurs until well after the classical period. There is no explicit statement in any ancient source on whether the iambic lines of the chorus were spoken only by an individual, or were chanted by a group. There is no statement on whether only the *koruphaios* would speak or whether other chorus members might have such solos. It is generally believed that there are (at least) three basic delivery styles – but even the standard modern handbooks on metre are opaque as to what these styles might have sounded like, or how clearly demarcated the divisions between them were.[17] There are a few passages where it is clear that the chorus is divided: in lyric there are hemichoruses in conversation; in iambics, there is at least one debate with multiple voices.[18] But it is unclear how often such devices were utilized by the dramatists, and editors are both arbitrary and divided amongst themselves as to when and how such separate voices should be indicated in the text. There is even a suggestion by modern scholars that some choral lyrics might have been sung solo by a chorus member, rather than by the ensemble, though again there is no explicit statement from ancient sources that this was ever an option.[19] The evidence for these most basic structuring units, then, is annoyingly weak, but, as we will see, the detailed interplays between speaking in

---

[17] See West (1982); Maas (1962); Dale (1968).

[18] See *Ajax* 866–880; Aesch. *Aga.* 1346–71.

[19] So e.g. Barrett (1964) on *Hippolytus ad* 362–72; and *ad* 565–600.

iambics and singing or chanting in lyric metres remain fascinating and highly significant.[20]

The first example will indicate why I think this interplay between lyric and iambic voices can be an important part of Sophoclean dramaturgy, and comes from the earliest extant play, the *Ajax*. (Ajax is an example central to Sarah Nooter's project, and her discussion of the hero is insightful.) The chorus enters with verses in marching anapaests (134–71) and move into their first *stasimon* (172–200). At this point, they are joined by Tecmessa: both she and they sing in lyric, an exchange about their intense worries for Ajax. They address each other; the chorus question her and she answers; they express their fears and she responds. They follow this lyric exchange with a dialogue in iambics in which the situation is outlined for the chorus by Tecmessa, but this conversation is interrupted by the offstage cries of the hero, and then the *ekkuklema*, if we trust the scholia, wheels Ajax into view. He cries out three times, and his fourth utterance is a pair of iambic lines (342–3), calling for his brother Teucer. It is this that prompts the chorus to comment that he seems to be sane (344 ἀνὴρ ἔοικεν φρονεῖν, "the man seems to be in his wits"), and to call for Ajax to be brought forth. It is this exposure of Ajax that interests me.

As Nooter has stressed, it is, first of all, significant that Ajax is now the one who sings lyric. In the prologue, he spoke iambics with Athene. He had even called for Teucer in iambics. Something has changed. He will at the end of this exchange revert to iambics with his exposition of his situation and his announcement of his decision to die in the first of his long and famous speeches (430–80). He will sing no more. Five of the six strophes and antistrophes which Ajax sings here, begin with *iô*, a cry of grief. His first great speech begins *aiai* (430), a cry of grief. But this *aiai* leads not so much into another outpouring of despair as into a reflection on how the cry sounds like his own name *Aias*, and the rational articulation of his situation. But for now, between his iambic conversation with Athene and his self-lacerating iambic account of his current dilemma, we have the less expected sight of the taciturn warrior of Homer breaking into song. Ajax's lyric voice marks a specific passage of transition for the hero.

But the chorus, who have been mainly singing (and will again sing their lyrics), stay resolutely in iambics throughout this scene – which are presumably spoken by the *koruphaios*. The anticipation of seeing Ajax produced emotional collective lyric, but his appearance stimulates apparently calmer speech from a single voice: maybe faced by a reality that is sobering; maybe to heighten

---

[20] "The modern literature on the subject of methods of delivery in Greek drama is as immense as the evidence is slight and inconclusive": Pickard-Cambridge (1968) 246. For his own account see 156–67. I will not indicate at every point that the evidence for these basic structuring units of performance is in itself so thin; and for the moment I will also write under the assumption that the remarks delivered in iambics attributed to the chorus were spoken by a single speaker, for whom the term *koruphaios* will be adequate. See Wilson (2000) 134–5.

the effect of Ajax's singing; maybe dramatizing their fear of or withdrawal from their maddened captain. So, Ajax begins by addressing the sailors as his *philoi* and as the only ones to stand by him in his disaster (348–51):

ἰώ,
φίλοι ναυβάται, μόνοι ἐμῶν φίλων
μόνοι ἔτ᾽ ἐμμένοντες ὀρθῷ νόμῳ,
ἴδεσθέ μ᾽ . . .

Io!
Friends, crewmen, alone of my friends,
You alone stand by me obedient to how things should be;
look at me . . .

The command *idesthe*, "look!", is the theatrical gesture *par excellence*, the creation of a spectator. But the chorus do not reply to Ajax (although they had addressed him in absentia throughout the *parodos*). Instead, they address Tecmessa, reflecting on their previous conversation (354–5), or rather the *koruphaios* alone speaks for them (again assuming that the iambic line is spoken by a single voice):

οἴμ᾽ ὡς ἔοικας ὀρθὰ μαρτυρεῖν ἄγαν.
δηλοῖ δὲ τοὔργον ὡς ἀφροντίστως ἔχει.

Oh! It seems you were all too right in your account.
The fact shows clearly that he is in no sane condition.

In terms of contact, the chorus are aligned with Tecmessa, and separate from, distanced from Ajax, like doctors observing a patient.[21] Although their use of *ortha* "right", barely echoes Ajax's *orthôi nomôi*, which I translated "obedient to how things should be" ("according to right law"), their comment, like their metre, puts a distance between them and him. Ajax addresses them again even more insistently (359–61):

σέ τοι σέ τοι μόνον δέδορ-
κα ποιμένων ἐπαρκέσοντ᾽.
ἀλλά με συνδάιξον.

You! you! alone of my carers I see
As sufficient.
Please help me die![22]

Se . . . se, "you! you!" is abrupt, commanding, and he demands they help him
to kill himself violently. This time the *koruphaios* does respond to him (362–3):

εὔφημα φώνει· μὴ κακὸν κακῷ διδοὺς
ἄκος πλέον τὸ πῆμα τῆς ἄτης τίθει.

Speak decently! Don't add ill to ill,
And don't make the disaster of your doom a worse pain.

He rebuffs Ajax's demands with imperatives that he should avoid such
uncontrolled, ill-omened speech, and should not threaten to make a terrible
situation even worse. The chorus' iambic distance and attempt at restraint is set
in opposition to Ajax's emotional appeals and despairing outbursts.

But this pattern begins to shift. For the second strophe (which runs from 356 to
376) is broken at 367–71 by four iambic lines and an *extra metrum* scream (364–72):

Αι. ὁρᾷς τὸν θρασύν, τὸν εὐκάρδιον,
τὸν ἐν δαΐοις ἄτρεστον μάχαις,
ἐν ἀφόβοις με θηρσὶ δεινὸν χέρας;
οἴμοι γέλωτος, οἷον ὑβρίσθην ἄρα.
Τε. μή, δέσποτ᾽ Αἴας, λίσσομαί σ᾽, αὔδα τάδε.
Αι. οὐκ ἐκτός; οὐκ ἄψορρον ἐκνεμεῖ πόδα;
αἰαῖ αἰαῖ.
Χο. ὦ πρὸς θεῶν ὕπεικε καὶ φρόνησον εὖ.
Αι. ὦ δύσμορος ὅς . . .

Aj. Do you see me, the bold, the brave,
The undaunted in fierce battles,
Terrible in strength against fearless wild beasts?
Alas, a laughing-stock! How I have been humiliated, I realise.
Te. Oh lord Ajax, don't say that, I implore you.
Aj. Outside! Go away from me!
Aah! Aah!
Ch. By the gods, yield and be in your right mind!
Aj. Oh, ill-fated, I who . . .

This is an intricately scored passage. Ajax begins in lyric (364–6), asking the
chorus to look on him, once so great and now a victim of humiliation. But at 367,
he speaks in iambics with a moment of intense self-recognition, marked by *ara*.
Speaks – as one would assume with iambics? Or possibly somewhere between
speech and song? The change of metre is abrupt: how abrupt is the change of voice?
But his voice, I assume, does mark this change of metre, this transition. At this
point, Tecmessa, who has been silent and unnoticed or at least unaddressed by
Ajax, comes in with a supplication, imploring her master, as the crewmen had, not
to say such things. But he sharply orders her out of his sight in a brusque iambic

line followed by a scream: direct contact, but only to break it. The chorus address him directly with a wish that he should be in his right mind (*phronêson* [371] recalls *aphrontistôs* [355] and *phronein* [344]), but this only leads to Ajax singing again, and singing of and to himself – a break in the contact that the iambics offered. Ajax seems to approach the expressive normality and self-recognition of iambics, only to be provoked by Tecmessa's appearance into even more intense grief.

The same metrical scheme occurs, of course, in the antistrophe, and again it is the (self-) recognition of laughter and abuse, the gestures of his humiliation, that lead him to the utterance of iambics (379–82):

> Αι. ἰὼ πάνθ' ὁρῶν, ἁπάντων τ' ἀεὶ
> κακῶν ὄργανον, τέκνον Λαρτίου,
> κακπινέστατόν τ' ἄλημα στρατοῦ,
> ἦ που πολὺν γέλωθ' ὑφ' ἡδονῆς ἄγεις.

> *Aj.* Ah, you see all, the instrument of all
> Evil, child of Laertes,
> Foulest knave of the army,
> For sure, you are laughing long and loud in delight.

The iambic last line here, with its strongly affirmative *ê pou*, "Aye, for sure" again marks Ajax's acute sense of humiliation. The verb *ageis* is explained by Jebb as indicating "continued derision"; Stanford adds the sense of "celebration"; we might also add the idea of "leading" a chorus of laughter, as Ajax sees himself as the object of the Greek camp's hostility.[23] But this iambic line continues the grammar of the lyric verses. How does the voice change here? What slippage is there between lyric and the verse closest to human speech? Is this Ajax sliding from his wilder emotional world to a moment of realisation? The chorus' ameliorating interventions that follow are not acknowledged by Ajax, and seem to pass him by as useless generalizations, locked as he is into his own despair. His next line is a iambic verse (384), "Just let me see him, even though I am so ruined . . .", but it is broken off (and Lloyd-Jones and Wilson punctuate it as an aposiopesis) with another cry of grief, and he slips back into lyric. As he turns again to lyric, the chorus comment – but receive no reply – "do you not know what point of misery you have reached?": they dismiss his self-recognition, though he will show all too clearly in the following scene that he is fully aware of where he has come to. The final lyrics of Ajax have him address the rivers and landscape of the Trojan plain, no longer seeking help from the chorus or rejecting Tecmessa. Alienated in lyric solitude and despair.

Ajax is singing a sort of lament here, and one might expect there to be a formal pattern of sympathy and solace from his collective listeners and Tecmessa.

---

[23] Jebb (1896), Stanford (1963) *ad loc.*

The comments of the chorus and Tecmessa receive short shrift from Ajax, and cannot echo his grief, nor frame it in mythic parallels: their disjunction from him, the failure of the *kommos*, is marked by the failure to share metre, the dramatic disjunction between the lyric voice in the mouth of the singular hero, and iambics in the mouth of Tecmessa and the representative of the collective, as well as by the failure of contact between the characters. But the transition which this scene marks, from the violent madness of the prologue to the rational despair of the second scene, is also performed in the slippage into iambics by the hero, precisely at moments of self-recognition and contact with his *philoi*. The voice of the hero is *moving*; and the beginning of the second antistrophe, starting with the paradigmatic lyric outburst of *iô* but ending with the iambic line, enacts this gradual hardening of the voice into bitter self-awareness and reasoning, before he returns to lyric, emotional alienation. The disjunctive and expressive use of metre, in short, is integral to the semantics of the drama, to the representation of the changing voice of the hero, struggling with his sanity and self-awareness. And integral to the chorus, in their dependent relationship with him. The chorus' shifts of metre contour the hero's, as they enact their role as horrified *philoi* drawn towards and alienated from their master. This is the central dynamic of the scene.

This variety of metrical delivery continues in *Ajax*. When the chorus return from looking for Ajax in two hemichoruses, itself a dramatically bold move, and enter a conversation with Tecmessa, we see a dialogue which swings between iambics and lyrics, and between the two half choruses (the first of which begins in lyrics [866–71], the second in iambics [872, 874] – if these lines are not spoken by a single *koruphaios*, it would be a good case for iambic lines spoken by a group rather than an individual). The whole chorus together (it seems) also sings (879–90); the *koruphaios* (892, 894–5) speaks; and an individual actor, Tecmessa, engages them in dialogue in both lyrics and iambics. The confused shifts of mood of hunting for the lost hero, anticipating and then recognizing disaster, the dispersed action, are embodied in the dispersed voices. Snatches of iambic conversation (904–7) are intercalated with lyric expressions of shock and grief (900–3, 908–14). This is a very striking use of multiple metrical forms to dramatize a confused scene of multiple shifts of emotion and viewpoint. It encapsulates – for dramatic effect – in the briefest of scenes the full range of the soundscape of tragedy.

Equally intriguing is the use of single iambic lines within an otherwise lyric stanza. When the chorus are thrilled that Ajax appears to have changed his mind, they sing two stanzas of joy (which I discussed briefly above). Each stanza begins with a single iambic line that directly sums up their hope (693: "I am thrilled with passion; and aloft with great joy"; 706: "Ares has loosed this terrible grief from his eyes".) Each of these opening iambic lines is followed by a wild exclamation: 694: *ἰὼ ἰὼ Πὰν Πάν*, "Oh! Oh! Pan! Pan!"; 707: *ἰὼ ἰὼ νῦν αὖ νῦν, ὦ Ζεῦ*, Oh! Oh! Now, again, again, O Zeus". It's as if the choral stanza begins in the flattest of metres and then explodes into a scream of joy. I wonder if the metrical contrast is to be fully articulated in performance to capture the outburst of their feelings? Iambic trimeters can, of course, appear in lyrics, but the only other example in Sophocles of stanzas beginning in this way with a iambic line is the *parodos* of the *Philoctetes*, where the sailors (again a subordinate group of men) enter to take their orders from Neoptolemus, but there the iambic lines flow grammatically and metrically into the rest of the *stasimon*.

Now, scholars have catalogued scenes where actors' monodies are combined either with iambic speeches from the chorus (starting from Aeschylus' Cassandra) or with iambic speeches from other characters (though analysis of such passages has been rather less forthcoming).[24] They have also listed scenes where actors shift between lyric and iambics (again starting with the long and complex scene of Aeschylus' Cassandra); other dialogues in different metres too have been collected. In Euripides' *Iphigeneia at Tauris* 827–99, *Ion* 1439–1509, *Helen* 625–97, three recognition scenes, in each case it is a female who sings lyric and a male who responds in iambics. This may suggest a generalized attitude towards the greater emotionalism of females,[25] though in each of these plays there is also an emotional asymmetry between the characters for other reasons too: in *Ion*, Creusa, who has lived long with the aftermath of her encounter with Apollo, is telling her son of her rape: he is only recently engaging with his family history and is listening to rather than sharing the emotions of her story; in *Helen* Menelaus is keen to know about Helen's departure from Sparta, and she has to recount a personally difficult story to her husband. In *Iphigeneia at Tauris*, both Orestes and Iphigeneia have barely escaped death, but it is Iphigeneia who breaks into an emotional account of her sacrifice and unmarried life among barbarians. But it may be that these scenes of female lyric emotion and male iambic restraint should be seen as a contrast with the *Ajax*, where, as Nooter has emphasized, it is the man's man Ajax who is singing, lamenting, humiliated, and the female prisoner and concubine, and the collective of ordinary sailors, who speak the iambics encouraging and displaying restraint. When Ajax sings, the chorus and Tecmessa are, as it were, reduced to iambics, and this change of voicing is fundamental to the scene's meaning in and as performance.

A second exemplary passage shows a similar technique in a single remarkable exchange, which has not been adequately appreciated, and which offers a further light on how Sophocles manipulates the potential of such metrical and thus representational possibilities. Although it does not involve the chorus directly, it shows how Sophocles uses the lyric voice itself for extraordinary dramatic effect – and will turn out finally to raise a question about the chorus' silence.

---

[24] See e.g. Finglass (2007) 117–121; 470–71; Dale (1967) 106–7 *ad* 625–97.
[25] So Finglass (2007) 470 *ad* 1232–87.

The recognition scene of the *Electra* juxtaposes a continuous lyric outburst from Electra (strophic, unlike the Euripidean scenes), and iambic lines from Orestes enjoining silence and caution (*Electra* 1231–88). This juxtaposition has been noted many times by commentators, and, typically for this most contentious of plays, interpretations vary between those who see this as a proper and expected female emotionalism in contrast to a proper and expected male efficiency and order, and those who see it as yet another wild explosion of Electra, out of place and dangerous verbally as ever, and a morally obtuse and even cruel Orestes, ignoring the opportunity for fraternal embrace.[26] The juxtaposition is clearly significant, however played, and strongly emphasized by the fact that Electra also talks about her overwhelming feelings throughout, whereas Orestes not only is more restrained, but also repeatedly demands restraint in the form of Electra's silence (1236, 1238, 1251–2, 1259), and specifically comments on her dangerously excessive emotional display (1251–2, 1271–2). As in the recognition scenes in Euripides which I have just cited, Electra's emotional response is motivated by more than her gender. It is Electra who has gone through the horror of believing her brother dead and the shock of finding him alive, whilst Orestes has been in command of the deception; it is Electra who has suffered daily anguished argument and bullying, as she says, while Orestes has been prepared for revenge by the Tutor over many years of exile.

What is more, the calmness of Orestes in the face of matricide is thematized, much as is Electra's violent psychopathology. So, Electra herself declares to the chorus that in her current circumstances "neither self-control nor piety is possible" because in "evil times, evil must certainly be practised" (307–9), and to her mother, as we saw in chapter 3, she has proclaimed that her "disgraceful behaviour has been thoroughly taught from the disgraceful behaviour" around her (621). Electra is fully aware of her own disgrace, her own unpleasantness, it seems. How like her mother Electra becomes, how wild and how decent she is becomes a question in the play – a question which goes to the heart of the troubling morality of the drama as it explores the costs of a consuming passion for revenge. Similarly, in contrast with the Orestes of Aeschylus or that of Euripides, Sophocles' Orestes is notably unreflective, unconcerned even, about the morality of matricide, a silence which grounds both the critical position of those who conclude that thus there is no doubt about the rectitude of the revenge, and also the opposite critical position of those who argue that it is precisely the failure to doubt in the face of matricide that constitutes the horror of Orestes' violence. The recognition scene's juxtaposition of Electra's emotional lyrics and Orestes' iambic restraint thus emblematizes this thematic nexus. This formal structure of monodic lyric and spoken iambic exchange *as a form* is fully and integrally part of the semantics of the play.

---

[26] See below chapter 8.

The contrast itself is picked up and mirrored in reverse, as it were, in the murder scene itself. As the cries of the dying Clytemnestra are heard from inside the house, not only is Orestes silent – we can hear neither doubt from him, unlike the Aeschylean Orestes, nor imprimatur from Pylades – but also the chorus screams out in emotional lyrics in horror, while Electra in iambics comments (1406) βοᾷ τις ἔνδον. οὐκ ἀκούετ, ὦ φίλοι, "Someone is shouting inside. Do you not hear, friends?". "Someone", *tis*, sounds as if she does not recognize her own mother's voice or cannot anticipate who might be screaming or why. This use of the indefinite *tis* is "primarily menacing"[27], when it is directed at a particular person in conversation (its usual form, as in "someone's going to get it"). But here she is addressing the chorus, and her menace is for her own pleasure – perhaps a chilly calm at a moment of long-awaited revenge, which is set in strong contrast with the chorus' dismay at a son killing his mother – an emotional *and* a moral contrast, I would suggest. The restraint of iambics in Electra's case is not a sign of *sophronein* and *eusebein*, "self-control and piety", but a sign of a dangerous passion differently manifested. The silence of Orestes, quite as much as Electra's passion, fully dramatizes the horror of an unquestioning commitment to violence. Sophocles displays the silent detachment of extremist violence as the uncanny double of the screams of extremist fervour.

This thematic focus on speech, control, passion and its relation to moral action makes the recognition scene's dialogue of monody and iambics especially charged. But there are two further questions about this exchange which have been less commonly debated. First, there is one small break in the pattern of iambics and lyrics (1275–80):

> Ηλ. . . . μή τί με, πολύπονον ὧδ᾽ ἰδών
> Ορ. τί μὴ ποιήσω; Ηλ. μή μ᾽ ἀποστερήσῃς
> τῶν σῶν προσώπων ἀδονὰν μεθέσθαι.
> Ορ. ἦ κάρτα κἂν ἄλλοισι θυμοίμην ἰδών.
> Ηλ. ξυναινεῖς; Ορ. τί μὴν οὔ;;
> Ηλ. ὦ φίλ᾽, ἔκλυον ἂν ἐγὼ οὐδ᾽ ἂν ἤλπισ᾽ αὐδάν.

> *El.* Don't, now you've seen me like this in despair . . .
> *Or.* What should I not do? *El.* Do not deprive me
> Of the pleasure of your face, don't take it away.
> *Or.* For sure, I would be angry if I saw someone else attempt it.
> *El.* You concur? *Or.* Of course.
> *Or.* O dear one, I have heard a voice that I could never have hoped for.

Orestes asks Electra what her broken and grammatically incoherent demand is: "what is it that you don't want me to do?". *Ti mê poêsô* is the first

[27] Bond (1981) *ad* Eur. *Her.* 747–8.

half of a iambic line (which Finglass analyzes as the first half of a syncopated, and thus lyric, iambic – though the syncopated part is not expressed).[28] She replies with a line and a half of lyric, which are iambic trimeter catalectics – iambic trimeters with an extra final syllable, as it were – asking him not to leave her again (it is almost as if she completes the metrical expectation of his half line – but goes beyond it). He concurs (with a single iambic line). But when she asks if he really does agree (*xunaineis*, metrically a bacchiac), Orestes replies *ti mên ou*, "of course", "why indeed not?", a bacchiac to match hers. Now a bacchiac can appear in a iambic line before the caesura, but this appears to be a metrical response to Electra's question. It's as if her direct demand prompts an emotionally heightened grace note from him (which might be anticipated in 276 if Finglass is right that this half line has a lyric timbre). His verse – his metre – seems to be infected by her emotional lyric, as even the strong man of revenge slips into a more emotional if laconic utterance. As he utters this three-word lyric – does he sing? does he break down? – Electra sings in response, "I have heard a voice that I could not even hope for".

This line of Electra's has prompted a good deal of discussion in the commentators. One problem is whether the vocative is *o phil'*, "o dear one", addressed to Orestes; or *o philai*, "o dear ones", addressed to the chorus. This has been inconclusively debated primarily as a question of metrics. Finglass adds reasonably enough, but also without settling the matter, that one might expect a superlative, *o philtate*, as an address between brother and sister in a recognition scene (it is inconclusive not least because Electra does address Orestes at 1285, two lines later, and a change of addressee so quickly here in the same speech would be surprising).[29] We will see in a moment that who is addressed also changes the semantics of the scene. The second and more pressing problem is the referent for *audan*: what voice is she referring to? Jebb argues it is "unquestionably" the "living voice" of the returning Orestes. Kaibel argued that it means "story" and refers to the tale of Orestes' death. Wilamowitz took it to indicate his agreement to her request.[30] The question might be raised most sharply by asking why the voice is mentioned here, almost at the very end of the exchange, when they have been in dialogue already for over 60 lines. Perhaps it should be seen as also a response to the three-word lyric utterance, that is, Orestes' briefest of slips into emotional symmetry, as well as his unexpected appearance. Electra did not expect to hear a lyric voice from Orestes. Whenever Sophocles draws attention to the voice it is for a purpose . . .

---

[28] Finglass (2007) *ad loc.*

[29] Finglass (2007) *ad loc* with a conspectus of opinions.

[30] Kaibel (1896) 268 (followed by Campbell, Lloyd-Jones and Wilson and Kamerbeek). Jebb (1894) *ad loc.* Wilamowitz (1921) 514.

The single phrases *ti mê poêsô* and *ti mên ou* constitutes the limit case for the transition between lyrics and iambics. The context could not be more marked, since not only is the pattern of male iambics and female lyrics strongly established, but also the thematics of emotion and control have been significantly underscored throughout the play. Is this a moment, as in 1174–5, where Orestes lets slip his self-control? Is this a moment when Electra's lyric outpourings finally persuade him to make an emotional connection with her?

The second brief point I wish to make on this scene takes us back to the chorus and concerns its silence. When Electra, wonderingly, is first sure she recognizes Orestes, she begs the chorus to look at him: ὁρᾶτ᾽ Ὀρέστην τόνδε, "Look at Orestes, here!" (1228). "We see him", they reply, and "a tear of joy runs from our eyes" (1230–31). But through the recognition lyrics, *and* then the next scene of iambics between Orestes and Electra *and* then the Paidagogus' intervention, *and* their exit into the palace, the chorus say absolutely nothing (1232–83), nor are they addressed by any character (unless the text of 1280 is read as *o philai,* and even if that reading were accepted, they do not respond: the silence of the chorus here should be part of the discussion of which vocative is to be read). By way of contrast, the recognition scene in the *Choephoroi* is ended by five iambics from the chorus (*Cho.* 264–8), and the scene shifts into the three-way *kommos* sung between Orestes, Electra and the chorus (*Cho.* 306–478). In Euripides' *Electra,* after the unwilling recognition, the chorus break into brief but excited lyrics (Eur. *El.* 585–95), which Orestes, with a typical Euripidean joke of characterization, breaks off with *eien,* "enough already; that's the dear pleasure of greeting done with" (Eur. *El.* 596–7). Here, however, in Sophocles the chorus remain silent.

This silence does create an unbroken emphasis on the brother-sister meeting, but I do not think that this is its sole dramatic function. Nor do I think that the chorus are just being functionally helpful to the avengers, keeping silent to avoid revealing the plot to those in the palace, even though Orestes and the Paedagogus both demand silence from Electra (unsuccessfully) to this end. Rather, this silence may also be understood as an example of what I termed in chapter 2 "the audience on stage". That is, the chorus are not just silenced and forgotten but are there watching (*horate*) the recognition (and following scene), and we watch them watching. We get two very different responses to the recognition from its leading actors, Orestes and Electra, and the chorus' silent observation encourages the audience in the theatre to see the difference, but gives us no guidance in how to read it. Their watching silence helps set up Electra's and Orestes' different responses as a problem for spectators in the theatre. What do they see here, or rather what do we see them seeing? As we will find in the *Philoctetes*, Sophocles is highly conscious of how to manipulate a chorus' silence. The chorus of the *Electra,* I would suggest, inhabits an increasingly difficult place as the murder approaches and takes place, and their silence here may well be part of that dramatization.

The flexibility and dramatic potential of the variation of iambic and lyric are also expertly manipulated by Sophocles at the highly dramatic moment of the entrance of the blinded Oedipus in the *Oedipus Tyrannus*, another play where Nooter has discussed the actor's singing tellingly. The *exangelos* announces the gates are opening to display Oedipus, a sight (*theâma*) to make even an enemy pity (1294–6). The sight (*idein* 1297) does indeed overwhelm the chorus, who sing a passionate lyric of pity, addressed to the king (1297–1306). They are overcome by trembling (*phrikên* 1306). The metre they use here is often described as "marching anapaests" ("recitative anapaests", "chanting anapaests") to distinguish it from the more highly wrought melic anapaests, in which Oedipus, as he stumbles in, cries out his pain (1307–11). It is often hard to distinguish with any rigour between the two forms, however (and in this case Pearson's *OCT* maintains some of the Doric features typical of melic anapaests (τλᾶμον 1299, μακίστων 1301, δύσταν' 1303), as found in many manuscripts, while Lloyd-Jones and Wilson's *OCT* emends them all away to help enforce the distinction (τλῆμον, μηκίστων, δύστην')). But even so the repetitions of the chorus (ὦ δεινόν/ὦ δεινότατον; "Terrible!"/"Most terrible!", τίς/τίς "Who?/who", φεῦ/φεῦ; "alas"/"alas", πόλλ'/πολλά/πολλά, "many", "many", "many"), their excited questions, and strongly articulated emotions, have great intensity – anapaests are also strongly associated with mourning, the obvious emotional and ritual framework here – and it is not even clear that this passage reveals "a more level and subdued strain of sorrow" rather than an intense shock. But in response to Oedipus' undoubtedly emotionally-heightened opening lyric, the chorus – the *koruphaios*, presumably – utters a single iambic line (1312):

ἐς δεινόν, οὐδ' ἀκουστόν, οὐδ ἐπόψιμον.

To a terrible place, beyond hearing, beyond sight.

Oedipus has asked where he is going, and the chorus answers. But the horror of their opening anapaests (whether chanted or sung) is replaced by the bare awfulness of the single iambic line by a single voice. The chorus of the *Ajax* had sung a frightened lyric of anticipation before the appearance of Ajax, but when they address their mad and lyrical master with iambics, they have been engaged in a long iambic dialogue with Tecmessa immediately before the display of Ajax. Here, the shift of voice from collective singing to an individual's spoken line is even more marked and dramatic. It is like a stage direction. Oedipus opens the first strophe still crying out in lyric (1312–4), the dochmiacs of high emotion, but he too shifts surprisingly and suddenly into iambics (1316–8):

οἴμοι
οἴμοι μάλ' αὖθις· οἶον εἰσέδυ ἅμα
κέντρων τε τῶνδ' οἴστρημα καὶ μνήμη κακῶν.

> Alas
> Alas once again. How the stab of these goads
> And the memory of evils sinks over me.

The phrase *oimoi mal' authis*, "alas once again" looks rather strange in English. It does not just indicate that the speaker is repeating *oimoi*. Rather, it is usually used when there is some specific doubleness at stake. Aeschylus' Agamemnon cries out *oimoi mal' authis* specifically when he is "struck a second blow" (Aesch. *Aga.* 1345). This is echoed when Sophocles' Clytemnestra is hit for a second time too: παῖσον, εἰ σθένεις, διπλῆν, "strike, if you have the strength, a double blow" (*El* 1415-6). Hyllus cries *oimoi mal' authis* (*Trach.* 1206) when he realises that his father's command is asking him to become *both* his father's killer *and* polluted with his blood (*Trach.* 1207). Here the double *oimoi* marks the double pain, the physical anguish from the blinding and the mental anguish from the recollection of the bad things in his life. As with Ajax's transition into iambics, the transition takes place specifically at a moment of self-recognition that takes the character beyond lament into reflection.

The chorus, still in iambics, pick up this sense of doubleness (a key note of the incestuous discourse of the *Oedipus*) immediately (1319-20):

> καὶ θαῦμά γ' οὐδὲν ἐν τοσοῖσδε πήμασιν
> διπλᾶ σε πενθεῖν καὶ διπλᾶ φέρειν κακά.

> Aye, no wonder amid so many pains
> That you lament double and bear double evils.

This engagement with his words and suffering prompts from Oedipus immediate counter-recognition in the antistrophe: *ô philos*, "O friend!". In this antistrophe too, Oedipus first sings out, and then, as one would expect from the metrical responsion, reverts to iambics – which is also constructed as a moment of recognition (1325-6): "You are not concealed from me, but I know your voice at any rate clearly, in darkness though I am", and the chorus again responds in iambics (1327-8), desperately asking about how Oedipus could have come to such a self-mutilating deed. But their next response to his continued lyric outpouring is harder to place (1336):

> ἦν ταῦθ' ὅπωσπερ καὶ σὺ φής.

> Things were as you indeed say.

This is an iambic dimeter (and there is a corresponding dimeter at 1356: θέλοντι κἀμοὶ τοῦτ' ἂν ἦν, "I also would have had things thus"). Between these two dimeters, the chorus have another pair of iambic trimeters (1347-8), separating two stanzas of Oedipus' lyrics. How are these dimeters to be voiced?

They could be seen as broken iambic trimeters, as if the chorus cannot complete a whole line in their shock – and both dimeters are lines that express a flat or numbed assent to Oedipus' intense and painful account. Or could they mark (also?) a raising of the emotional tenor of the voice – into recitative or even singing? Dimeters are a regular part of lyric, and the chorus may even be echoing Oedipus' lyric dimeters (1332/1352). Collectively articulated or individually? Again, even if we cannot be sure of how the change of metre precisely marks a change of voice, we can see an implicit stage direction.

This section of the *Oedipus Tyrannus* is a useful example of what I mean by choreography. The chorus begin collectively in trembling lyric mode at the appearance of Oedipus, revert to a single, shocked iambic line, an individual's voice, and then respond to his mixture of lyrics and iambics, with iambics of sympathy and questioning horror. As Oedipus sings, so too the chorus start to mix iambic dimeters and trimeters in their responses – dimeters that express a numbed assent. The collective lyric voice becomes a single voice of response, which may become something else again with the dimeters. The scene has sometimes been likened to a *kommos*, where one would expect a pattern of alternate lament, a performance of sympathy. What we see is an emotional counterpoint where Oedipus sings a more and more articulate and pained account of what has led him to where he is, and the chorus respond with increasing restraint and even distance. "How I wish I had never known you", they state at the beginning of the final antistrophe (1348), and in that last stanza Oedipus no longer addresses them as *philoi* (as he had at 1321, 1329, 1339), or indeed addresses them at all. They introduce the next scene tellingly by declaring to Oedipus that his decision was bad, and he would be better off dead than living blind (1367–8). There is a narrative here, not just a reflection on Oedipus' life – a narrative of how the chorus' response to the blinded king is changing, as well as how Oedipus is retelling the story of his life. Again, the form of exchange, the shifting in and out of the lyric voice, is integral to the narrative development.

My final example in this section is also an almost *kommos*, and is particularly tricky. At an extremely tense moment in the *Trachiniae*, after Deianeira has entered the house in silence and the chorus has sung an uneasy ode, a scream is heard inside, and the nurse comes out with the news of Deianeira's death (862–95). There are several small but vexatious issues in this passage, which I will need to discuss briefly, but the overriding point is simple and clear. For at least the majority of the scene, and probably all of it, the chorus sings in lyric, asking distraught questions, and the nurse replies in iambics. Unlike the scenes we have focused on so far, which highlighted Ajax's lyric voice against a chorus' and Tecmessa's iambics; or the chorus' silence while Electra sang and Orestes spoke; or Oedipus' lyric outpourings responded to primarily by a chorus' iambic trimeters and dimeters; here in *Trachiniae* it is the chorus which has the lyric voice in the exchange and the actor who speaks. The nurse's direct message and repeated blunt assertions that she is being direct (875, 876, 892) are set in dramatic contrast with the chorus' emotional confusion – a single, speaking character, whose previous scenes with Deianeira colour her role as messenger, in contrast with the collective singing of the chorus. As the chorus finally realise what the Nurse is saying, they too speak in a single iambic line (898), which leads into the Nurse's long account of the queen's death. Sophocles' dramaturgy again makes the formal qualities of the exchange, its different metres or voices, an integral part of the dramatic narrative.

There are, however, two specific issues which need to be built into this picture, each of which raises questions of considerable importance for our understanding of the choral voice in Sophocles. The first concerns the opening lines of the chorus (863–70) which crank up the tension by hearing some commotion in the house, wondering what it is, and then seeing the nurse come out in distress. The lines are iambic trimeters with two parallel insertions (τί φημί; "what am I to say?" (865), ξύνες δέ, "Mark!" (868)). Jebb assigns 862–5 to one hemichorus [half chorus], 866–7 to a second hemichorus, and 868–70 to the chorus as a whole – that is, he imagines three different groups of voices speaking. Pearson's *OCT* divides the lines slightly differently but also proposes three separate voices, as does Easterling's commentary. The new *OCT* of Lloyd-Jones and Wilson suggests no division of speakers, and Davies, unhelpfully making no judgement, prints the new *OCT* and merely notes that "some scholars . . . envisage a change of speakers", without further discussion.[31] The response of the chorus to the death cries of Agamemnon in Aeschylus' *Agamemnon* is usually seen as ten separate voices, a fragmented scene which dramatizes both the chorus' doubt and inefficacy in a striking manner, and also vividly represents the dissolution of social bonds which the murder in the palace constitutes. In Euripides' *Heracles Furens*, Diggle's *OCT* (and many other editions) suggests that three voices might be used: particularly at 815–21, where the chorus panic at the appearance of Iris and flee in confusion, there is a special import to the fragmentation; but in the *stasima* that precede this *coup de théâtre*, where there is a particularly complex interweaving of iambic and lyric passages, different speakers are also indicated by editors, to express, as in the *Agamemnon*, a multiform response to a murder in the palace from outside – though in this case, of course, responses in support of the killing.[32] Here in the *Trachiniae* too the chorus is responding to the sound of a royal death within the house, and is responding in confusion, a confusion that will be the keynote of their response to the nurse. So there is certainly a good enough reason for

---

[31] Davies (1991) *ad loc*; Easterling (1982) *ad loc*.

[32] "It is fashionable with scholars of the present time to multiply instances of this [multiple choral voices] by splitting up choral systems into individual ejaculations, but this may easily be overdone, and the process is anyway guided mainly by the scholar's personal fancy": Pickard-Cambridge (1968) 245.

those scholars who divide the lines between different speakers (and a case to answer for those who suppose some sort of internal discussion, as it were, of the *koruphaios* alone).

But there are two general points that this discussion underlines. First, between the choral collective, lyric voice (sung or chanted), and the *koruphaios'* individual speaking voice, there is the potential for another element in the soundscape, the fragmented collection of individual voices. We can see dialogue within the chorus, or even, as in *Hercules Furens* 815–21, the possibility of a confused babble of individual voices in panic. This technique is used sparingly and for moments of particularly high tension, where the collective voice fragments into multiple responses to the dramatic events offstage (or on the *theologeion*). Second, this technique, I would argue, is not only part of the experimentation with the potential of the chorus but also part of the politics of tragic representation: there is in democratic texts a considerable anxiety about dissension within the collective and how it is managed.[33] The representation of the fragmented chorus, the collective breaking into individual voices under social pressure ("dramatic tension"), is an integral aspect of how the chorus can be said to represent the collective within a democratic framework.

The second issue also concerns the division of parts. In the following lines (871–95), the confused chorus ask for information about the death of Deianeira, and the nurse provides the answers. But the manuscript sequence is difficult to follow in detail, and several solutions have been proposed, of which Henderson's has justly received the most support from recent scholars.[34] The fundamental question is whether 882–8 are given wholly to the chorus, or whether they are divided between the chorus and the nurse. Jebb and Pearson's *OCT*, typically for pre-War editions, split 882–8 between the nurse and the chorus. Lloyd-Jones and Wilson, Easterling, and Davies follow Henderson in giving the lines all to the chorus. What interests me is one of the arguments on which those who give all the lines to the chorus rely, namely, Paul Maas's claim that "characters of low social standing (except the Phrygian in the *Orestes*) are never given lines in sung metres, but are given instead anapaests, like the Nurse in the *Hippolytus*, or hexameters like the Old Man in the *Trachinae*".[35]

Now Maas is a very fine scholar of all things metrical, and his handbook on Greek metre is a fundamental work, and it would be a rash person who disagreed with him without great caution. But this dictum (and there is no more argument offered by Maas other than this quotation nor any counter case considered in his book) does need a little more nuance. First, for clarity's sake, by "characters" obviously Maas must mean individual actors, since many choruses are made up of figures of low social standing who sing lyric.

---

[33] See Barker (2009); Ober (1999).
[34] Henderson (1976).
[35] Maas (1962) 53–4.

Second, one must be rather generous in one's understanding of "social standing". The boy who sings in *Andromache* is the son of a slave, and would be certainly not of good status in Athens; but he is also the son of Andromache, a Trojan princess, and, especially in the heroic world of tragedy, may well be regarded at very least as touched by nobility. Even so, it is striking to have a child sing lyric, and since the play is also concerned with this child's status, his singing may be seen within that frame of contention. Similarly, in Aeschylus' *Supplices*, the chorus exchange lyrics with someone whom they address in the singular (836–70), and the most likely candidate is the Herald who is certainly on stage unannounced at the end of the lyric exchange (873). Here, Maas proposes a chorus of Egyptians as the addressee, and Henderson, seeing the weakness of the case for a battle of choruses, suggests weakly – to save the rule – that Heralds may not be really of low social standing, even if they are clearly not heroes or kings (it is hard to justify this on social terms even if a herald is sometimes associated with the poet, and is treated with some respect by virtue of his role).[36] The *Supplices* is also a play obsessed with the social status of its characters and especially the chorus. Nor is Polymestor, who sings pained lyrics in *Hecuba*, of aristocratic status (as Hall points out)[37], nor Greek (as Barner incomprehensibly suggests).[38] Indeed, his ambiguous status grounds Agamemnon's treatment of him. Third, one must also note that it is not wholly clear whether the Phrygian Eunuch is an allowed exception, rather than a full-scale counter case, because he is Phrygian (but barbarians sing on stage), or because he is a Eunuch (but this is untestable), or just because Euripides liked to shock.

Another obvious possible exception, however, is in the transmitted text of this passage of the *Trachiniae*. The lyric phrase (886) στονόεντος ἐν τομᾷ σιδάρου, "by the cut of iron that brings grief", is given to the Nurse by the manuscripts (as is 883–4 by some editors), but it is re-attributed to the chorus by Paul Maas himself, so that thus the Nurse is not allowed to sing. It would seem that some special pleading is necessary to maintain the "rule" of "low social standing", and it might be better to admit that the exceptions are broader and more dramatically motivated than Maas envisaged. Even here the Nurse at 892 still has a single bacchiac (σαφηνῆ, "clear") in response to the chorus' bacchiac question (τί φωνεῖς; "What do you say?") – a lyric metrical unit. This need not sink the general observation, however, but encourage us rather to see the playwrights working with such a tendency. So, for example, Teucer in *Ajax* is dismissed by the Atreidae because of his low birth, and he indeed never sings, even when he joins in the *kommos* over the body of Ajax. The chorus there do sing lyrics; and he responds with *extra metrum* cries of grief and,

---

[36] Henderson (1976).
[37] Hall (2006) 317–8.
[38] Barner (1971) 262–3.

otherwise, iambics (exactly when one might expect an antiphonal response in lyric). This representation of iambic mourning may prepare us for the Atreidae's snobbishness, as well as contrasting Teucer with Ajax. Teucer's performance, that is, his *voice* confirms the status the Atreidae denigrate him with. Similarly, Ion in Euripides' *Ion* appears first as a temple attendant sweeping the steps, and, though of lowly status, he sings lyric – but as we already know from the prologue and will see fulfilled in the course of the play, his real identity is very starry indeed. Again, his lyric voice may well prepare us for the identity which is to be revealed.

But it is a fourth point where I think most care is needed. To give Maas' claim its full weight, one must also feel very clear about the division between (marching) anapaests and melic anapaests – between, that is, chanted and sung anapaests – and feel very clear about whether it is the social status of the character which keeps them from full lyric, or whether other attendant causes are more relevant. We have already seen how a text can be emended to help enforce the distinction between marching anapaests and other melic anapaests, and we have seen too that there are places where the status of the anapaests is harder to categorize than Maas' strictures would suggest.

So, it is worth recalling how often the scenes we have considered have involved asymmetrical exchanges which are not necessarily based solely on social standing. The case of the Nurse in *Hippolytus* certainly presents us with a division of social standing between Phaedra, the queen, and her nurse – but the opening scene's long exchange of anapaests has different levels of speech and singing (if it does) because the queen is represented as mad, and out of control, while the Nurse is arguing rationally with her and trying to find out what she wants. Similarly, if there is a difference in quality of voice in the anapaests of Heracles, Hyllus and the Old Man as they enter in the *Trachiniae* (974–1003), and it is far less clear in this case how strongly marked such a difference is, it is not a question so much of social standing as of the anguish of the dying, monstrously great Heracles in contrast to the grief of the Old Man and the grief and guilt of Hyllus. It might be better to conclude that there is not a hard and fast rule that characters of low social standing do not sing lyric, and rather that lyric's intensity is usually reserved for the characters having particularly intense experiences (who are not usually individuals of lower social standing in the hierarchical world of Greek tragedy), but that the playwrights explore the differences of different styles of utterance for dramatic purposes, to create specific contrasts and colours.

Now, on the balance of evidence, it seems to me that Henderson's emendations (with or without Lloyd-Jones and Wilson's small correction of 881) construct the most likely text of *Trachiniae* 879–95 – but the better reason for this reading is not because the Nurse can't sing according to a postulated law about social standing, but rather because the scene is constructed as a dialogue between a confused and emotional chorus, and a figure, the nurse, who is about to deliver a long messenger speech describing the death of Deianeira and who in this introductory passage as in the scene to come is direct, in control, and sharply articulate. This conclusion is based on the balance of probabilities, however, not on a certain rule; and counter arguments (a nurse struggling to control emotions and slipping between lyric and iambic, for example) are evidently available.

We do not know exactly how any actor delivered iambics in contrast to marching anapaests in contrast to melic anapaests; we do not know what differences in articulation there were between different styles of anapaests or, indeed, how much they overlapped and were played with in performance; nor can we be sure how strongly articulated the movements between lyric and iambic verses were in a single actor's performance. Pseudo-Aristotle's *Problems* claims that *parakataloge* is especially tragic (*Prob.* 19.6), and this is usually translated as "variation", which may direct us towards an ancient recognition of change of voice as a particularly dramatic resource, and a particularly moving part of tragedy's repertoire. But ancient sources are all agreed that specific metres are associated with specific genres, with particular emotional registers, and with precise forms of stimulus for an audience. This should encourage us to be especially attentive to how the tragic playwrights worked their uniquely variegated medium.

What I have suggested in this chapter is that Sophocles manipulates transitions and juxtapositions between lyric voices and iambic voices, between sung and spoken voices, between collective and individual voices, and even between sequential or fragmented individual voices and collective choral voice, in order to construct a score in which the chorus interrelates with the actors in a fully and integrally dramatic manner. There is more flexibility and experimentation with the lyric voice than is customarily allowed, especially by generalizations about The Greek Chorus. Metre, as an essential element of the choral voice, acts as a system of stage directions for the chorus' narrative – and Sophocles manipulates these formal elements of the language of the chorus to create a remarkably labile and powerfully expressive lyric voice.

{ 5 }

The Chorus in Action

I The *Kommos* and Emotional Narrative

Pseudo-Aristotle's *Problems* is no better than the genuine Aristotle on the performance of the chorus in tragedy: ἔστι γὰρ ὁ χόρος κηδευτὴς ἄπρακτος· εὔνοιαν γὰρ μόνον παρέχεται οἷς πάρεστι, "For the chorus is an inactive interested party; for it provides only friendliness to those on stage" (19.48). The term *kêdeutes* which I have translated "interested party" is neat for the chorus: it means "someone who cares", "guardian", and often implies someone who cares for the dead, which nicely suits the chorus which is often a witness to the death of a hero or leader. It is easy to see how the author of the *Problems* could term the chorus *apraktos*, "inactive", "passive", since they do not act in the manner of heroes, Hollywood or ancient; but it is equally easy to point out types of counter-example: Aeschylus' *Suppliants*, who fight and run and eventually kill; or the Furies of the *Eumenides* chasing, and singing the binding song over Orestes before speaking in court. The same examples could be used to question the inevitable "friendliness" of the chorus towards the actors, too. The generalization of the *Problems* is as distorting as it is insightful. This section will explore two examples of a scene where *eunoia*, "friendliness", "good intentions" is precisely what is expected, but where in each case Sophocles has created a far more complex and interesting dramatic narrative. What is more, the dramatic narrative has the form it does because the chorus takes part in the action.

Both examples are *kommoi*, mourning songs. The traditional form of the *kommos* has been much discussed in recent scholarship.[1] The understanding of *kommos* as a social ritual, and as a political act; the literary re-use of *kommos*,

---

[1] See Alexiou (2002); Holst-Wahrhaft (1992); Foley (2001); Dué (2003); Swift (2010).

in tragedy and in other genres, such as epic, have been well analysed in recent criticism, and these discussions ground what follows. The presence of elements of the *kommos* in tragedy, where response to disaster and death seem endemic, is hardly surprising. We have already seen how the lament of Ajax as he comes to (or towards) his senses, and the entrance of the mutilated Oedipus, and even the arrival of the Nurse with the news of Deianeira's death, have each been analyzed as rehearsing in fragmented form the ritual of antiphonal lament which typifies the formal aspect of the *kommos*. Each extant play of Sophocles has been seen to include a form of *kommos*. My two exemplary scenes, each of which is more formally definable as a lament – though each has very untypical elements – reveal how the pattern of *eunoia* which might be expected to flow between mourners, is manipulated dramatically by Sophocles.

My first example is *Antigone*. After the chorus have sung of the power of *Eros*, Antigone enters processing as in a funeral march, but singing her own funeral dirge (802–943).[2] Here is an immediate sign of the oddness of her ritual action, allowed by her strange circumstances: it is not normal to sing one's own *kommos*. The traditional *kommos* is antiphonal, and involves consolation from the group to the individual mourner as well as shared, often incantatory, expressions of grief. The exchanges between the chorus and Antigone in this scene construct a delicate and subtle interplay as she mourns, and they switch between consolation and condemnation, and she asks for sympathy by her laments but also successively alienates herself from her surroundings. She sings her lyrics (in a metre very close to the chorus' previous ode on *eros*), and the chorus respond with anapaestic stanzas, a common form of antiphonal lament.

Antigone in her first stanza (806–16) marks herself as "the bride of Hades", the conventional sign of the virgin who dies before marriage.[3] The chorus respond with a standard consolation for premature death (usually expressed for a young man, however) that she will have fame (*kleinê* 817) and praise (*epainon* 817) for her death.[4] But they add: ἀλλ᾽ αὐτόνομος ζῶσα μόνη δὴ θνατῶν ᾽Αἴδαν καταβήσῃ, "but of independent will, alive, alone, bereft of mortals, you will descend to Hades" (821–2).[5] The *alla* "but" marks a transition

---

[2] See Dittmars (1992) 104–31; Kitzinger (2008).

[3] See King (1983), (1998); Seaford (1987); and for the significance of the role of the Parthenos for Antigone, see Goldhill (1990).

[4] These lines have been much discussed. On the difficulty of this praise see Knox (1964) 176–7 n8. Denniston (1934) 436 suggests that the "livelier οὔκουν seems more appropriate . . . while the quieter interrogative οὐκοῦν is also possible" and translates "Well, are you not dying a glorious death?". He adds that Jebb's strong reading "therefore" here is "inappropriate".

[5] Jebb translates "No, mistress of your own fate, and still alive, thou shalt pass to Hades, as no other of mortal kind hath passed". This translation is in line with his wholly positive image of Antigone; αὐτόνομος, however, is not a simply positive term: it means more nearly "self-willed", "using one's own law", which in democratic terms, especially for a woman, is not as grand as "mistress of one's own fate",

from praise. She has brought about her death by her own actions, her own self-willed activity. *Autonomos* is a positive term in political theory and political rhetoric when applied to states, which can with *autonomia* set their own laws and are not subject to a tyrant's imposition. It can thus become a rhetorical blind for less high-minded military activity. But it is not a positive term when applied to an individual, especially when set against the state. The figure who gives law by and for himself (to his own family) is the Cyclops, the epitome of barbarism (*Od.* 9. 114–5): they do not care for one another, which is the opposite of civil society. By being *autonomos*, she has set herself apart, and hence is *monê dê thnatôn*. The phrase implies her death is unique "alone of mortals" – something Antigone will herself immediately challenge; but also implies "quite on her own" – and Antigone's "isolation" becomes "overwhelming" in this scene.[6] Their use of *zôsa* seems prompted by Antigone's paradoxical self-description as a "living" (*zôsan*) bride of death (811), but the addition of *autonomos* reminds us that she is herself a complicit cause of her unique death. As Griffith notes laconically, "their tone is hard to gauge". While they console (one function of the chorus in a *kommos*), they also distance themselves from her behaviour.[7]

Antigone finds a parallel for her death in Niobe (824–33, the antistrophe), turned to stone in her grief. But the chorus respond with "But she was a goddess and god born. We are mortal and born of mortals. And to be sure it is a great thing for one who has passed away, even to have it said of her that she received shares with demigods while living and after she died" (834–5). The recognition of inevitable mortality is a cliché of consolation (as used at *El.* 1171–2); if it sounds like a mild correction of Antigone's likening herself to Niobe (*alla . . .* "but"), the remainder of their words still (*kaitoi*) recognize the glory of being like a demi-god. Again they both pull away and draw closer to Antigone. But she is outraged by their utterance: οἴμοι γελῶμαι. τί με. . . ὑβρίζεις, "Alas, I am mocked! Why do you humiliate me?", she explodes (839–41). She rejects any of the consolation as an insult. Where the chorus called her "quite alone", she declares herself to be "unwept by friends" (847), and, in an extraordinary phrase,

---

nor as positive. μόνη δὴ θνατῶν is usually taken to mean "the only one of humans [to suffer this]". Not only is this simply untrue – how can Antigone be the first person to be put to death like this? – but also and more importantly the word μόνος has been a thematically marked word for Antigone, in her separation from the community, from her sister and from her family. See *Ant.* 941. One might even translate thus "alone – bereft of – human beings", that is, she goes "self-willed" and "without any humans to support her". On Antigone's moral status, see especially Foley (2001) 172–200; also Sourvinou-Inwood (1990) with Foley (1995).

[6] Griffith (1999) 261.

[7] On the *kommos*, a much discussed passage, see Reinhardt (1979) 80–4; Winnington-Ingram (1980) 136–46; Knox (1964) especially 176–7; Whitlock Blundell (1989)147–8; Burton (1980) 118–27; Segal (1981) 177–83; Gardiner (1987) 91–3; and Blake, Tyrrell and Bennett (1998) 97–121; all with the background of Foley (2001) 19–56; 172–200. I will not add a bibliography here on Antigone's long final *rhesis*, which is not relevant to my current discussion.

a "resident alien among neither mortals nor corpses as a corpse, neither with the alive nor the dead", βροτοῖς οὔτε <νεκρὸς> νεκροῖσιν μέτοικος, οὐ ζῶσιν, οὐ θανοῦσιν (850–1). Antigone is truly separated here from all bonds: she cannot find a home either with the living or the dead.

The chorus respond with their most outspoken condemnation of her behaviour: "You stepped out to the furthest extreme of boldness; you smashed your foot against the high pedestal of Justice. You paid for your father's sin" (854–7). She committed a transgression and in so doing indicated her inheritance from her transgressive father. Matching her (self-)isolating expression, the chorus distance themselves strongly from her justification. What she did was wrong. But their remark about her father prompts from Antigone a lament for her family's woes. The chorus respond to this with a deeply ambivalent comment σέβειν μὲν εὐσέβειά τις, κράτος δ', ὅτῳ κράτος μέλει, παραβατὸν οὐδαμᾷ πέλει· σὺ δ' αὐτόγνωτος ὤλεσ' ὀργά, "There is a certain piety in showing pious reverence. But to one whose business is power, power cannot be transgressed. Your self-willed temper has destroyed you" (872–5). They allow a certain (*tis*) piety in what she has done: the play between *eusebeia* (which I have translated "piety") and *sebein* ("show pious reverence") recognizes Antigone's claim that what she has done is morally required (*sebein*) and may have a claim on an abstract positive idea of a relation to the gods and to the hierarchies of social order ("reverence"). But they also recognize that what she has done transgresses the dictates of power, which cannot be brooked by those in authority. There is a hesitancy, a striving for qualification in this double evaluation. But their judgement on her attitude is unswerving. Her temper is self-willed (*autognôtos* clearly echoes *autonomos*): it is a further gloss on *monê*: her temper has left her separate from the community. Hence Antigone's lament that follows: "Unwept, unfriended (*aphilos*), unmarried I am led forth . . . No friend (*oudeis philôn*) laments my uncried fate" (876–82). Antigone, who had proclaimed herself born to *sumphilein*, "to share in the bonds and obligations of mutual relations" sees herself finally as deprived of *philoi*, isolated even from sympathy or consolation.[8]

The *kommos*, then, maps a flowing relationship between chorus and young girl, from conversation and consolation through to moral equivocation and even condemnation, and isolation. The chorus is engaged in a dialogue that is far from simply *eunoia*, on either side, and which is integral to the plot's central problem of evaluating the action of Antigone. As we saw in the previous chapter, this nuanced response of the chorus is in marked contrast with that of Creon: it is also part of the plot's evaluation of Creon's behaviour as ruler. Helene Foley in her fine piece on the politics of tragic lamentation argues that Antigone "uses lamentation to carry her point assertively in a public context that might otherwise have silenced her speech", a gesture she sees within her

---

[8] See below chapter 9 for further discussion of Antigone's sense of collectivity.

general description of "the potentially revolutionary force of women's role in rituals performed for the dead".[9] Antigone does attempt to make a point (though it is less clear she carries it), and she is assertive, but the public context is certainly far more complex than Foley allows. The chorus, as one version of the public, is far from simply moved to pity her, or even to recognize her political claim, even if they do still feel distress at her impending death (933–4) and regret Creon's obstinacy, which is powerfully in evidence in his (now lyric) reaction to their distress (931–2, 935–6) directed at both the girl and the king, as the scene reaches its increasingly emotional climax; and Antigone herself is increasingly isolated rather than increasingly assertive. Her final clarion call (940–4): "Behold me, rulers of Thebes, the only remnant of the royal line, how I suffer at the hands of such men, because I reverenced piety [τὴν εὐσεβίαν σεβίσασα]", declares her religious conviction of her own rectitude, but, apart from the silencing of Ismene (as discussed more broadly in chapter 9), these lines also strikingly and directly echo the chorus' earlier more guarded comment, σέβειν μὲν εὐσέβειά τις, "There is a certain piety in showing pious reverence" (872) – which immediately led to their corrective addition, "your self-willed temper has destroyed you". She is assertive, but can the counter-voice be silenced? Are we to forget that for the chorus her piety is linked to her self-destructiveness?

The audience in the theatre is faced, then, by a multi-voiced score of shifting sympathies from a group of individuals, and it is this complexity which has helped produce the multi-voiced and often polarized evaluations of *Antigone* in the critical tradition. Sophocles takes the form of the *kommos*, and specifically the expectations of the role of the collective as an antiphonal and sympathetic or consoling voice, and from it constructs a complex scene: it is triangulated through the watching tyrant as well as the theatrical audience, and ends in fragmentation rather than consoling unity; and, above all, it constructs an emotionally and intellectually conflicted exchange, which engages, provokes and upsets the audience on stage and in the theatre. This tragedy has no place for consolation.

The second scene of a *kommos* that I wish to analyze is the opening of the *Electra*, which has long been recognized as one of the most subtle pieces of Sophoclean exposition, and for which, as Winnington-Ingram observed, it would be extremely difficult indeed to provide "a full analysis of all the trains of thought and emotion, of all the aesthetic relationships" that it displays.[10]

Electra's first offstage cry interrupts the prologue with its three men earnestly plotting revenge (77). The Tutor assumes it is a maidservant at the door (78–9), but Orestes wonders if it is Electra herself and whether they should

---

[9] Foley (2001) 32–3.
[10] Winnington-Ingram (1980) 335.

wait and listen to the lament (80–1). That is, he asks if they should follow the plot of the *Choephoroi*, where Orestes first conceals himself with Pylades to hear the lament of his sister, who enters with offerings for the grave of his father, and then reveals himself for the recognition scene. But here the Tutor dismisses this idea instantly: *hêkista*, "not at all" (81). *Electra* is written through the *Oresteia*, and the first entrance of Electra is constructed in and against the expectations of Aeschylus' masterpiece. Where Electra in Aeschylus processed with the chorus, bearing offerings, here Electra enters alone, bearing nothing but her misery, and performing a lamentation. (Now the tomb is offstage, and the offerings will, of course, appear later in different form; the relation of this entrance to Euripides' Electra, on her own, at night, bearing a water jug rather than a religious offering, will depend on the irresolvable issue of the respective dating of Sophocles' and Euripides' plays.) Her opening anapaests (86–120) brilliantly demonstrate the fecundity of the potential slippage between marching and melic anapaests. Finglass provides an excellent guide to this. On the one hand, most aspects of the metre, as one might anticipate for the opening entrance of the play, show the expected qualities of marching anapaests. On the other hand, there are also elements associated with melic anapaests, typical as this form is of mourning. (The lines could even be printed as a responding strophe and antistrophe, each of 17 lines). Thus, Finglass concludes, we have here "a system of recitative anapaests which at 88–9 and 105–6, moves towards lyric, probably as a mark of Electra's intense emotion".[11] At 88–9, with the repetition familiar in lament (*pollas, pollas*), she both announces and performs her mourning; at 105–6 she says she will not give up mourning "while I look on the flashing swings of the stars, and this daylight" – that is, she again talks about and enacts the lament (*thrênôn* 88, *thrênôn* 104 [cf *thrênô* 94]). Electra's first anapaestic speech (recitative?) threatens to break into song, as already her emotions overtake her, precisely at moments when she describes and performs her solitary lamentation. A woman already on the edge of lyric . . .

The chorus, by contrast, enters not with anapaests but with a fully lyric strophe, to which Electra replies with lyric verses of her own, to begin what will prove a complex metrical and emotional interchange. If Electra was constantly on the point of boiling over into an outpouring of (lyric) grief in the opening anapaests, the arrival of the chorus leads her to a further pitch of expressiveness. The dramatic technique of this opening is a director's dream. First, the opening discussion of male speakers, plotting seriously the revenge, ends with a female scream – and the Tutor's immediate control of the younger hero's desire to see if this is his sister; then, the solitary entrance of a desperate Electra, in lyric mode, precariously on the edge of something uncontrolled, who moves to address her dead father in despairing pity (101), and then to pray to the gods of the underworld for revenge; then the collective of older women, in full lyric mode, entering to bolster and

[11] Finglass (2007) 118.

comfort, and try to persuade the younger Electra away from the constant weeping. Where the prologue had insisted on the precision of the right moment, Electra seems locked into the timelessness of endless repetition.[12] The contrasts of voice and atmosphere are especially emotive.

This *parodos* is longer than any other in Sophocles or Euripides (who also experimented with single female voice, singing or in recitative, joined by a female chorus in interchange, in the *parodoi* of *Troades*, *Hecuba* and *Helen*). It also has perhaps the most developed and clearest dramatic structure. The opening section (121–92) has the formal structure of a *kommos*: it is antiphonal and revolves around consolation. "Why do you constantly bewail the long dead Agamemnon?", open the chorus. While this underlines that Electra's mourning is transgressive in that it has not followed the normal time restrictions of ritual, it also has the familiar structure of consolation ("Why mourn . . .?"), and Electra recognizes it as such (130–1): ἥκετ᾽ ἐμῶν καμάτων παραμύθιον· οἶδά τε καὶ ξυνίημι τάδε, "You have come to console my toils. I know and understand this. . .". So too her reply has the shape of a cliché ("I must . . ."), but has an unnerving intensity as her description turns into self-announced performance (135–6):

> ἐᾶτέ μ᾽ ὧδ᾽ ἀλύειν,
> αἰαῖ, ἱκνοῦμαι.

> Let me rave like this:
> Aiai! I beg you.

Both the choice of the word *aluein*, "rave", "rant" for her own grief, and the demonstration of her raving, *aiai*, stretch the *topoi* of lamentation towards an extreme. *Aiai*, "alas", introduced by *hôde* "like this", is marked as an exemplary performance of a (ritual) grief, in the disturbing self-consciousness of her own behaviour that Electra reveals again and again in this play. Look at me, I will now do a lament . . . So, too, in the antistrophe (136–43), the chorus observes that no mourning will bring back the dead – adding the pointed comment that she is travelling "from due bounds to a pain beyond help" (ἀπὸ τῶν μετρίων ἐπ᾽ ἀμήχανον ἄλγος 140–1). That is, they take up the standard trope of lamentation and make it a personal criticism of Electra's refusal to stay within the ritual and social bounds of mourning. Electra responds by also taking up a standard paradigm of mourning – the myths of Niobe and Itys – and assimilates herself to their model: as Itys, turned into a bird constantly weeps, so too will she. Indeed, she regards Niobe as a divinity "because in your rocky tomb, you weep, aiai". In the same place in the last line of her stanza, she repeats *aiai*, again marked off as a performance: "Let me rant thus, 'aiai'" is paralleled by Niobe "you weep, 'aiai'", as her likeness to the figure of myth is proclaimed. Electra thus defends her constant weeping as if she were the petrified Niobe or metamor-

---

[12] See Hutchinson (1999) especially 51–8.

phosed Itys. The rhetoric of consolation becomes here the rhetoric of self-assertion. One way in which her later mourning over the urn is so moving is the lack
there of any such signs of self-consciousness or performance. The chorus may
think that she has crossed the boundaries of propriety in her mourning already,
but she will discover a further level of intensity of grief as the plot unfurls.

The next stanzas have a similar pattern. The chorus begin, "Not for you alone..."
(153) – the most familiar of consolatory motifs – but personalize the story by comparing Electra to her sisters, who have borne the same situation with a quite different attitude, and who like her wait for Orestes. Electra responds by emphatically
describing her unwed, tear-filled, woe-racked life, and adding Orestes to her lament
(164–72). The chorus try the traditional comfort that the gods oversee the world
slowly but surely – adding another complaint that she should not thus "be excessive
in grief" (μήθ'... ὑπεράχθεο 178). She replies (185–92) with a particularly grim
and moving description of her hopeless life and unremitting misery.

There is a marked pattern to this opening sequence: the chorus in each of four
stanzas take up a traditional motif of the *kommos* as consolation, and add to it a
specific criticism of Electra's excess. Her continual mourning over many years
requires a change in the logic of consolation, from generalized comment on the
inevitability of death to complaint about the ritual distortion and emotional incon-
tinence that Electra's behaviour represents. In response to each of these stanzas,
Electra begins by also adapting familiar tropes of the *kommos* – the paradigm of
Niobe, say – to defend her own commitment to never-ending grief, but in the last
two of her four stanzas describes her own life with unremitting negativity.

At this point, however, there is a marked shift in the metre and tone. The
chorus start to sing in anapaests, the lyric associated closely with mourning,
and Electra responds in the same rhythm. Instead of consoling or criticising,
the chorus seem to have been pushed by Electra's intense misery into joining
her perspective, her imaginative world. They begin to describe the night of the
murder of Agamemnon (193–200). Their language adopts the repetitions and
incantatory style of lament (193–8):

> οἰκτρὰ μὲν νόστοις αὐδά,
> οἰκτρὰ δ'ἐν κοίταις πατρῴαις
> ὅτε οἱ παγχάλκων ἀνταία
> γενύων ὡρμάθη πλαγά.
> δόλος ἦν ὁ φράσας, ἔρος ὁ κτείνας
> δεινὰν δεινῶς προφυτεύσαντες
> μορφάν

> Pitiful the voice on return,
> Pitiful in father's bed,
> When the blow of the all-bronze axe
> Rushed at him.

> Deceit was the guide, lust the killer,
> Terrible progenitors of a terrible
> Form . . .

Mourning sets out ritually to reintegrate the individual into the group, but here the group has become subordinated to the individual's view of things. The chorus' voice has changed as it enters this anapaestic lament. The strange impressionistic expression "progenitors of a terrible form" may recall Clytemnestra's claim in Aeschylus that it was a *daimon* in the shape of a woman (*phantazomenos gunaiki* Aesch. *Aga* 1500), who killed Agamemnon, motivated by blood lust (*eros Aga* 1478), a sign of the deception that never leaves the house (*dolia* 155).

Electra re-doubles her grief at this awful murder (201–12), responding to the chorus' change of tone; but they immediately back off, in the strongest yet expression of their distaste for Electra's emotional outpouring. "Don't speak any further!", they demand (213–5), "Do you not realize where the current problems come from? You are collapsing shamefully into disasters of your own" [οἰκείας εἰς ἄτας ἐμπίπτεις αἰκῶς]. This is a severe rebuke. And they are quite clear that it is her excessive commitment and uncontrolled hatred that is causing the disaster (217–9):

> πολὺ γάρ τι κακῶν ὑπερεκτήσω
> σᾷ δυσθύμῳ τικτούσ' αἰεὶ
> ψυχᾷ πολέμους

> You have greatly increased your troubles
> Constantly breeding conflicts
> In your dispirited soul.

Again, their criticism is direct and even brutal. She has aggravated her troubles (*huperektêsô*: a hapax, "to obtain excessively"); she gives birth to conflicts – and the language of birth is not only a commonplace for the creation of disaster in Greek moral writing[13] but also a precise and jarring term for Electra who has already repeatedly harped on her unwed state. Her soul, the site of this warring, is *dusthumos*, spirited, but in a negative way.

Electra responds to this with equal strength or even violence of expression – but also with self-recognition (221–5):

> δείν' ἐν δεινοῖς ἠναγκάσθην.
> ἔξοιδ', οὐ λάθει μ' ὀργά.
> ἀλλ' ἐν δεινοῖς οὐ σχήσω
> ταύτας ἄτας
> ὄφρα με βίος ἔχῃ.

---

[13] Tragic *locus classicus* is Aesch. *Aga.* 750–71, where it is marked as a *palaiphatos logos*. See also Fraenkel (1950) I *ad* 386.

I have been compelled to terrible things in terrible circumstances.
I know this fully. I recognise my rage.
But things are terrible; so I will not hold back
these disasters,
while I have life in me.

The phrase "these disasters" bitterly picks up the chorus' description of her self-destructive behaviour (Finglass surprisingly does not see this when he proposes to read ἀχάς with Blaydes).[14] She knows what she is doing (she claims) and because her situation is so dire she is intent on following the course of action that they call a disastrous outcome of a disastrous infatuation (to translate *ate* fully). So she wishes away her consolers (229) ἄνετέ μ᾽ ἄνετε, παράγοροι, "Let me be, let me be, consolers". Her problems are insoluble, and her mourning unlimited, uncountable (231–2).

This extraordinarily passionate rejoinder cows the chorus. Up until this point, the chorus and Electra have replied to each other with stanzas of approximately the same length. In the last twenty-nine lines of the *parodos*, Electra sings two stanzas of thirteen lines each, and the chorus offers one three-line interjection. And their interjection is in a wholly different tone from their powerful ethical complaints in the previous stanza (233–5):

ἀλλ᾽ οὖν εὐνοίᾳ γ᾽ αὐδῶ.
μήτηρ ὡσεί τις πιστά,
μὴ τίκτειν σ᾽ ἄταν ἄταις.

Well anyway I am speaking with good will at least,
Like a trustworthy mother,
When I say don't give birth to disaster on top of disasters.

All' oun . . . g[e], "Well, anyway", indicates the concession they are making here. They have left off their criticism. And as Pseudo-Aristotle would have it, they are, they say, just speaking with *eunoia*, good will. They insist that they are on her side, even in their criticism, like – in an obviously charged phrase for this play – a "trustworthy mother".[15] But even so they recall the bone of contention with the repetition of *tiktein* and *ate*. They still see her behaviour as self-destructive and excessive.

This prompts yet another extreme riposte from Electra who asks with intensity (236) "And what measure is there to evil/my troubles?!", καί τί μέτρον κακότητος ἔφυ;. This is the opposite of the Delphic *mêden agan*, "nothing in excess". For Electra, evil, or her evils, know no limit, and hence her response knows no limit. It is not by chance that the chorus that spoke up so fiercely earlier begins the next scene rather crushed. "We came to support you", they remind her (252–3): εἰ δὲ μὴ καλῶς λέγω, σὺ νίκα· σοὶ γὰρ ἑψόμεσθ᾽ ἅμα, "But if my words are misplaced, then let your opinion prevail. We will follow you." Electra has dominated her comforters.

---

[14] Finglass (2007) 167–8 *ad* 223–4.
[15] On the Homeric echoes in these lines see Davidson (2006) 35.

This *parodos* is a dramatic narrative. It is narrative that is built out of the *topoi* of the *kommos* at one level, especially at the beginning, but it is also built out of the social or emotional expectations of the *kommos* at another: consolation, exchange, integration of individual and group, deployment of myth, recalling the past. It performs a changing relationship between the individual Electra and the collective of women – a changing relation of power, authority, emotional dominance. The chorus moves through comfort, to rising concern, to sharing lament, to stark ethical criticism, to submissive hesitation. Electra in turn moves through lament for her father, to despair over Orestes and her own condition, to passionate and angry defence of her own perspective. The elements of the *kommos* as a form are dispersed and redeployed into an emotional and intellectual score, as the group and individual approach and pull away and come together. The *kommos* as a ritual is designed to unite a community in grief and re-organize the community around a loss, and to reintegrate the mourners into the community. But here the group of women end up beholden to the individual: the power of Electra's misery holds sway.

In both *Antigone* and *Electra*, the form of the *kommos* is adapted to particular and strange circumstances, the singer marching to her own death, the mourner who won't stop mourning. In each case, elements of the traditional ritual and poetic form of the *kommos* are re-deployed in dramatic exchanges, which construct shifting, developing dynamics between the collective of the chorus and the transgressive individual character. In both scenes, the chorus criticize the heroine starkly for her transgressiveness; in both scenes, there is a complex and changing relation of power, judgement, affiliation between chorus and individual – and for each play, the evaluation of the heroine has become the central question of modern criticism. In short, Sophocles manipulates the language and forms of choral performance from outside the plays (the *kommos*), to construct dramatic narratives, which are essential both for our understanding of the ethical and emotional status of his heroines, and for exploring the relations between the collective of the chorus and the individual. These are plays that are terrified and fascinated by the self-commitment of their heroes, which always tips precariously or disastrously towards *ate*, self-destructive obsession. The lyric voice of the chorus, in these active engagements with the heroes, is an integral part of the performance of this terror, this fascination.

II The Chorus as Actor: Experimenting With Form in the Philoctetes

Philoctetes is perhaps Sophocles' most experimental play.[16] It is one of very few tragedies not to be set in a city or the military camp, the city on the move, as it were. It is the only extant play without a female character. It stretches the

---

[16] Apart from the standard books cited below, see for representative studies also Falkner (1998); Garvie (1972); Kittmer (1995); Rose (1976); Taplin (1971), (1987); Worman (2000), each with further bibliography.

formal expectations of tragedy to the limit, with hugely long, varied scenes, with all three actors in play. Its double ending and its engagement with the values of archaic heroism have provoked an unresolved and probably unresolvable debate over the moral issues the play raises about trust, commitment and duty. Central to all these issues is the remarkable treatment of the chorus, which embodies most fully the idea of the chorus as actor. Critics, in response to Aristotle, have repeatedly listed the moments in Sophocles where a chorus directly interacts with and influences the actors – the chorus of the *Antigone*, for example, persuading Creon to commute his sentence of death on Antigone. I have already argued that the engagement of the chorus in a *kommos* is as a full partner in an emotional narrative of power and alienation. In this final section of the chapter, we will see how a chorus can be fully part of the action of a play, even through their silence.

The chorus' entrance immediately indicates their engagement with the action. After the opening scene's intense iambic discussion between Odysseus and Neoptolemus, exploring the scene, preparing the plot of deception, and establishing the striking character difference between the wily Odysseus and young, inexperienced and idealistic Neoptolemus,[17] the chorus of sailors enter with a strophic song (whose first line is actually a iambic trimeter, as we saw above), to which Neoptolemus replies in (marching) anapaests. The difference in metre is matched in tone – by the excited questions of the chorus, full of repetitions, some pleonasms, and a directness of interest, which contrasts with Neoptolemus' explanatory answers and calmer commands (as well as with Odysseus' earlier rhetorical care). As Pucci has noted, this chorus is not just a group of "the people", but figures who significantly do not share their leaders' ethical qualms, political ideals or vision.[18] As with the annoying garrulousness and political simplicity of the Guard in the *Antigone*, the chorus' pragmatism, emotional insensitivity, and their crassness even, contrasts tellingly with the protagonists in the ethical intrigues of the drama. Their first question vividly shows the dramatic technique of Sophocles in this. In its excited tones, the entrance is matched by the entrance of the chorus in *Oedipus Coloneus*, and in its direct engagement with the lone character on stage it is matched by the entrance in the *Electra*: that is, in these later plays (and I take *Electra* to be late, whatever its relation to Euripides' *Electra*), Sophocles explores the interaction of a protagonist and the collective of the chorus from the very first moment in fully dramatic, engaged exchanges, a technique quite different from any extant Aeschylean play (135–7):

> τί χρὴ τί χρή με, δέσποτ', ἐν ξένᾳ ξένον
> στέγειν, ἢ τί λέγειν πρὸς ἄνδρ' ὑπόπταν;;
> φράζε μοι.

---

[17] See above chapter 3.
[18] Pucci (2003).

What must I, what must I hide, master, a stranger
In a strange land? Or what should I say to a man of suspicions?
Tell me!

The chorus are already in on the plot, though we have only just seen Neoptolemus accede to Odysseus' intrigue. They already know Philoctetes will be suspicious, that they have a role to play in the verbal web. But the phrase *en xena xenon*, "a stranger in a strange land", although it is a standard jingling *polyptoton*, recalls the repeated language and type scenes of the *Odyssey*, where Odysseus so often needs concealing language, as a guest before a suspicious host. The arrival at the cave of Philoctetes has long been recognized as playing off the Cyclops' cave.[19] Here the chorus seem to recall Odysseus (or perhaps his crew, who never quite learnt the lessons of concealment). They are here to act in a plot.

The second strophe (after Neoptolemus has given them their orders and thereby done some essential exposition for the audience) adds a new note (169): "I pity him . . .", they begin. They have looked at the cave, and imagined Philoctetes' grim life (170–90). They have not yet seen him or his pain, and their pity is generalised. But it still contrasts with the prologue, where the exploration of the scene displayed Odysseus' focus on the dangers of the plot, and Neoptolemus' paraded concern with his own morality.[20] Indeed, Neoptolemus' response to the chorus here is blithely accommodating (197–200): "it is nothing to be surprised at", "it is god's plan he should suffer", "when the time is right, things will change". The chorus' instant and superficial pity, and Neoptolemus' lack of concern and naïve theodicy are the grounding from which the play's emotional journey starts. The chorus are an integral part of the drama of response, changing sentiments and shifting sense of duty.

Integral – but sparingly articulated. In the long and extraordinary first scene, which runs to 675, they sing only two short stanzas, which are strophic but separated by over a hundred lines. Each little ode develops our understanding of deception through remarkable performances. The first stanza (391–402) begins as a sort of holy prayer to Earth the mother of Zeus. It invokes her through her traditional epithets and haunts, and, in standard mode, recalls previous times that they have called on her – in this case, when the Atreidai insulted Neoptolemus by refusing him the arms of Achilles, his father – though they do not in fact reach any actual moment of request, which would be the normal ritual form of a prayer: it begins with prayer formulations but ends as no more than an invocation. Reinhardt back in 1933 brilliantly observed how the situation of a prayer has been perverted in the world of Odyssean deception so that "what should be most holy has become a means of betrayal" – which he

---

[19] See e.g. Schmidt (1973) 19; Pucci (2003) 156–7; and in general, Davidson (1995).
[20] On pity, see Konstan (2001).

links to the corrupting social conditions of the end of the Peloponnesian War.[21] The dochmiac metre is often taken as a sign of passionate emotion, here acted, deceptively imitated. But the fact that this is the chorus who utter a false and manipulative invocation is also significant, and disturbing, I think. There is no other case in extant tragedy where a chorus utters such a false prayer or so easily distorts ritual. (The closest parallel may be the Danaids in Aeschylus' *Supplices* who threaten to hang themselves on the altar, though this will not happen: but it is an early sign of the violence they will perpetrate.) The chorus is a familiar part of Greek ritual, singing, praying: the community reaching out to the gods. Sophocles dramatizes this pious scene as an easy front for manipulative self-interest.

The second stanza is no easier (506–18). The chorus, in line with the plot, call on the deceitfully hesitating Neoptolemus to pity the hero, and to take him home to escape the wrath (*nemesis*) of the gods. As Reinhardt puts it beautifully, "the betrayal of all that is inviolable in human life does not hesitate to take cover under the religion of inviolability".[22] How, then, does this call to pity relate to their earlier statement that they pitied Philoctetes (169)? Is this a "lie like the truth", as Homer's Odysseus proffers? Merely an opportunistic piece of acting that happens to echo their transparent emotions of before? Their encouragement to Neoptolemus to pity Philoctetes will also bear strange fruit, however. For it will be precisely the growing pity of Neoptolemus that will derail the deception. As we saw in chapter 2, it is hard to tell from his own use of *palai*, "for a long time now", when Neoptolemus' pity starts. With the retrospective temporality of re-judgement we discussed in chapter 1, the imperative of the chorus becomes touched with irony.

What's more, at the end of this scene when Neoptolemus and Philoctetes retire to the cave, and the chorus sing the only traditional ode in the play, alone on stage, they reflect movingly on the horrors of Philoctetes' solitary life. This is a performance of pity, which ends with the (self-)satisfaction that their arrival means Philoctetes will now be saved and can go home (719–29). It is an ode on which much ink has been spilled.[23] Why, now that they are alone, do they sing as if they were still part of the deception? Does this *stasimon*, addressed to no one, except, indirectly, the audience in the theatre, and thus removed from the deception, indicate a continuity of their feelings, in which their injunction to pity addressed to Neoptolemus takes on the air of sincerity? Does now the chorus' part in the deception (also) look like the chorus persuading Neoptolemus towards sympathetic feelings? Or are we to assume that the characters offstage can still hear the chorus, or, at any rate, that the chorus fear they

---

[21] Reinhardt (1979): 171 ([1933] 180).

[22] Reinhardt (1979): 171 ([1933] 180).

[23] See e.g. Tarrant (1986) with extensive bibliography; Ussher (1990) 134 *ad* 721–6; Visser (1998); Dobrov (2001) 31; Pucci (2003) *ad* 719–29.

might be overheard?[24] (Overhearing has already been dramatized as part of the plots of communication in the False Merchant scene.) How sincerely are we to hear their words? This very question, which underlies all the critical concern on this ode, indicates how the audience in the theatre is presented with a desta-bilizing and rather worrying scene, where the very authority of the chorus' voice qua chorus seems uncomfortably at stake. The audience, that is, becomes enmeshed in the doubts about truth and communication, hearing and over-hearing, being the master or victim of the deceptiveness and persuasion of language, which the characters on stage experience. The *stasimon* sung alone on stage is exactly when we might expect the chorus to reach towards the voice of traditional authority. Sophocles, in this play where the chorus is most like an actor, makes this the moment when the audience is most unsure about the status of the chorus' voice.

They begin precisely as if from within the repertoire of traditional myth. "I know of no other man", they declare (682), "from what I have heard or seen, who has encountered a fate more hateful than this man's". They have heard the stories of myth (the ode begins "I have heard in the stories . . ."), and have seen the heroes of the Trojan War. But even in comparison with these exemplars, they are shocked by the injustice to Philoctetes, who has suffered so terribly despite hurting nobody. The expression οὔτ' ἔρξας τιν', "not having done any-thing [violent] to anyone" (683) was recognized by Eustathius as echoing a Homeric turn of phrase (οὔτε τινα ῥέξας, "not having done anything [unjust] to anyone" *Od.* 4. 690, part of Penelope's angry description of how Odysseus always behaved like a just king and yet was requited now by the suitors' out-rages). Since so much of the play is concerned with articulating its moral doubts in and against a tradition of Homeric values, it is not by chance that this Homeric language of human (in)justice and theodicy is echoed here in the description of the founding injustice of the situation, in the chorus' eyes.

Indeed, the first antistrophe and second strophe (691–717), the heart of the ode, imagine the conditions of Philoctetes over the last ten years. They had imagined his life in pitying terms in the *parodos*, before they had seen him. Now, after they have heard the hero's own story and seen him with their own eyes, there is a marked increase in intensity in their expression. Where before they had marvelled at a life "alone, apart from others" (183), now they shudder because he had οὐδέ τιν' ἐγχώρων κακογείτονα παρ' ᾧ στόνον ἀντίτυπον βαρυβρῶτ' ἀποκλαύσειεν αἱματηρόν, "no neighbour from the place in his misery, to whom he could bewail a lament, an echoing exchange, heavy gnaw-ing, bloody." My translation strains to capture the difficult Greek here, which is dense in the extreme. The word *kakogeiton*, which must mean something like a "neighbour in" or "neighbour for" evils, does not occur elsewhere in extant fifth-century literature, and combines the senses of having no neighbour, and

---

[24] See Schmidt (1973) 132–3.

having no person who could share or respond to his troubles. The lament (*stonon*) has three adjectives, which again pack a set of relations into a compacted lyric expression: *antitupon*, which has its root in *tupos*, a "blow", "impression", "figure", here seems to mean something like "which invites response", as, indeed, a lament is usually antiphonal, or as a story of woe stimulates a story in return. But it may also remind us, with *stonos*, of the beating (*tupto*) of breasts in lament. Perhaps it may even hint at its sense of "type" or "character", and the place of profound grief in Philoctetes' character. But it remains a difficult term, where the sense has to be stretched here in context from any other usage of the word. *Barubrôt'* is also an unparalleled word: the sense "deeply gnawing" is transferred from the disease (that which is lamented) to the lament itself – though the metaphor of "gnawing grief" is also at work. *Haimateron*, "bloody" takes the symptoms of the disease into the performance of its lament. This language is powerfully impressive, as it strains to capture the horror of Philoctetes' solitary pain as a failure of human exchange, a physical, social and ritual anguish, in words and grammar that stretch and push the boundaries of sense.[25]

This heightening of the choral language prepares us for the coming scene, where for the first time Philoctetes will be ravaged by the bloody, gnawing disease before our eyes. It is part of the growing tension of the play. But it is also an integral element in the chorus' own narrative. Over the first scene, while they have remained silent, they have moved from their first encounter with the cave, where they tried to imagine Philoctetes' life, to this passionately sympathetic imaging of his condition. Their shifting narrative of emotional engagement with Philoctetes acts as an interwoven background to Neoptolemus' more consequential and more wrenching turmoil. "Its function is both to echo and to contradict, to harmonize at one moment, to conflict melodramatically at another".[26]

The chorus contributes no words to the following scene (one of the most physically arresting exchanges in all Greek tragedy), and the choral interlude that follows Philoctetes' collapse (827–64), demonstrates how Sophocles' formal innovation in the choral performance contributes to the growing ambiguities of the play. Neoptolemus asks the chorus to leave Philoctetes to his exhausted rest, and their first stanza opens with a little prayer to Sleep, which has clear signs of the Paean (which Haldane has detailed)[27], as one might expect for a song for healing, a hymn, with an appeal for epiphany (827–32):

> Ὕπν' ὀδύνας ἀδαής, Ὕπνε δ' ἀλγέων,
> εὐαὲς ἡμῖν
> ἔλθοις, εὐαίων εὐαίων, ὦναξ·

---

[25] See Worman (2000).

[26] Reinhardt (1979) 182 ([1933]: 191).

[27] Haldane (1963).

ὄμμασι δ᾽ ἀντίσχοις
τάνδ᾽ αἴγλαν, ἃ τέταται τανῦν.
ἴθι, ἴθι μοι παιών.

Sleep, stranger to pain, to anguish, Sleep,
with gentle breath, we beg,
come now, blessed ! blessed! lord.
keep upon his eyes
the gleam that spreads over them now.
Come! Come! please, healer.

This is a good example of how forms of choral lyric from elsewhere – the cultic hymn – are brought into and transformed by the chorus of tragedy – but not just at the level of its highly literary language (the opening address "Sleep, stranger to pain, to anguish, Sleep" is a carefully braided expression, for example, and the vocative *euaies*, "with gentle breath" (828), suggests an etymological or at least phonic link with the ritual address in the next line *euaion, euaion*, "blessed", "blessed".) For, after the prayer to Earth in the previous scene, the semantic or veridical status of this hymn is hard to appreciate with certainty. Pucci suggests that the cynicism of the previous prayer fades here, as the chorus are happy to invoke sleep both to comfort the tortured hero and to advance the plot.[28] Reinhardt, at the opposite pole, calls it a "song of gentle enticement to deceit, all the more forceful for its gentleness"[29]; or Segal, a contradiction of "their earlier compassion", a "voice against which Neoptolemus must defend himself."[30] Once deceit has been introduced into communication, it is hard to rediscover trust. Is this hymn delivered with at least half an eye on the possibility that Philoctetes is listening? Or is it more triumphantly marking the unconsciousness of the enemy? Or luring the young Neoptolemus towards corrupt dealing? The audience in the theatre finds the insecurity of interpretative mistrust veining *their* engagement with the chorus.

The second part of the stanza does not quite resolve this tension. The chorus turns to Neoptolemus, now that it is clear that Philoctetes *is* asleep ("he sleeps" 835), and ask their master what the plan now is.[31] This seems to them the right moment (*kairos*) for action. There is no question of any sympathy for Philoctetes blocking the plot (yet), though, once again, their questioning – joined with a gaze at Philoctetes (*horâis?*) – "Look where will you stand, where will you go, what's the intention? Do you see?" – will turn out to have been pregnant with the possibility of Neoptolemus' change of mind. But Neoptolemus' answer to the chorus is wholly unexpected. He starts to speak in hexameters (839–42), and

---

[28] Pucci (2003) *ad loc.*
[29] Reinhardt (1979) 181 ([1933]: 191).
[30] Segal (1995) 107.
[31] The text here is difficult, though not perhaps as desperate as Dawe suggests.

declares that their expedition must bring the hero *and* the bow together. As commentators have rightly noted, hexameters are the metre of prophecy, and this speech is a recollection of the oracular utterance which has motivated their venture. It also gives his speech great authority: *horô*, "I see", he declares in emphatic response to the chorus' question *horâis*, "do you see?".[32] In the previous scene, Neoptolemus had fallen silent, and, pushed by Philoctetes, had confessed (806), "For really quite a long time I have been in pain, lamenting your troubles". In the next scene, Neoptolemus will break down, and tell Philoctetes about his true destination (895–916). His prophetic voice is both authoritative-sounding – and part of his journey of doubt: perhaps a way of now firmly resisting the chorus' suggestion of action, decision time (*kairos/prassein*), with a commitment to divine authority in the face of increasing human confusion.

But if this seems like a stalwart answer to the chorus, their second stanza and the epode (843–64) slide away from any easy acceptance of the boy's authority. ἀλλά, τέκνον, τάδε μὲν θεὸς ὄψεται, "But, boy, god will see to that", they answer (843). Kitto notes the "empty sententiousness" of this remark, and no doubt it has a formulaic, even rather dismissive ring. But where they had said "do you see?" and Neoptolemus had replied "I see", now they echo this precisely with *opsetai*, [god] "will see". They respond to Neoptolemus' prophecy-like hexameters by reverting to god, thereby bypassing Neoptolemus' decision-making. The rhetorical force of the sententiousness is to close off discussion of the oracular – only to sidle round to suggesting what they had hinted at in the first stanza: that now is the time to pick up the bow, and make a run for the ship (855–64), oracle or no. Their sententiousness is not just a bit of characterization, but also plays a role in their performative rhetoric; it's a step towards their working to find a place from which to try to persuade Neoptolemus of what they actually think he should do. Their language continues to be veiled and cautious ("You know what/whom I am talking about; if you have the same opinion towards this man, it's for the wise to foresee innumerable problems" [852–4]). This is partly because they are explicitly afraid that Philoctetes will come to ("speak quietly . . ." [845–6]), but also because they are talking around their subordinate position and Neoptolemus' strong expression in the hexameters in order to disagree with their leader. At 865 Neoptolemus shushes them because Philoctetes is stirring, and we see no more of such disagreement. ("I order silence . . .") But this brief choral exchange shows the chorus "most closely connected with the intrigue".[33] They suggest action to their leader whom they see as dilatory, and they try to avoid his apparent scruples with curt directness: "A good wind, child, a good wind; the man is sightless; got no help; stretched out like a night's sleep" (855–7). The contrast of the chorus' lyrics, with their re-working of a cultic hymn, and Neoptolemus' hexameters,

---

[32] See *Ajax* 118 and 125: "Do you see?". . ."I see . . .", discussed in chapter 2 p41–2.
[33] Reinhardt (1979) 182 ([1933]: 191).

with their reworking of an oracular pronouncement, together with the further contrast between the chorus' cautious and subordinate insistence on pragmatic action, and the already doubting Neoptolemus' on god's word, constructs a dramatic exchange in which the chorus plays a full and active role. Where we might have expected a choral ode, a *stasimon* sung by a chorus alone on stage, we have the hushed and power-laden conversation between a crew and a young commander about what to do: this, I take it, is what Aristotle meant by having the chorus perform as an actor.

Jebb adds another line to the argument. He suggests that the strophe and the antistrophe are each sung by a different hemichorus. It is unclear to me on what evidence he says this is certain: in the *Ajax* [866ff], his parallel, the conversation between two different groups is clearly marked; here there are no such clear markers.[34] Were Jebb's suggestion to be correct, however, it would introduce a division within the chorus, the first group hymning Sleep and asking at best leading questions about action; the second group more forcefully encouraging a swift, physical response to the opportunity provided by Philoctetes' sleep. It might suggest division within the collective about what should be done, complicating further the moral pressures on the boy. Neoptolemus would be faced by two groups, each counselling action in different ways, with different purchase on his wavering. As far as I am aware, Jebb's suggestion has been neither adopted by any subsequent editor, nor further discussed in the scholarly literature (though Campbell back in 1881 has an even more complex and fragmented distribution of parts).

In the next scene – the hugely dramatic revelation of the intrigue by Neoptolemus, Philoctetes' outraged and despairing response, to the point of trying to throw himself down the rocks and being restrained, and Odysseus' powerful direction of the situation – the chorus have only a few lines. But each of their three speeches demonstrates Sophocles' concern with their status as actors. They respond to Philoctetes' long, emotive plea to Neoptolemus (927–62) with (963–4):

> τί δρῶμεν;; ἐν σοὶ καὶ τὸ πλεῖν ἡμᾶς, ἄναξ,
> ἤδη 'στι καὶ τοῖς τοῦδε προσχωρεῖν λόγοις.

> What are we to do? It is in your hands now, lord,
> Whether we sail or cede to this man's arguments.

It is very rare indeed in tragedy for a chorus to ask the paradigmatic tragic question "What to do?". They see themselves as actors, even as they cede the authority for decision-making to their lord. The *koruphaios* here speaks for the chorus as a collective – but his words seem to stretch to include Neoptolemus. They will all sail or yield, on his word. There is, however, also a performative

---

[34] Jebb (1898) 134 *ad* 827–64.

force to their little speech. They recognize the possibility of yielding to Philoctetes' arguments (and in Homer, the second of two options is usually the one chosen . . .). This prompts Neoptolemus' response: "In my case, [*emoi men*], a certain strange pity for this man has fallen, not now for the first time, but for some time since" (965–6). The *men solitarium* emphasizes *emoi*, but also gives an implied contrast, which seems to draw out the implication of the chorus' comment: Neoptolemus recognizes an emotional motivation for the second of their options. The anguish of Neoptolemus continues with him asking first (969) οἴμοι, τί δράσω, "alas! what am I to do?" – taking on himself the responsibility for action, and then (974), as Philoctetes intensifies his appeal, he asks τί δρῶμεν, ἄνδρες, "What are we to do, men?". He makes the crew party to his decision; he recognizes them as shared agents, as his *drômen* echoes their use of the same word – and significantly it is exactly at this point that Odysseus enters to take control of the fragile plot. The chorus' words are few, but their exchange with Neoptolemus is crucial in articulating the boy's insecurity, and starts to engage them as actors in the decision-making – only to be bypassed by Odysseus' entrance.

Their second remark follows another of Philoctetes' long rants, this time against Odysseus (1004–44). The first part of Philoctetes' speech uses second person singular forms and is directed specifically at Odysseus (1007, 1008, 1009 etc.); the second part of the speech (1029–44), apart from 1031, uses second person plurals, leading up to his prayer for revenge on "all of them" (1042). The chorus comment (1045–6):

> βαρύς τε καὶ βαρεῖαν ὁ ξένος φάτιν
> τήνδ' εἶπ', Ὀδυσσεῦ, κοὐχ ὑπείκουσαν κακοῖς.

> The stranger is bitter, and this is a bitter speech
> He has spoken, Odysseus; not yielding to his woes.

Barus, which, with Jebb, I have translated as "bitter", implies not merely "vehement" but also "freighted with import", "weighty". The emphatic repetition of the term, applied to Philoctetes and his speech, encourages some care in understanding. The chorus, after all, are included in Philoctetes' curse, and may be thought to feel its weight. But there is no evident sign of pity here. In the careful patterning of the emotional appeals in the play, it is important to note when Philoctetes' extreme expression alienates his listeners and when it engages them. Here the chorus are pushed away by the curse and violence of his attack. The direct address to Odysseus is demanding a reply from him. This is the first and only time in the play that Neoptolemus' men speak to Odysseus. This is not just a recognition that Philoctetes' execrating rage needs an answer; it is also a recognition that only Odysseus is to give it. Neoptolemus' silence in this scene, as we saw in chapter 2, is a dramatic performance of his internal turmoil. The chorus' address to Odysseus, especially after the curse on "them all" and the second person plurals, has the effect of setting up Odysseus as spokesman, leader, authority figure – in contrast to Neoptolemus' silence: a stage-direction for the dynamics of the scene.

Their final comment in the scene is in response to a direct question from Philoctetes. He asks (1070–1) – with considerable emotion ($\mathring{\eta}\ \pi o\upsilon\ \ldots\ \delta\acute{\eta}$) – "Will I really in this way, strangers, be actually deserted by you; will you not pity me?". The chorus immediately turn towards Neoptolemus (1072–3):

> ὅδ᾽ ἐστὶν ἡμῶν ναυκράτωρ ὁ παῖς. ὅσ᾽ ἂν
> οὗτος λέγει σοι, ταῦτά σοι χἠμεῖς φαμεν.

> This youth is our commander. Whatever he says
> To you, this we too say to you.

This remark cedes authority to Neoptolemus, and forces him to break his silence, as we saw in chapter 2. The chorus, finally, will not act without Neoptolemus' explicit command. As Philoctetes turns directly to them and appeals for pity, they turn away from him, and direct the emotional thrust of the scene on to the vacillating boy.

Each of the chorus' comments in this scene is thus a prompt: in each case, they ask the lead characters to make a decision, to make a speech, to take control. In each case, the speech is designed to do something rather than merely to comment on the action. But as Odysseus leads Neoptolemus offstage, the chorus are now left alone with Philoctetes, and now it is their turn not to sing a *stasimon* commenting on the action but to act as the leading interlocutor with the hero – in the *kommos*, which, as we might expect, brilliantly dramatizes the interaction of group and hero as a performance of persuasion and alienation, engagement and refusal.

The *kommos* is long (1081–1217) and complex, but has a clear structure, marked by metre and by the nature of the exchange. It falls into two parts. The first (1081–1168) consists of four strophic stanzas sung by Philoctetes, interspersed with four shorter stanzas from the chorus. Philoctetes, in each of his stanzas, expresses his grief and rage by addressing the landscape, lamenting his fate, bewailing the plot.[35] He takes no notice of any of the chorus' comments, nor addresses them. He appears totally alienated. The chorus, in turn, sing in reproof and persuasion. "It is you, you who have made this decision: this lot does not come from somewhere else from a superior force . . ." (1095–7); "Turn your hated, ill-fortuned curse at others. Do not reject my friendship!" (1119–22). They offer a competing version of his story, and sing of reciprocation, integration, connection as they appeal for him to join them. So their fourth stanza implores Philoctetes to approach a friend "who draws near with all kindness

---

[35] Knox (1964); Segal (1981); Rose (1976) have all deepened our understanding of Philoctetes' relationship to the landscape.

[*eunoia*]" and to recognize that it is "within your own power to escape this doom". Again Pseudo-Aristotle's comment on what a chorus does looks jejune, even and especially as the chorus is claiming to treat an actor with *eunoia*, precisely as Ps-Aristotle would expect: the claim of *eunoia* is a self-aware strategy of persuasion, an act of self-presentation, and not simply the standard performance of choral good will. At exactly this point (1169) – the second section of the *kommos* – the metre and the structure of exchange alter completely. Philoctetes starts to address the chorus, as they have demanded; the metre varies rapidly; there is no symmetry as the dialogue flows jaggedly with lines and speeches of varying lengths. It is the chorus' final throw: they start to leave; he begs them to stay; they state their terms: "to Troy"; he bitterly rejects them; they make a further move; he demands a sword to kill himself – and, as the conversation drags through its intense but inconclusive course, they are stopped by the return of Odysseus and Neoptolemus, thus preserving the convention by which a chorus does not leave the stage during the play's duration, a convention already breached in the *Ajax*.

We have seen already how the *kommos* enacts a pattern of emotional, moral and physical integration and separation of individual and group. Here, first Philoctetes is quite separated from the chorus: they address him but he speaks to the unfeeling landscape. They address him, and talk both of how he is responsible for his alienation, and how they are offering friendship. Second, Philoctetes is drawn into fragmented and vehement dialogue with the chorus, which can only re-stage the failure of his integration. They start to move away and offstage – physical separation – while offering to integrate him into their journey. He resists, and rejects them – though he is now speaking with them. The chorus here follows on from Odysseus and from Neoptolemus in attempting to persuade Philoctetes to leave off his rage and come to be cured at Troy; they engage in a protracted and intricate scene of persuasion, and end by making a move to leave (as Odysseus and Neoptolemus have done). Here, then, above all, we see the chorus as an actor.

The chorus will say nothing further until the last three lines of the play. "Let us go all of us together, with a prayer to the nymphs of the sea for a safe journey home". Closural formula, no doubt – but the phrase "let us go then all of us together" closes by marking precisely what had proved impossible for them to achieve without Heracles' help: a shared, collective journey.

It is easy to see why *Philoctetes* might be summoned in evidence for the Aristotelian teleological history towards *embolima*. The chorus sing only one *stasimon* in traditional style, alone on stage; they have few interjections, and are silent for long stretches of the action. But what we have seen here, first of all, is how integral to the action of the play they are. When they ask *ti drômen*, "what are we to do?" it is a pointed question because of their engagement in the deception, the plot. The chorus too has a narrative in this play, drawing closer to and moving away from Philoctetes, finding a shifting range of emotional responses to him. This is a fundamental part of the chorus' score. The more complex and consequential responses of Neoptolemus and Odysseus are in counterpoint to the chorus. Part of the wonderfully dense texture of this play's dialogues comes from the interweaving of the different emotional journeys of the characters and chorus, interacting. What's more, the chorus' involvement in the intrigue produces a peculiarly difficult status for their language. When they pray, it is hard to know if there is any sincerity in it; when they promise friendship to Philoctetes, is this acting out their role in the intrigue still, a strategy of persuasion, or a statement of their changing feelings and hopes for the hero's salvation? That is, the audience in the theatre has to respond to the chorus as it would to an actor, and as we find it hard to see exactly when and how Neoptolemus is changing, so too with the chorus. In short, Aristotle's celebrated comment that Sophocles made the chorus an actor finds its fullest embodiment in the *Philoctetes*.

III Conclusion: A Politics of the Collective?

Two conclusions should be clear. First, the performance of the Sophoclean chorus, the scoring of its lyric voice, is far more complex and nuanced than many generalizations about "the chorus" have allowed, and far more dramatically involved and expressive than many modern performances have managed to access. The shift of voices within the chorus, especially between iambics and lyrics (a variety of performance introduced only with tragedy, it seems), between a collective and individual or half chorus, between sung and spoken, is a fundamental element for choral performance in the *polis*. The narrative development of the choral performance between odes, and within odes, is a dramatic journey in itself. The distinguished American composer Philip Glass recently (summer, 2009) wrote the music for the *Bacchae*, directed in New York by his former wife, Joanne Akalaitis. The much-anticipated production was a disaster in almost all respects, and it was particularly unfortunate that the music for the choral odes had no sense of the modulation within any particular chorus, and, even more damagingly perhaps, between different odes, so that the ode which sings of the holiness of the god, on the humble place of man, and which ends with a statement that the chorus will always follow what the ordinary people think and do (370–431), had a similar rhythm and similar musical language to the wild hunting song where the Bacchants ecstatically encourage their sisters on the hills to destroy King Pentheus (977–1023). The sameness of the choral voice, enforced by the sameness within the music, distorted Euripides' narrative with crass oversimplification. A monotonal chorus produces monotony in the theatre, and misrepresents the more fluid story of the chorus as a group, which responds to and engages with the actors – and in the case of the *Bacchae* is climbing towards a climax of exuberant and frightening aggression.

This engagement is especially telling when the choral voice adapts the language or form of other choral institutions, such as the *kommos*. The *kommos* is by definition not just a mourning song but an antiphonal performance, where the group responds to the individual's grief with gestures of consolation and reintegration. It is a *topos* of the *kommos* for the group to demand recognition from the mourner that everyone dies, that myth shows the doom-laden nature of man's lot, that they are not the only ones to suffer. These expressions of consolation, which can sound like correctives, are adapted in Sophocles into scenes where the chorus criticizes, attempts to persuade, or comments on the moral transgressions of the characters. In *Antigone*, the male elders are drawn towards, but still need to criticize, Antigone's self-willed behaviour; in *Electra*, Electra's supporters are cowed by her intensity away from their well-intentioned criticism of her everlasting and extreme laments; in *Philoctetes*, the chorus fail to persuade Philoctetes to leave with them, as they criticize his self-destructive attitude. In each case, the chorus enacts a dialogue which shifts, develops and plays through a power relation. It is an exchange which redeploys the form of another choral institution to construct a dramatic dialogue of intensity and purpose, central in each case to the plotting of the play and to the evaluation of the characters' behaviour. Here is one way we can see what Aristotle meant by saying that Sophocles used the chorus as an actor.

The second conclusion concerns the broader political implications of this representation of the chorus. We have become accustomed in the scholarship on Sophocles to a concentration on the hero. From Reinhardt to Knox to Winnington-Ingram and Segal, the lineaments of the type of the Sophoclean hero have been drawn out with a good deal of sophistication (and we will see the roots of this focus on the individual in chapter 7 in particular). This discussion has developed a political slant especially since the 1980s. The hero's fierce commitment to self, and often violent expression of it, has been seen in general terms to interrogate democracy's sense of collective enterprise, and the relationship between the traditional heroic values of Homer and the new framework of the democratic *polis*. For a modern audience, faced as we are by the violent extremism of current political activism, Sophocles' interrogation of the tragic politics of excessive commitment has never been more timely. In this contemporary critical discussion, the chorus as a collective group, its mobilization of mythic, traditional stories, its opposition to or support of the hero, have all been seen as essential elements in the representation of the hero: a foil to the hero's extremism. Or ignored: as we will see in chapter 7; modernity has all too often removed the chorus from the stage and from critical discussion. I would like to suggest that the more nuanced reading of the chorus' performance that I have been developing here, should be seen also as part of a political understanding of tragedy. The chorus, as a group, struggling to assimilate, comprehend, negotiate with excessive, demanding, transgressive individuals, was good for the Athenians to think with, politically. That is, in the same way that the portrayal of the hero's extreme commitment was one way of thinking about the boundaries of the normal, so the portrayal of the chorus' response to the hero and the hero's story is one way of thinking about the difficulties of integrating such figures into the collective enterprise.

Such an argument takes politics in its most general definition. It suggests no more than that when the chorus try and fail, as friends, to persuade Philoctetes to give up his rage and come to Troy, the drama of this scene may have something to say to the citizens of the *polis* as political actors, not least in the recriminatory and mistrusting aftermath of the oligarchic coup.

But there is one final twist to the political argument that also seems worth underlining. The critical oversimplification of the chorus may find a parallel that goes back all the way to Plato and Thucydides, whose negative representations of the crowd, the people, the collective, have been so influential on political thinking, especially anti-democratic thinking. It is always easy to slip into rather dismissive stereotypical descriptions of "the crowd" as a block, simple, easily led, dangerous in judgement. One consequence of our attraction to the destructive heroes of the genre of tragedy may be that we, like the heroes, find it hard to hear the lyric voice of the chorus with proper attention. The portrayal of the chorus in Sophocles' plays offers a place where the group may emerge in a more sophisticated light, and where the drama of being part of a community might be more intricately explored.

The Language of Tragedy

{ 6 }

Generalizing About Tragedy

Personam tragicam forte vulpes viderat:
quam postquam huc illuc semel atque iterum verterat
"O quanta species", inquit, "cerebrum non habet".

A fox once saw an actor's tragic mask:
He turned it this way and that, once and again.
"What an amazing sight!", he said, "but it's got no brain".

PHAEDRUS' FABLES OF AESOP

The first five chapters of this book have explored what I regard as essential for any discussion of Sophocles' use of tragic language. Irony and the reversals of narrative, the conflict embedded in *stichomythia*, the dialogic dynamic of chorus and actors with its multiple voices and exchanges, the interpretative and dramatic performances of watching, listening, judging, on and offstage – a structuring made possible by the introduction of the third actor – provide the fundamental framework through which Sophoclean tragedy finds its particular form.

No doubt this range of topics could have been further extended and deepened. The variation and power of the messenger's role in Sophocles, for example, a topic which I have touched on several times in passing in the first half of this book, has often been underappreciated in the critical literature. A generalized picture of the messenger as (mere) dramatic device – the anonymous man who brings news from outside – obscures the extraordinary and specific ways in which the messenger is fully integrated into the play's dramatic and thematic structure in Sophocles' plays. Think of the Paidagogos of *Electra* whose deceptive speech is part of the plot of revenge and also part of the play's fascination with role-playing, (self)-deception and performance; or the messenger of the *Oedipus Tyrannus*, who has been a part of the plot of Oedipus' early life and whose message of release fully rehearses this play's obsession with the impossible dangers of language and knowledge; or Hyllus in the *Trachiniae*, the son forced to tell his mother the story of how she has murdered his father, a message that leads to her own suicide: a family's killing words. A messenger, in Sophocles' hands, fully dramatizes how a discussion of the language of tragedy leads inexorably towards a recognition of how language itself – the perils of words, communication and interpretation – plays an integral role in the unfurling of tragedy. Similarly, I could have drawn out more systematically how often the first or last words of characters – words of greeting and parting – are especially freighted with tragic import and charged with unrecognized significance: from Oedipus' "My children . . .", to Hyllus' "Teach me . . .". Sophocles' characters already dwell within tragic language.

I have tried to indicate in this first section – and I will return to it in more detail in the coda – the areas where Sophocles' language and dramatic strategies seem to me to be particularly distinctive, even though irony, the drama of silence, the exchanges of *stichomythia*, the role of the chorus, can be said to form the common matrix of all our extant Greek tragedy. These chapters have tried, that is, to articulate how Sophocles develops his own particular engagement with the language of tragedy.

In the second half of the book, however, as I indicated in the introduction, I shall be developing a different sense of the phrase "the language of tragedy". I want to start to unpack the critical tradition that underlies – even in negation – the critical vocabulary with which contemporary critical reading approaches the genre of ancient Greek tragedy. This tradition starts for us from – and obsessively returns to – the philosophical fathers, Plato and Aristotle, with the occasional snigger from Aristophanes, whose critical hooliganism some classicists insist on taking with a rather too po-faced seriousness (rather than the seriousness comedy does deserve). Through Seneca in particular, a diffused and oblique affiliation to Athenian tragedy also enters European culture and repeatedly complicates any sense of direct linear engagement with the ancient Greek genre. There is also an intricate and influential history from the Renaissance through to the Enlightenment, with a particularly interesting French investment through the *ancien régime* and the Revolution. The intellectual world of Goethe and Lessing too engaged profoundly with tragedy as a form. The richness of this conceptual and dramatic legacy is evident and potent.

In this second section of my book, I wish to turn my gaze elsewhere, however. For there is no post-classical set of writings that has had such an influence on modern ideas of tragedy and on the modern performance tradition as the works of the German Idealist philosophers and their readers in the nineteenth century. Across Europe, the influence of Hegel, Schiller, Schlegel, Schelling in the first instance, and then Schopenhauer, Nietzsche and Wagner, has been so pervasive that after the 1820s it becomes hard to find any significant and extended response to tragedy that is not mediated through a German, philosophically tinged lens – even in the performance tradition where the re-discovery of tragedy as a staged, theatrical event finds its beacons in Schiller's *Bride of Messina*, Tieck/Mendelssohn's *Antigone*, Reinhardt's *Oedipus*, Hof-mannsthal's *Elektra* (and so forth), with the result that even a landmark French production such as Mounet-Sully's *Oedipus* needs to be seen within this German-led intellectual tradition, through which the cast and audience alike viewed the performance and its significance. To an extraordinary degree, the earlier post-Renaissance writing on tragedy was silenced by this nine-teenth-century discourse: even earlier German writing on tragedy in Ger-man-speaking regions faded into increasing insignificance. Despite the continuing presence of Goethe and especially his *Iphigenie*, or the buried influence of, say, Lessing's *Hamburgische Dramaturgie* (1769), or the tradition of Trauerspiel celebrated later by Walter Benjamin, it was now largely through a self-consciously post-Kantian agenda that tragedy was approached within German-speaking countries – and across the rest of Europe.

In the following chapters, I will be looking at how the German Idealist tra-dition created a new sense of the chorus, and how this entered the perfor-mance tradition in part at least through opera (the rebirth of tragedy from music); then at how the interpretation of a single play – Sophocles' *Electra* – is constructed within an intellectual tradition, how this tradition can change, and how the performance tradition interacts with and ignores and appropri-ates such scholarly interventions; and, finally, at how the *Antigone* has become a set-text for feminist political analysis in particular as a response to Hegel and the German tradition. But in this first chapter of the section, I shall begin by looking at the very broadest terminology of the critical language of tragedy and its modern formation, namely, the word *tragedy* itself and the concept of the tragic. How does this language take shape in the nineteenth century and how does it affect the reading of Sophocles in particular? What agenda was set for tragedy by nineteenth-century criticism?

The long tradition of Western writing about tragedy might make it seem natural for both critics and artists to reach towards an abstract and general concept of "the tragic" in their discussions of dramatic literature or of the structured comprehension of the pain and turmoil of the world. Defining "tragedy itself", "true tragedy", has become a shared and competitive game (with Schelling, Hegel, Nietzsche, Kierkegaard, Jaspers and many others as its most valuable players). The lure of seeking for such a general and abstract understanding is evident and pressing, especially for nineteenth-century Ger-man thought, and for its heirs today: the grand, epideictic arguments of Steiner, Szondi, Eagleton – and many others – self-consciously debate and continue the tradition of nineteenth-century obsession with the tragic. Tragedy, for the nineteenth century in particular, became a structuring prin-ciple of the self-understanding of modernity. In the wake of this tradition, *the tragic*, alas, has become a staple of university courses and exam questions . . .

But, as ever, what seems natural has a full cultural history behind it. A broad – or more narrowly circumscribed – intellectual history could, of course, be written for each of these searches for the tragic essence, and scholars have lovingly traced the construction and refinement of the (German) commitment to finding the place of suffering in modernity's self-awareness. So, Nietzsche's construction of the tragic, for example, has been repeatedly analysed within his own growing philosophical thought, especially with regard to his stormy relationship with Wagner, within his reading of his predecessors, especially Schopenhauer, and as an influence on later writers, especially through the Cambridge Ritualists, but also throughout modernist approaches to the genre.[1] Similarly, the role of Hegel's thinking on tragedy within his philosophy and his religion is complex and fascinating, as indeed is its impact, explicit and unacknowledged, on later critical writing.[2] In the next chapter we will be looking in more detail at how German Idealist philosophers concentrated on the *Sittlichkeit* – the ethical self-positioning – of the individual, and on the narrative of the suffering individual as basic to an appreciation of the tragic. What's more, as we will see in detail also with the discussion of the chorus in the next chapter, tragedy as an idea became central to the self-conscious *historical* understanding of modernity, how man's place in history is to be conceptualized. "First as tragedy, second as farce", as Marx in the *Eighteenth Brumaire* famously summed up the repetition of history, a phrase intimately and manipulatively redolent of Hegel's understanding of the dialectics of history and the importance of tragedy in it. If tragedy was an aesthetic battleground in the argument between the ancients and moderns in the eighteenth century, for the nineteenth century it became an integral element in the profoundest thinking about history and the suffering of humankind.

In this opening chapter of the section, however, rather than a straight doxographic approach, itemizing how each nineteenth-century philosopher constructed his sense of the tragic, I am interested in taking a different tack towards a cultural history of the language of tragedy and the tragic. I shall be exploring the prior question of what it might mean to appeal in this way to "the tragic" as an abstract concept: what are the implications and costs, that is, of generalizing about tragedy? What is at stake when a particular narrative of suffering becomes the paradigm of an abstract notion of the tragic? How does the definition of the tragic affect the appreciation of tragedies? This chapter will explore not only what is at stake in the hypostatisation of the tragic, but also how a more nuanced sense of the exemplary can be traced from within Greek tragedies themselves in order to question an essentialized sense of "the tragic". How do the texts of the genre of tragedy engage with the issue of the paradigmatic status of its exemplary narratives? In short, how has the critical

---

[1] Exemplary here is Silk and Stern (1981). See also Schmidt (2001).
[2] See, for example, Schmidt (2001); Steiner (1984).

language of tragedy developed, and how does the language of the tragic texts relate to this development?

I

There is a repeated pattern of rhetoric in claims to recognize the truly tragic. It usually starts with a rather easy commonplace: dismissing the modern journalistic love of the term "tragic" as a trivialization, used as it is for any upsetting event from the broken bone in a footballer's foot to the natural disaster of a tsunami. This critical rejection of the journalists' promiscuous recognition of tragedy is part and parcel of an attempt to reserve the vocabulary of "the tragic" not just to denote the grandest genre of the Western theatrical tradition, but also to describe and to privilege a particular sense of the human condition: a suffering that sets man against the otherness of the world, "call it what you will: a hidden or malevolent God, blind fate, the solicitations of hell, or the brute fury of our animal blood".[3] Generalizing about the tragic is one strategy for introducing a hierarchy into perceptions of human suffering – downplaying your mundane misery in the name of my truly tragic. Only some suffering can be really tragic . . .

The rhetorical exclusion of the not-really-tragic has deep intellectual underpinnings in both religion and politics. One crucial frame for this hierarchizing of tragic experience is Christianity's re-valorisation of the discourse of suffering (*pathos/passio*) through the passion of Christ and the martyrdom of his saints.[4] In Christianity, suffering evokes a fully theological perception of the world, man's place in it, as well as an understanding of the body and spirituality. When suffering becomes so charged a term, there is inevitably a great deal at stake in how pain or misery is narrativized (and valued), and thus policing the tragic becomes in turn far more than a philological nicety – especially in the troubled interrelations between German Idealism and Christianity, which lead through Schopenhauer, Nietzsche and others to extended arguments about pessimism and promise. Nationalism in the nineteenth and twentieth centuries (and beyond) has also fed repeatedly on a narrative of the suffering of the people – or, more precisely, on the claim of a specific and special tragic suffering of a particular people – just as bourgeois identity politics so often locates authority in a tale of a group's or an individual's personal suffering. A

---

[3] Steiner (1961) 9.

[4] Eagleton (2008) 343 writes "the New Testament regards suffering as an evil to be abolished, not a condition to be heroically endured. Jesus never once counsels a sufferer to be reconciled to his or her illness". This may be true, but it wholly ignores the logic of imitation of Jesus' suffering in saints' lives, the practice and theory of the mortification of the flesh, theological reflections on the passion, and much writing of the Protestant and Catholic church encouraging forbearance, which Eagleton may deplore but which is deeply influential on thinking about suffering, as well as artistic representations of it.

recognition of "real pain", "genuine suffering" becomes a political self-justification, where all too often the claim to tragedy – the tragedy of the rape victim, the tragedy of illness, the tragedy of the Palestinian people – is an attempt to arrogate an unimpeachable status. There is a politics in defining tragedy, which aesthetic arguments about "the tragic" have tended to repress. The rhetoric of suffering is always a weapon in the contests of justice.

Although few discussions of "tragedy and the tragic" refuse a return to classical Greece, few actually consider how the term "tragic" is used in antiquity: how it is linked either to the dramas of the genre or to a broader concept of tragedy. For the ancient term *tragikos*, "tragic", has a different rhetorical force, and quite different intellectual underpinnings from its modern usage. *Tragikos* is used in ancient Greek (first of all) as floppily as "tragic" is in modern journalism. It is used, of course, in a technical sense (as it is in modern English) to apply to any aspect of the dramatic performances of the festival of the Great Dionysia in Athens: "tragic stage", "tragic mask", "tragic costume" and so forth. But when Plato's Socrates refers to "tragic talk" (*tragikôs legein*), "speaking in a tragic manner", he indicates a language which is grander and more pompous than usual.[5] It implies nothing about suffering, but a sense of the majestic or stately. This can be a source of humour, and making fun of tragedy's grandeur is a staple of Aristophanic comedy. In the mouth of the Platonic Socrates, "tragic" marks a wry self-recognition that his language is getting a little overheated. So Aristotle's celebrated definition of tragedy includes the stipulation that tragedy should be expressed "in language which is embellished" (*Poet.* 6.2). A heightened language is integral to tragedy in this definition. In a similar way, many centuries later the Greek novelists reserved the terms "dramatic", "theatrical", "tragic", for scenes of heightened emotion, usually the conflicting feelings of the novel's characters at some surprising denouement – or for the rhetoric of grief, which some disaster calls forth from the protagonists, highly educated as they are in the formal arts of rhetoric. "The tragic" here implies little more than grandly poetic and emotional – and garlanded with the literary prestige of the classical.[6]

When Aristotle in the *Poetics* calls Euripides "the most tragic" of playwrights (*tragikôtatos* 13.10), it is therefore difficult to tell how hard the term is to be pressed. At the most basic level, it indicates that Euripides is the poet who produces in his audience the deepest feelings of pity and fear: he is especially emotive. There may be a further implication that Euripides is particularly good at constructing a narrative that ends in extreme and unmitigated misfortune (though Aristotle seems himself to prefer a pattern where a character is led towards a familial murder which is avoided at the last). But Aristotle also uses

---

[5] *Republic* 413b4: "but I run the risk of speaking tragically". Cf 545e and *Meno* 76e.
[6] Froma Zeitlin's Sather lectures deal with this with her customary intelligence and perception: their publication is eagerly awaited.

the term *tragikos* much like other writers. He dismisses some metaphors as being "too grand and tragic" for good oratory (*Rhet.* 3.3.4). Even in the *Poetics* his use of "tragic" does not seem to imply a closely defined or theoretically rigorous category. So, when he criticizes the plot device where a character is led knowingly towards committing an act of violence against someone who is known, but then retreats from the violence, he explains (14.7) that "this is repulsive and not tragic [*miaron . . . ou tragikon*]: for it lacks suffering" [*apathes*]. The "not tragic" is glossed as that which "lacks suffering", because nobody is the victim of violence, and even the violent emotions are held in check. It does not seem to imply a world-view or a metaphysics, but rather something unsuited to a genre which thrives on suffering. In a similar way, the plot where a good man is brought into adversity is said (13.2) to be "neither pitiful nor fearful, but repulsive [*miaron*]", just as the "most untragic" [*atragiko-taton*] plot, that of a bad man reaching prosperity, is untragic precisely because it is "neither moving, nor pitiful nor fearful". The tragic is linked to the emotional registers of "pity and fear", and Aristotle wants to avoid the "repulsive", but Aristotle "shows no inclination to enlarge the experience of pity and fear from tragedy into anything resembling a world view".[7] Indeed, Stephen Halliwell persuasively denies that we should be "moving towards a formulation of what Ar[istotle] considered to be the essence of 'the tragic', taken as a complete vision or experience of at least one face of reality. . . . Such an expansion of the idea of tragedy has no place in the *Poetics*".[8]

Aristotle does offer in his typical style an opening and famous definition of tragedy – "the representation of an action which is serious, complete and of a certain magnitude – in language which is embellished in various forms in its different parts – in the mode of dramatic enactment, not narrative – and through the arousal of pity and fear effecting the *katharsis* [cleansing/purification] of such emotions" (6.2). But this is a formalistic definition of the dramatic form *tragoidia*: it indicates that tragedy is drama (an enactment rather than just a story-telling); that its language is heightened (by which he also means it includes song and other lyric poetry, as well as that its diction is grander than usual speech); that it takes as subject matter something which is not flippant, funny or trivial; that it causes emotional responses in an audience, and that such responses have a psychological effect (to offer as neutral as possible a version of *katharsis*, which I will not translate here).[9] Pity and fear are the primary emotions of tragedy, and this is borne out in the comments I have already cited above. It is important that Aristotle does not here mention

---

[7] Halliwell (1987) 126. His views are greatly expanded in Halliwell (1986), where the linkage in Aristotle between ethics and aesthetics is convincingly established.

[8] Halliwell (1987).

[9] See Belfiore (1992) for a good account of the difficulties of this passage. Also Halliwell (1986) 168–201.

pathos,[10] and at no point in the definition does he give any indication that his definition of tragedy is extendable from the dramatic form to a view of the world, or that a view of the world is inherent in or integral to tragic form.

Plato stretches the language of tragedy more than any other Greek writer.[11] In the *Philebus* (50b1–4) Socrates says that "pleasure and pain are mixed not just in drama but also in the whole tragedy and comedy of life". This is the first example in extant literature of the now familiar cliché of life as a tragedy (or comedy). But it is worth noting that this bold metaphor does not specify at all what the tragedy or comedy of life might consist in, beyond a mix of pleasure and pain,[12] and the language is motivated by the immediate context of the discussion of the strange mix of pleasure and pain in drama. Similarly, when the Guardians of the Republic dismiss the tragedians from the *polis*, they say "we aspire to be the makers of the best tragedy, because our whole constitution [*politeia*] is constructed as a *mimesis* of the finest and best life – which is what *we* count as the finest tragedy" (*Rep.* 7. 817b1–8). The Guardians are explicitly in competition with the tragedians, and hence they appropriate the language of tragedy – rather strangely – for their constitution. (It is strange since there appears to be no sense of suffering or misery in the perfect constitution.) This has sometimes been taken to imply that the philosophical worldview is different from the tragic world-view, though it does not progress beyond bald dismissal at this point in Plato's argument.

The long discussion of the censorship of poetry in *Republic* 10 does go on to attack Homer and tragedy for its representation of the world – as part of Plato's establishment of philosophy as a master-discourse over and against all the authoritative languages of the city. But this general case that poetry, in philosophy's austere view, is an inadequate moral representation of the world is the closest we come in ancient Greek writing to using the language of tragedy to construct an abstract view of the world, and even here what is at stake for Plato (apart from the attack on poetry's *mimesis*) is the failure of poetry to encourage a proper, philosophical self-control (*sôphrosunê*).[13] Far from introducing a privileged notion of human suffering, Plato dismisses the *pathos* of tragedy as undignified at best, and at worst as morally corrupting for indulging lazy and destructive emotionality.

Despite the long history of Platonism, a more developed sense of "the tragic" does not follow on from Plato's metaphors in later Greek, either. In fact, its dismissive, ironic usage seems the prevalent tone. Lucian – who regularly opposes the laughter of Democritus to the tears of Heraclitus[14] – describes

---

[10] On the importance of *pathos* in Plato and Aristotle on tragedy see Gould (1990).

[11] For a full discussion with bibliography see Halliwell (1996); see also Tarrant (1955).

[12] Itself a familiar notion powerfully and paradigmatically expressed in the famous scene of Priam and Achilles in *Iliad* 24 524ff.

[13] See Else (1986); Murray (1996); Asmis (1992); Ferrari (1989); Nightingale (1995) especially 60–92.

[14] See Branham (1989); Halliwell (2008) 428–70.

Peregrinus as a man who "played a tragedy the whole of his life [*etragôdei holon ton bion*], beyond Sophocles and Aeschylus".[15] This does not mean that Peregrinus had a "tragic outlook on life", but that he was a pompous charlatan who was constantly acting out a false role of self-dramatizing despair. So his appearance in the guise of a poor Cynic philosopher, with long hair, dirty cloak and stick, is described as "altogether a complete tragic get-up [*holôs mala tragikôs eskeuasto*]".[16] So, too, as he prepares to immolate himself on a pyre at the Olympic Games, Peregrinus calls on all men to play Philoctetes to his Heracles – not just to light the fire but to play out a tragic role.[17] All this is grist to Lucian's merciless and scornful satire: he laughs uproariously even at the final suicide of Peregrinus as a bit of bad tragic posturing. If Peregrinus tries to present his final act as a tragic drama, it is viewed as a risible self-delusion by Lucian. Peregrinus is also described at length as a Christian leader – it is, for Lucian, another sign of his hypocrisy and unreliability – and the Christians, Lucian tells us, despise death and go willingly into prison. Lucian, however, also dismisses any attempt to see Peregrinus' tale as a religious martyr act (though later critics have been very uncomfortable with Lucian's scorn here). Peregrinus is not to be taken at all as a (positive) example – and describing him through the language of tragedy is one way of mocking his pretensions to exemplarity.

In ancient Greek, then, you simply can't say "this event was truly tragic" in order to authorize one form of suffering over any other. From Socrates' self-deprecation to Lucian's scorn at self-delusion, "tragic" is a mark of rather overblown self-regard, a self-styling gesture rather than a world-view, even when habitual. The difference from modern usage – both the "truly tragic" and the idea of "the tragic" as a fully developed world-picture – is striking and significant.

Aristotle's *Poetics*, in short, is a theory of tragedies, not a theory of the tragic. It moves in typical Aristotelian manner from examples towards a general model, and puts the general model in a teleological and hierarchical structure, as he does elsewhere with parts of animals or constitutions of city-states. Poetry – including tragedy – is a more philosophical, a higher form than history, he writes, because it tends to focus on the general – that is, Aristotle's privileged category of *eikos*, "the likely", "the probable", "what usually occurs" – rather than the singularity of what did take place, history's realm. This remark, which turned out to stimulate later theorists immensely, allows us to connect tragedy and an idea of the general – but this is not the embracing "tragic" world-picture of the nineteenth century, nor is the category *eikos* specific or integral to tragedy. Tragedy as a form culminates in Sophocles' *Oedipus*

---

[15] Lucian *de mort. Peregr.* 3.
[16] Lucian *de mort. Peregr.* 15.
[17] Lucian *de mort. Peregr.* 33.

Tyrannus, and it declines through Aristotle's own era of the fourth century. This history remains formal: tragedy declines in its use of character and the chorus, as earlier tragedians had excelled in these aspects of the dramatic art. Aristotle throughout the *Poetics* is in debate with his master Plato, most obviously in his support for the beneficial educational value of the emotional impact of tragedy. Plato attacks tragedy because as a genre it has power over the imagination and emotions of the citizens, and thus an authority he wishes to arrogate for the new discipline of philosophy. Aristotle's refusal to see tragedy and its conflicts as a threat to the order of philosophy is perhaps the deepest level of his opposition to the Platonic project. As Aristotle defines tragedy, there is no reason to ban it from the city. Both Plato and Aristotle write as philosophers, and their views of tragedy are constructed within a philosophical system, but neither offers a coherent theory of the tragic as a world-view.

Our first preliminary conclusion, then, is to underline that the philosophical construction of a metaphysical world-picture in which the tragic has a place as a privileged form of suffering and a privileged guide to the narratives of the subject in history is not an ancient but a more recent conceptualization. "The tragic" is a modern conceit.

II

None the less Aristotle has repeatedly been taken as the father of the tragic as theoretical abstraction, and the German Idealists often write in dialogue with both Aristotle and Plato.[18] The complexity of the process by which Aristotle became such an authority after the Renaissance precludes any attempt at a full history here. Terence Cave's magisterial *Recognitions* focuses on one term from the *Poetics*, *anagnorisis*, and traces its construction in largely seventeenth- and eighteenth-century theoretical manuals, as well as in recognition scenes in drama and other literature.[19] (It also treats contemporary theoretical approaches.) To discuss the inheritance of even the less scandalous terms of Aristotle's treatise, let alone the whole thesis of the *Poetics*, would require a study of a truly monumental scale. We can note here the continuing authority of Aristotle (to whom I too will return in this chapter), but, for the purposes of the argument of this chapter, I want to move on by pointing towards two particular interrelated strands of eighteenth- and nineteenth-century thinking which will help frame my argument about the move towards generalization in discussions of the tragic.

The first of these strands concerns the huge influence of Kant and especially the aesthetics of the *Critique of Judgement*. In recent years the Third Critique

---

[18] See Gellrich (1988).
[19] Cave (1988).

has increasingly been seen as central to Kant's thinking, and Kant's aesthetics has become an intensely debated area.[20] I want here merely to note that the four basic "moments" of the Third Critique stand behind a good deal of how Greek tragedy has been thought of as an art object, and, in particular, how a response to a tragedy is formulated as a response to "the tragic". It should be clear that my concern here is not with the difficulties or precisions of Kant's argumentation, but with the diffuse and sometimes indirect (and even incoherent) influence of Kantian thinking on the criticism of Greek tragedy.[21] The intense nineteenth-century response to Kant, especially in the German-speaking world, not only redirected the discussion of tragedy and the tragic, but also had the effect of effacing earlier debates and agendas.

The principle of "disinterestedness", when it is taken to imply a separation from an interest in the good, demands not only a response to form above all, but also a rejection of a concern with the political – and, indeed, a rejection of an audience's conflicted engagement with conflicting moral debate in their response to beauty. Judgement should be "universal", and "purposive without purpose" (that is, should attempt to abstract itself from knowledge of the purpose of production), and "necessary"; and this in turn constitutes how the object of studious attention is conceptualised – at least that is how Kant was often read through the nineteenth century (although much modern criticism has worked tellingly to break down such barriers between the political, the moral and the aesthetic in Kant's thinking).[22] The sublimity of tragedy transports its readers into a disinterested contemplation of the universal, the necessary and the purposive without purpose. That is the power of "the tragic". The abstract and general concept of the tragic allows the Kantian subject to view Greek tragedy as a privileged aesthetic object.

Friedrich Schlegel, the most cited of nineteenth-century theorists of tragedy, especially by handbooks on tragedy, is exemplary in demonstrating the Kantian pull on the criticism of tragedy: "the study of Greek poetry . . . is and always will be the necessary duty . . . of all experts who want to arrive at universal judgements, and of all thinkers who seek to define once and for all the pure laws of beauty and the eternal nature of art".[23] For Schlegel, the study of Greek is the necessary duty of those who want to fulfil the Kantian ideals of aesthetic judgement. The language of duty, of universal judgements, and pure laws of beauty, echo with a fully Kantian force. Schlegel, however, historicizes Kantian theory by projecting into antiquity an idealized condition "where a disinterested

---

[20] From a huge bibliography, see Caygill (1989); Crowther (1989); Cohen and Guyer eds (1982); Allison (2001); Wenzel (2005) – each with further bibliography.

[21] A useful start on this is Pinkard (2002) especially 131–213.

[22] See the works cited in footnote 20 above.

[23] Schlegel (2001). Schlegel's *Über das Studium des Griechischen Poesie* (1795–7) was written without knowledge of Schiller's *Naïve and Sentimental Poetry*, with which it has many points of contact.

pleasure supposedly ruled": "the study of antiquity – the study of that phase of culture in which culture was characterized by disinterested pleasure – provides the historical content for aesthetic contemplation".[24] For Schlegel, the turn back to classical antiquity is an essential move – one Kant himself resists – in making Kantian aesthetics part of his literary criticism. The ideal he finds in tragedy is the ideal of a past world, recoverable by an act of imaginative criticism – and not just the contemplation of an artwork of beauty.

The lectures on Greek poetry and on aesthetics by Friedrich Schlegel and his brother August Wilhelm Schlegel had a powerful effect on Schelling, who read and discussed Kant in the 1790s with his student friends Hegel and Hölderlin. Schelling, paradigmatically, sought to define "the whole essence of tragedy", the "genuinely tragic", the innermost spirit of Greek tragedy".[25] Like Schlegel, he saw in tragedy a privileged art form in which the conflict between the freedom of the subject and external force is a fundamental dynamic.[26] Schelling demonstrates vividly how the abstract notion of tragedy produces an abstract, normative and challenging narrative of suffering: "This is the most sublime idea and the greatest victory of freedom: voluntarily to bear the punishment for an unavoidable transgression in order to manifest his freedom precisely in the loss of that very same freedom, and to perish amid a declaration of free will": this "is the innermost spirit of Greek tragedy".[27] It would take a good deal of time to tease out the complex connections between this programmatic statement and a Protestant theology of will and punishment and transgression. For both Schelling and Hegel, with regard to tragedy as with regard to their wider philosophy, their engagement with Christianity has often been underexplored[28] – but Schelling's desire to see in the form of tragedy an essential patterning of *Sittlichkeit*, of ethical action, depends on a sense of freedom and external necessity that is moulded by the revolutionary political thought that runs through German Idealism from the French Revolution through 1848 and beyond, and which is in constant tension with a principle of disinterestedness and contemplation of beauty. In response to Kant, tragedy thus becomes the site where aesthetics, politics and history are most intimately intertwined.

And for no one more than Hegel. Tragedy is "a testing ground and validation for main tenets of Hegel's historicism, for the dialectical scenario of his logic, and for the central notion of consciousness in progressive conflict".[29] For Hegel, tragedy is a route into questioning Kant, and developing his own sense of the

---

[24] Barnett (2001) 9–10.
[25] Schelling (1989) 253, 254, 258.
[26] Schelling (1989) 251. See below p176–7.
[27] Schelling (1989) 254.
[28] See Beckmann (1999) – with further bibliography.
[29] Steiner (1984) 21.

historicity of ethics and its relation to what could be called "collective" normative values, and the compulsions under which a human subject works – a
process which goes to the heart of Hegel's sense of a human self-consciousness
divided against itself, and yet in progress through this division and its transcendence. So closely interconnected are the structure of tragedy and the structure
of Hegel's thinking that critics have declared that the *Phenomenology of Spirit*
"is a tragic text"; it has "a tragic conception of truth"; its dialectic is "structurally
tragic".[30] Now, within his historicizing teleology Hegel strives to construct a
universalising view of *the* family and of *the* state as abstract and general principles, but it is through his insistence on conflict as the essence of tragedy that
Hegel's model continues to have a profound affect on contemporary criticism,
not just in the clash of systems of belief or commitments, but in the internal
conflicts of the ethical agent in historical context. For Hegel, tragedy is a door-
way to re-thinking Kant's notion of the subject.

The power of the response of German Idealism to Kant is that "tragedy and
the tragic" becomes a way of exploring central questions of human freedom,
political autonomy, self-consciousness and ethical action, which repeatedly
integrates the tragic into a philosophical regime. Generalizing about the tragic
takes tragedy from the sphere of literary genre and establishes it as a means to
comprehend the self as a political, psychological and religious subject. Tragedy
is a route to the self-definition of modernity.

Our second preliminary conclusion, then, is not simply that German Idealist readings of tragedy are framed as a response to Kant, but rather that in
responding to Kant the generalizations about tragedy which characterize nineteenth-century critical discourse are necessarily and integrally part of a systematic approach to history, religion and the aesthetic. "The tragic" takes shape
within these grand agendas and speaks to them. To open the question of "the
tragic" is to take up a position within such ideologically laden narratives.

The second strand of eighteenth- and nineteenth-century thought follows
on directly from this broad Kantianism – the criticism of tragedy in response
to Kant – and concerns Romantic Philhellenism and its particular investment
in the perfection of Greek art.[31] The tyranny of Greece over the European
imagination develops a specific rhetoric of art – a rhetoric for which Winckelmann is integral to the plastic arts, along with Lessing, and for which Hegel,
Schelling, Schlegel have a major impact on the language of literary criticism. In
all spheres of the arts, there is an extraordinary emphasis on what Ernest Renan
called "beauté eternelle, sans nulle tache locale ou nationale" ["an eternal

---

[30] Eagleton (2003) 41; de Beistegui (2000) 28; Gasché (2000) 39.
[31] See from a huge bibliography Butler (1935); Butler (1981); Webb ed (1982); Clarke ed (1989);
Ferris (2000). I have had my own go at this in Goldhill (2002).

beauty with no stain of the local or the national"].[32] Greek art and literature are repeatedly praised as being timeless (as Hofmannsthal wrote of Antigone "Dies strahlende Geschöpf ist keines Tages!" ["This glorious creature belongs to no given time!"]).[33] Greek culture speaks across the ages to contemporary artists because it is not limited by the time of its production. It is ageless. Because it is divorced from any sordid or trivial engagement with the mundane, it escapes from the accusation of being tied to the local. Because it is not marked by the disturbing politics of nationalism, it is universal. Greek art epitomizes the transcendental and the sublime, and is the standard by which modern art is judged (and judged to fall short): that is what "classic" means.

It is hard for nineteenth-century critics to escape from this framing of praise. So when Matthew Arnold suggests that "An action like the action of the Antigone of Sophocles, which turns on the conflict between the heroine's duty to her brother's corpse and that to the laws of her country, is no longer one in which it is possible that we should feel a deep interest", his worry is aimed precisely at the criticism that the local and the national will prevent an audience from profound concern.[34] George Eliot responded by re-asserting that *Antigone* encapsulates "that struggle between elemental tendencies and established laws by which the outer life of man is gradually and painfully brought into harmony with his inner needs".[35] She declares that *Antigone* speaks to the "elemental", "the life of man", an abstract and general understanding of human life that precisely transcends the local and the national. It is by virtue of its appeal to the universal and the timeless that Sophocles' play is both attacked and defended.

Yet particularly for German-speaking critics, engaged inevitably in the nineteenth century with German nationalist thinking, the universal needs to be linked to the national. There are three standard argumentative moves in such a linkage. The first is to assert the necessary and profound connection between an artist and his nationality – his race, the people, the blood of the nation. Herder provided the fundamental theory of *das Volk* for these claims: that a nation has a language of its own, a land of its own, a historical narrative of its own.[36] *Das Volk* should, in this way, be *rooted* (unlike the wandering Jew, the other to these nationalist ideals), and the artist should be the spokesman of *das Volk*. So Sophocles can – simply – be proclaimed a "*national* genius",[37] or,

---

[32] The phrase is taken from E. Renan's celebrated "Prière sur l'Acropole" (1865) first published in *Souvenirs d'enfance et de jeunesse* (Paris 1883), and many times since. This piece is beautifully discussed by Leonard (forthcoming).

[33] Hofmannsthal (1953) I. 284 [*Vorspiel zur Antigone des Sophokles* (1900)].

[34] Arnold (1853) 12.

[35] Eliot (1963) 264.

[36] See Lincoln (1999).

[37] Anthon (1853) 54, my emphasis.

at greater length, be seen as a particular voice of the nation. Here is Hölderlin's characteristic version:

> Sophocles is right. This is the fate of his time and form of his nation [*Vaterland*]. One can well idealize, for example, choose the best moment, but the national [*vaterländisch*] ways of imagining should not, at least according to their subordination, be changed by the poet who portrays the world in a reduced measure. For us such a form is suitable precisely because the infinite, like the spirit of states and of the world, cannot be grasped any other way than from an awkward point of view. The national [*vaterländisch*] forms of our poets, where such are, are however to be preferred because they are not merely there to learn to understand the spirit of the time, but to hold it fast and to feel it, when it once has been comprehended and learned.[38]

Sophocles is the epitome of the *vaterländisch*, the national spirit, a way of imagining the world from a nationalistic perspective.

The second move is to assert that German art is a privileged aim and ideal within the hierarchies of national traditions: there is a *Sonderweg*, a unique path which the German nation and its art are travelling. If German art is not yet a perfected form, such a national ideal is the teleological conclusion of the history of artistic forms. Wagner's history of opera – in which the history of the form culminates in Wagner's German art – is iconic here – including the famous dedication of the *Ring* to the German Spirit.

The third move is to assert a genealogical link between Greek art as the most perfect form of the past and German art as the promise of contemporary art.[39] Greece is for Germans, as Riehl put it, "a second homeland", so that one could feel, with Wagner, "more truly at home in ancient Athens than in any condition the modern world has to offer",[40] a sentence replete with the ideological associations of *Heim* and *Heimat*. These moves, which need not appear altogether in sequence, allow two ideas, apparently in tension with one another, to be asserted in the same breath: Greek art is privileged as the ideal and timeless model; yet a national model of art must be developed. The language of imitation, regeneration, return, inheritance – in multiple forms and combinations – recur again and again, expressing this linkage and mediation between a classical Greek past and a German promise of the future. "The tragic" in nineteenth-century German writing is deeply implicated with a nationalist historical and political teleology. "The tragic" unfolds – and this is our third preliminary conclusion – between the claims of universalizing, timeless art, and the demands

---

[38] Hölderlin (1946–85) vol 5: 272.
[39] See Lincoln (1999), Hall (1997), Gossman (1994).
[40] Riehl is cited by Gossman (1994) 11; Wagner (1911) 412.

of nationalist exceptionalism. What is more, as we will see, this continues in the most recent critical debates where the questions of whether tragedy is to be seen as a solely Western genre, and, if not, how tragedy takes shape within a post-colonial tradition, and, most specifically, how ancient Greek tragedy is appropriated and adopted in African, Eastern and other cultures, have become dominant issues in the contemporary academy.[41]

The examples of such generalizing critical diction addressed to tragedy could be multiplied dozens of times from both the intellectual leaders of the nineteenth century and from the school books and journalism of the period. What should be clear even from these very truncated and inevitably oversim-plified snapshots is that the prevalent view of the excellence of Greek tragedy (the Greek ideal) is deeply implicated with the (post-)Kantian project (German Idealism), and with a response to Kant in a turn to national, political thinking. From Kant it is argued that tragedy's timeless sublime engages the reader's sense of disinterestedness, the universal, the necessary, and the purposive without purpose. Tragedy is for contemplation (the lack of regular perfor-mances certainly helped this perspective), and how the beauty of tragedy is expressed strives to embody the ideal of aesthetic judgement expounded by Kant. In response to this drive, Hegel in particular uses tragedy, a privileged genre, to explore a different historical teleological concern, and a model of the subject – for both of which arguments conflict is central (a sense of conflict and progress linked to a political perspective of the state in its possibilities forged in reaction to the French Revolution). The difference between the nineteenth-century construction of the tragic and the Greek view of tragedy is marked. Szondi captures the contrast nicely, by way of a conclusion to this scene-setting: "seit Aristoteles gibt es eine Poetik der Tragödie, seit Schelling erst eine Philosophie der Tragischen", "after Aristotle we have a poetics of tragedy, only since Schelling a philosophy of the tragic".[42]

III

This very brief framing of the nineteenth-century construction of the idea(l) of the tragic allows us to see two different ways of answering the question of how the critical term "tragedy" is used. First, it can be an expression of literary history. In this form, the idea of Tragedy becomes a way first of all of construct-ing a link between Greek tragedy, the Latin tragedies of Seneca, the English tragedies of Shakespeare, the French tragedies of Racine and Corneille, the Spanish tragedies of Calderon, the Norwegian tragedies of Ibsen and so forth.

---

[41] A concern already in Nietzsche and Hegel who insisted tragedy is alien to the Jews: see the splen-did Leonard (forthcoming) from which I have learnt a great deal.

[42] Szondi (1961) 151. See also Lesky (1966a) 213–9.

As with any discussion of genre, this connection must recognize tacit and explicit linkages by the respective artists as well as the genealogical lines drawn by critics. Seneca translates and transforms Greek tragedy into his Stoic milieu, just as Racine and Corneille knowingly respond to both literary tradition and critical exposition of the form of tragedy in their compositions. Each of these authors works with a set of expectations formed in and by a generic history (and most would happily use the term "tragedy" on a title page). When in Seneca's *Medea* we hear *Medea fiam* "I will become Medea" [171], a threat which is fulfilled at the point of killing her children, when Medea declares *Medea sum* "I am Medea", [910], Seneca offers us a knowing glance back to Euripides: his readership knows the role model his character is fulfilling. When Shakespeare's Hamlet asks "What's Hecuba to him . . .?", his reflection on grief displayed at a fiction is a self-reflexive comment on tragic drama for which the reference to Hecuba opens a significant vista back to the Greeks. Although there are innumerable proclamations of the rules of tragedy, the way in which any particular play instantiates a generic affiliation is far more complex than a simple model of law and transgression might suggest. What is at stake in determining the boundaries of the genre of tragedy, as with any such boundary dispute, involves issues of critical authority and ideology, to which we will return shortly. It is enough for the moment to note that the term "tragedy" in this first sense acts thus as a self-conscious marker of generic affiliation. For the nineteenth century, this is a genre which is headed by Greek tragedy as the pinnacle of the form (with Shakespeare close behind, followed by Calderon: the constant search for "the modern tragedy" takes shape in the light of this genealogy). And the pinnacle of Greek tragedy for the nineteenth century, as for Aristotle, whose classical authority bolsters such a judgement, is Sophocles.

The second use of the term "tragedy", however, and the more important for the current argument, is to promote a particular view of man's place in the world and a particular understanding of the narratives of suffering and conflict. Nietzsche marks the strategic move clearly when he immediately glosses his approach to tragedy with "One of the cardinal questions here is that of the Greek attitude to pain"[43]. Such a vision aims to link tragedies not through formal qualities or self-affiliation to a genre, but through a shared sense of the order of things. Thus what links Aeschylus to Ibsen in this account is their shared expression of "the tragic" – an attitude to pain, broadly conceived. "'Tragedy' is a dramatic representation, enactment or generation of a highly specific world-view", writes George Steiner paradigmatically, a world-view which is "summarized in the adage 'It is best not to be born, next best to die young,'" which "entails the view that human life *per se*, both ontologically and

---

[43] Nietzsche (1956) 7.

existentially, is an affliction. . . . The proposition implies that men and women's presence on this earth is fundamentally absurd or unwelcome . . . that our lives are . . . a self-punishing anomaly".[44] There are, states Steiner, few tragedies that capture in full this pure and simple sense of the tragic, but that is all the more reason to turn back to them and to "be humbled by their strangeness".[45] In the nineteenth century (and beyond) the privilege of the genre of tragedy is intimately connected with the power of the tragic as a world-view. It stems from the German Idealist models, which made tragedy integral to a sense of the historical and philosophical subject, and which made tragic suffering a window onto the condition of humans, and tragic language a sublime expression of that suffering.

It is not always clear when a critic writes "tragedy" or "(the) tragic" whether it refers to the genre, to a vision of the order of things, or to both. The slide between recognizing the genre as a genealogy of modernity (modern tragedy as the heir of ancient tragedy) and declaring a tragic vision as determinative of modernity (the shared world-view of ancient and modern tragedies) is formative of many an argument about literary authority in the nineteenth century. But what concerns me here is not whether overlapping these different uses of tragedy necessarily leads to confusion. It seems clear that part of the self-affiliation to a genre could be precisely through a shared recognition of a view of man's place in the world – in the way that the genre of detective fiction, for example, repeatedly and knowingly utilizes the image of the self-marginalizing and alienated hero or heroine, in conflict with the negotiations and corruptions of society in its institutional forms (and hence so often unmarried). Rather, the question I wish to explore is how does this nineteenth-century construction of the abstract and general notion of "the tragic" affect – and distort – the critical understanding of ancient tragedy and Sophocles in particular.

There are two particular and major areas of this interaction between a general understanding of the tragic and the specific plays that I wish to consider. The first is the sphere of the political. Let us start again from Aristotle. It is striking that the *Poetics* barely mentions the *polis*,[46] despite the fact that tragedies were performed first and foremost at a festival of the *polis*, the Great Dionysia, and were funded by the *polis*. Not only were the playwrights selected and funded by the state through the process of liturgy, but there was also a fund, known as the theoric fund, which paid every citizen to attend (so that for theatre, as for jury service, and, eventually, for the assembly, no one could claim loss of income as a reason not to participate in the political event). What is more, the festival was the largest gathering of citizens in the calendar, and

---

[44] Steiner (1996) 535–6.
[45] Steiner (1996) 544.
[46] Hall (1996).

was perceived to be a stage for political celebration and display, as well as for the more challenging dramas.[47] It is in part because of the sheer scale and impact of the drama festival on the imagination of the city that Plato is so intent on banning the tragedians from his Republic. Yet Aristotle, with his focus on the individual's practical reasoning, has no time for this political framing, and when he dismisses *opsis*, spectacle, as the least important part of tragedy, he is also giving a normative direction, I would suggest, for our view of the whole festival and not just for the staging of plays.

Aristotle's silencing of the civic frame of drama may have several reasons. By the fourth century, tragedy had spread throughout Greece via repertory companies and the building of theatres in other cities.[48] Its fifth-century links to Athens and democracy had been greatly dissipated. Aristotle's major intellectual interest is in the educational benefit of tragedy for the citizen through the staged display of practical reasoning, which is not merely a rejoinder to Plato but also links his ethics and aesthetics in an integral manner. This focus on the individual is also reflected in the treatment of the chorus, which, he notes, should be "handled as one of the actors" (18.7), in the manner of Sophocles, ever the example of excellence; that is, he makes no mention of the chorus as a collective or as a different authoritative voice of the community in the drama. It has the effect of further reducing any impact of the civic frame. But Aristotle's authoritative stance has had a long-term influence on the criticism of tragedy – especially when combined with the Romantic insistence on universality and disinterestedness of aesthetic judgement.

Indeed, one immediate result of this critical movement away from civic interests is the devaluing of tragedies which do reveal most insistently a concern with a more immediate and messy sense of politics: the creation of a canon within the canon. The claim to take a broad view of the tragic has had the paradoxical effect of restricting which plays, which scenes, or even which lines, are allotted a place on the honour roll. The plays of Euripides which have the most densely focused and localized political themes – the *Phoenissae*, the *Children of Heracles*, the *Suppliants* are paradigmatic examples – rarely receive extended critical appraisal, let alone praise, in the nineteenth century (and beyond), and are very rarely staged.[49] So, too, with Aeschylus' *Persae*. Sophocles, as the apex of the tragic art, is mainly shielded from such slurs, though the strain is often clear enough. The *Antigone*, as George Steiner has shown so well, becomes treated as great precisely to the degree it can be shown to escape

---

[47] On tragedy and the city see Goldhill (1990); (2000b); Easterling ed (1997); Csapo and Slater (1995); Wilson (2000).

[48] Easterling (1997b); Taplin (1999).

[49] More recent exceptions include Zuntz (1955); Mendelsohn (2002) who notes (2) how often these plays are treated as anomalous failures within the tragic canon.

the taint of the parochialism of politics, and, as in Hegel's analysis, it can enter the abstract and general world of "the family", "the State", "the individual" – as transhistorical categories.[50] The *Philoctetes* results in some embarrassed denials of its political importance ("the play itself is the best proof that, having chosen his subject, he treated it for itself alone"), and some regrets at the "less elevated strain" of its language, concerned as it is with the wranglings of power and persuasion; but also prompts an admiring recognition of the representation of Philoctetes' heroic suffering – praise led by the aesthetic masters, Winckelmann and Lessing.[51] The debates between Teucer, Agamemnon and Menelaus in the *Ajax*, even when they are seen as dramatically and conceptually integral to the play, are also "wholly repugnant to modern taste".[52] The whole and steady gaze of Sophocles is thus set in a hierarchical contrast with the rhetorical contemporaneity of Euripides. What German idealist thinking most sought for in the tragic was most consistently found in Sophocles, and consequently his iconic status, enshrined in Aristotle, as the apex of tragic form was both proof of and proved by their critical judgement.

"The tragic", then, has been a strategic and persuasive definition which has worked to keep the most evidently and directly political of ancient tragedies from the elite of the great books tradition, and which has re-aligned the political as abstract, transcultural discussion. Even for Hegel, never less than a political thinker, who privileged *Antigone* as the greatest achievement of Western art, and who saw all of tragedy in terms of a dynamic relation between the individual's suffering, learning and ethical positioning, on the one hand, and the collectivity of the State and its knowledge, on the other; even for Hegel, who saw *Antigone* as taking shape within a particular moment in the history of spirit, within a particular moment in the development of the ethical life of a community – even for Hegel the politics of tragedy is an abstract and generalized concern.

A corollary of this is that an increased recognition of the political engagement of ancient tragedies both changes the critical definition of the canon and changes the evaluation and performance history of particular plays. So through the twentieth century, partly in response to the critical tradition of the nineteenth century, tragedy has been increasingly placed within political rather than religious frameworks, and staged explicitly to comment on political matters. It is not by chance that Jean-Pierre Vernant, whose work has been so instrumental in current critical interest in how tragedy is integrated into classical Athenian political discourse, describes his work as a reaction against German Idealist thinking.[53] Both in scholarly criticism and in the performance tradition, the

---

[50] Steiner (1984). On Hegel and Antigone and his use of familial terms see the fine discussion of Leonard (2005).

[51] Quotations from Jebb (1890) xli.

[52] Jebb (1896) xliv.

[53] Vernant and Vidal-Naquet (1981) 28–62. For this turn, see Goldhill (1986); Zeitlin (1996); Wiles (1997); Meier (1988). Many studies of particular plays or authors could be cited here.

twentieth century has seen a long, slow and fragile re-evaluation – rejection, disengagement, restatement – of the nineteenth-century construction of the tragic and its politics.

A paradigmatic and particularly striking case of this process of re-evaluation, which throws a fascinating contrastive light on Sophocles, is Aeschylus' *Oresteia*, a text Sophocles wrote through again and again. For much of the eighteenth and nineteenth centuries, the *Agamemnon* was circulated and performed separately from the other two plays of the trilogy, and it is a commonplace of criticism that the *Eumenides* is flawed as a play precisely because of its turn to Athenian politics and the all-too-sharp business of the politicised courtroom.[54] The difficulty of maintaining the universalism and disinterestedness demanded by the tragic when faced by the threat of civil strife and the frank persuasions of the political solution to the drama make it harder to see how the *Eumenides* is a fully integrated conclusion to the tensions set in place by the *Agamemnon*.[55] But in the second half of the twentieth century, the *Oresteia* as a complete trilogy has become a necessary masterpiece: in the single year 1991 there were more performances of the *Oresteia* in America alone than in the whole world between 1800 and 1865.[56]

The two different productions of this trilogy by Peter Stein in Berlin and Moscow, to take merely one celebrated example, were widely perceived to be contributing to the changing politics of Eastern Europe before and after the collapse of the Berlin Wall and the Soviet Union – and praised and evaluated precisely in such terms.[57] Similarly, Yael Farber's production of an *Oresteia*-based play, *Molora*, as a commentary on the truth and reconciliation tribunals in South Africa combined a culturally embedded African dramatic style with the authority of the classical to create a politically charged (and deeply moving) engagement with the psychological and social dynamics of revenge as a force within political change. Tragedy in the twentieth century has in this way opened itself to a broad re-politicization, and with it plays like the *Persians* of Aeschylus or Euripides' *Children of Heracles* have re-entered the repertoire as politically charged performance events. For the nineteenth century Sophocles was praised because he did not write political plays like Aeschylus' *Eumenides*, or *Persae*. In the twentieth century, *Antigone* has become a commonplace of commentary on the troubles in Northern Ireland. . . .

---

[54] With the notable exception of Karl Ottfried Müller, on whose edition of the *Eumenides* see Most (1998) with the background of the other essays in Calder and Schlesier eds (1998).

[55] Sir Hugh Lloyd-Jones epitomizes this difficulty when he states that Athene's reason for voting for Orestes – that she supports the male and has no mother – "has nothing to do with the issue being judged", Lloyd-Jones (1971) 92.

[56] These figures are taken from Amanda Wrigley's catalogue of performances usefully printed in F. Macintosh, P. Michelakis, E. Hall, and O. Taplin eds (2005).

[57] See Bierl (1999). Trubotchkin (2005) is disappointing in that it barely mentions Stein.

The question of how political tragedy is, or of how it is political, continues to be one of the most contentious issues of contemporary scholarship and theatre. The very framing of this debate betrays its origin in nineteenth-century discourse and our continuing responses to it. The canon of the tragic – and consequent attempts to move the boundaries of the canon – is an inheritance of regimes of thinking set in place by German Idealist agendas.

The second major area where it seems to me that generalizing about the tragic has had worrying consequences for appreciating ancient tragedy and Sophocles particularly, concerns generalizing itself. Here we move from the broad issue of the politics of tragedy to the question of its rhetoric. Now, it should be clear that I have certainly not been attempting to construct a teleological history whereby the modern world triumphs in critical perception over earlier generations' blindness. And it would be crass to suggest that generalizing about tragedy *per se* is a necessarily flawed project, not least because ancient tragedy loves to generalize and to generalize about its own tragic narratives. The potential for generalizing readings of tragedy has always been there. As Oliver Taplin has reminded us, ancient Athenian tragedy was almost immediately an exported genre, which spoke across national boundaries, and the plays of the fifth century became repeated and studied classics within fifty years of their first productions, and, indeed, entered the school system as classics, where they have remained ever since.[58] Tragedy was perceived to be literature to inform and form the imagination: from the beginning, "they [ancient Greeks] believed that tragedy was somehow offering them insights into the human condition".[59] Tragedy is indeed often quoted by other Greek writers as a source of wisdom and understanding – a cultural evaluation which is exploited with brilliantly self-conscious *Witz* by Philostratus in the third century CE, when he has his hero Apollonius of Tyana travel to the mysterious East to seek for the ultimate truth from the Sages of the Orient, only to find that they quote Euripides to him.

But even as it struggles with insights into the human condition, Greek tragedy itself is already highly (self-)conscious about the role of the general, the exemplary and educational – and exposes it to a probing scrutiny. As we have seen in the first five chapters of this book, fifth-century tragedies ruthlessly anatomize the rhetoric of grief, of self-understanding, of the comprehension of downfall. It is the power and subtlety of this self-awareness of rhetoric within tragedy that seems to have been occluded in the search for the tragic.

So Sophocles' *Trachiniae* begins with a generalization about the tragic nature of life – a cliché marked as such (*Trach.* 1–6):

---

[58] Taplin (1999).
[59] Taplin (1999) 55.

λόγος μὲν ἔστ᾽ ἀρχαῖος ἀνθρώπων φανεὶς
ὡς οὐκ ἂν αἰῶν᾽ ἐκμάθοις βροτῶν, πρὶν ἂν
θάνῃ τις, οὔτ᾽ εἰ χρηστὸς εἴ τῳ κακός·
ἐγὼ δὲ τὸν ἐμόν, καὶ πρὶν εἰς Ἅιδοι μολεῖν,
ἔξοιδ᾽ ἔχουσα δυστυχῆ τε καὶ βάρυν...

There is a saying among men, from of old,
That you cannot fully understand whether a human's life
Is good or bad until a person dies.
But I know fully that my life, even before I have gone to Hades,
Is ill-fortuned and grim ...

Deianeira, the wife of Heracles, quotes from Solon – "count no man happy till he is dead" – only to contradict the proverb with a recognition that she is fully aware already that her life is miserable. The irony here, typically for Sophocles, is not a presentiment of reversal – her life is miserable and will continue to be so – but rather that she thinks she knows fully how the misery of life unfurls. Knowing not quite enough, knowing too late, knowing not fully . . . that is the space of the Sophoclean subject which Deianeira does not yet recognize for herself, but that she will brutally and fatally come to see in the course of the drama. The exemplary generalization, even with its critical correction, is only an introduction which itself contributes to a tragic narrative.

The play ends with a similarly fractured and painful attempt to sum up what the exemplary tragic message has been. Heracles, agonized by the poison Deianeira has unwittingly given him, has forced his son Hyllus to swear that he will place his father on a pyre and set fire to him, and that he will then marry Iole, Heracles' concubine, who has been the passive cause of the violence that has destroyed the family. Hyllus is horrified by both charges. The final lines of the play are uniquely bitter for the closure of any ancient Greek drama (1264–77):

Υλ. αἴρετ᾽, ὀπαδοί, μεγάλην μὲν ἐμοὶ
τούτων θέμενοι συγγνωμοσύνην,   1265
μεγάλην δὲ θεῶν ἀγνωμοσύνην
εἰδότες ἔργων τῶν πρασσομένων,
οἳ φύσαντες καὶ κληζόμενοι
πατέρες τοιαῦτ᾽ ἐφορῶσι πάθη.
τὰ μὲν οὖν μέλλοντ᾽ οὐδεὶς ἐφορᾷ,   1270
τὰ δὲ νῦν ἐστῶτ᾽ οἰκτρὰ μὲν ἡμῖν,
αἰσχρὰ δ᾽ ἐκείνοις,
χαλεπώτατα δ᾽ οὖν ἀνδρῶν πάντων
τῷ τήνδ᾽ ἄτην ὑπέχοντι.   1275
Χο. λείπου μηδὲ σύ, παρθέν᾽, ἐπ᾽ οἴκων,
μεγάλους μὲν ἰδοῦσα νέους θανάτους,
πολλὰ δὲ πήματα <καὶ> καινοπαθῆ,
κοὐδὲν τούτων ὅ τι μὴ Ζεύς.

Hy. Lift him, attendants. And grant me great
Fellow-feeling for these things;
Recognize the great lack of feeling of the gods
Towards these deeds as they are being done.
They sire children; they are hailed as fathers;
They oversee sufferings like this.
No-one foresees what's to come.
But the present circumstance is mournful for us,
Shameful for them,
And actually, of all men, hardest for him
Who bears this disaster.
Ch. Maidens, you too, do not stay at the house.
You have newly seen great deaths,
And many sorrows, full of strange suffering;
And of all this, there is nothing that is not Zeus.

This ending could not be further from Ezra Pound's celebrated Sophoclean conclusion, "IT ALL COHERES". Hyllus struggles with his bitterness
to see anything whole and steady. He begs for *suggnômosunê* from the mute
and insignificant attendants. I have translated it "fellow-feeling". It implies, I
think, a sense of shared recognition, tinged with forgiveness (*suggnômê*): it
seems to be a neologism, a strange word to capture the strangeness of his
feelings and position, as the son, complicit with his mother's suicide, about
to oversee his father's immolation, and marry his cast-off concubine. He
reaches out for a form of contact that has been notably missing in the play's
interactions, where husband and wife communicate only through poisoned
gifts and curses across the divide of their separation. The term echoes jar-
ringly against the *agnômosunê*, the lack of recognition and feeling, with
which he accuses the gods of looking down at things. Both are overwhelming
(*megalê*). The gods "oversee" (*ephoran*) but no human can "foresee" (*ephoran*) the future: the same verb expresses the fundamentally different perspectives of gods and men, a different way of looking at things. The shared
vocabulary marks the dissonance between god and man, and the aspiration
of humans for the vision that is not marred by its failures and blindness. In
contrast to his mother's opening statement, for Hyllus the future is opaque,
and the present a table of horrors. This is the most outspoken and emotive
accusation of divine indifference, and unparalleled in its extremity in
Sophocles. Yet if there is a hint in these lines of the divine translation of
Heracles from the pyre to Olympus ("no one foresees what's to come",
picking up earlier possible intimations), then Hyllus' anatomy of grief is
ironically misplaced, just as he cannot know that the descendants of his
union with Iole will be one of the great clans of archaic Greece. The gods do

have Heracles in their view. Hyllus' summary of events may be as ironically flawed as his mother's.

The final four lines may be spoken by Hyllus or perhaps by the chorus. There was uncertainty already in antiquity.[60] Whoever speaks them, they are in some sort of dialogue with the previous verses. So the deaths represented in the play are described as "great" (*megalous*), as were the "fellow-feeling" Hyllus demands and the "lack of feeling" of the gods – as the violent events of the drama and the responses to them share a heroic magnitude. The *pathe*, "sufferings" (1269) of the tragedy are further glossed now as *kainopathê* "full of strange suffering" (1278). But, most memorably, the final, ringing line of the play offers a theological perspective that all has been Zeus, his will, his immanent planning, his power, at work. If this is Hyllus speaking, the claim seems less aggressive than his previous denunciation of the gods' indifference, and even if we were to agree with Budelmann that "there can be no doubt, the last line of the *Trachiniae* is accusatory", the vagueness Budelmann also notes equally opens the way for a more resigned recognition of some sort of divine order to events.[61] As Hyllus' horror at his father's final wishes sinks into resigned acceptance, so his railing at the gods' indifference slides finally into a bare acknowledgment of their power. If these last lines are spoken by the chorus – as I have printed them – then this final line can seem an ironic corrective of Hyllus' outspokenness. The chorus in their earlier consolation of Deianeira had encouraged her not to give up hope because (139–40) "Who has seen Zeus thus without care [*aboulon*] for his children?".[62] At the close, then, the irony is at least three-fold. From one perspective, their encouragement now seems shockingly undermined as Heracles struggles in the agony caused precisely by his wife's hopes: how is this scenario Zeus' care for his children? From another perspective, although the chorus cannot fully know this, the recognition of Zeus' all-embracing agency looks forward to god's plan being fulfilled precisely by Heracles' transformation, his transcendence of his current agony: god's care, precisely. From a third perspective, their grand recognition sounds discordantly against not merely Hyllus' profound disquiet, but also the play's multiple causations: *all* is Zeus? How satisfying a conclusion can the chorus provide?

---

[60] The scholia note that both attributions are possible. The debate is unending: see Finkelberg (1996); Holt (1989) and, of course, the standard commentaries. I have followed the reasoning of Easterling (1982) here in the distribution of lines.

[61] Budelmann (2000) 170.

[62] Wecklein suggested reading ἀγνώμον᾽ for ἄβουλον here, precisely, I assume, to link it with Hyllus' final lines. ἄβουλον may, with whatever irony, recall *Iliad* 1.5 – another example of the plan of Zeus which is fulfilled in tragic violence.

Trachiniae not only reveals violence, miscomprehension and failing control at the heart of human social interactions, but also shows humans to be contributing to their own unstable and self-destructive narratives precisely at the moment that they offer generalizations about the tragic nature of life. Whether it is a cliché about misery or fate, or an impassioned complaint against the world's apparent injustice and violence, this tragic language is undermined by its own insufficiency, its ironic misprisions.

The violence of the exemplary is displayed most garishly by Euripides, who provides an illuminating contrast for Sophocles in this. So in Euripides' *Electra*, the chorus explicitly and even cynically discuss the value of mythic exempla for inculcating decent behaviour, the recognition scene plays intertextual havoc with the example of Aeschylus, and Electra dismisses the idea that Orestes may have returned in disguise, because that does not conform to her paradigm of the hero. And, above all, Orestes is led into the crime of matricide by the forcefulness of Electra's commitment to a model of revenge. For Euripides, the myths of the past, the ideological and emotional lures of how to be a hero, combine with a man's weakness to enable a scene of brutal tragedy to take place. The *Electra* explores how commitment to the examples of the past and the lauding of general models of heroism become part of the inexorable, chaotic slide into disaster.[63] Self-consciousness about tragic form is part of this play's exploration of the flaws of critical judgement and the dangerous appeal of self-serving ideologically laden images of the past. The *Orestes*, the *Ion*, the *Hippolytus* – each drama plays similar snide, flamboyant and ultimately wrenching games with the lure of the exemplary. It is precisely such self-consciousness that leads to Nietzsche's declaration that Euripides represents the death of tragedy.

Classical Athenian tragedy takes up stories from the epic cycle and from Homer and rewrites them for the fifth-century theatre, to speak to a fifth-century audience. The institution of tragedy is a machine to turn epic myth into the myths of the *polis*. A dialectical relationship between the heroic past and the contemporary world is built into ancient tragedy, and, again and again, how the exemplary past functions as a model for the present is brought into a critical spotlight. The German Idealist tradition enshrined Greek tragedy as the paradigm of the tragic and of the potential of tragic drama to encapsulate the tragic. It declared it exemplary, an idealized classical past to guide the present. Perhaps inevitably, such foundational, strategic thinking found it hard to assimilate Greek tragedy's profound anxiety about the role of the exemplary, the role of the past, the insufficiency of generalizations, and the destructiveness of inheritance.

Greek tragedy searches towards the general and finds its scope in the common state of mankind. The exemplary of tragedy is to be for all, always:

---

[63] See Goldhill (1986) 245–59 for more detailed discussion and bibliography.

as the chorus of Sophocles' *Oedipus Tyrannus* sings (*OT* 1186–8), "With your example, yours, Oedipus, I count nothing of the human blessed." Yet not only were Athenian tragedies written for a particular political context, and firmly located within it, but also the plays themselves repeatedly question the value of the exemplary or explore the blurring between the general and the specific. As the body of Ajax lies on stage through the second half of Sophocles' *Ajax*, the debate is precisely whether this corpse is the corpse of a man who deserves respect as all men do, or the corpse of a violent traitor, a specific individual who deserves humiliation. Every character in an Athenian tragedy who thinks he can escape from the specific family into which he was born, discovers, like Sophocles' Oedipus or Antigone, that the curse of the family never leaves. How often are the generalizations of a chorus set in ironic or horrific tension with the action that follows on stage? How often are the moral generalizations of characters on stage revealed as the self-serving rhetoric of the politician?

Generalizing about the tragic within the framework of German Idealist thinking has had the paradoxical effect of threatening to take the sword to this complex sense within Greek tragedies themselves of the dynamic between generalization and the messy, specific, self-interested, turmoil of human activity. So Steiner, as we cited him, sums up the tragic with the adage "It is best not to be born, next best to die young" and concludes that this "proposition implies that men and women's presence on this earth is fundamentally absurd or unwelcome . . . that our lives are . . . a self-punishing anomaly". Andromache in Euripides' *Trojan Women* echoes Steiner's words, both for herself and for her sister Polyxena, recently sacrificed at the tomb of Achilles (Eur. *Tro.* 636–37): "I declare that not to be born is the same as death, and death is preferable to a bitter life". She concludes that Polyxena is better off than she is, as her sister is at least dead. "As for myself", she finishes (681–3) "I do not even have hope, the last refuge for all humans, nor do I delude myself that I will fare well. It is sweet, though, the seeming". This speech has often been criticized as inappropriate, disappointing, or largely banal. But its very numbness is essential to the drama of the scene. Shortly after it, comes the news that her son, Astyanax, will be taken from her and thrown to his death from the city walls. Andromache breaks down into one of the most moving and heartfelt scenes of desperate farewell. She had not before realised how far she was from the depths of sorrow. Even her previous recognition that she will not fare well seems now a pathetic delusion in its inadequacy. Her silent exit realises Shakespeare's "The worst is not so long as we can say 'tis the worst". The summary adage that Steiner offers is already a cliché, exposed as such in tragedy, an all too easy response which is viciously shown up as hollow by the play's unfurling horror. Her generalization about the hopelessness of her life shows merely that she has not yet grasped where she has actually invested her hope. The audience of this bitter drama may reach a range of conclusions about the nature of human life and suffering, but a recognition of the inadequacy of generalizations about the tragedy of life should be part of any such response.

The texts of ancient Athenian tragedy repeatedly explore causes of suffering, responses to suffering, misprisions about suffering, and in each of these areas general statements about the nature of human suffering become part of the rhetoric of the play, part of how tragedy happens. How the wisdom of generalizations functions is part of tragedy's questioning, which has been largely repressed in the search for "the tragic".

IV

The question remains, then: in continuing the debate about the tragic, to what degree are critics committed to the ideological frameworks in which the debate is formulated in the nineteenth century? Defining the tragic, it seems, depends not so much on aesthetic discrimination or formal literary arguments as on taking a stance about religion, politics, the self, nationalism. Eagleton is exemplary in his generalizing panache: "Tragic art is on the whole a Western affair", he writes, trying and failing to step outside the nationalist thinking of the nineteenth century in the name of a more sensitive multiculturalism, "Only Western cultures need apply".[64] So, too, he adds, it is "a mistake to believe with George Steiner that Christianity is inherently anti-tragic".[65] "Steiner makes the same mistake about Marxism".[66] "Tragedy represents . . . a spiritual experience for the metaphysically minded few".[67] And so forth. To make tragedies the locus of the tragic requires a view – a declaration, it seems – of the grandest lineaments of human self-definition within history and culture, in a way which Aristotle's *Poetics* or eighteenth-century fussing about the rules of the unities (say) eschew. That is both the lure of defining the tragic, and its danger: the lure, that it enables us to talk transculturally and transhistorically about some profound and significant literature, and a tradition of intense and serious criticism, at an engaged and serious level of abstraction; the danger, that it crushes cultural difference and literary variety and political specificity in the name of such generalization.

"'The tragic' is a central concern to anyone who wishes to come to terms with tragedy, Greek or other", writes Michael Silk.[68] I have suggested that one crucial move towards coming to terms with "the tragic" is to historicize the term, and thereby to see what the consequences are when it is applied with its

---

[64] Eagleton (2003) 71. See contra Goff and Simpson (2007); Hardwick and Gillespie (2007)
[65] Eagleton (2003) 39.
[66] Eagleton (2003) 39.
[67] Eagleton (2003) 46 – he is describing modern critical tradition "from Hegel" here.
[68] Silk (1996) 2.

full panoply of German Romantic associations to the genre of ancient Athenian tragedies, where "the tragic" as an abstract notion does not develop, for all the self-awareness of genre within the tragedies and the incipient critical tradition. The challenge for the critic remains to pay due attention to the specific socio-political context of ancient drama, while recognizing the drive towards transhistorical truth both in the plays' discourse and in the plays' reception. This double attentiveness should in turn inform each stage of the literary history of the genre – the fragmented and incremental development of the genre through social institutions of theatre, self-affiliation of writers and the strictures of critics. Here too the local, the political, and the polemical are in tension with the grandest gestures towards the long durée of the genre of tragedy. At each stage, tragedies and "the tragic" are in a productive and dialectical tension, a tension for which the idea of "the law of the tragic" and its failing/succeeding test-cases is likely to prove an unwieldy and distorting methodological model. What's more, Greek tragic texts relentlessly shine a harsh light on the platitudes and general wisdom with which its characters try to come to terms with the political turmoil and personal suffering with which they are faced. There is a message there too about the humbleness with which we might stand as critics before the tragedies of ancient theatre: before we write a sentence that begins "the tragic is . . .", "the essence of tragedy is . . .", we should recall how often ancient tragedies show up the inadequacy of such generalizations as a response to the violent narratives of human conflict.

In the chapters that follow I will try to instantiate this new agenda, an agenda that departs significantly from the tradition of thinking about tragedy and the tragic that is embodied in Szondi, Steiner and Eagleton (and many others), who have continued in full complicity with the German Idealist project in their search to define the tragic, and to reveal its dark authority in a privileged literature. The high intellectual history of German Idealist thinking will certainly play a major role in my work too. But this philosophically led discussion of the tragic will be framed by a broader cultural history, which traces how this notion of the tragic also becomes part of cultural history – in the handbook, schoolroom, university lecture; in the performance tradition, as Greek tragedy becomes staged with greater frequency and greater social impact; in the opera hall, as thinking about tragedy and drama is interlaced with the popularity and high theory of music in the nineteenth century; in the world of gender politics, as feminist theory takes on the dual patriarchal cultures of Greek tragedy and nineteenth-century German thinking. In this, my aim is not just to reveal how the language of tragedy has developed, but also to explore the potential of resisting the inheritance of its agendas. Can we as critics find a position that will both recognize the continuing influence of nineteenth-century agendas and yet write beyond them?

{ 7 }

Generalizing About the Chorus

I

It is a remarkable fact that in Terry Eagleton's book-length discussion of tragedy and the tragic, *Sweet Violence*, there is absolutely no discussion of the chorus. It is remarkable not only because in this silence Eagleton stands out against the long tradition of theorizing about tragedy from the eighteenth through the nineteenth century, an intellectual tradition in which he locates his work again and again,[1] but also because, as he himself would like to point out (*mutatis mutandis*), it is striking that a critic who throughout his book parades a maudlin love for the huddled masses, when faced by the collective voice, the collective voice, what's more, so often of a group of slaves, women or victims of violence, should have nothing to say. Yet in a way which *Sweet Violence* certainly never expresses, this silence may turn out to be a fitting culmination of an intellectual history, formed between theorizing about tragedy and opera, word and music, and between philosophical system and performance, which made the chorus a particular *problem* for the long nineteenth century. No one doubts that the chorus is integral to the classical tragedies, and, since Aristotle, the marginalization of the chorus has been taken as a sign of a falling away from the ideals of classicism – into a degenerate modernity or a necessary modernism. Yet it was in the long nineteenth century that theorizing about the chorus became essential to philosophy, to opera, and to theatre. The project of this chapter is to try to disentangle the intricate relations between the philosophical theorizing about the chorus and the increasing performance of Greek tragedy itself. Here we move on from generalizing about tragedy to generalizing

---

[1] As well as Eagleton (2003), see Eagleton (1990) for the more general argument about aesthetics.

about one crucial element of ancient tragedy – and pick up the discussion of the Sophoclean lyric voice from the first section of the book. How did the chorus become such a concern in the nineteenth century? How did answers to this concern become embodied on stage?

There are four elements of background that are essential to pursuing such a project, each of which has been discussed at lesser or greater length within a specific disciplinary formation, but which have less commonly been brought together. The first of these narratives concerns the status of tragedy within the tradition of German Idealist philosophy, to which I have already alluded in the previous chapter. There is certainly no need here to rehearse the well-known position – the tyranny – of Greece in the German imagination: as a model of perfection, an ideal, an inspiration, Greece held an extraordinarily privileged status in the German-speaking community across intellectual disciplines, political discourse, and artistic culture.[2] Greece was Germany's "second homeland"; there was a genealogical link between Germany and ancient Greece, which for Nietzsche at least, even took on a physical imperative: "we must become Greek in our *bodies*".[3] For the generation after Kant, the thinkers who had such an impact on the continuing intellectual and political life not just of Germany but of the whole of Europe – Schelling, the Schlegel brothers, and, above all, Hegel, along with the self-consciously renegade Schopenhauer and his two most passionate readers, Wagner and Nietzsche – Greek tragedy held a uniquely privileged place even within their philhellenic idealism.[4] On the one hand, tragedy stood at the apex of a hierarchy of artistic forms. As Schelling put it: "The most perfect composition of all the arts, the unification of poesy and music through song, of poesy and painting through dance, both in turn synthesized together, is the most complex theatre manifestation, such as was the drama of antiquity."[5] Tragedy surpassed, because it synthesized the national, objective, heroic voice of epic, and the personal, emotional, voice of lyric. For each of these writers, tragedy *as a form* was the supreme artwork of antiquity.

On the other hand, tragedy was integral to the *philosophical system* of each of these writers, and each lavished many pages on it as a genre. Tragedy revealed something essential about conflict within the world, and, above all, about the *Sittlichkeit*, the ethical self-positioning, of human actors within the world. As we will see, the tension between inner freedom – free will – and

---

[2] See Butler (1935); and for a selection of the modern debates, Gildenhardt and Ruehl eds (2003); Marchand (1996); Potts (1994); Morrison (1986); Schmidt (2001); Gossman (1994); Lincoln (1999); Silk and Stern (1981); Goldhill (2011) ch 4.

[3] Nietzsche (1988) vol VII 3, 413, discussed in Goldhill (2000). It is, says Nietzsche, his "hope for the German character", "meine Hoffnung für das deutsche Wesen!".

[4] The 19th-century itself and much later criticism has tended to efface its 18th-century (and earlier) predecessors: see Hamilton (2008) and on *Oedipus* Lurje (2004), and in general the exemplary Cave (1988).

[5] Schelling (1989) 280.

external necessity, between the individual as moral agent and the collective as normative, are fundamental to this debate, and it might well be said that the constant work of twentieth-century criticism of tragedy, especially in the wake of Vernant, has been an attempt to escape from or to redraft the dominant force of this German discourse. The understanding of the chorus takes place within this broad philosophical positioning.

Within this idealizing tradition, Sophocles stands at the apex, the summation and perfection of the form of tragedy (as Aristotle had already suggested). Sophocles is contrasted with the explosive, gigantic, mountainous Aeschylus, with whom he is often linked in opposition to the already corrupt and degenerate Euripides (who, for Nietzsche, heralded the death of tragedy – but it was a death long foretold in the critical discussions of early scholars). The description of Sophocles the playwright (a pious man who served the state) and the description of his poetry as calm, sublime, grand – and the other terms of Winckelmannian classicism – make Sophocles the icon of classical art (the consequences of which will be discussed in the next chapter). The chorus of Sophocles becomes thus the type of the chorus, and this is essential to understanding how so many abstract descriptions of "the chorus" seem not to fit the great works of Aeschylus or Euripides.

The second narrative background concerns the political. The debate around inner freedom and external necessity was not just an aesthetic or philosophical issue, but played directly into the political understanding and activity of the period. The era I am discussing is mapped by the fixed beacons of 1797, 1848, and 1914 (with many smaller fires, and many local topographies in between). Again, here is not the place to re-tell the history of the revolutions of the long nineteenth century, but it is worth recalling the impact of Hegel, say, on the so-called young Hegelians and on Feuerbach and Marx in particular (or, to reverse the perspective, the impact of the events of 1848 on Wagner), and the degree to which the French Revolution is a central political stimulus to German writing in this period.[6] Through these political upheavals, there is a changing sense of what community, the crowd, the collective, the voice of the people, can mean, and this dynamic inevitably affects the conceptualization of the chorus, not just by virtue of a potential politicization of its group dynamics, but also, and perhaps more stridently, by virtue of the insistent impact of ideals of the freedom of the individual on the understanding of the heroes of tragedy in relation to the chorus. How does the celebration of *das Volk* in national history relate to the chorus as the voice of the people? When we turn, say, to

---

[6] A vast bibliography could be given, starting with Engels, Gramsci, Marcuse, Althusser and so forth: starting points are McLellan (1969) (clear and direct – as is the introduction to Burns and Fraser eds (2000) 1–34), and, in more detail, Moggach ed (2006), with further bibliography; Nauen (1971); Ritter (1982); Kain (1982) (good on the Philhellenism); Beckman (1999) (good on the religious angle); Kavoulakis (2003) (for a modern Marxian approach).

Reinhardt's celebrated production of *Oedipus Tyrannus* at the beginning of the twentieth century, where the massed ranks of his chorus were perceived both as a discomforting manifestation of the "primitive", "ritual" crowd (Nietzsche here was the immediate philosophical Urtext), and as a precursor of Nazi rallies, it is important to recognize that there is a long history behind this moment, a history of how the representation of the chorus in public culture enters a domain of politics – thanks in part to its conceptualization within the German Idealist tradition and the reception of that tradition within revolutionary political thinking of the mid-century and beyond.

The third narrative concerns performance and the parallel medium of opera. The history of the performance of Greek tragedy is wholly intertwined with the history of opera.[7] Opera, repeatedly, has seen itself as the reconstruction or rediscovery of the genre of ancient tragedy: so, at the beginning, with Monteverdi; so the revolutionary opera of Gluck; so Wagner's *Gesamtkunstwerk*. Yet even this familiar point conceals a far more complex and contested story. Hegel states that nobody stages Greek tragedy today.[8] That is, despite the scattered performances of Greek tragedies lovingly collected by Hall and Macintosh (and others) before the nineteenth century, as far as the great philosopher was concerned, tragedy was an event of the imagination, and there is no indication he ever expected to see a Greek play reconstructed or performed, even in translation.[9] By the end of the nineteenth century, however, performances of Greek tragedy were significant cultural events, though not yet in the profusion that the end of the twentieth century has witnessed. One narrative, then, would recount the rediscovery of Greek tragedy as a genre for performance through the nineteenth century.

But this is not simply a teleological tale of growth towards the current day where performing Greek tragedy is part of every acting student's expectations. First, there were many attempts to re-invent Greek tragedy in a different, modern guise. Particularly important in this chapter's account is Schiller's *Bride of Messina*, a now largely unread and unperformed work, but which is explicitly discussed by Schlegel and Schelling, precisely because of its use of a chorus in a modern play.[10] Schiller indeed wrote a long prose preface to the play in which

---

[7] General accounts such as McDonald (2001); Ewans (2007) are rather unsatisfactory; more critically sophisticated, if selective, is Brown and Ograjensek eds (2010); more provocative are thematic accounts such as Hughes (2007). For more detailed snapshots, see Ewans (1982) and, better, Foster (2010); for my take, Goldhill (2002) 108–77; Goldhill (2011) chs 3 and 4, with further bibliography. Hegel remained dismissive of the potential of opera and ballet for tragedy: Paolucci and Paolucci (1962) 41–3; 43–4.

[8] Paolucci and Paolucci (1962) 33: "we no longer see them on the contemporary stage".

[9] See especially Hall and Macintosh (2005); Macintosh, Michelakis, Hall and Taplin eds (2005), and especially Flashar (1991). The eagerly awaited publication of Helene Foley's Martin lectures will revolutionize our understanding of early American performances of Greek drama.

[10] Schiller's play was translated into English by Irvine in 1837 and by Lodge in 1841 [Schiller (1841)] and by Towler in 1851; most modern publications of the play are reprints of these, especially Lodge. The play is discussed specifically with regard to Hegel by Pillau (1981), and Prader (1954) 79–91.

he discussed and defended his use of the chorus as a form, and the manner in which he handled it. Both Schlegel and Schelling thought the experiment a failure (and it never achieved the broad popularity of Goethe's *Iphigenie*). But even as a high-profile failure it set the question of the modernity of the chorus on the agenda – and it remained an issue for the self-definition of modernism throughout the century. Contemporary drama, then, was also exploring how tragedy could be made modern, as the performance of Greek tragedies themselves are beginning to be staged.

At the same time, opera itself was a battleground where modernist aesthetics and its imbrication with the classical ideal were being fiercely contested. At the end of the eighteenth century, the revolutionary operas of Gluck were lauded precisely as the recreation of the experience of music as described by the theorists of antiquity, and attending his operas was celebrated as the equivalent of being in the theatre of antiquity: "Every time I listen [to Gluck], I feel myself cast back to the days of ancient Athens, and I believe that I am sitting at productions of the tragedies of Sophocles and Euripides", as one eighteenth-century pamphleteer gushed.[11] Yet by the nineteenth century Gluck was already largely forgotten (though not by Berlioz or Wagner), and the status of opera as the experience of tragedy was aggressively challenged by the idealist philosophers as their imagination of tragedy resisted the gaudy world of the theatre. So, for Schlegel, opera was not a *Gesamtkunstwerk*, not "the perfect composition of all the arts" which Schelling sought, but an "anarchy of arts, where music, dancing, and decoration are seeking to outvie each other by the profuse display of their most dazzling charms".[12] To compare tragedy and opera "betrays an utter ignorance of the spirit of classical antiquity. Their dancing and music had nothing but the name in common with ours".[13] Yet for the young Nietzsche, it was only in Wagner's music that the full Dionysiac experience of tragedy at its best could find modern expression – a view fully endorsed by Wagner's own voluminous prose works. He dismisses opera as a trivial entertainment in comparison to his artworks, his "music theatre", where the Bayreuth Festival will act as a modern experience of the ancient festival of the Great Dionysia. One of the figures Wagner criticised with most vitriol was Mendelssohn: one of Mendelssohn's most frequently played pieces was his music for *Antigone*, which as we will see, is a turning point in the history of the performance of Greek tragedy. (Wagner, after visiting England, wrote that oratorio, as opposed to his own music, "is closely intertwined with the spirit of English Protestantism": this is fundamental to the success of Mendelssohn's

---

[11] Lesure (1984) I, 245. This, and the remainder of the comments on Gluck, are taken from Goldhill (2011) ch 3.

[12] Schlegel (1846) 64.

[13] Schlegel (1846) 64.

piece in England and to Wagner's disdain.[14]) What Mendelssohn wrote was not so much incidental music as choruses, which were most often staged in the concert hall, or in a domestic setting. Was this, then, the music of Greek tragedy? What is to count as true music theatre is as violently a self-interested and self-assertive question as what tragedy is truly tragic.

These intertwined stories of the development of opera, the development of drama – in dynamic tension with each other and in relation to an ideal of ancient theatre – and the discovery of a performance tradition for Greek tragedy, together provide an intricate matrix for understanding the changing ideas of the chorus. As I said in chapter 5, when ancient tragedies started to be staged, the chorus became a different sort of problem. The chorus of the Idealist philosophers was not easy to put on stage, and was not easy for an audience to see. The tension between the intellectual conceptualization of the chorus and its staging in performance becomes central to its reception.

The fourth background narrative brings together two elements that might seem at first sight rather surprising bedfellows. The first of these elements is the opposition of words and music, and the important place of the idea of the lyric in Romantic thinking. The second is religion. Let me try to explain why these two elements come together in an interesting way for the chorus.

The opposition of words and music as expressive media goes back a long way for sure (and there are well-known arguments within the church about the dangers of polyphonic textures making the Word of God unintelligible, a background which offers one immediate link between my two elements).[15] But the opposition of words and music has a particular place in the secular philosophizing of the era with which I am concerned. It finds a direct – even crude – articulation in the pronouncements of Leclerc, a leading figure at the centre of the French revolution. He wanted to have all music *without* words to be banned because of its potential for uncontrolled expressivity (an argument based on his reading of Plato): "A military march", he declares, "however well characterized, does not adequately determine ideas."[16] But among the idealists, music takes up an integral and significant role. Indeed, for Schopenhauer – to take the opposite pole from Leclerc – "whereas words can never move beyond the world as representation, melodic moving forms can reach into the "innermost soul" of any representation they accompany".[17] Music, that is, is transcendent, words earthbound. For Schopenhauer, music is the supreme art form, above even tragedy (which is nonetheless the greatest of art-forms beneath the purity of music, not least because it has music in it). Where Schopenhauer is close to Schelling's thinking, is in the belief that music is revelatory

---

[14] Smither (1977–2000) vol IV 262. See also Eatock (2009) especially 133–9.

[15] For a stimulating discussion of the immediate eighteenth-century precursors see Hamilton (2008).

[16] Leclerc (1796) 23.

[17] Goehr (2008). See also Dahlhaus (1989).

of inner meaning. Both Wagner and Nietzsche picked up and quoted this sentence from Schopenhauer: "The internal relation that music has to the true nature of all things can also explain the fact that, when music suitable to any scene, action, event, or environment is played, it seems to disclose to us its utmost secret meaning and appears to be the most accurate and distinct commentary on it".[18] Since – to put it in an overly simple way – the chorus has a role in Idealist thinking as the revelatory frame and as moral commentator, it is easy to see not just how the chorus' role as music becomes an insistent theoretical issue, but also how – finally – Wagner could claim that the orchestra itself takes over the role of the chorus in his music drama. How music is conceptualized deeply influences the conceptualization of the chorus. It was for Schelling a knock-down argument against Schiller's dramatic chorus that it had no music.

How, then, is this related to religion? We will see specific connections between the chorus and religion later, especially in Schelling, who states with unnerving directness that Calderon is a better tragedian than Shakespeare because Calderon wrote in a Catholic community, Shakespeare in a Protestant one. But it is fascinating to note that the more the chorus became a problem for performance, the more choral performance became a significant cultural form. That is, the nineteenth century is the great age for the oratorio[19] (and Mendelssohn's rediscovery of Bach's *St Mathew's Passion* may be a turning point here).[20] Handel's *Messiah* is an eighteenth-century composition but a nineteenth-century phenomenon. Community choirs extended beyond the church. Choral performance in the concert hall was a commonplace. Cheap editions of choral parts allowed practice at home for the enthusiastic amateur. So for some philosophers, the church in particular provided a model for thinking about the ancient chorus in a way which would have outraged Nietzsche. So Schelling writes "The only trace – and a highly distorted one at that – of the music of antiquity still resides in the *chorale.*"[21] He even goes so far as to declare "The ideal drama is the worship service, the only kind of *truly* public action that has remained for the contemporary age, and even so only in an extremely diminished and reduced form".[22] Schopenhauer, late in life, praised the Mass as a great musical form (in so far as the words did not distract from the pleasure of the music!). It is impossible to overestimate the importance of Christianity in the thinking and practice of the nineteenth century, both as a spiritual resource

---

[18] Schopenhauer (1958) I 262.

[19] See Smither (1977–2000) vol IV who draws out well the role of the oratorio in German nationalism.

[20] See Geck (1967). The historian Droysen, whom we will meet later, wrote (*Berliner Allgemeine Musikalische Zeitung* 6 (1829) 205) that the oratorio "belongs not only to art and its history, rather, as the true purpose of art can only be, to the community, to the nation [*das Volk*]".

[21] Schelling (1989) 113.

[22] Schelling (1989) 280.

and as a battleground of ideas. Greece, however ideal, was still the pagan world. Typically, Schlegel sets as a principle at the head of his lectures on the literature of antiquity, with their constant idealization of ancient Greece, "This sublime and beneficent religion [Christianity] has regenerated the ancient world from its state of exhaustion and debasement".[23] The association or disassociation of the Greek chorus from modern choral singing and its religious framework is also part of the reception of the chorus. The shock at the "primitivism" and "violence" of Reinhardt's chorus was partly because it was so different from the religious choir, a difference that was hard to negotiate with the blithe assurance of Schlegel. The success of Mendelssohn's choruses was partly because they fit so easily into the oratorio tradition.

Now, these four background narratives, which I have separated for heuristic purposes, clearly overlap in multiple ways. When Schelling writes that "A work by Sophocles possesses pure rhythm, and presents only what is necessary. It has no superfluous dimensions", he is engaged in an idealization of tragedy as a form as well as a discussion of music and expressiveness.[24] When Wagner establishes the Bayreuth festival, he is self-consciously bringing together a grand perspective on tragedy and antiquity in a modern guise, the role of music in politics, and, in the construction of the theatre as much as in his compositions themselves, a commitment to a specific idea of musical expressiveness; with *Parsifal* he ties this into a profoundly religious framework. But it is also the case that the relation between any author or production of a play and these ideas is rarely direct: that is, there is a very varied dissemination of such broad ideas, particularly in their most complex and abstruse form. For the English, figures like Coleridge at the beginning of the century and A.C. Bradley at the end were fundamental to the spread of Hegelian ideas in particular, and in the coda we will see the importance of Connop Thirlwall in this history. Schelling has never been widely read in English-speaking countries.[25] Nietzsche found a conduit into British theatre via the Cambridge Ritualists. What's more, artists have always been willing to take up snatches of arguments and ideas without any commitment to a system, and audiences bring different perspectives and different ranges of knowledge and expectation into the theatre with them. One part of the audience formation on tragedy comes through their education not just in school or university but through the circulation of handbooks and other studies of ancient literature: in these, German idealist philosophy is often circulated in a trivialized and even unrecognized form. A *bon mot* of Schlegel may

---

[23] Schlegel (1846) 24–5. See also Beckman (1999) for the complex relations between Hegel, Christianity and Hegel's followers. Steiner (1961), of course, as we saw in chapter 6, makes Christianity an integral element in the death of tragedy.

[24] Schelling (1989) 115.

[25] See Bowie (1993), for suggested reasons for this (as well as a rather particular take on Schelling's philosophy).

be cited as an authority again and again in these educational manuals: but there is rarely any discussion of him, and there is an evident slippage (as we will see) between Schlegel's analysis and his reception in the lower levels of scholarly production in particular. One of the complexities of discussing the reception of the chorus is that the aesthetic, theatrical and political discussions of the chorus have an influence on the productions that are staged, but that this influence is often highly *mediated* through routes which are hard to trace with any surety. It is important as well as funny to remember that, when Isadora Duncan proclaims that Kant's Third Critique was the inspiration of her dance in Greek dress, she may not be the most insightful or truthful guide to it, but she was apparently taken seriously by her German audience.[26]

This framework could no doubt be extended, but enough has been offered by way of background, I hope, to give an adequate context for the questions which this chapter sets out to investigate: first, how does the chorus fit into this dominant tradition of largely German thinking, and, second, how does this tradition then have an impact on theatrical life – and, indeed, go on to draw on it, as theory and practice, especially in musical theatre, enter into a dynamic relationship with each other. In exploring how the chorus became a specific problem for nineteenth-century theatre, we will see articulated the set of questions with which contemporary theatre is still struggling.

II

Now, there would no doubt be some advantage here in offering a standard doxographic approach that looked at each of the German writers in my roll-call of theorists, and analysed their philosophy of tragedy, and the place of the chorus in this philosophy, and then compared such schemata. Apart from the fact that such an approach would require a book in itself (or probably two volumes with one saved for Hegel alone), the danger of such a strategy is that the general issues of most interest are always likely to be swamped by the sheer weight and complexity of the detailed arguments, and by articulating differences between philosophical positions which often seem to be fine, even when stridently expressed. Rather, since my focus is on the reception of the chorus and how this philosophical material informs theatre, I intend to look at some of the central lines of argument, which have had the greatest impact on other writers and on the theatre.[27]

---

[26] Duncan (1968) 89, 151, discussed and contextualized in Goldhill (2002) 115–6, 147–8.

[27] Kant, despite his overwhelming presence in the general philosophical writing of all the figures who follow (see e.g. Pippin (1988) on Kant and Hegel), will play little role here, as he contributed so little to the discussion on music: see Parret (1998), who is not really contradicted by Bowie (2003) 84–90, 96–7.

Let us begin, therefore, with a set of reflections about generalization and the chorus (which continues from chapter 6's discussion of generalizing about the tragic). It is striking – though I have not seen it commented on in any of the standard discussions of the chorus – that in the many hundreds of pages about tragedy in Hegel, there are barely a dozen (generously counted) about the chorus. Schlegel, who is so often quoted on the chorus, writes only two pages on the subject in his long general discussion on tragedy, and barely a paragraph in his detailed discussion of the three tragedians and their plays. Schelling gives us two pages on the chorus in his extended systematic aesthetics, which uses tragedy again and again as an example. Even Nietzsche, who might be thought to be especially committed to the chorus as an expression of the Dionysiac is remarkably chary in the *Birth of Tragedy* with comments on the chorus itself as a form in tragedy. In each case, the chorus as form and as performance is argued to be absolutely integral to the theory of tragedy promulgated (as we will see), but the chorus is also repeatedly marginalized or ignored in discussion.

Can we hazard a reason why this is so? I would suggest, first of all and in the bluntest manner as the basis of an answer, that the overwhelming interest of these philosophers is in the individual – the individual, that is, as a moral agent, as a site of moral conflict, and as a political figure. And, as Schelling states paradigmatically, the individual is "the negation of the larger group".[28] Let us look briefly at how the individual features as the key term: again, this material has been well traced in philosophical discussion, but rarely brought to bear in any literary analysis of the genre of tragedy.[29] Schelling is exemplary of how the chorus is marginalized by the focus on the individual. For Schelling, the "innermost spirit of Greek tragedy"[30] – with all the force of the idea of "*inner*" truth that Schelling as well as Schopenhauer privileges – is located in the struggle and fate of the hero. It is in the hero that we perceive the tension between inner freedom and the external necessity that sums up why tragedy is such a powerful representation of the *Sittlichkeit* of humans. That Oedipus freely bears the punishment, which an inscrutable but necessary fate has decreed for him, constitutes him as the archetypal tragic hero. So, in lines already cited in the previous chapter: "This is the most sublime idea and the greatest victory of freedom: voluntarily to bear the punishment for an unavoidable transgression in order to manifest his freedom precisely in the loss of that very same freedom, and to perish amid a declaration of free will."[31] For Schelling, the individual hero is the *only* location of such moral sublimity:

---

[28] Schelling (1989) 69.
[29] The only discussion of this material with regard to the chorus is Silk (1998). For the basic lines of argument in the philosophy, see – from a huge bibliography – Pinkard (1994) (with Pinkard (2000) for the biographical material on Hegel); Nauen (1971); Siep (1979); Beckman (1999); Patten (1999).
[30] Schelling (1989) 254.
[31] Schelling (1989) 254 – lines also cited above in ch 5 p148.

"This is also the only genuinely *tragic* element in tragedy".[32] The hero achieves his sublime state by calmly bearing the disasters fate sends him, and it must be *necessity* and not mere bad luck or misfortune that faces him:

> The hero of tragedy, one who nonetheless calmly bears all the severity and capriciousness of fate heaped upon his head, represents for just that reason that particular *essential nature* or unconditioned and absolute in his person. . . . It is essential that the hero be victorious only through that which is not an effect of nature or chance, and hence only through inner character or disposition, as is always the case with Sophocles.[33]

Sophocles is the perfect and constant example of what Schelling seeks in tragedy. So, Shakespeare is inferior to Calderon by virtue of the fact he lives in a Protestant community. For a Catholic, sin is necessary; a Protestant is expected to struggle against temptation and even to defeat it: thus there is less inevitability in the Protestant tragic hero's fall, less of the *tragic*. So too the *deus ex machina*, the exemplary sign of arbitrary closure, is "against the essence of tragedy",[34] however many tragedies it appears in. The tension between the exercise of free will and the compulsion of necessity produces the paradox of tragic revelation and makes the hero the sole paradigmatic figure, not least by virtue of his solitude.

The chorus, for Schelling, takes up the roles of secondary, minor characters in modern plays – to set the hero in the most telling light – but does so "more idealistically, symbolically".[35] The chorus responds to the hero, but because it anticipates the spectator's own reaction, it also blocks the spectator from a free response, but rather encourages through art a higher form of reflection in the audience:

> The chorus acquired the function of anticipating what went on in the spectator, the emotional movement, the participation, the reflection, and thus in this respect, too, did not allow the spectator to be free, but rather arrested him entirely through art. To a large extent the chorus represents objectivized reflection accompanying the action.[36]

By displaying its own pain, the chorus mitigates the audience's pain, and reaches a calmer, more serene reflection of the hero's condition:

> the spectator was guided toward more serene reflection and thereby relieved, as it were, of the feeling of pain by that feeling being placed into an object and presented there as already mitigated.[37]

---

[32] Schelling (1989) 254.
[33] Schelling (1989) 89.
[34] Schelling (1989) 258.
[35] Schelling (1989) 259.
[36] Schelling (1989) 259.
[37] Schelling (1989) 260.

The chorus has roles on stage, for sure: "It counsels peace, seeks to ameliorate, laments injustice and supports the oppressed, or it reveals its participation in the misfortune through gentle compassion",[38] but the chorus is primarily *functional*. It is a device to enable the audience to reach a more serene reflection of the hero: it is a glass through which our perspective is focused. The chorus is integral to tragedy, but only in so far as it mediates the crucial relationship between the spectator and the hero. Schiller, the dramatist and theorist, in a similar way links politics, psychology and dramaturgy. Like Schelling, his general point – "Man's freedom only comes when he is able to distance himself from the world so that he is free to contemplate it"[39] – is linked directly to the functionality of the chorus: by blocking passion "the chorus restores to us our freedom".[40]

Hegel too establishes "essentially free individuality", the "self-sufficiency of the citizen",[41] at the centre of his vision of tragedy, though his idea of the individual is developed in far more complex ways than Schelling, and with a far more involved sense of what "self-consciousness" might entail for a historical subject. "The feeling accordingly of subjective self-consciousness in relation to necessity is this sense of repose which abides in the region of calm, in this freedom, which is, however, still an abstract freedom. . . . Whoever has this consciousness of independence may be indeed outwardly worsted, but he is not conquered or overcome".[42] The sense of independence and necessity is basic, for Hegel as for Schelling, to understanding the tragic hero: "Those individuals are in a special way in subjection to necessity and have a tragic interest attaching to them, who raise themselves above the ordinary moral conditions, and who seek to accomplish something special for themselves."[43] Now Hegel's views on tragedy are encoded through a vast set of arguments, which develop and change over time.[44] But it is clear that although the structure of his most basic argument is similar to Schelling's in this opposition of independence and compulsion, he takes both "internal freedom" and "external necessity" in a far more complex manner than Schelling. For Hegel, individual law and universal law provide a matrix in which freedom and compulsion are conceived, as do the normative structures of family duty and the citizenship of a state. Here, for example, as Leonard and others have discussed, gender plays a formative role in the construction of an ethical subjectivity.[45] Above all, Hegel is concerned with the move towards the established state and the ethical role of the individual as citizen. This concern provides a direct political frame for his discussion – lacking in Schelling – and leads to the

---

[38] Schelling (1989) 260.
[39] Kain (1982) 23.
[40] Schiller (1841) 13.
[41] Paolucci and Paolucci (1962) 165-7.
[42] Paolucci and Paolucci (1962) 323.
[43] Paolucci and Paolucci (1962) 323.
[44] See e.g. Schmidt (2001).
[45] Leonard (2005) 96-147.

influence of Hegel on the political movements of the middle years of the century. "The community" plays a part here absent in Schelling, not least because Hegel typically finds a dialectical relation between the community and the individual as a motive force in world history: "The community, however, can preserve itself only by suppressing this spirit of individualism; and because the latter is an essential element, the community likewise creates it as well, and creates it, too, by taking up the attitude of seeking to suppress it as a hostile principle".[46] It is against this sense of community and the heightened notion of the self-consciousness of the individual that Hegel's views on the chorus resonate.

For Hegel, the chorus has a structural role, which advances Schelling's functional model. The chorus is, first of all, as in Schelling a frame for the hero: "Just as Greek theatre itself has its external terrain, its scene, and its surroundings, so the chorus, the people, is as it were the scene of the spirit; it may be compared, in architecture, with a temple surrounding the image of the gods, for here is an environment for the heroes in action".[47] The chorus' inaction, however, functions as a "general ground"[48] for the movement of tragedy, and as such is invested with a certain knowledge, a knowledge tied to their role as "the people": "the chorus confronts us as a higher consciousness, aware of the substantial issues, warning against false conflicts, and weighing the outcomes".[49] This is not a sort of divine, perfect knowledge, but the normative, traditional voice against which the hero discovers his own destructive and creative freedom of self-consciousness. "The chorus is the actual substance of the heroic life and action itself: it is, as contrasted with the particular heroes, the common folk regarded as the fruitful soil, out of which individuals, much as flowers and towering trees from their native soil, grow and whereby they are conditioned in this life".[50] The chorus, however, despite this initial sense of a dialectic of power and knowledge between the community and the individual, appears as weak and ineffectual: "in the powerlessness of the chorus the generality finds its representative, because the common people itself compose merely the positive and passive material for the individuality and the government confronting it. Lacking the power to negate and oppose, it is unable to hold together and keep within bounds the riches and varied fullness of divine life".[51] It "produces the empty wish to tranquilize and feeble and ineffective talk intended to appease." The best the chorus can do is "helpless pity", the "empty peace of resignation".[52] This is in contrast to the heroic individual, with his "self-consciousness", "determinateness of character", "effective

---

[46] Paolucci and Paolucci (1962) 284–5. Quotations from Hegel are cited from this volume for ease of reference.

[47] Paolucci and Paolucci (1962) 66.

[48] Paolucci and Paolucci (1962) 292.

[49] Paolucci and Paolucci (1962) 65.

[50] Paolucci and Paolucci (1962) 65–6.

[51] Paolucci and Paolucci (1962) 292.

[52] Paolucci and Paolucci (1962) 293.

activity" – and all that this entails for understanding the individual as a political and, above all, ethical subject. The discussion of the chorus is wholly subordinate to a paean to the individual as a force in world history. The repeated return to Sophocles as the paradigmatic apex of tragedians – Sophocles with his focus on the individual hero committed to a form of self-assertion to the point of self-destruction – inevitably re-enforces this focus on the individual as the site of the tragic.

One consequence of both Schelling's and Hegel's generalizing about the individual and the chorus in tragedy is that it is hard to find in any of the idealist philosophers any description of any specific chorus in any particular play. There are barely any analyses either of individual odes or of the action of any chorus within a play. *A* chorus is of minimal concern, only *the* chorus deserves attention. (The play of Sophocles where the chorus is most obviously and directly in action with the characters, the *Philoctetes*, is declared "uninteresting" by Hegel, and not discussed further.[53]) The chorus emerges as an object of generalization. To discuss the "character" or the "action" of a named and particular chorus would be thus a distraction. It has become a familiar cliché in literary critical considerations of the chorus to rebut such general theories with counter-examples: the Furies in the *Eumenides* (the Bacchants in the *Bacchae*, the Sailors in the *Philoctetes*) are not an ideal spectator, a generalized voice of the people, an elevating comforter of the hero, and therefore the general theory must be insufficient at best and simply wrong at worst. I think this form of rebuttal runs the risk of ignoring the force of such generalizing models about the chorus.

Take the case of the single most quoted sentence from the tradition of German Idealists on Greek tragedy, Schlegel's apophthegm that "That is, the chorus is an ideal spectator".[54] It is a phrase which has launched a thousand essays, and many hundred sniffy comments: it is cited in handbook after handbook on tragedy, either as a simple assertion, or for simple contradiction. Yet it is far from clear to me that due attention has been paid to what Schlegel actually means by it. We should note from the outset that it begins, "That is" – in other words, the famous apophthegm is a lapidary restatement of what has preceded it. What precedes it is the assertion that the chorus represents "first the common mind of the nation, then the general sympathy of all mankind". That is, what makes the chorus an ideal spectator is first of all their rootedness in *national* thinking, and second the relation of this national thinking to a more universal *human sympathy*. The representation of general "human sympathy" is predicated on the ability of the chorus to "incorporate statements" of the poet, who speaks "as a spokesman

---

[53] "The malady of Philoctetes . . . [is] as little likely to awaken the genuine interest of a modern audience as the arrows of Heracles" Paolucci and Paolucci (1962) 33 – not Hegel's most astute judgement.

[54] Schlegel (1846) 70.

of the whole human race".[55] This grand claim alludes to the role of the poet in Romantic thinking as the authority of the sublime, the unacknowledged legislator whose language and insight speaks to and for humankind. The generalizations, which the chorus utters, are not just "the views of the poet" in that they express the happenstance opinions of an individual from Athens in the fifth century; but rather they reach towards the sublime, to touch us all, and embody the authority of the poet as seer. Behind this appeal to the universal lies a nationalism, equally of the moment in nineteenth-century culture (though Schlegel does not fully explore here the potential gap – or dynamic – between the general and the national). Schlegel is full of nationalist fervour throughout his lectures, which end with an appeal to the unity of his audience as Germans. He is assertive that there is an especial affinity of Germans to the highest art form, tragedy, because of the "peculiar character of the nation", its "German national features". There is something especially *vaterländisch* about the chorus.

What makes the chorus ideal, then, is its ability to represent something uniquely Greek (which will be especially appreciated by the German nation, its descendants). The chorus is not an ideal spectator because it watches and gets things right.[56] It is ideal because it links the *Geist* of the national character with the profundity of poetic authority. Now the relation of nationalism to dramatic form will remain a theme of this chapter as we approach Wagner's *Ring*, dedicated on its title page to the German *Geist*, as will the role of poetic authority and the ability of the chorus to speak for the author. Schlegel is not saying that the chorus simply gets things right, and serenely watches, and thereby tells us how to react. Rather, he is contributing to what he thinks an ideal engagement with art looks like, an engagement from a nationalist perspective that finds in tragedy an authoritative statement about the world. It is surely telling that when he discusses Euripides he calls his chorus an "unessential ornament"[57] (turning an Aristotelian observation about *embolima* into a more pointed critique of degeneracy), and when he discusses the chorus of the *Antigone*, he offers a critical account of their moral engagement in the action – "On a first view the chorus in *Antigone* may appear weak, acceding, as it does, at once, without opposition to the tyrannical commands of Creon" – which he then qualifies with a functional explanation of their role – "But to exhibit the determination and the deed of Antigone in their full glory, it was necessary that they should stand out quite alone, and that she should have no stay or support".[58]

---

[55] Schlegel (1846) 69–70.

[56] Typical of the handbook (mis)appropriation of Schlegel is Browne (1853) 217 – a prebendary of St Paul's and the Professor of Classical Literature at King's College, London: the chorus "often represents the reflections of a dispassionate and right-minded spectator, and inculcates the lessons of morality and resignation to the will of heaven. . . . As Schlegel says, the chorus was the spectator idealised".

[57] Schlegel (1846) 115.

[58] Schlegel (1846) 105.

In the same light, Schelling is fully aware that the Furies in the *Eumenides* do not immediately conform to his theory, but neatly declares that because this chorus has the role of an actor, here "the spectators constitute the chorus themselves". But even in this case the exception is not total, as the chorus is impartial and "always takes the side of right and of fairness". The chorus for Schlegel is a "personified reflection of the action"; as with Schelling it has the function of "elevat[ing the real spectator] to the region of contemplation".[59] It does so by virtue of its national and universal sentiment: it is this which makes it ideal, within an ideal model of tragedy. He offers an ideal chorus to explore our artistic ideals, not to describe the genre of Greek tragedy comprehensively.

Here, then, is my first conclusion: the chorus is discussed in the most lapidary form in the German idealist tradition, and is discussed primarily as an ideal form, separate from any performance and separate from any particular chorus and without reference to any particular set of choral stanzas. The focus on the individual hero as the locus of tragic conflict and ethical or political freedom repeatedly reduces the chorus to a functional role in constructing this focus. The functional role establishes the chorus primarily as a mediator between the spectators and the heroes, rather than as figures in dialogue with the heroes. Its role is to raise the spectators to a level of profound reflection. This generalised chorus will appear again and again in later discussions, both in the intellectual tradition of scholarship on tragedy and in the theatrical tradition. But because the chorus is conceptualized in such a generalized form, when it comes to the instantiations of the model in the messiness of specific performance, what the audience repeatedly recognizes is the gap between the model and what is embodied on stage. From this dynamic, the "problem of the chorus" on stage takes shape. Simply put, the more ideal the chorus is in the imagination, the less satisfying the real chorus on stage is likely to be.

III

The second and briefer area I wish to discuss concerns music and dance, media which are integral to the chorus in performance and in conception. My first section focused at one level on how the chorus becomes a problem for modernity by virtue of its collectivity: how can the community be represented? What is the value of the community's mediation of individual striving, and what wisdom is encapsulated in the reflection of the group? Is the chorus necessarily a sign of antiquity? How do modern ideas of the people relate to the ancient chorus? Music and dance form the second great problem for modernity's

---

[59] Schlegel (1946) 66.

thinking on the chorus. As productions of Greek tragedy come to be staged with more regularity, the chorus becomes the most vexing difficulty for directors and audiences alike, a difficulty not just of the conceptualization of the collective on stage but its very form of performance and voice: singing and music, or chant, or speech? Dance, rhythmic movement, or stillness? Collective singing/speaking or individual voices? How to move between choral voice and actors? How can the intimacy and personal violence of the exchanges of tragedy be played out in front of an apparently inactive group of spectators, constantly on stage? This section will end by moving towards the solutions to the performance of the chorus broached in the nineteenth century, but it is essential first to explore the intellectual context that grounds these solutions. Music itself was a major theoretical concern for German philosophy, and the chorus was one key focalization of the issue.[60] Dance, too, needed its theorization (which is why Isadora Duncan could cite Kant to an audience of German journalists): in contrast to Nietzsche's famous celebration of the dance – the dance of the body, the dance of the pen, the dance of thinking – Hegel stolidly dismisses such physicality: "The choric songs were accompanied by the dance, a procedure which can only appear frivolous to us Germans".[61] Between the sublime and the frivolous, between the irrational and the profoundly expressive, between argument and emotion, music poses a question to the discourse of philosophy – much as the physical embodiment of dance poses a question to philosophy's intellectual rigour.

Perhaps the key term, linking the theory of music, the tragic, and performance is *das Musikalisch*, "musicality", "the musical" (a term applicable to poetry and the plastic arts as much as to works for the concert hall). When Nietzsche entitled his provocative volume *The Birth of Tragedy from the Spirit of Music*, his connection of tragedy and music was not as shocking as it might seem. Not only was the assumption that tragedy developed out of Dionysiac choruses a commonplace, in line with Aristotle's authoritative history of the genre in the *Poetics*, but also German philosophy had discussed the conceptualization of music, with specific reference to ancient tragedy, for fifty years and more. Here is not the place for a full-scale treatment of the philosophy of music, an intricate and often abstract debate; rather, I want to draw attention to a single line of argument that runs through Hegel, Schelling and above all Schopenhauer, and which leads via Nietzsche and Wagner into the practice of performance with profound effect in theatre and opera-house. It is here where the connection between abstract theory and staging is especially vivid and insistent.

---

[60] See Goehr (2008) with Goehr (1998); Goehr follows Johnson (1991) closely; Dahlhaus (1989); Krausz ed (1993); Parrett (1998).

[61] Paolucci and Paolucci (1962).

It is music's power to reveal *Innerlichkeit*, "the inner", "inwardness", that fascinates the German idealists. As Lydia Goehr, who has explored these ideas most pertinently, puts it: "'musicality'" connotes some sort of pure *Innerlichkeit*, or powerful preconceptual or predeterminate expressivity, an emotional energy or drive of deep aesthetic, moral, cultural, religious or social significance".[62] So for Hegel, music's proper element "is the inner life as such . . . music's *content* is constituted by spiritual subjectivity in its immediate subjective inherent unity, the human heart, feeling as such". Now, Hegel's thinking here is tied into music's temporality, and it may be that "the inadequacy of Hegel's understanding of music is not hard to demonstrate",[63] but in his interest in *Innerlichkeit*, he picks up on Schelling's grand claim that "only an *inward*, ideal drama can unite the people".[64] For Schelling, the chorus is fundamental in this search for the inward: or rather, its musicality provides the inner, ideal face of drama. The essential role, he writes, of the ancient chorus is to draw outer attention to what is inner, within the total symbolic appearance of the artwork. Schopenhauer, however, offers the fullest account – an account that reaches a conclusion Hegel certainly would not support – which has its most long-lasting effect by enabling the separation of *das Musikalisch* from the chorus. These are the lines I have already cited, but which we can now see in a richer context:

> The internal relation that music has to the true nature of things can also explain the fact that, when music suitable to any scene, action, event, or environment is played, it seems to disclose to us its innermost secret meaning and appears to be the most accurate and distinct commentary on it.[65]

Music – by virtue of its relation to the nature – the innermost Will – of the world, has the power to reveal something otherwise concealed to the spectators. Music is the route to a transcendent insightfulness. The chorus' role as commentator and as medium for an audience to reach a new level of reflectiveness has been taken over by music itself. Schopenhauer has little time for "programmatic music" where music imitates the sound of the world.[66] Rather, music aims not at specific, particular, definite feelings but feelings "*themselves* to a certain extent in the abstract, their essential nature, without accessories, and therefore without their motives".[67] Music should escape from mere representation to

---

[62] Goehr (2008) 50: here she follows Johnson (1991).

[63] Johnson (1991) 152.

[64] Schelling (1989) 280.

[65] Schopenhauer (1958) I 262.

[66] Schopenhauer (1958) I 264: "all this [Haydn's *Creation* e.g.] is to be rejected".

[67] Schopenhauer (1958) 261; in the weakest form this was a cliché: "In the nineteenth century, the idea that feelings or affections were expressed by music 'only in their form' was a music-esthetic commonplace" Dahlhaus (1989) 72.

become the most spiritual of the arts. Indeed – most grandly – "We could just as well call the world embodied music as embodied will".[68]

I have raced through here what could be explored at far greater depth because it seems to me that, for my current argument, the importance of this line of thinking about music's revelation of inwardness is not its philosophical depth so much as its influence on both Nietzsche and Wagner, and the impact it turns out to have in the theatre itself. The specific lines of Schopenhauer I quoted above are quoted by both Nietzsche in *The Birth of Tragedy* (at far greater length: Nietzsche quotes fully three pages of Schopenhauer!)[69] and by Wagner, and the influence of Schopenhauer's writing on both men has been extensively analysed by later scholars.[70] For Nietzsche, the link between philosophy and music is fundamental, of course: "To what does this miraculous union between German philosophy and music point if not to a new mode of existence, whose precise nature we can divine only with the aid of Greek analogies?".[71] Music and philosophy have a "miraculous" interrelationship, and this must be understood both as a national phenomenon (it is true of *German* philosophy and music) and as a genealogical imperative: it needs the analogies of ancient Greece to be comprehended. And it is a harbinger of the future, of the *Zukunftsmusik* in all its cultural glory. The chorus thus for Nietzsche is crucial because in its dithyrambic form (from which tragedy comes) it embodies the "transport of the Dionysiac state with its suspension of all the ordinary barriers of existence". . ."This chasm of oblivion separates the quotidian reality from the Dionysiac".[72] The performance of the chorus requires music: "Music alone allows us to understand the delight felt at the annihilation of the individual".[73] For Nietzsche, tragedy's juxtaposition of the chorus and the actors' struggles embodies the tension between the Apollonian and Dionysiac forces – but the dialectic between them privileges the Dionysiac:

> Dionysiac art . . . forces us to gaze into the horror of individual existence, yet without being turned to stone by the vision: a metaphysical solace momentarily lifts us about the whirl of shifting phenomena.[74]

---

[68] Schopenhauer (1958) I 262–3. Compare Schlegel: "Are architecture and metre perhaps only embodied music? or are *all* arts that?": *Philosophische Lehrjahre (1796–1828)* (*Kritische Friedrich Schlegel Ausgabe* 18, Munich, Paderborn, Vienna) (1963), 244, cited and translated in Bowie (2003) 101. On Schopenhauer, see the (brisk and historically decontextualized) account of Budd (1985) 76–103: "We must now decide how much truth there is in Schopenhauer's theory of music. Unfortunately, there is very little." (96).

[69] Nietzsche (1956) 98–101.

[70] See the elegant and clear account in Silk and Stern (1981).

[71] Nietzsche (1956) 120.

[72] Nietzsche (1956) 51.

[73] Nietzsche (1956) 101.

[74] Nietzsche (1956) 102.

The chorus as Dionysiac art, that is, may seem, as in Schelling, a route for the audience to reflection. But it is a very different experience from the distance required by Schelling:

> For a brief moment we become, ourselves, the primal Being, and we experience its insatiable hunger for existence.[75]

And, however intense the feelings are which Schelling, following Aristotle, predicates of the audience through the chorus, for Nietzsche we experience a certain wild joy in Being itself:

> Pity and terror notwithstanding, we realise our great good fortune in having life – not as individuals, but as part of the life force with whose procreative lust we have become one.[76]

Nietzsche does not name Hegel at any point in the *Birth of Tragedy*, although his rejection of the theory that the chorus "represents the populace over against the noble realm of the set" has been taken as an indirect attack on him.[77] Yet it seems to me that Nietzsche's attack on the individual as the figure of Apollonian art, and on Apollo as the *principium individuationis,* constitutes a significant and pointed reversal of Hegel's view of subjectivity and history. For both writers, there is a tension between the group and the individual, yet where for Hegel the tragic is located within the individual as ethical subject, for Nietzsche the individual is to be annihilated joyously within the group. Where for Hegel the chorus is an ineffective voice of commonality to be transcended by the hero's self-consciousness, for Nietzsche it is precisely the loss of such self-consciousness that constitutes Dionysiac wisdom: "The metaphysical delight of tragedy is a translation of instinctive Dionysiac wisdom into images. The hero, the highest manifestation of the will, is destroyed, and we assent, since he too is merely a phenomenon, and the eternal life of the Will remains unaffected. Tragedy cries, 'We believe life is eternal!', and music is the direct expression of that life".[78]

Nietzsche's appropriation of Schopenhauer leads through music's transcendent expressivity to a re-valuation of the chorus as the true inwardness of the Dionysiac within tragedy. Nietzsche's provocation consists thus not in stepping outside the tradition of German thinking on tragedy but on using its resources to reverse what was – as he himself notes – becoming commonplace opinion, and thus turning the chorus from spectator to prime participant in the experience of the tragic. Nietzsche's argument has had, of course, a profound influence on drama, not just on directors and playwrights reading his

---

[75] Nietzsche (1956) 102.

[76] Nietzsche (1956) 103.

[77] Notably by Silk and Stern (1981) 68–9 [see Nietzsche (1956) 47]. Nietzsche's own final critique of *Birth of Tragedy* repudiates it actually for "smell[ing] offensively Hegelian" *Ecce Homo* ch 1.

[78] Nietzsche (1956) 102.

words, but also more indirectly, as his celebration of the Dionysiac was cross-fertilized with later anxiety about the limitations of language in contrast with the expressivity of ritual and music (the so-called *Sprachkrise* of modernism), and with the awareness of so-called primitive cult fostered by the new discipline of anthropology.[79]

Wagner also read Schopenhauer with deep attention and commitment, and from the morass of Wagner's prose, I want to extract a single extension of Schopenhauer's theories which has a particular purchase on the works I shall be considering later in this chapter. Now Wagner had a far more politically inflected view of tragedy as an event and as a genre than Schopenhauer. For Wagner, "Greek tragedy denoted the culminating point of the Greek spirit" and "the entry of the artwork of The People upon the public arena of political life".[80] Like Schelling, Schlegel and Hegel, he idealized tragedy as the supreme genre of art, and saw himself, as its inheritor, in a national and aesthetic gene-alogy. "This flower was the highest work of Art, its scent the Spirit of Greece; and it still intoxicates our senses and forces from us the avowal that it were better to be half a day a Greek in the presence of this tragic Art-work, than to all eternity an – un-Greek *God*".[81] He intended his masterpiece, *The Ring*, per-formed at the Bayreuth Festival to be such "a reflection of unified nationhood and enduring spiritual vitality". Wagner's myth of Greece grounds his myth of a German nation, and his own *Gesamtkunstwerk*, or "total work of art", is designed to be the artistic means by which such a myth could become an embodied reality. Yet the *Ring* (unlike earlier Wagnerian operas) is without the traditional operatic chorus. Wagner had written how the orchestra now had taken on the role of the chorus: it provided, as Schopenhauer demanded, the revelation of the innermost secrets of things and a commentary on the action on stage. He constructed the Festspielhaus at Bayreuth with the orchestra con-cealed beneath the level of the stage in a "mystic abyss", so that the music emerged, disembodied, as it were, pure and abstract, without the visual dis-traction of its actual means of production. Wagner's reading of Schopenhauer led to the removal of the chorus as a physical, staged presence in music drama, while yet claiming that the full force of the tensions of tragedy obtained. Wag-ner inherited a tradition that declared the operatic chorus to be the new em-bodiment of the ancient chorus of tragedy (and contested it in the same terms). He made it possible to have a chorus without a chorus.

There is a tension within Wagner's thinking, then, between the chorus as a potentially idealised form of the voice of the People, linked intimately to the

---

[79] See Stocking (1987), Detienne (1981), Zimmerman (2001).

[80] Wagner (1982–9) I 135–6.

[81] Wagner (1892–9) 1. 35. Foster (2010) is good on the repeated flower imagery in Wagner's Helle-nism.

nationalist ideals of Das Volk, and the ideal of absolute music as an expression of the true inwardness of emotion.[82] His commitment to the people, a combination of early socialism and later Herderian notions of the race, does not lead to a direct representation of the people on stage, but rather,– via perhaps an equally Herderian notion of the voice as sign of identity, a genealogy marked in the physicality of expressiveness – to an abstracted, ideal form of musical expression. The collectivity of the people becomes the collective of the orchestra.

IV

Wagner was recognized famously by Nietzsche "to sum up modernity". His music drama as a form was lauded and lambasted precisely for its novelty as a sign of the modern – aesthetically, politically, emotionally. One essential argument about the chorus is its potential as an ancient form within modern theatre: can the chorus be modern? Hegel gives a characteristically political answer: "Consequently, the chorus is peculiarly fitted to a view of life in which the obligations of State legislation and settled religious dogma do not, as yet, act as a restrictive force in ethical and social development, but where morality only exists in its primitive form of directly animated human life, and it is merely the equilibrium of unmoved life which remains assured in its stability against the fearful collisions which the antagonistic energies of individual action produces".[83] The chorus is a form suited in its collectivity to an earlier, more primitive stage in the ethical and political development of humankind. Nietzsche, by contrast, finds the return to the Dionysiac, in Wagner above all, a promise of a "new mode of existence" when "All that is now called culture, education, civilization will one day have to appear before the incorruptible judge, Dionysus".[84] Because the chorus is so fully associated with the ancient theatre, and because the re-production of ancient theatre was an arena where cultural modernism was fought out so intently, the chorus becomes a key test-case in thinking through modernity and its relation to antiquity. By the end of the nineteenth century, the question of self-conscious affiliation to modernity is inevitably raised in staging a chorus.

Schiller's *Bride of Messina* (1803) helped set the question of modernism and the chorus on the agenda, both in the preface to the play and in the drama itself, which has two half choruses, sometimes of named individual voices, supporting different households, who clash through the action as well as

---

[82] See Foster (2010) on the lyric voice in Wagner.
[83] Paolucci and Paolucci (1962) 66.
[84] Nietzsche (1956) 120.

commenting on it.[85] For Schiller, the chorus of antiquity was "in and of nature" ("sie fand ihn in der Natur"), but the modern chorus, an instrument of art ("Kunstorgan"), was a modern necessity, the barrier that kept drama from naturalism, and turned the stilled audience to reflection (in contrast to Schlegel, who found no place for the chorus in modern theatre). It was a widely discussed experiment, not least in relation to Schiller's celebrated political artistic credo that "When we gain and experience a national theatre, then we will become a Nation". For the German idealists (and Carlyle, one of the routes through which German philosophy reached a British audience, was another reviewer of the piece), Schiller was to be praised because he declared that the great value of the chorus was precisely that it defeated any realism or naturalism, and thus drew literature towards the ideal.[86] But the failure of the play as an experiment was also the standard response of critics, and Schelling dismissed it simply for its lack of music. More successful in terms of performances and reception was Mendelssohn's *Antigone* (1841), which deserves a place as a turning point in the history of the performance of Greek tragedy, and specifically in the relation between music, opera and theatrical staging.

Mendelssohn was invited by the new king of Prussia, Friedrich Wilhelm IV to Berlin: the Prussian ruler was passionate about the arts and about the classical world. He commissioned *Antigone* first for a private performance at Potsdam, and then it played in Berlin to great acclaim (and some satire), and, from there, the score travelled across Europe and America (where Edgar Allan Poe saw a disastrously under-rehearsed performance in New York and lambasted it, and all productions of ancient drama).[87] The production was directed by Ludwig Tieck, a celebrated writer, theatre maven and critic,[88] and the translation, which was metrical and followed the Greek verse forms, was undertaken by Donner, though the classicist August Böckh was consulted and his translation, which was being completed at the same time, had some impact on the final published version.[89] Tieck was already in his seventies, an old-style Romantic writer (and rather sniffed at by the younger members of the audience

---

[85] On Schiller in general see Kain (1982); on the *Bride* (and Hegel) see Pillau (1981) 155–90. The half chorus, each attached to a particular character, reflects contemporary opera, not merely Gluck but also (as Roger Savage pointed out to me) André Grétry's *Andromaque* (1779–80) with libretto by Louis Guilloume Pitra, which had four semi-choruses each attached to and supporting a lead figure.

[86] "The introduction of the chorus . . . serve[s] this end – namely to declare open and honourable warfare against Naturalism in art . . . a living wall which Tragedy had drawn around herself, to guard her from contact with the world of reality, and maintain her own ideal soil, her poetical freedom" (Schiller (1841) 7).

[87] See Seaton (2001); Steinberg (1991), and in particular the excellent Geary (2006), reprised in a new context in Geary (2010). For the European distribution see Boetius (2005) 262–79; for the English productions see Hall and Macintosh (2005) 318–50.

[88] On Tieck see Paulin (1985).

[89] See Andraschke (1997); Flashar (2001).

for it), but not only did he epitomize the "passion for the theatre" as "the symptom of a generation nurtured on feeling",[90] but he had also written influentially if not wholly coherently about music from the perspective of his Romantic concern for inwardness and, above all, feeling. As with Schlegel and Wagner, "the pursuit of national identity"[91] was integral to Tieck's thinking. He was closely connected with the Schlegels in particular, Humboldt, and Jacob Grimm. This was a production (self-consciously) from the (self-appointed) centre of the German-speaking cultural world.

Mendelssohn wrote a brief orchestral prologue (the equivalent of an operatic overture) and then settings of the *stasima* for a chorus of sixteen male voices, scored with a small orchestra including brass. He initially considered using "Greek" instrumentation (flute, harp, tuba [*aulos, kithara, salpinx*]), but found the restriction wholly debilitating: finally the addition of a harp to the orchestration is the one sign of "Greek" coloration to the scoring. He used sixteen voices because he believed, incorrectly, that the chorus of fifteen was augmented by the chorus leader. He also included recitative or melodrama: a bare musical accompaniment to the actors' voices, especially carefully marked for the transitions between *stasima* and scenes. There are also solo parts for Antigone and Creon in the *kommoi*. The chorus sings in unison, in two half choruses, and in quartets and with solo voices (in the style of the oratorios that were so popular in the nineteenth century), but the musical line is always simple and single; there are no overlapping polyphonic harmonies, no verbal repetitions (except *weh*), and no passages where the chorus and soloists sing together. Tieck, like so many Romantics, was heavily influenced by Rousseau: and Rousseau had argued that antiquity knew no harmony (that is, polyphony): "all our harmony is but a Gothic and barbarian invention".[92] The direct melodic line of Mendelssohn's *Antigone* is part of its historically self-aware classicizing.

Mendelssohn had attended Hegel's lectures as a young man; he was related to the Schlegel brothers through marriage; Tieck was a close friend of, and collaborator with, the Schlegels, too. This was a fully Romantic production – by which is meant not just that Creon appears as a more sympathetic figure than a stage tyrant, to allow some sense of Hegelian opposition of right and right, as has been argued.[93] Rather, its Romanticism is fully integral to the musical conception. Mendelssohn wrote to his friend, the historian Droysen

---

[90] Paulin (1985) 10.

[91] Paulin (1985) 132.

[92] Rousseau (1969) 242. Schlegel too followed Rousseau: see Dahlhaus (1989) 48 for discussion. This commitment to monody – and even the disparaging term "Gothic" – did not originate with Rousseau but goes back to the Camerata in sixteenth-century Italy (see e.g. Savage (2010), but for Tieck and Mendelssohn, it is most likely to have been Rousseau who was the major influence on their thinking.

[93] By Steiner (1984) 182, tempered by Hall and Macintosh (2005) 321.

(whose translations had a great impact on Wagner's Hellenism), that "the moods and the prosody are so genuinely musical throughout that one does not have to think about the individual words and only needs to compose those moods and rhythms; then the chorus is finished."[94] In this letter we can hear striking echoes of Schelling and Schopenhauer – and even Tieck himself.[95] The poetry is "echt musikalisch", and this comes via "Rhythmen". But the music is not representative, imitative: rather, the specific words are subordinated to a *Stimmung*, a voice, a mood. The music, that is, brings out the true inner meaning of the chorus. Mendelssohn's *Antigone* was perceived, and sometimes celebrated, as an attempt to recover the music of antiquity, not in an imitative manner – the orchestration makes this clear enough – but in a manner mediated through German idealist philosophy.

There were major productions of Mendelssohn's *Antigone* in Dresden, Paris and in London, where the Covent Garden show had a lasting impact on the history of the performance of Greek tragedies.[96] The chorus in this production, however, was not a great success if the snide cartoons of *Punch* are anything to go by – despite Mendelssohn's lengthy letter to the director, Sir George Macfarren, on exactly how the choruses should be staged and sung, including support for the decision to raise the number of chorus members to sixty, which greatly increased the sense of the piece as an oratorio. Fascinatingly, Mendelssohn was intent that the chorus should not appear on the stage, but "where the orchestra usually is, viz. Before the stage".[97] This, Mendelssohn notes, "enhances the effect of the voices, the distinctness of the words, and the beauty of the scenery most wonderfully", but it also separates the chorus from the actors, associates them with the orchestra, and links them as mediators for the audience: they can play a Schellingesque role far more effectively from this position, placed between the audience and the stage. The production was a success in part because it drew so clearly on familiar ideas even as it claimed its own modernity.

The score, however, was most widely re-performed by oratorio societies and amateur groups as a separate set of choruses, for which a piano score was

---

[94] Droysen (1959) 72: "die Stimmung und die Versrhytmen sind überall so echt musikalisch, daß man die einzelnen Worte nicht zu denken und nur jene Stimmungen und Rhytmen zu komponieren braucht, dann ist der Chor fertig".

[95] Dahlhaus (1989) 58–87 discusses the contribution of Tieck (and Wackenroder) to music theory in their *Fantasies on Art*.

[96] It was "received with a furore that showed how extensively Classical tastes are diffused among the educated classes in England", wrote Charles Bristed in his diary. He went to the show (with a copy of Theocritus in his pocket – self-consciously one of the "classically educated"), and also reports that "One line which drew down the house, There is no State where only one man rules, afforded a ludicrously melancholy example of popular inconsistency. The very people who cheered this sentiment had, but a few weeks before, been hooraying for His Majesty Emperor of all the Rooshas." Stray ed (2008) 216.

[97] The whole letter is in Mendelssohn Bartholdy (1872) 128–32; also quoted in full at Seaton (2001) 203–5.

published. The price of four shillings for this vocal score prices it for the extremely broad, largely middle class, domestic market, well used to piano reductions of oratorios as well as other orchestral pieces. There were also more deluxe editions like the Ewer and Co. edition of *Antigone* and *Oedipus at Colonus* at 15 shillings. It is in this form that "to most lovers of music Mendelssohn's *Antigone* is too familiar to permit any word of comment here", as Jebb put it in 1888, two generations after the Potsdam opening.[98] For classical scholars, the metrical skill of Mendelssohn's setting still had an interest, but these choruses were sung first as the music of an extremely popular composer, second as music with the cachet of an ancient Greek classicism. So in London there were editions produced for teaching purposes (*Translated in Tonic Sol-Fa Notation*), and for domestic music making (*Gems from Antigone arranged for Harp and Pianoforte*, and extracts for *Piano Forte Duet*) and, most tellingly, there were at least nine separate editions of single choruses for male voices. Indeed, by the 1880s, despite Jebb's comments, the cutting edge of self-consciously modern musical criticism had begun to despise Mendelssohn as "The Enemy".[99]

Within this context, the girls from Girton College in Cambridge decided to use the piano score of the *Antigone* for their production of Sophocles' *Electra* in 1883. For any musically minded audience members the disjunction between the associations of the familiar music and the very different plot acted in front of them must have been jarring, even if perhaps the familiar strains made some spectators feel comfortably at home with the Greekness of it all, and it no doubt helped the audience see Electra as similar to Antigone in her sense of duty and constancy to her family. But the decision of the Girton girls does indicate how far from its original conception the success of *Antigone* had drawn it. The prologue in the piano score is technically stretching but not impossibly hard for an amateur pianist; the choruses, much simpler to play, sound remarkably like chorales or hymns, which no doubt helped the easy assimilation of the piece into a domestic setting, but which today make it very hard to hear any "Greek" element in the music.[100] Indeed, to modern English ears the piano accompaniment sounds now rather too much like a grim and old-fashioned school assembly. The wide dissemination of Mendelssohn's music should not be taken as a sign of the wide dissemination of German philosophy. Yet for many in the second half of the nineteenth century, the sound of the Greek chorus evoked Mendelssohn's music: what began as an experimental and informed engagement

---

[98] Jebb (1988) xli-xlii.

[99] Shaw (1937) 251. For the shift in evaluation and its unsavoury roots, see Eatock (2009) 115–50.

[100] Geary (2010) 61 links this to Wilhelm's desire "to establish a Christian-German state". Napolitano (2010) 39 calls the music "wonderful": despite the piece showing some evidently Mendelssohnian elements, I find it rather easy to see how it has dropped out of the repertoire.

with German philhellenism eventually circulates in British culture as a thoroughly domesticated musical experience.

Indeed, the philosophical material I have been discussing disseminates in more and less marked ways throughout the theatrical milieu – and enters even the world of modernist theatre design and its theory. Probably the leading theatrical designer in the German-speaking world through the last years of the nineteenth century and into the twentieth century was Adolph Appia. He published his programmatic artistic credo in 1899 under the title *Die Musik und die Inszenierung*:[101] would any designer from the second half of the twentieth century use the word "Music" to make such a statement about his craft? Appia marks his intellectual genealogy clearly enough: he opens his work with two epigraphs, one from Schopenhauer and one from Schiller – and dedicates the volume to Houston Stewart Chamberlain, Wagner's son-in-law (and horrid racial theorist, whose most influential work, *Grundlagen des Neunzehnten Jahrhunderts* was published the same year to huge success[102]). The dedication is apt both because Appia makes Wagner's *Gesamtkunstwerk* the icon and model for his modernist theories of theatre, and because the racial comments in Appia's work are unpleasantly nasty. As one of the high priests of modernist theatre, working with Craig from England as well as European artists, he sees the accompaniment of *music* to the stage action as integral to the ideal of *staging* and sets himself thereby explicitly and justifiably in a long German tradition back through Wagner and Schopenhauer to Schiller. In this sense, Appia is, as he is so keen to assert, fully a German artist. The spirit of music is an inevitable theatrical question for nineteenth-century German theatre, even for a designer.

V

When tragedy came to be staged, then, in the nineteenth century, the chorus emerges as a problem, and perhaps could not have appeared otherwise. No production of tragedy can escape the three great questions posed by the German idealist tradition and its reception through opera: Can the chorus be modern? Can it be ideal? Can it be musical? In short, will the very staging of the chorus inevitably result in it falling short of its idealist imagining? How overdetermined is the reception of the chorus?

I will conclude this chapter, therefore, with a very brief glance at three paradigmatic productions, each of which has been very well analysed in contemporary scholarship as exemplars of the reception of Greek tragedy in

---

[101] Conveniently translated in Appia (1962).
[102] See Field (1981).

the performance tradition. In each case, I want to explore how the chorus is conceptualized in and against the agenda for choral performance dominated by the tradition of German intellectual reflections on the form of the chorus.

The first is Mounet-Sully's *Oedipus* (1888), which, Hall and Macintosh declare rather grandly, was "responsible for shaping twentieth-century definitions of self".[103] Mounet-Sully's *Oedipus* was celebrated for the performance of Mounet-Sully in the title role. Lillah McCarthy, the beautiful actress who appeared in Reinhardt's *Oedipus* in its English company and was married to its English producer Granville Barker, recalled that the production at the Comédie-Française was "cold, classical. Chorus: two women dressed in French classical style. No movement, the figures of the actors motionless, carved in marble".[104] Hall and Macintosh seem to take this as an accurate description of the production.[105] There were two young women cast (though the script seems to expect three, all young women), along with a chorus leader (male), but this was expanded with a large group of non-speaking male and female extras, who formed a human backdrop to the action. There is a small film clip still extant of Mounet-Sully playing the role (many years after it first opened) and the male *koruphaios* darts in to try to catch the stumbling Oedipus in the blind scene, only to pull back in horror, as the crowd also sways towards and away from the shocking image of Oedipus: they physically articulate his movement as a sort of mirror. The opening scene has a large group of men and women, kneeling with their backs to the audience in supplication of Oedipus who stands above them, facing out into the auditorium.[106]

McCarthy is no doubt influenced in her perception by her long association with the Reinhardt production, but she is right, it seems, from the accounts that are available, that the acting of Mounet-Sully dominated the production wholly, and that although the chorus could not be said to be "nothing", it was constructed as a backdrop to the hero's narrative: the reduction of the chorus from fifteen city elders to two young women surrounded by silent masses changes the dynamics of the drama to focus even more closely on the hero as the site of tragedy: the change of gender and age in particular works to heighten the gravity and authority of the hero's lead role. The chorus, speaking and silent, was instrumental in the spectacular nature of the drama, it seems, but not to its tragic narrative. Here, then, is a good test case for the reach of the questions of German philosophy. In a French provincial, republican festival,

---

[103] Hall and Macintosh (2005) 494.

[104] McCarthy (1933) 302.

[105] Hall and Macintosh (2005) 524. Macintosh (2009) 87–108 is more circumspect.

[106] There are spectacular photographs of the production in DuQuesnil (1901) and Janvier (1895), with verbal descriptions, which show the full chorus to good effect. The clip on line (*YouTube*) is very brief and shaky, and entitled Rare Video – French Royal's, but it shows an active and multi-gendered chorus.

how should this focus on the individual hero be appreciated? Is this not the apotheosis of the nineteenth-century fascination with the tragic hero as the site of self-consciousness and as the subject of history? When Freud and many other notables responded so strongly to Mounet-Sully's performance, was it not in part because it fulfilled so powerfully a model, a model of the individual hero that was deeply engrained through the study of Greek tragedy in school and elsewhere? Is this not an example of the instrumental chorus, aiding the audience's emotional response to the hero?

The contrast between Mounet-Sully's *Oedipus* and Reinhardt's *Oedipus* has been repeatedly made, not least since, as Hall and Macintosh note, Reinhardt's production was constructed with an eye firmly on the celebrated French show.[107] Reinhardt's chorus was huge: it invaded the audience's space; it dominated the action. As J.T. Sheppard commented: "Reinhardt's actors . . . raged and fumed and ranted, rushing hither and thither with a violence of gesticulation which, in spite of all their efforts, was eclipsed and rendered insignificant by the yet more violent rushes, screams, and contortions of a quite gratuitous crowd."[108] Reinhardt's chorus "to add to our discomfort" were directed "to utter meaningless yells and to clash strange cymbals and other instruments of brazen music. The appeal was to our senses".[109] At one level, Sheppard is recording his deep discomfort at the thoroughly un-Winckelmannian performance: this was the opposite of calm dignity, of sublime restraint, of profound simplicity. But, at another, more pointed level, Shepherd's physical distaste – matched by many reviewers – to the chorus' invasion of the audience space is because it destroyed the role of the chorus as a "living wall", in Schiller's terms, between the audience and action: it broke down the wall, it disturbed the physical calm of the spectators, it was, in this sense, thoroughly, unideal. The commitment to Nietzsche's view of the Dionysiac crowd, with an admixture of the anthropology of primitivism that followed Nietzsche, is evident in Reinhardt's staging, and evidently disturbed Sheppard as it did many of the English audience – and did so in part at least because it went against the inherited theory of the chorus from the German idealist tradition. But Sheppard also adds that he learnt from Reinhardt's production one overriding lesson: that the dynamic between chorus and actors should not be allowed thus to be overwhelmed. To "make the dialogue Romantic" instead of filled with "clear and logical simplicity" is as damaging a mistake as changing the chorus' language "full of metaphor, rich in the

---

[107] Hall and Macintosh (2005) 522.

[108] Sheppard (1920) ix. "We do not want pageantry intruding into Sophocles", sniffed the *Daily Telegraph*.

[109] Sheppard (1920) ix. Ihering (1929) 12 is nicely sardonic about such remarks: "When Reinhardt's chorus was let loose, it was unanimously reported that several maidservants screamed and went into hysterics".

direct and musical expression of emotion".[110] To destroy the relationship between the actors' dialogue and the chorus' lyrics loses Sophocles' tragic form.

Reinhardt's production reversed Mounet-Sully's emphasis on the individual, and demanded that the audience respond first and foremost to the suffering crowd – the politics of which did not go unnoticed to an audience in 1912.[111] Reinhardt called his work the theatre of 5,000, and he talked not just of bringing drama to the people, but also of creating "a festival theatre . . . in the spirit of the Greeks".[112] But its success and its scandal were so marked because it hit a moment when theories of the violent savagery of the primitive and theories of the dangerous crowd were becoming especially trendy, and when Nietzsche, in part thanks to Gilbert Murray and the Cambridge Ritualists, had become an icon for new thinking about myth and ritual. In Germany too, the so-called *Sprachkrise*, the anxiety that civilized language was an inevitable distorting representation of the world, which could be bypassed by ritual, dance, and the emotiveness of music, was central to modernism's rejection of what it saw as outmoded aesthetic models. The intellectual response to Isadora Duncan's dance, or the new music of Stravinsky, say, whose *Rite of Spring* of 1913 also brought primitive and violent ritual and primitive and violent musical rhythms to the stage, or the influence of African art on Picasso and other artists of modernism, are all testimonies of the general turn of the first decades of the twentieth century away from Hellenism's noble simplicity and quiet grandeur as ideal and as genealogical root. Reinhardt's *Oedipus* with its chorus as ritual crowd fits precisely into this milieu. The chorus is "Nietzschean" in a very general sense, but mediated through a range of other intellectual influences and art forms.

The *Electra* of Hugo von Hofmannsthal was also directed by Reinhardt, and it comes from the same period (1903) and reflects similar influences. As I have discussed at length elsewhere, this rewriting of Sophocles' play was a *succès de scandale* from the moment of its first performance, which resulted in a storm of protests against its "unGreek" nature – and especially against its ending, when Electra, in a wild ritual dance, dances herself to death. Its combination of violence – psychological and physical – disturbed emotions, and self-conscious resistance to any calmness or quietness amply fulfilled the author's aim to "let shadows emerge from the blood" – and it changed the whole

---

[110] Sheppard (1920) x.

[111] On Reinhardt, see Marx (2006) (with useful further bibliography); Braulich (1969); Styan (1982); Jacobs and Warren eds (1986); and, for contemporary responses, see e.g. Herald (1915), though Greek tragedy is discussed only 91–4; and Carter (1914), with rather unimpressive discussion of the *Oedipus* 209–22. Hostetter (2003), despite its naïve Marxism, is useful on the later development of the Großes Spielhaus.

[112] Kahane (1928) 120. The Wagnerian tone of these comments is patent.

approach to Sophocles in the twentieth century.[113] The blood of violence and the new perspective on the blood of the German Hellenic inheritance were both threatening challenges to the comfort of German Philhellenism. Hofmannsthal saw his play as a scream against Goethe's *Iphigenie*, the one German drama from the Greek to have attained classic status. His *Elektra* attacked not just the classical tradition but its most cherished German form.

Hofmannsthal dispenses with the chorus entirely. Reinhardt made the point with a brilliant modernist gesture: he began the play's first production with the overture from Gluck's *Iphigeneia*. That is, not only did he open with music which at that time summed up classicism in its most conservative guise, before the shock of Hofmannsthal's aggressively anti-classicising antiquity, but also this overture evoked a very particular model of the chorus to come. Gluck was celebrated in the eighteenth century for the way in which his music as a whole and his choruses in particular recaptured the essence of the music of antiquity, the *experience* of the music of antiquity.[114] The overture raised expectations that were drastically overturned.

The effect of removing the chorus entirely from the plot of the play is to fundamentally alter the drama. First of all, it must be remembered that after a century of discussion of the possibility of a chorus for modernity, this is a direct and stark answer: no chorus here. This is a play of psychological turmoil and conflict, where the inner lives of the figures on stage are exposed mercilessly. For Hofmannstahl "the Ancient world of Greece" is a "ghost world, pregnant with life, within us ourselves, our true, internal Orient, an open, imperishable secret".[115] Classical antiquity is a secret inside the self, awaiting decipherment, an Orient within even the anti-Eastern souls of the German-speaking audience, which functions as a sort of subconscious for modern civilization, destabilizing as it grounds. The chorus and its music acted in the dominant German intellectual tradition as a mediation between audience and actors, its music revealing the inner life of the scene, its words and music allowing the audience a space for reflection by virtue of its distancing; for Hofmannsthal, not only is Greece a violent, primitive, bloody terrain rather than an idealized past, the open secret, the other within the apparently civilized West, but also the lack of the chorus brings the audience into direct contact with this image of horror. It was this immediacy of nastiness that so provoked his first audiences.

Secondly, however, the chorus in Sophocles' *Electra* has a particular role: as we saw in chapter 5, in the opening *kommos* it has a complex relation of support

---

[113] See Goldhill (2002) 108–77. I am baffled why Braulich (1969) damns this dark, modernist production as "neu romantik".

[114] See Goldhill (2010) ch 3 for discussion of testimonia (collected in Lesure (1984) and bibliography.

[115] Hofmannsthal (1952) 135.

for the heroine, and it continues to bolster her throughout. By removing the chorus altogether, Hofmannstahl focuses our attention on the raw individuality and fragility of the heroine, as she enters the conflict with her mother and her misery and triumph of revenge, without any prop or stay of female support. With no chorus – neither a Schlegelian spectator, nor an embodiment of Hegelian community nor a Nietzschean Dionysiac group – the site of tragedy becomes an internal, psychological battle untouched by the social forms of community, uncomforted, unpitied. The chorus' absence leaves the heroine and the audience exposed.

This leads, thirdly and inevitably, to the absence of the reflective, lyric role of the chorus. In Sophocles' play, the choral *stasima* reflect on revenge, on the relation of parents and children, and try to find some generalizing discourse in which to comprehend the events unfolding around the chorus. Without these moments of lyric reflection, the unremitting intensity of the action allows the audience no space for such generalizing reflectiveness. The absence of the chorus removes a level of mythic and moralizing framework from the play, and the consequence is that once again the audience is driven towards enacting the role of the chorus, to produce its own commentary, its own emotional response, without guide, help or mitigation. When Hofmannstahl removes the chorus from his tragedy, he is not simply dispensing with an outmoded resource of ancient tragedy; he is precisely and in the most extreme manner reversing a century of thinking on the chorus. Or – with an eye on Wagner – one could say that Hofmannsthal is the *culmination* of the interaction of opera and theatre, as the rethinking of the chorus as orchestral music in opera becomes a marked *silence*, an *absence*, in the theatre.

Reinhardt is now best known for the *Oedipus*, which travelled broadly and was much discussed in the British as well as the German press.[116] But there is a strong case to be made that his production of Hofmannsthal's *Electra* is even more revolutionary. It is striking that two of the most extreme and powerfully influential expressions of the chorus – the mass, ritualized, Dionysiac crowd and the total absence of the chorus – should have been produced by the same director. Both productions had the stunning and long-lasting effect they did because they manipulated in particularly aggressive and thoroughgoing ways the expectations of the choral form developed within the German intellectual tradition. And audiences were shocked and thrilled by both productions because they so threatened the idealized image of Greece as the origin of Western and German civilization, an image nourished by that same intellectual tradition. Just as the image of the chorus was integral to the conceptualization of

---

[116] His production of *Midsummer Night's Dream* is actually more discussed and said to be more influential by contemporary sources (and some later critics): see Marx (2006); Braulich (1969); Herald (1915); Carter (1914). This should not distract from the evident impact of the *Oedipus*.

the (privileged) antiquity of Greek tragedy, so the chorus had an especially highly charged potential to proclaim the modernity of a production.

When Strauss composed his *Electra*, with a libretto by Hofmannsthal based on his own play, the question of the chorus once more was re-framed. The absence of the chorus from an opera had been long prepared by Wagner's writing and Schopenhauer's reflections on music as revelatory commentary. Yet Strauss used this tradition wonderfully in his epigonal and brilliant engagement with Wagner. I have discussed the first performance of Strauss' *Electra* in London in 1910 at great length elsewhere.[117] Here I wish just to add two small points specific to the chorus. First, when Electra enters, there are three servants, the fragmentary trace of a chorus, who sing a few disjointed lines before being dismissed. Electra then sings her first great soaring aria which begins "allein, weh ganz allein . . .", "alone, oh, quite alone". The opening scene dramatizes the removal of the chorus and the solitude of the heroine. Second, Strauss knows well both Schopenhauer's and Wagner's notion of the revelatory power of the orchestra as chorus, but he uses it also with extraordinary bitterness and irony. When Electra sings her great song about her father, the words of grief are ironically pointed and psychologically traumatized by the love music to which they are set. The revelation of inner world as a process is ironized and sexualized by Strauss' music. Hofmannstahl was vitriolically criticized in the German press for the psychologically twisted and eroticized portrait of Electra. Strauss, following Wagner's lead, disturbingly uses the music as a mirror for the deepest internal emotional life of the heroine. In this sense, through the orchestral music, he brings back the role of the chorus.

Peter Szondi's celebrated book, *An Essay on the Tragic*, like Terry Eagleton's *Sweet Violence*, does not mention the chorus, although, like Eagleton, he too sees Schelling, Hegel, Schopenhauer and the other luminaries of the German philosophical tradition as central to the defining of the tragic as a notion.[118] It may seem that their projects reflect a teleological understanding of modernity that moves through Schopenhauer to Wagner to Hofmannsthal, high priests of the modern all, whose engagement with the classical past involves the redefinition of the chorus and then, through its very musicality, its removal as a form from the tragic stage. It could be argued, too, that their search for the tragic – as outlined in the previous chapter – does not need and even resists any such concern with the generic form of any particular tragedies. But I would argue that both scholars, despite the range and impact of their analyses, are wrong to silence the chorus in this way – and for three main reasons.

First, the German idealists needed to theorize the chorus in order to construct their accounts of the theatrical experience, their concept of the community

---

[117] Goldhill (2002) 108–77.
[118] Szondi (2002) [first published in 1961].

and the importance of the individual as a historical subject, and their ideas of musicality as an expressive medium. The chorus is integral, if sometimes only briefly adumbrated, to German idealist writing about tragedy. There are costs not just to understanding this intellectual tradition but also to how tragedy can conceptualize the political and the communal, if the chorus is silenced.

Second, this tradition of thinking was hugely influential in writing about tragedy, theatre and opera across the nineteenth and twentieth centuries. Schlegel's construction of the chorus as idealized spectator finds its way into the standard handbooks on the history of literature; Hegel's influence is pervasive across a range of literary criticism, partly in his evaluation of *Antigone*, partly in his conceptualization of the clash of right and right as a model of tragic conflict, and partly in his understanding of tragedy as a revelatory form for understanding world history, the development of ideals of community and self-consciousness. Schopenhauer, who is closer to Schelling than either would care to admit, had a particular influence on thinking about music and thus the choral role as the embodiment of musicality in tragedy. From Nietzsche and Wagner, both of whom affiliate themselves to Schopenhauer, two quite different (if related) lines emerge: for Nietzsche, the chorus becomes the embodiment of the Dionysiac within tragedy, the potential loss of individuality in the group, the ecstatic experience of the life force through music (and, in modern times, Wagner's music); yet for Wagner, in his prose and more tentatively in his operas, the chorus is replaced by the orchestra, articulating a commentary, a narrative, a journey of meaning that is interwoven with the actors' voices and actions on stage. The two contrasting productions of Reinhardt, the *Oedipus* and Hofmannsthal's *Electra*, are iconic theatrical expressions of these two lines of comprehending the chorus as a form for modernity. Silencing the chorus will prevent us from appreciating the interplay of ideas of the tragic and modern theatrical and musical performance.

Third, as the example of Reinhardt underlines, it is hard to trace single lines of influence from the philosophical tradition to particular productions. Not only are theatre practitioners magpies who pick up elements of contemporary and past thought without any requirement of systematicity, and without necessarily even any direct contact with the theoretical texts themselves, but also the audiences who came to the shows brought different ranges of expectation and knowledge. Yet, as we have seen, one narrative that is essential to understanding the development of tragedy as performance in the nineteenth century is articulated by the tension between philhellenic idealism (as developed by German idealistic philosophy and nationalist claims of genealogical authority from the classical past) and the challenge to that idealism by a further self-conscious modernism (also fostered by a German-speaking intellectual tradition that would include the philosophy of Nietzsche, the psychology of Freud, and the anti-humanist anthropology of the Berlin group, for all that each has its own engagement with antiquity as a privileged model). The chorus, its presence or absence, its construction as a group or as individual voices, its relation to music and to speech, is one focalization of this self-defining tension of modernity.

This account of the conceptualization of the chorus, along with the inter-twined performance histories of opera and theatre, reveals how *overdeter-mined* the reception of the chorus is. The chorus in performance is no doubt always affected by local exigencies, financial, theatrical, intellectual; there are different national stories too, as there are different stories of nationalism. Yet the broad dissemination of strands of German intellectual understanding of the chorus, and the wide circulation of the literature and productions deeply influenced by such thinking, have transcended such contingencies to prove hugely and lastingly influential. When we look at the chorus of Greek tragedy on stage, we are always viewing it through German-tinted spectacles.

The Language of Tragedy and Modernity

HOW ELECTRA LOST HER PIETY

At some juncture, as the Victorian nineteenth century turned into the twentieth century of modernism, the figure of Sophocles' Electra changed from a sympathetic, tender, loving, constant heroine into an over-emotional, murderous, disturbed woman, violently perverted by her own hatred. In nineteenth-century Europe, schoolbooks, university lectures, scholarly criticism, and the more diffuse world of the journals and newspapers, produced a remarkably uniform view of Sophocles' heroine as a sublime and constant moral force – though there are a tiny number of telling exceptions, as we will see – and the expectations formed by such a discourse were fulfilled and supported by the few performances of the play both in the professional theatre and at schools and universities. In the years before the First World War, however, the Reinhardt production of Hofmannsthal's *Elektra* and then Strauss' opera produced a shocking, new figure of a dangerously unhinged Elektra, dancing herself to death in bloody ecstasy, a figure that now haunts the critical expectations of Sophocles' tragedy. The heroically suffering girl emerged as a blood-stained hysteric.

The challenge of this image provoked an intense reaction in audiences and commentators, and prompted critical attacks, still sporadically in evidence, on the grounds that such a portrayal of Electra desperately misrepresents Sophocles, and misunderstands Greek tragedy. But it is striking that within the performance tradition there has been no turning back. Celebrated stagings of the opera and the play have extended the portrayal of Electra as an exploration of the distorting effects of the passion for revenge, and actors' accounts of the disturbing power of playing the role have added to the lustre of this view of the tragic heroine. In the theatre, sublime, moral purity has been thin on the ground. Reinhardt, Strauss and Hofmannsthal were each influenced by the master disciplines of modernism – psychology, anthropology, linguistics, dance as an expression of physicality – but it is their performances which have had a profound effect on the literary criticism of tragedy: the language of tragedy has changed, and changed in reaction to what happened on stage in the theatre, as much as in reaction to the broader shifts of culture over the century. It has now become a commonplace in the scholarly work on *Electra* to note that there are two interpretative lines on the play, one dark, disturbing, morally unsettling, the other, optimistic, morally assertive, Homeric. This cliché is usually followed by the critic declaring an affiliation to one of the two critical positions and arguing for it vociferously: so, to start things off, paradigmatically the play opens either in "a mood of destructive violence" or in "a bright dawn, loud with optimistic birdsong".[1] Sophocles' *Electra* has become the play where the fissures of the critical language of tragedy are most evident and most insistently debated.

This chapter sets out to explore how this change in the language of tragedy took place, and what its implications are for understanding the genre. How did the sunny and the sublime become the dark and the disturbing, the "bright dawn" turn to "destructive violence"? I will look first at how the general expectations of *Electra* were formed through the nineteenth century – looking at a very broad range of writing from the schoolroom to the university to the theatre to the newspapers; I will then explore how this consensus was challenged, and the impact of this on contemporary critical approaches. After looking in the previous two chapters at how tragedy itself and the chorus as an integral element of ancient tragedy were part of a generalizing discourse about suffering, the self, music, collectivity and the individual and so forth, it is time to look at how a single Sophoclean play was read – how its comprehension is formed within such a language of tragedy. Finally, as in chapter 1 and, indeed, in the book as a whole, I will try to show how what appears as a simple structure – before and after, light to dark – turns out to be rather more complicated and in need of some greater nuance. The deliberately vague phrase with which I started this chapter – "at some juncture" – will turn out to be pregnant with a complex historical narrative.

I

This story begins *in medias res* with a minor but archetypal hero of nineteenth-century education, Arthur Gilkes, whose life (1849–1922) stretches across precisely the years with which I am most concerned.[2] Gilkes, the son of a chemist, was educated at Shrewsbury School. He went on to take a double first in classics at Oxford. He returned immediately to Shrewsbury School where he worked as a teacher between 1873 and 1885, rising to Assistant Master. He then became headmaster of Dulwich College, a school in south London,

---

[1] Gellie (1972) 107; Leinieks (1982) 115.

[2] For Gilkes's life see Leake (1938) which is rather too interested in sports results.

which he built up into a celebrated public school, particularly well known for its forward-looking emphasis on science teaching, though Gilkes himself publicly supported the privileged place of classics during the heated controversy about the national curriculum at the end of the century. After his retirement, he was ordained and acted as a vicar in Oxford from 1917. This stellar career captures a good deal of the idealism of Victorian education – a middle-class boy who progresses through hard work and scholarship to a good Oxford degree; returning to the school where he was taught to teach in his turn, faithfully embodying the claims of the school tradition and of social duty; rising to become a pioneering headmaster in the Thomas Arnold tradition, instilling high-minded ideals of scholarship and public service, and transforming a very old traditional school (Dulwich was founded in 1619) into a modern institution (the college became an independent senior school only in 1882, when the foundation was contentiously split by the Charity Commissioners). He also founded the College Mission in the poorest area of Camberwell, and his ordination only confirmed the long and deep-seated connection between his religion and his life's work – between church and school as institutions of instruction. His earnestness is encapsulated in getting his pupils to work in the mission to help the poor of London through religious and social support, an unusual social programme among schoolteachers, though colleges at Oxford and Cambridge supported such missions. Like F.W. Farrar, churchman and schoolteacher, or Thomas Hughes with his celebrated *Tom Brown's Schooldays*, Gilkes also wrote novels embodying his educational agenda. Gilkes's career finds easy parallels in the biographies of many other great teachers – F.W. Farrar at Wellington, Edwin Abbott Abbott at City of London, say – and his combination of religious, educational and institutional commitment, encapsulates nineteenth-century principles.[3]

Gilkes wrote and published *School Lectures on the Electra of Sophocles and Macbeth* in 1880, while teaching at Shrewsbury. As a set of school lectures, it is an especially clear guide to what one might expect to be said about the play, a summation of the critical views thought suitable for young men to absorb. Gilkes clearly knew his way round the German tradition I discussed in the last chapter, probably by reading August Schlegel (whose lectures had been translated as early as 1815 and reprinted many times), perhaps indirectly from university days. So, he tells his pupils, the chorus' "office is the same always, namely, to direct the minds of the spectators to the thoughts which are most proper to each situation", the chorus "constantly, as the action proceeds, passes upon it the judgment that would suggest itself to the highest human authority, to the educated man" – he even sees the chorus, more daringly, in the modern

---

[3] "Gilkes was in most way[s] a Victorian, a Victorian of the best type" Leake (1938) 229. Koven (2004) is a good introduction to Victorian work in the East End; see Stray (1998) on the educational background; and Goldhill (2011) on Farrar.

world as "an orchestral accompaniment".[4] Edmund Morshead, the assistant master at Winchester, in his school edition of Sophocles takes much the same line, with the added regret that if only they could act – with the vigour of an English schoolboy – the chorus would not be so reflective: "the chorus is . . . an 'ideal spectator' . . . their words represent . . . the unuttered thoughts which would pass through our minds at a crisis, if our hands were tied."[5] A plucky English lad, given a free hand, would not faff like the chorus of the *Agamemnon* or stand with eyes averted like the chorus of the *Medea*.

Gilkes's views of Electra herself, however, come from the very centre of Victorian thinking. "She is possessed of a genuine politeness of the heart", he writes – a fascinating phrase that links inward emotional life to external form through the ideal of "politeness", a notion that, as ever, goes beyond etiquette in Victorian social life towards a fuller sense of socially embedded propriety, a real sense of selfhood and morality.[6] This hint that Electra lives up to Victorian social values continues: "Electra also had a tasteful liking for all the appurtenances of life and person, that make the delight of a woman's life. . . . She appreciated fine dresses, golden ornaments, soft living, and the beauties of her person. . . ."[7] The normative force of "tasteful", as well as the more obviously slanted expectations of female ambition, underlines the judgemental basis of his description of Electra as a woman. The boys who were taught by Gilkes certainly picked up the lesson. One remembered how "He could turn a Greek drama into a living thing without any fuss or antics, just by making us realise how vivid the characters were"; another, who went on himself to be a headmaster, caught the moral emphasis more precisely: "I remember too the contrast he drew between the two sisters: Electra, with her unselfish devotion to what she believed to be her duty, and her pleasure-loving sister, who made a compromise with her father's murderess."[8] Gilkes hated selfishness almost as much as conceit: like Evelyn Abbott, he admired Electra precisely for her "abnegation of self" in the cause of her dead father.[9] Indeed, despite her own evaluation of her actions, for Gilkes Electra "has no sins", and the sympathy of

---

[4] Gilkes (1880) 39–40, 40, 42.

[5] Morshead (1895) 7, 8.

[6] Gilkes (1880) 18. He is probably thinking of Goethe in *Elective Affinities* ch 5: "There is a courtesy of the heart; it is akin to love. From it springs the purest courtesy of outward behaviour." And – making the point I have been emphasizing – "There is no outward sign of courtesy that does not rest on a deep moral foundation". Gilkes was very fond of the phrase: in his best novel [Gilkes 1894] the working class hero declares: "Good manners must spring from a heart of courtesy; but these manners you teach are manners which are good on the outside only and cover a barbarous heart" (249). In Gilkes (1905) 3, a lightly fictional account of a day at Dulwich School, he disdains "a varnish of politeness, but often somewhat rotten at heart".

[7] Gilkes (1880) 18.

[8] Leake (1938) 230; 101 (F. Griffin, headmaster of Birkenhead School).

[9] Abbott ed (1880) 40. So, too, "Victorian Antigone became a study in the selfless quality of appropriate feminine public action". Winterer (2007): 195.

the spectators is thus clear and assured: she "has won the love of the audience by her patient faith, by her courtesy, by her sorrow".[10] Of all values to ascribe to Electra, courtesy is perhaps the most surprising – regular though it is in the vocabulary of school requirements. Electra emerges, in short, as a perfection of the Victorian mourning woman in the eyes of a Victorian schoolmaster: steadfast and emotional but always within the bounds of politeness, courtesy and taste. Killing Clytemnestra is "an act of piety towards the gods" – "So judges Electra, and so also every Greek in the theatre, cruel as the deed is".[11] Here, then, is Electra as the icon of moral steadfastness, in crinolines.

Gilkes's book, designed for sixth formers and undergraduates, duly appears in the bibliography of the prize-winning essay of L.G. Horton-Smith in Cambridge in 1894. Horton-Smith was not exactly an ordinary undergraduate. His essay for the Members' Classical Essay Prize was written in Latin, and went on to be published (by request of his friends and advisors, as the rhetoric of the preface has it) in 1896; it was reviewed by the distinguished professor from St Andrew's, Lewis Campbell, in the *Classical Review* within the year.[12] Horton-Smith went on to publish works of technical philology, although he practised as a lawyer and was a noted propagandist for the expansion of the British navy. He was elected a fellow of St John's College, Cambridge, as were his father, his grandfather, his uncle, and his brother, all of whom also were awarded first class degrees. He was helped in his career at each point by the distinguished classical scholar, Sir John Sandys, by now a friend of the family. (Sandys recommended Gilkes' volume fulsomely in a work written expressly for Cambridge undergraduates, as "a book which ought to be in the hands of all who desire to read that play [*Electra*] with profit".[13]) Horton-Smith could not have been more warmly embedded in Cambridge college life and hierarchy.[14] His essay "if expressed in English might have appeared commonplace", noted Campbell, though, he added generously, "it will be unfair to him if his ample citation of authorities should be allowed to derogate from his originality".[15] Campbell was impressed with Horton-Smith's reading ("Much of what has been written on Sophocles especially is little read – still less acknowledged."[16]), but the bibliography still looks very much like a clever undergraduate's attempt to impress. That is, it does put together some less common works in German and French – that's the flashy part – but in fact is largely made up of handbooks and school guides to tragedy, which have the most pervasive influence on his writing.

---

[10] Gilkes (1880) 48.
[11] Gilkes (1880) 76, 82.
[12] Horton-Smith (1896); Campbell (1897).
[13] Sandys (1880) lxii n.1.
[14] See Horton-Smith (1915).
[15] Campbell (1897) 119.
[16] Campbell (1897) 119.

So what would the clever undergraduate show off as his reading in 1894? Along with Gilkes, there is an eighty-year-old review of Schlegel; some works on Shakespeare, in English and German; the usual reference works on the ancient theatre as an institution (Haigh – for whom Electra seeks "righteous retribution about which there could be no doubt or scruple"[17] – Donaldson, Gow[18]), and a handful of books on tragedy, which reveal a fascinating snapshot of how Sophocles is to be read. Although there are some pieces which would be recognized as scholarly,[19] the vast majority are books for a general, educated audience. At one level, there is the standard French work on tragedy of the period, Patin's *Études sur les tragiques grecs, Sophocle*, first published fifty years earlier. In Patin, Horton-Smith found repeated reference to Schlegel as an authority, and a careful reading of *Electra* which presented the revenge as a divinely inspired and morally justified action. Similarly, Lewis Campbell's respected editions of Sophocles were used, along with Jebb, of course.[20] Campbell later summed up his view of the play for a general audience as "dominated by divine law: a scheme imperfectly comprehended but bearing the impress of the Supreme Disposer".[21] This argument – that the play may have grim aspects but nonetheless represented the divine order of things – is a commonplace of Victorian theology, as a description of our life in this world (as is the term "Supreme Disposer", applied usually to the Protestant God); but it has had a very long shelf-life in the criticism of Sophocles' *Electra*, as Kitto in 1961 and Gellie in 1972 fully exemplify. Horton-Smith also read Churton Collins's *Sophocles*, where he came across the stirring words of Edward Bulwer-Lytton, author of *The Last Days of Pompeii*, and successful modern dramatist. For Bulwer-Lytton, as for Collins, the matricide is a holy act: "poetical justice elevates what on the modern stage would have been but a spectacle of physical horror into the deeper terror and sublimer gloom of a moral awe; and vindictive murder, losing its aspect, is idealised and hallowed into a religious sacrifice".[22] The paucity of such religious vocabulary in Sophocles, in contrast, say, to Aeschylus' *Oresteia*, is no bar to Bulwer's religious and moral awe. Bulwer-Lytton catches the *mot juste* as ever: this reading *idealizes* the action and *hallows* it. Horton-Smith also read Moulton's *The Ancient Classical Drama: a Study in Literary Evolution*, a work I shall come back to shortly, which tells us that Sophocles "naturally throws into the background the unpleasant topic of matricide", as the avengers move towards "the unmingled triumph of their

---

[17] Haigh (1896) 191.

[18] Donaldson (1860) – seventh edition; Gow (1888) – third edition – a good example of the factual primers available for pupils, which also has a good deal of technical material in it.

[19] Jebb's commentaries, for example; or S. Lichtenstein's 1850 study *Shakespeare und Sophokles: ein Beitrag zur Philosophie der Geschichte* (Munich).

[20] Campbell (1871); (1881); (1879); (1891).

[21] Campbell (1904) 65.

[22] Collins (1871) 180–1, quoting Bulwer-Lytton (1837) II 568.

cause".[23] So Moulton does not even mention the death scene . . . Symonds's *Studies of the Greek Poets*, now in its third edition, is in the bibliography too, and Symonds does discuss the death of Clytemnestra, but the murder also appears for Symonds as a righteous act: "when the cry of the queen is heard in the palace, he shows his heroine tremendous in her righteous hatred and implacable desire for vengeance".[24] When Horton-Smith followed Gilkes in finding Electra an upright and constant heroine, he could cite a considerable weight of authoritative opinion in support of his considered, undergraduate judgement.

The one book in the bibliography which might have added a contrary note was J. P. Mahaffy's *A History of Classical Greek Literature*. Now Horton-Smith did note Mahaffy's views on the chorus, which add a striking twist to the orthodoxy from Schlegel: "The chorus . . . was . . . by Sophocles degraded to be a mere spectator of the action – sometimes an accomplice, sometimes a mere selfish, sometimes an irrelevant observer."[25] The word "mere", along with "selfish" and "irrelevant", sniffily undermines the idealistic model of the chorus, and attacks the claim, from Aristotle onwards, that Sophocles treated his chorus like an actor. Campbell surprisingly singled out Horton-Smith's views on the chorus, which are no more than a polished Latin version of Mahaffy, for special praise. But Mahaffy also found Electra harder to take than did the other handbooks I have considered. There is, he wrote, "a hardness amounting to positive heartlessness in Electra, who, when she hears her brother within murdering his and her mother, actually calls out to him to strike her again". This is a "revolting exclamation".[26] Despite this challenging reading of the death scene, Mahaffy nonetheless also agrees with the commonplace that Sophocles wants to fix our sympathy on Electra and Orestes, and that the oracle of Apollo provides an absolute justification of the killing. This leads Mahaffy to an awkward conclusion: the play is "truly Homeric, but . . . a retrograde step in the deeper history of morals".[27] The suggestion that Sophocles does not epitomize the poet as moral authority goes against a long tradition of the privileging of antiquity.

But this was Mahaffy.[28] He had already reviewed Jebb's *Attic Orators* with derisive scorn and personal animosity, and entered into a long-running hissy fit of public argument with the greatest of English Sophoclean scholars. Jebb was further incensed by Mahaffy's declaration that Sophocles was inferior to Euripides, and was incompetent in his portrayal of female characters. Mahaffy even included Sophocles in a list of those committed to Greek love in what was then

---

[23] Moulton (1890) 158, 160.
[24] Symonds (1879) 231.
[25] Mahaffy (1883) I: 317.
[26] Mahaffy (1883) 289.
[27] Mahaffy (1883) 290.
[28] See Stanford and McDowell (1971).

the most outspoken treatment of male desire in a handbook in English.[29] Between Jebb and Mahaffy, the evaluation of Sophocles bit deep into their sense of *amour propre*, scholarly principle, and attitude to the pleasures of the world. It was, in all senses, a *personal* row. The fall-out from this spat between the renegade Mahaffy and the establishment Jebb (Irishmen both) was still being felt many years later when Mahaffy was not elected to the British Academy nor honoured with an honorary degree from Cambridge (as he was by Oxford and other universities).[30] As Basil Gildersleeve, the great American classicist and apologist for the slave-owning Confederate States[31], noted, "Jebb knew how to hate".[32] Mahaffy's comments on Electra were not picked up and followed by other scholars (or by the young Horton-Smith). *A History of Classical Greek Literature* was rather well received, and quite suitable for Horton-Smith to include – in contrast to some of Mahaffy's later books which received reviews of some of the nastiest and most crushing pieces of Victorian vitriol[33] – but the idea that Electra might be heartless and even revolting, let alone that Sophocles is morally retrograde, does not appear again for some years. Mahaffy, Oscar Wilde's guide to Greece, and great sportsman who played cricket for the Gentlemen of Ireland and was besotted with horse racing, was regarded as something of a slipshod and opinionated scholar, whose views could easily be marginalized, and his revolting Electra seems to have been passed over with discreet silence.

Richard Green Moulton (whom I said I would return to) leads us in a different direction from Horton-Smith's well-connected route through Cambridge into the legal profession. Moulton came from a Methodist family, and his three brothers each made a career in public service, and had connections with St John's, Cambridge, the law, and maths, which might have helped draw Horton-Smith's attention to the book.[34] Richard Moulton, also eventually a lawyer, acted as an extension lecturer for Cambridge, that is, he went out to give lectures on academic subjects in working men's clubs and other public institutions. He was particularly proud that his course on Greek tragedy in the industrial city of Newcastle attracted on average 700 participants a week.[35]

---

[29] See Mahaffy (1874) with Stanford and McDowell (1971) 156–7.

[30] Well told by Stanford and McDowell (1971) especially 159–66.

[31] See Lupner and Vandiver (2011).

[32] *American Journal of Philology* (1920) 40: 448.

[33] "The principal draw back to his work, next to the absence of any comprehensive or philosophical view of his subject is the characteristically national one of a spirit of disparagement and detraction. . . . Pericles could not have safely entrusted Mr Mahaffy with an oyster-shell" *The Examiner* Feb 13, 1875: 4. "The manner in which the subject is treated is quite unworthy of a scholar. . . . He is clever, even brilliant, but he lacks reasonableness, moderation, style and charm". *Pall Mall Gazette* Nov. 9 (1887).

[34] John Moulton, who was at St John's and Senior Wrangler in 1868, became a leading judge, and eventually was made Baron Moulton; William Moulton was the Headmaster of the Leys School in Cambridge; James Moulton was a Methodist minister and headmaster in Sydney, Australia, who translated the bible into Tonga.

[35] Moulton (1890) vi.

Churton Collins, whose book on Sophocles Horton-Smith also read, held a similar post in Oxford, as did Arthur Sidgwick in London. Sidgwick, best known today for his *Introduction to Greek Prose Composition*, campaigned against compulsory Greek, and for wider admission into the universities (including women), and was, by all accounts, an outstanding and inspirational teacher. Richard Moulton too was a campaigning educationalist, whose book on ancient drama is provocatively subtitled "a study in literary evolution" – as though Greek drama was not the ideal from which everything could only descend – and it is forthrightly aimed at "readers in English or the original". Moulton, Collins and Sidgwick helped take Greek tragedy to the people, and thus to spread the standard image of Electra outside the closed circles of school, university and the inns of court. (The happily snobbish Mahaffy, by contrast, although he wrote for a general audience, was "outspokenly contemptuous" of extension schemes.[36]) The student at university gratefully relies on the works designed for the general public – and the public receives views which are grounded in the university environment.

At the same time as he was reviewing Horton-Smith's essay, Lewis Campbell was producing his own *Sophocles for the use of schools*, written together with Evelyn Abbott, two volumes of all seven plays, with a Greek text and commentary (the *Trachiniae* and *Oedipus Coloneus* were later published as single volumes). The commentary is largely philological, and is a good reminder that most schoolboys and university students encountered the text of Sophocles first and foremost as a piece of Greek to be translated, and secondly as poetry to be appreciated for its beauty. Far more time was spent in writing Greek verse in the style of Sophocles than reading or writing essays about Sophocles.[37] Gilkes at Dulwich was a rarity as a teacher in that he read and discussed a passage of literature every week with his sixth formers. In such an educational framework, the brief introductions to translations or commentaries, as well as the occasional literary comment within the commentaries, have an increased impact, not least as they might be the only interpretive remarks a student might encounter. Campbell and Abbott's school edition sums up the standard view of Electra, once more. Like Mahaffy, they recognize that the moment of the murder of Clytemnestra is grim: "It is indeed a terrible moment when we hear the cry, 'Strike again, if strength is left'. The chorus shudder. Orestes himself appeals to the command of Apollo; but Electra is unshaken", and they recognize too that this might affect one's judgement of Electra: "It has been sometimes thought that Electra and Antigone are more harsh and repellent than becomes their sex".[38] But this is quickly scotched. Electra's emotion is "unhesitating confidence in a righteous cause." Sophocles is on a mission: "His

---

[36] Stanford and McDowell (1971) 50.
[37] See Stray (1998). Learning by heart was also a major part of the educational process.
[38] Campbell and Abbott (1886) xvi; xvi-xvii.

purpose is to set forth a revelation of Divine justice, in the punishment of the guilty, the vindication of the dead, who have been wronged, and the restoration of the oppressed. This purpose is maintained by him with perfect simplicity."[39] So Electra might have some apparent demerits: she "is past the flower of her age; she has no lover", and when she cries out "Strike her again!", "no doubt this is terribly unchristian".[40] But such forcefulness is a demonstration that Clytemnestra's guilt has destroyed "even the claims of natural affection", and we can safely conclude that Electra is "absolutely in the right".[41] Boys and students at school and university are to see in Sophocles' play a revelation of divine justice, a proof that punishment follows crime, and, in Electra herself, an ideal of righteousness under trying conditions. Lewis Campbell was an active minister of the church, and his religious certainty underlies this reading of tragedy. Electra's confidence is "unhesitating", her cause is "righteous", and she is "absolutely right".

Campbell's religious tone is not by chance and not simply because he is a clergyman. Since George Grote's hugely successful and influential *History of Greece* (1846), tragedy was repeatedly discussed within a specific Christian, religious history. Grote's work is usually and properly discussed as a magisterial contribution to the politicization of ancient history, moving the discussion of Athenian democracy in particular towards a liberal comprehension and away from the conservative account that had dominated the historiography of ancient Greece before him.[42] But his discussion of myth and religion also had a long lasting effect on British scholarship. Grote's critical historical and rationalist approach to myth, which followed Niebuhr's analysis of Roman mythography, not only sought to separate historical narrative from mythological legends, but also saw a developmental model at work, in which myth was redrafted by Greek thinkers towards a higher conceptualization of ethical and spiritual matters. Myth was a "mode of thought", to be transcended eventually by philosophy in the progress of mankind.

Grote's *History* changed its readers' lives: as E.A. Freeman, the Regius Professor of History at Oxford recalled, Grote's work was "one of the glories of our age and country": "to read the political part of Mr. Grote's history . . . is an epoch in a man's life".[43] Mahaffy read Grote as a child and praised him throughout his career. Jebb thought Grote's *History* had done more than any other book "to invest his subject with a vivid, an almost modern interest for a world wider than the academic".[44] It was reviewed enthusiastically by John Stuart Mill, George Cornewall Lewis, A.P. Stanley, and became a major best-seller.

---

[39] Campbell and Abbott (1886) 307.
[40] Campbell and Abbott (1886) 312.
[41] Campbell and Abbott (1886) 312.
[42] See Turner (1981) for a fine discussion of Grote; also now Goldhill (2011).
[43] Freeman (1856) 172. On Freeman, see Momigliano (1966).
[44] Jebb (1907) 534.

The reading of Sophocles was repeatedly drawn into the orbit of Grote's developmental model. So Symonds's *Studies of the Greek Poets* might "lead one to suspect that he wrote his lectures with Grote's first volume open on his desk".[45] For Symonds, while Pindar had added to the old Homeric religion a "deeper and more awful perception of superhuman mysteries", Sophocles in particular had added an ethical dimension that made religion "more impregnable within its stronghold of the human heart and reason, less exposed to the attacks of logic or the changes of opinion".[46] He forced inherited myths "into new moulds such as their authors had never conceived".[47] Sophocles was a sign and symptom of the changing ethical status of mankind.

Evelyn Abbott, who collaborated with Lewis Campbell, was explicit in this developmental model: "The Greeks did not allow the mythology which stood to them in the place of doctrine to restrain them from the endeavour to bring their conception of the Supreme Being into harmony with their conceptions of justice and law. Their religious conceptions became ethical at an early period, and continued to be so to the last, ever growing higher and higher as the conception of life and duty became more elevated".[48] Through religious thinking, ethics became more elevated, and duty, that key Victorian value, grew higher and higher. So Sophocles "accepts the mysterious fact that the guiltless do suffer, but seeks to explain it by taking a higher view of the nature of such suffering".[49] For Abbott, Sophocles is crucial testimony of a Greek journey towards reconciling abstract principles of justice and law with a notion of the Supreme Being (a monotheistic term which is more suited to later Greek or to Anglican Britain than to the polytheistic fifth-century *polis*). With an even more direct Christian teleology, the widely used book, Plumptre's *The Tragedies of Sophocles*, not only argued that Sophocles aimed "to turn [the mythology of Homer], as far as it could be turned, into an instrument of moral education, and to lead men upwards to the eternal laws of God, and the thought of His righteous order"– again the Anglican tones are not hard to detect, along with Grote's developmentalism – but also saw in Sophocles "testimonium animae naturaliter Christianae", "evidence of a naturally Christian spirit" – the phrase the early Church Fathers used to rehabilitate certain pagan authors who deserved, they felt, a continuing place in the canon.[50] Sophocles, concluded Plumptre, with a portentous turn into Greek, "may have become, to those who followed his guidance rightly, a παιδαγωγὸς εἰς Χριστόν", a "Guide to Christ".[51]

---

[45] Turner (1981) 100.

[46] Symonds (1879) 327, 427.

[47] Grote (1846) 1: 364.

[48] Abbott ed (1880) 38.

[49] Abbott ed (1880) 65.

[50] Plumptre (1865) lxxxix.

[51] Plumptre (1865) xcviii. There is, as ever, a German thesis, at the Gymnasium level – very short and in Latin: Wassmuth (1868).

For Christian writers, from the beginnings of Christianity, the status of the pagan authors was always an issue for negotiation. In Victorian England, Classics dominated the curriculum, while Christianity provided not merely a foundational institutional structure for British society but also the battleground where earnestness, spiritual value, and notions of modern progress clashed with an intensity unparalleled since the Reformation. Consequently, how the Judaeo-Christian tradition and classical antiquity were to be brought together was a question that produced a great deal of speculative, developmental history, which entered public debate with a certain force.[52] Paradigmatically, Prime Minister Gladstone's long pamphlet on Providence, arguing for a connection between Homer and the Hebrew bible, and constructing a link in the divine plan between early Greece and Christianity, sold over 100,000 copies.[53] So, Bishop Westcott, normally a severely sober scholar, makes the connection between the Church and the institution of Greek tragedy absolutely explicit in a quite extraordinary manner. The tragedians are "national preachers" in a "national temple", he writes, and the "sermon" of the *Oresteia* is "'a natural testimony of the soul' to the reality of sin and inevitable penalty which it carries in itself".[54] Aeschylus emerges as a bishop with a national pulpit, not wholly unlike Westcott himself, and the *Oresteia* appears as a *testimonium animae naturaliter*, and, though his translation of the standard phrase coyly leaves out *Christianae*, the "reality of sin" can only be heard as the familiar trope of nineteenth-century preaching. The *Oresteia*, where Orestes, the matricidal murderer, is exonerated in court, is read as proof of the Christian certainty that sin will be punished. Sophocles is not, for Westcott, a truly religious figure, but Euripides – bizarrely – prefigures the Christian revelation in a startlingly extreme version of the developmental model: "We can then study in Euripides a distinct stage in the preparation of the world for Christianity".[55]

We can now appreciate the full force of Mahaffy's assertion that Sophocles' *Electra* represented "a retrograde step in the deeper history of morals". His impugning of Sophocles' drama is not just an aesthetic or localised ethical judgement, but a precisely calibrated rejection of how Sophocles had been incorporated into a Grotean paradigm of the development of Greek thought towards higher planes of Christianity. Indeed, contrary to the prevailing expectations of social development, Mahaffy was sceptical about progress in general: it was inevitable, he thought, that we should recognize "schemes of injustice, violence and cruelty in the most civilized countries of the world" – that "inequality is and must be the first condition of every society".[56] There is a

---

[52] See Goldhill (2011) for discussion and bibliography.

[53] Brilliantly discussed by Gange (2009).

[54] Westcott (1891) 52, 94.

[55] Westcott (1891) 140. Shakespeare also received aggressively Christianizing readings in the same period: see, for example, Ellis (1897), (1902), discussed briefly by Poole (2004) 162–3.

[56] Quoted in Stanford and McDowell (1971) 49.

broader perspective behind Mahaffy's apparently dismissive take on the *Electra*. Mahaffy was taking a provocative and pointed stand against the grandees of Sophoclean criticism in the major universities of England and Scotland.

There was no grandee more grand than Sir Richard Claverhouse Jebb, Regius Professor of Greek at Cambridge, Member of Parliament, public intellectual of dignity and distinction, and greatest scholar of Sophocles in Britain, whose editions of the plays of Sophocles impressed even the grandees of German scholarship.[57] It is easy to oppose Jebb and Mahaffy as characters (as they did themselves): Jebb was a precise scholar, where Mahaffy was slapdash; despite his public roles, Jebb was a quiet and withdrawn man, where Mahaffy was flamboyant; Jebb would never have taken Oscar Wilde on holiday; Mahaffy missed out on many of the greatest positions of status for which he aimed. Jebb had no time for sports. Mahaffy even by his own admissions talked too much and told too many ribald anecdotes; Jebb's lectures were described by the scholar A.S.F. Gow, scarcely an intellectual peacock himself, as excruciatingly boring: Jebb would "read out in a monotonous inaudible voice from a notebook or proofsheets strings of references which nobody would look up and which would not have profited them if they had."[58] Yet for most scholars at the end of the nineteenth century, Jebb epitomized Sophoclean scholarship. Gratingly for Mahaffy, his colleague at Trinity College, Dublin, Robert Yelverton Tyrrell, praised Jebb to the skies as "characteristic of the English school of criticism at its best" (a combination of German learning and French brilliance) – in the course of a long-running skirmish between Tyrrell and Mahaffy, which replayed the dispute between Mahaffy and Jebb in equally personal as well as scholarly terms.[59] (Tyrrell was close to Jebb and reported Mahaffy's setbacks gleefully to him.) Jebb was the scholar whose views on Sophocles could not be ignored.

Jebb's Electra shows her heroism and loyalty in a "union of tenderness and strength".[60] The play is "pervaded by an under-current of divine co-operation . . . the bright influence of Apollo . . . prevails from the first. Those sights and sounds of early morning with which the play opens are fit symbols of his presence . . . the god of light and purity."[61] Jebb's view of the opening of the play is cited by Campbell; and more tellingly by Verrall. Verrall edited Munk's standard history of Greek literature, translated from the German by D.B. Kitchin, not least because Munk's views "represent very fairly the current opinion".[62] Verrall's Munk quotes a full page of Schlegel, emphasizing how there is a "divine innocence amid such terrible surroundings, the fresh bloom of life and

---

[57] Standard biography by his wife (Jebb [1907] will be replaced soon, it is hoped.
[58] Gow (1945) 240.
[59] Tyrrell (1909) 41–84.
[60] Jebb (1894) xlii.
[61] Jebb (1892) xlv-xlvi.
[62] Verrall (1891) v.

youth pervades the whole. Apollo, the bright sun-god, at whose bidding the deed was done, seems to shed his brightness throughout; even the day-break with which the play opens is full of meaning".[63] Schlegel, quoted by Munk, edited by Verrall, echoed by Jebb, praised by Campbell (through Jebb), and then cited by Haigh "the scene is bright and cheerful, opening with the rising sun and the matin songs of birds"[64] and so on . . . It would be hard to demonstrate more clearly the circle of mutually confirming critical opinion stemming back to Schlegel's authoritative lectures. Between Germany and England (and France, if we return to Patin and his quotations of Schlegel), there is by 1900 a tradition of how to read Sophocles. Jebb stands for the hierarchy of the University world, the world of professional scholarship, in determining the significance of Electra for his culture. Electra was a set text at Cambridge and elsewhere, and there was a set way of reading it.

Matthew Arnold was a grandee of Victorian cultural value if ever there were one. As essayist, poet and educationalist (following his great father's footsteps), and in particular through the trend-setting, *Culture and Anarchy*, with its opposition of Hellenism and Hebraism as general models for understanding modern culture, he was established as an arbiter of taste, of how taste could and should be talked about – he popularized the category of the Philistine as a term of cultural scorn – and, above all, as a judge of why high culture mattered.[65] For Arnold, Sophocles was a cornerstone of the value of Hellenism, and Arnold, perhaps more through his poetry than his essays, also helped determine the standard view of Sophocles. In his poem "To A Friend", he provides the most famous Victorian description of Sophocles: "He saw life steadily and he saw it whole". In "On Dover Beach", a poem far more tense with uncertainty and ambiguity, Sophocles appears as an ancient touchstone: "Sophocles long ago / Heard it on the Aegean, and it brought into his mind / The turbid ebb and flow / Of human misery. . .". The modern world is riven with dark conflict, personal affections with longing and unease, but amid the pessimism and doubt there is still the faint glimmer that in the past Sophocles heard in the seas the rolling waves of human misery too, an artist's saddened perspective on the world rather than suffering within it. This is the darkest image of Sophocles in Arnold's many comments on the tragedian: elsewhere it is an untrammelled serenity that attracts him. Arnold's poetry and essays, very widely circulated among the general reading public, helped fix the Victorian image of Sophocles and his tragedies. He helped place Sophocles as a serene, reflective figure, whose tragedies captured the sublimity of Greek poetry. The echo of Winckelmannian Philhellenism along with Schlegel's critical

---

[63] Verrall (1891) 175.

[64] Haigh (1896) 191.

[65] On Arnold see – from a huge bibliography – Faverty (1951); Anderson (1965); de Laura (1969); Carroll (1982); Gossman (1994); Collini (1994) with Collini (1991).

apparatus is part of Arnold's dependence on German thinking; his focus on Sophocles part of his own presentation of Hellenism as a matrix for understanding contemporary culture. Judging Sophocles was an integral element of English intellectual self-placement.

The undergraduate Horton-Smith was too young to have seen the first production of *Electra* in Greek performed by the young ladies of Girton College in Cambridge – and since the only men allowed into the audience were dons and members of the council, he would not have been able to attend anyway. This production, which took place in the gymnasium of the all-women college in 1883, was covered in the national press as well as local Cambridge magazines. It led to a performance of the same play at Smith College in America in 1889.[66] In the eighteenth century *Electra* had appeared through a series of adaptations, and, typically for the century which had drastically re-written even Shakespeare to its sense of manners, Electra's aggression was toned down or removed entirely: "Electra's harshness and unbecoming behaviour . . . repelled most eighteenth-century gentlemen".[67] But by the 1880s performances of Greek plays in the original language, with appeals to authenticity of dress and staging, had become something of a society craze (which helps explain in part why papers like *The Times*, *The Academy* and *The Women's World* saw fit to cover a student production).[68] Edith Hall has attempted to see this production within the context of "a new interest in female subjectivity going beyond the hackneyed expressions of maternal and conjugal devotion".[69] But, as Prins has convincingly demonstrated, the dominant context for this production was the changing world of female education and claims for women to be able to learn Greek, and, indeed, perform it. So, the reviews of the Girton production, written by men and women, emphasized the surprise – and surprising success – of a female student production of Greek tragedy in Greek, but when they offered any detailed evaluations, they praised the beauty, serenity, and, above all, the grace of the performance, as if they were experiencing a Greek frieze through Winckelmannian eyes. The emotion of Electra – played by Janet Case, the future teacher of Virginia Woolf – was certainly applauded, but within the powerful expectations of Victorian female mourning. The choice of play was appreciated because of its number of female roles and its qualities as a drama – and, one might add, because it was a *safe* play for the girls to do. It was Sophocles and

---

[66] Both productions are very well covered by Yopie Prins in her forthcoming book *Ladies' Greek*. I follow her analysis here.

[67] Hall and Macintosh (2005) 179, in a particularly fine discussion of the eighteenth-century adaptations: 152–82.

[68] Earlier classical burlesques such as Talfourd's *Electra in a New Electric Light* (1859), although they have some licensed fun and some more pointed engagements with the ideology of classicism, as Hall and Macintosh (2005) 350–90 and Richardson (2003) have shown, did not meddle with the continuing decency of Electra. "I am Electra not a lecturer", puns Talfourd's heroine, with typical burlesque wit.

[69] See Hall (1999) especially 288–91.

one of his best plays, and, as we have by now seen repeatedly, for its nine-teenth-century readers focused on a constant, faithful, pious, girl with a deeply ingrained courtesy of the heart.[70] So, too, Mendelssohn's score for *Antigone* adapted for this performance was musically as safe as could be: chosen, as Shaw, at the cutting edge of critical dismissal put it in 1888, for "his conven-tional sentimentality and his despicable oratorio mongering".[71] When the au-thorities carefully considered giving permission for this performance, the choice of play was no doubt in their minds.

So far, then, I have traced the school-teacher's talks and his pupils' re-sponses; the student's reading, with a professorial review of it; the publishing world of the handbook and the outreach lecture for a non-university audience; the elite world of the highest scholarship and the broader cultural world of poetry and essays; female students staging the play under the auspices of their university teachers, reviewed in the local and national press. Across this very wide range of writing – itself not just a fluke of the uniquely rich Victorian archive but a sign of the cultural importance of an education in Sophocles – a remarkably uniform picture of Sophocles and his *Electra* have emerged, as have the typical nineteenth-century social networks of influence between dif-ferent figures of the story, and between different levels of intellectual ambition. This congruence is clear, despite the equally evident critical infighting and scholarly odium that can always erupt. In a period when so many disciplines are internally divided and when so many disciplines are in contest with one another, especially over the materials of the past, it is telling that Sophocles and *Electra* can emerge in such apparent consensus. But most importantly, the criticism of Sophocles is embedded within broader concerns of Victorian cul-tural and personal self-definition. The evaluation of Electra as a figure is, of course, tied up with stereotypes of gender and violence (with its characteristic nineteenth-century alibis of politeness, duty, and selflessness), but, more strikingly, the play and its heroine's moral status are read within a develop-mental narrative of the religious growth of mankind, that makes Sophocles a test-case and demonstration of how myth is turned into a higher level of com-prehension and expression through philosophy, spiritual value and ethical understanding. This is a narrative which has a Christian teleology, which makes it all the easier to assimilate into the educational establishments of school and university, with their close connection with the church as an insti-tution and with Christian values as principles of education. Grote's liberal and intellectually revolutionary historiography has become assimilated to an insti-tutionally embedded and intellectually conservative normativity. The image of "pious Sophocles" is fully formulated within this Christian developmental

---

[70] *Antigone*, for exactly these reasons, became the most popular Greek play on American campuses, see Winterer (2007) 192–206.

[71] Shaw (1937) 69. See Eatock (2009) 115–50 for the change in Mendelssohn's reputation from the 1840s.

understanding. But Sophocles is also read within an intellectual perspective that explicitly finds its source and authority in the German idealism of Schlegel, and the influence of Schlegel in particular is diffused throughout the British response to Sophocles, from schoolboy to professor to lecturer for the working man. The commitment to the continuity and moral strength of the suffering hero – as opposed to a more complex and provocative possibility of shifting patterns of sympathy or fissured characterization – is integral to the model of tragedy within German idealist thinking, as we have seen.[72] At one level, British scholarship is struggling to align itself with the status and success of the German models of higher education; at another level, as is shown by Arnold, who compiled the government report on the German education system, the idea and ideal of Hellenism maintained in such a critical tradition provide a window onto the cultural self-awareness of the British, caught, as Arnold anatomizes, between Hebraism and Hellenism, between England and a less parochial cultural world. Sophocles is an icon of Hellenism, and an icon of the cultural value of literature, the classical literature of the past, the continuing and contested centre of the British educational curriculum. There is, therefore, a great deal at stake in the evaluation of Sophocles, and the congruence of views on Sophocles across the system is testimony to the power of the forces at work in keeping the system in place. The consensus on Sophocles is doing a job of work, politically, in British society: part of the glue trying to hold institutions and ideology together.

II

The weight of cultural and institutional authority invested in the icon of Sophocles – which represents so much more than the cliché of the "pious Sophocles" – provides one explanation for the intensity of the reaction to the modernist Electra constructed by Hofmannsthal and Strauss. Hofmannsthal's *Elektra* was first produced in Berlin in 1903. It was a *succès de scandale*, bought for twenty-two theatres within four days of its opening, and five editions of the script were required in short order as sales of the book followed the large and shocked audiences. It was produced in English in London in 1907 with a fine cast including Mrs Campbell, but there, surprisingly, it caused barely a notice in the press, and certainly no fuss, especially in contrast to the massive furore over Strauss' opera only three years later. I have discussed at length elsewhere the background to Hofmannsthal's writing and the cultural history of the opening of his play and its transformation into Strauss' opera – and the second wave of

---

[72] Tycho Wilamowitz's attack on consistency of character in Sophocles is best seen as the aggressive and almost parodic inversion of this commonplace of idealist thinking on character: Tycho is the bastard son of German idealism. . . .

scandal, where the combination of the new music and the new portrayal of Electra caused such heated debate in intellectual circles and the popular press across Europe and the United States, and especially in London in 1910.[73] I do not want to rehearse that analysis of the impact of the performance as an event again here, though the sheer excitement over Strauss in England in particular is a crucial frame for the remainder of this chapter. Rather, I want to look first at some of the intellectual roots to Hofmannsthal's modernism, and then at how this modernism seeped into English scholarly and popular responses to Sophocles, eventually to become a critical orthodoxy in itself. My interest here is primarily in the *afterlife* of the radical redrafting of Electra by Hofmannsthal and Strauss, especially in English-speaking responses to Sophocles.

When Lewis Campbell wrote, "Much of what has been written on Sophocles especially is little read – still less acknowledged", he was referring primarily to British academics and their precarious engagement with German scholarship. Schlegel was indeed an acknowledged authority (as well as a constant second-hand influence), but since Schlegel had been translated into English, there had been seventy-odd years of German work on Sophocles and tragedy in general.[74] This more modern discussion was indeed only very slowly and sporadically absorbed into British writing in the Victorian university (exhaustive bibliographies did not yet have the prestige they have since garnered). There is even less general awareness among British classicists of the growing modernism in Vienna and other centres of the German-speaking world, although the Cambridge Ritualists' affiliation to Nietzsche in the early twentieth century once again would link classics, continental thought, and anthropology in a productive synthesis. It was from within this environment, however, that Hofmannsthal developed his degenerate, maddened, bloodthirsty, dancing Electra.

Now, Mahaffy was not the only critic to be repelled by Electra at the scene of the matricide. Haigh called her cries "unnatural and repelling".[75] Munk in Germany wrote, "Certainly the ease with which the terrible matricide is accomplished, and the complete absence of any scruples in daughter and son, is revolting to modern feeling, and marks the weak spot in the play".[76] Even Campbell and Abbott had noted, as we saw, that some find Electra (and Antigone) "more harsh and repellent than becomes their sex". But Hofmannsthal's portrayal of Electra was most influenced by a book which took such hints far further, namely, Erwin Rohde's *Psyche*. Rohde was a friend and fellow student with Nietzsche under Ritschl (and who supported Nietzsche against Wilamowitz); he rose in his career to be a distinguished professor of

[73] Goldhill (2002) 108–77 – with further bibliography.
[74] On Schlegel and Euripides, see Behler (1986) and Henrichs (1986).
[75] Haigh (1896) 192.
[76] Verrall (1891) 175.

classics. *Psyche*, a study of ancient Greek views of the soul and immortality, was written in the 1890s, with a full second edition in 1897. It is a very learned study of ancient cult practices and beliefs, collecting, as one might expect from this period of German scholarship, a huge range of sources, discussed in detail, in service of a broad argument about social evolution. It is also a book, however, which was deeply influenced by the new disciplines of anthropology and psychology (as well as by Schlegel again, when he turns to tragedy). Anthropology – again within the familiar nineteenth-century commitment to developing broad models of the evolution of social forms – had uncovered parallels between the myths of Greece and the myths of other cultures, in a way which challenged the simple privilege of the classical past as the origin of the West and its values; and, equally disturbingly, anthropology had also emphasized the brutality and savagery of these early stories, Uranus' castration by Cronus rather than the light of Apollo, as it were. Mythology and the civilization or savagery of the archaic past had become deeply contentious issues.[77] The study of psychology in Freud's Vienna – or Charcot's Paris – also placed nasty violence and worrying desires at the base of its developmental models, and offered a perspective on female psychology in particular which was hard to assimilate to the normative Victorian stereotypes we have seen at work in the standard nineteenth-century interpretations of Electra.[78] Rohde's interpretation of Electra shows the influence of both fields.

At one level, Rohde offers what could be seen as an extreme version of the familiar account of *Electra*, which perceived in it the plan of God, however grim the action might become. So, Divine Purpose is fulfilled in tragedy, Rohde argues, "though human happiness may be destroyed in the process, and though pain, crime, agony, violent death may overwhelm the individual". Electra is the epitome of this: "only tragically extreme characters can have a tragic fate".[79] Here is one germ of the new Electra: Rohde sees Electra as an *extreme* character, destined to be overwhelmed by crime and agony. He adds to this mix, however, a psychological reading of myth. For Rohde, the Furies, who appeared on stage in Aeschylus' *Oresteia*, were to be conceived as psychological forces: "In reality, these horrid figures only exist in the imagination of the mentally diseased".[80] From Rohde, Hofmannsthal discovered the Furies as the violent psychological disruption of the mentally diseased, leading to the crushing of the individual, the extreme individual, in pain and suffering and crime. This image forms the central strand of Hofmannsthal's portrayal of Electra.

---

[77] See in general Stocking (1987), Detienne (1981), Zimmerman (2001); Massin (1996).

[78] Schorske (1980) in general is supplemented by Rudnytsky (1987) and Armstrong (2005) specifically on Freud and the classical past.

[79] Rohde (1925) 427.

[80] Rohde (1925) 434.

Rohde's work, like that of his friend Nietzsche, is a sign of the shift in the evaluation of the ancient roots of civilization, and with it, a shift in the idealised image of classical Greece that underpins German Philhellenism. The response to Hofmannsthal's *Elektra* marks the moment of this shift with remarkable vividness. There were those who loved the play, of course, especially his friends in the media in Vienna; but those who hated it, particularly in the conservative press, did so precisely in terms of the standard image of Electra they had imbibed at school and university over the past twenty-five years and more.[81] So, Wilhelm Schmid, paradigmatically, wrote some years later with continuing intense distaste "The noble, deeply suffering heroine" – what he had been led to expect and admire, from Schlegel onwards – "is turned into a disgusting, hysterical mad woman for a public of instinct wallahs": he hated not only the figure of Electra but even the audience tainted by their appreciation of the play.[82] Many called the play "unGreek", "ungriechisch". They lamented that the sublime and noble girl had been eroticised, bestialized, psychoanalyzed. One lamented the loss of the *Lichtgestalt* of the girl and thus the play – its "character of light", its "luminosity". Schlegel's vocabulary of sunniness lives on in the expectations of the journalists a century later.[83] Newspapers are often taken as evidence of contemporary reaction; they are also as often evidence of the long-lasting impact of an earlier education on the restricted expectations of audiences.

The re-evaluation of Electra, however, is beginning to sound more broadly in classical scholarship too as Hofmannsthal's radical Electra is emerging on stage. It begins with the moment of the matricide. So in France, Allegre in 1905 declares that at the moment of the murder "the heroine loses our sympathy and becomes hateful; more hateful even than the murderer" (*le meurtrier*, that is, Orestes).[84] Charles Vaughan gave public lectures in Leeds in 1906 where he complained "there is, in fact, nothing to indicate that Sophocles felt the horror of the deed, the appalling tragedy of the situation with which he had set himself to deal" and, remembering the *Oresteia*, asked of Orestes, "Where is the tragic pleading between him and his mother, the instant's hesitation, the bitter cry of remorse that follows on the irrevocable deed?".[85] So – rather later, in 1920 – the elderly Thomas Dwight Goodell, professor of Greek at Yale, in his popular book *Athenian Tragedy: a Study in Popular Art*, nods backwards towards the "constancy" praised by the Victorians he grew up with, but also sees Electra as disturbed and unpleasant: "years of resistance, suffering and waiting, her thoughts bent always on mourning and on vengeance,

---

[81] Reviews are collected in Wunberg (1972) 76–144; Jens (1955)b) 152–4; Renner and Schmid eds (1991).

[82] Schmid (1940) 501. The date adds a further racial nastiness to the charge of decadence.

[83] See the works cited in footnote.71.

[84] Allegre (1905) 220.

[85] Vaughan (1908) 55, 54.

have developed qualities that are abnormal and in themselves repellent, however much we admire her constancy".[86]

J.T. Sheppard is a fascinating test-case of this shift. He studied at Dulwich
College under Gilkes (with whom this chapter began), starred in the Greek
play there, and went on as a student and don to a very active role as actor and
director in the Cambridge Greek play (before becoming a long-serving and
eccentric Provost of King's College, who addressed every acquaintance, even
female students, as "dear boy"). Like Gilkes, he was not seen as an "exact
scholar", but was celebrated for his flamboyant lectures, and his willingness to
explore vivid characterization in performance. We saw his dismissive reaction
to Reinhardt's chorus in the *Oedipus* in chapter 7. He staged *Electra* in Cambridge in 1927, a play he saw as a character study "of a noble spirit, first tortured
and then ruined by the cruelty of circumstances and a vicious creed".[87] He
argued that Orestes asked the wrong question of the oracle, and his subsequent
actions were criminal: "Only fools and criminals suppose that, if an oracle
appears to sanction crime, the crime is justified".[88] Electra was not so much a
heroine as "a tragic victim, driven to destruction by a fatal loyalty to a false
creed",[89] her speech was "appalling in its blasphemy and pitiful in its despair".
Sheppard may not have appreciated Reinhardt, but twenty years later his
interest in performance and in characterization leads to an interpretation
which follows the extremism of Rohde to paint a portrait of a violent and misguided woman – a portrait which boldly reverses the religious pieties of his
nineteenth-century training by terming loyalty "fatal", her ideals "false", her
politeness and courtesy "blasphemy" and "despair".

There are, then, voices raised in scholarship following Rohde and Hofmannsthal, to match the performance tradition, fuelled by modernist concerns.
The Victorian consensus no longer holds. These voices will become dominant,
however, only in the last quarter of the twentieth century. It is much easier, in
fact, to trace a continuum from the nineteenth century in shared phrasing and
judgements. So – to take a sample of English and German handbooks, which
often cross-reference each other, and whose influence could easily be traced
into student essays and newspapers, as we have for the Victorian evidence – for
H.J. Rose (1934), Orestes "receives nothing but commendation"; Moses Hadas
(1950 in America) "Sophocles is shutting out as extraneous to his tragedy of
character any consideration of the moral order . . . or he is defending the justice
of Apollo as the guardian of that order"; Albin Lesky (1966): "The ethical problem of the matricide remains firmly in the background"; Dihle (1994): "The
problem of matricide . . . is suppressed by Sophocles". Waldock (1951): "Sophocles

---

[86] Goodell (1920) 231.
[87] Sheppard (1927a) i. These remarks follow his treatment in Sheppard (1918) and Sheppard (1927b).
[88] Sheppard (1927a) vii.
[89] Sheppard (1927a) viii.

is dramatizing . . . the story of Electra . . . [Matricide] is excluded as irrelevant";
Musurillo (1967): Electra's and Orestes' actions are "perfectly in accord with
both human and divine justice, and demanded by private feeling and decency".
Bowra (1944): "The divine powers of vengeance are on the side of the execu-
tioners . . . [This is] justifiable homicide".[90] Gilbert Murray – famously – talked
of the rare combination of "matricide and good spirits" – a phrase that looks
back to Schlegel's tag, the "happy matricide" (as if Orestes was a character from
Lehar, like the "Merry Widow").[91]

I say there is a continuum from the nineteenth century in so far as these
critics, like their nineteenth-century predecessors and teachers, agree that
Sophocles in contrast to Aeschylus focuses on Electra, and in so doing removes
attention from the matricide, which is an act ordered by the divine, and thus
irreproachable. Yet there is also a fundamental difference between nineteenth-
century authorities and their latter-day pupils, however close the choice of
phrasing or judgement may seem. In none of these more recent critics, not
even in those critics who, like Musurillo, identify their own active role in the
church, is there any indication of the framework which supported Victorian
critical assessments of the play. There is no indication of tragedy as a stage in
human ethical development towards Christianity. There is no assimilation of
Apollo to the Supreme Disposer. Nor is there the same concern for Sophocles
as a lodestone within national cultural awareness. If the critical language of
tragedy appears to have continued unchanged, what is (to be) comprehended
by this language has significantly altered.

There are multiple, converging explanations for the loss of the Victorian
frame of reference, which can be pointed to here – beyond the familiar rejection of "the Victorian" as a self-serving self-definition of modernism's modernity. If there is a steady decline in the influence of the Church in society over
this period, there is a drastic collapse of the intimate institutional intertwining
of University and ecclesiastical authority. This is shadowed by the diminution
of Christianity as an inevitable, vociferous and informed context for the serious
wranglings of students and the public and private debates of academics. Evolu-
tionary models of society or ethics are less willing to take Christianity as their
teleological culmination. Marxism and socialism (for example) constructed
other teleologies that lured the debating students and their mentors. At the
same time, Classics has gradually declined from its position as central to the
curriculum in schools and universities, and with it, the position of Sophocles as
a sign of cultural value has become less iconic. The growth of the institutions of
literary criticism, with the rise of English literature as a subject, has shifted the
potential of classics to speak for the lineaments of national identity. The two

---

[90] Rose (1934) 167; Hadas (1950) 90; Lesky (1966b) 288; Dihle (1994) 112; Waldock (1951) 195;
Musurillo (1967) 104; Bowra (1940) 259.
[91] Murray (1905) vi.

world wars fundamentally altered the relation between German and English scholarship, especially where nationalism and literature are concerned – and changed some attitudes towards war, violence, and the costs of revenge. Sophocles, and Sophocles within the history of ethics, no longer matters in the same way, nor, I think, with the same embracing consequence and intensity. Where the Victorian judgements on *Electra* formed a national consensus and a glue for culture, the same judgements when repeated in the 1960s seem more like tired and marginal echoes of old lessons from a lost schoolroom.

III

By the end of the twentieth century, a sea-change has taken place, however. The so-called "dark" reading of Electra – and of tragedy in general – has become an orthodoxy[92]: tragedy is seen as a democratic genre which does not so much aim to give a national sermon from a national pulpit – despite the form's well-known passages of Athenian jingoistic fervour – as to put before the people a set of challenging questions, which go to the heart of Athenian structures of self-definition. R.P. Winnington-Ingram is an exemplary leader of this transition in England. The son of a rear admiral, he came from a solid family of clergymen. His uncle was Bishop of London for 38 years, and a profoundly conservative churchman, who died in 1946, with his views unchanged, he himself claimed, from the start of his ministry in the 1880s. These views included "an unquestioning trust in the civilizing mission of the British Empire", expressed in language which "verged on xenophobia",[93] especially through the First World War, which he termed a "holy war": for him, the British soldier's slaughter was "the consecration of a martyr's death".[94] The bishop was an "essentially Victorian moral character" who was "increasingly an anachronism in the interwar years".[95] In sharp contrast with his uncle the bishop, the classicist Winnington-Ingram, although he acknowledged the long-lasting influence of his schoolteachers on his thinking, was also profoundly affected by the political turmoil of the 1930s and the Second World War. By his own account, his study of the *Bacchae*, drafted in the late 1930s and published in 1948, is haunted by the nightmare of the Nuremberg Rallies, and he remained passionately committed

---

[92] "Only a few critics currently hold a view which sees matricide as unproblematical", Macleod (2001) 10 – who has a good conspectus of opinions.

[93] These quotations are from the entry on Winnington-Ingram in the *DNB* written by Jeremy Morris. Both the autobiography (Winnington-Ingram [1940]) and the official biography (Coulson [1935]) are painfully hagiographic. There are interesting comments on Winnington-Ingram's social work in Koven (2004) s.v. Winnington-Ingram.

[94] Winnington-Ingram's terms cited by Wilkinson (1978) 169, 253 – a useful book for the context of Winnington-Ingram's patriotism.

[95] Morris's judgement: see n.93.

to international politics and social justice (as indeed had been Gilbert Murray before him).[96] As early as 1954, Winnington-Ingram, already Professor at King's London, argued that Electra was an "agent and victim of the Furies" in a play he called "grim".[97] Without following Rohde to the extreme of regarding any appearance of the Furies as nothing more than a psychological delusion, Winnington-Ingram saw a complex relation between the justice of the Furies and the fury of Electra's pursuit of justice. "It would be perverse", he went on to argue, "to deny that there is a sexual component in Electra's hatred of her mother".[98] The eroticized psychology of Electra that had seemed disgustingly perverted to Schmid in 1904, now, fifty years on, seems "perverse" to deny. In 1951 in America, Cedric Whitman with similar robustness dismissed as "fallacy and sterility"[99] all earlier – and continuing – attempts to argue that the matricide was not a moral crisis in the play – and reported that Jebb himself had told his students that the *Electra* had always seemed a deep problem to him, an anxiety that scarcely surfaces in Jebb's published writing. For Whitman, Electra appears to the characters of the play as "stubborn, sullen, insanely rebellious, even masochistic".[100] Yet Whitman too thought that Sophocles must have approved of Electra, as there was no trace of her punishment in the play: for him, Orestes arrives "full of confidence and hope"[101]; Electra, "heroic [in her] self-destruction" makes "victory" "an achievement of the divine within her own life".[102] Later critics removed even this prop, as Electra's psychological torment is seen as punishment in itself for her hate-distorted soul: "eine innerlich gebrochene Frau", as Friis Johansen puts it, "a maiming – an inner disfigurement".[103] In Germany, Karl Reinhardt's *Sophokles* (1933, reprinted in 1941 and 1947) presented Sophoclean heroes as "lone, uprooted, exiled creatures"[104] (language bound to recall Nietzsche's modernism); the play as "a drama of suffering, powerlessness, cruelty, noble immoderation, both in hate and love".[105] His fascination with dissolution, dissonance, illusion – all good modernist concerns – led him to find the murderous ending "muted" – though still "discordant, repellent".[106] Orestes – "so untragic a character, so unburdened, so cheerful, so un-Orestes-like" – is contrasted with Electra's mountainous emotions, and the "liberation of slavery" finally emerges as "the execution of divine

---

[96] See West (1994).

[97] I take these quotations from the later expansion of the article Winnington-Ingram (1980) 228; 246. See for the first version Winnington-Ingram (1954)-5).

[98] Winnington-Ingram (1980) 231.

[99] Whitman (1951) 153.

[100] Whitman (1951) 156.

[101] Whitman (1951) 155.

[102] Whitman (1951) 167, 171.

[103] Friis Johansen (1964) 32; Segal (1966) 543.

[104] Reinhardt (1933) 10; (1979) 2.

[105] Reinhardt (1933) 145–6; (1979) 135.

[106] Reinhardt (1933) 170; (1979) 161.

justice rather than as the personal responsibility of the murderers" – a view of the morality of killing that may have read differently in 1948 than in 1933.[107] Reinhardt, who lived through the Nazi regime in post as a professor in the German system, had a long-lasting influence on German (and indeed European and American) scholarship on Sophocles. In post-war Europe, Britain and America, it was proving harder to see the violence of Electra as pious, murder as hallowed sacrifice, the avengers' psychology as calm and sunny, even when the revenge was still seen as divinely ordained. There was now a marked and insurmountable difference between scholars who rehearsed their Victorian teachers' judgements, and scholars who heard the screams and saw the torment. Paradigmatically, in 1966, Charles Segal, who had studied with Whitman and always shared his humanist commitments, wrote in debate with Thomas Woodward – two influential articles – and began by stating: "there has been little agreement on the meaning [of the *Electra*] or even on the fundamental issue of whether its tone is one of hope and confidence or one of pessimism"[108] – a view which would have seemed absolutely baffling in 1890. The general public consensus on how to read *Electra* from the nineteenth century had become a consensus that there is no consensus.

Forty years after Segal's article, the critical battle-lines have been drawn up in a different formation again. In the last twenty years of the twentieth century, tragedy emerged as a genre which "challenges", "questions", "problematizes". The *Cambridge Companion to Greek Tragedy* edited by Pat Easterling, the first woman to hold Jebb's position as Regius Chair of Greek at Cambridge, may stand for a string of companions and guide books which have explored how tragedy can be seen to dramatize the "tensions and ambiguities", to use the title of Vernant's seminal article, of Athenian civic discourse.[109] Academic monographs and articles support such work for a broader audience, and find support both in the performance tradition – where ancient tragedy has had a new golden age on stages across the world – and in the teaching of schools and in the newspapers, mediating such thinking for the public. Post-war criticism – influenced by the interwar work of critics like Richards and Empson – has not only come to value ambiguity and doubt over certainty and the sublime, but also has fostered a deep suspicion of Victorian interest in the classical world, and a sharp awareness of the violence of the grand claims from the national pulpit. Just as Hofmannsthal's *Elektra* was fostered through anthropology and psychology, through Nietzsche and Freud, so modern literary critical discourse has sought its genealogy in anthropology and psychology, Nietzsche and Freud, and consequently it must seem overdetermined that the dangerous, violent, self-destructive Electra should be a figure who appears so dominantly

---

[107] Reinhardt (1933) 147; 170; (1979) 137; 161.
[108] Segal (1966) 473. See Woodward (1964) and (1965).
[109] Easterling ed (1997). Vernant and Vidal-Naquet (1972); (1981).

in modern literary readings of Sophocles. To argue for the unblemished moral probity of Electra, agent of divine justice, is now swimming (desperately) against the tide; and just as Sheppard, when he argued for his heterodox reading in the 1920s, was recognized as offering a rhetorically over-exaggerated case, so today to argue for the piety of matricide produces a somewhat frantic exaggeration. Jenny March is exemplary of this when she states, "The uncomplicated punishment of evil would have formed a very large part of the audience's expectations of the story", a view which requires the audience and the critic to forget about Aeschylus' *Oresteia*, so clearly quoted at the moment of the matricide itself (and Euripides, if he wrote his *Electra* before Sophocles), to ignore that the major Athenian festival of the Anthesteria was focused on the arrival of the polluted Orestes in Athens, to deny that tragedy as a genre has expectations of morally complex issues ("Alas, what should I do?" is the archetypal tragic question), and to ignore that in Homer Clytemnestra's death is not attributed to Orestes, and that tyrannicide and matricide cannot be simply assimilated.[110] That Athenian defendants in court were given the benefit of the doubt if the votes were equal, was given an aetiological explanation from Athene's casting vote in the case of Orestes: the paradigmatic "tied", "difficult", "complicated" case. March argues for what was a commonplace of Victorian criticism, but the commonplace has been refigured by the history of criticism and can now seem only a very strangely "out of date" view. For the Victorian critics, tragedy in general and *Electra* in particular could be seen as a step in humankind's moral improvement; nowadays, to describe matricide as "uncomplicated punishment for evil" is likely to seem morally crass.

I have raced through the interwar and post-war years – where a much fuller historical account could, of course, have been developed – because my concern is not with the precise cultural and intellectual contexts of these scholars, interesting though such an account is bound to be for me and for any other critic interested in the genealogy of contemporary concepts as well as the family history of classics as a field; nor is my concern so much with the shifts of political and intellectual frameworks which underlie the contemporary comprehension of tragedy as a genre, important though the Second World War and shifts in the focus of literary criticism outside classics are. I want rather to end with a general point about the historical locatedness of the critical language of tragedy that follows from this story of the changing status of Electra and of Sophoclean drama.

The collapse of the Victorian consensus could be expressed positively as the emergence in post-war Europe of a critical language which has replaced the self-reflection of religion with the self-reflection of psychoanalysis, the self-conscious analysis of national identity and cultural value with the self-conscious analysis of rhetoric and the suspicion of the institutions of power.

---

[110] March (1996) 77, remarks further embodied in her edition: March (2001).

The Electra of 2000 can be seen to be as much a figure of her time as the Electra of 1900. When Westcott speaks of Greek tragedy as "a distinct stage in the preparation of the world for Christianity", modern surprise at such an opinion is testimony to the cultural change between Westcott's intellectual environment and a contemporary context. That Westcott's views raised no eyebrows when they were published (except perhaps for his choice of Euripides as a model of ethical thinking) indicates how much his work is located within his time and place, within his intellectual context as a late nineteenth-century historian and theologian. It seems easy to say that he represents something of his era; he is representative. It is equally true that when Josh Beer states that Sophocles' *Electra* "presents a world in which hatred is so deeply ingrained and traditional moral values so debased that no-one even stops to ask the moral consequences of their actions",[111] he offers a summary that will surprise no contemporary critic, even if there scholars exist who would wish to disagree. It is representative of the contemporary comprehension of Electra, and located within contemporary discourse about ethics, tragedy, language, power, and constitutes a horizon of expectation for performance and literary comprehensions of the play.

At one level, it should seem obvious to state that critics are figures of an era, and that the critical language of tragedy is overdetermined by its formation within a specific cultural and intellectual context. (And, no doubt, such relativism should be seen as a product of my own critical locatedness.) Yet what it means to be "of one's time" is actually rather more difficult to disentangle than this generalization about the inevitable historical contextualization of criticism suggests.

There are, first of all, different frameworks which do not seem to follow the same chronologies or developments; there are different velocities of cultural change. So, in the case of *Electra*, the performance tradition changed radically before the First World War, and has maintained its trajectory in the theatre where Fiona Shaw's Electra famously drew blood from her own scarred flesh in her torment (a fine piece of technical drama), and in the opera house where Susan Bullock's Electra in Strauss' opera had a mask fixed by Orestes to her face, which, when the mask was removed, ran copiously with blood as she danced to her death in the ruined landscape of the war-damaged palace. But at the same time, the scholarly community has discarded its Victorian consensus more slowly and discontinuously: for many critics writing through the twentieth century – and, consequently, schoolboys and students within the academy – the work of reading Sophocles goes on as if Hofmannsthal's Electra had never existed. Within this disjunction between scholarship and theatre, newspaper reviewing, when undertaken by professional journalists, tends to reflect their early education and in turn often lags well behind the scholarly thinking – while maintaining a stronger grasp of the theatrical tradition. Yet reviewers

---

[111] Beer (2004) 131.

can also set the terms of contemporary debate – think of Bernard Shaw and Ernest Newman debating Strauss[112] – in a way which leads both audience expectations and the state of the art.

The education system itself contributes to these time lags. Schoolteachers, churchmen and university lecturers, who were educated according to nineteenth-century principles in the Victorian era, were teaching into the 1940s, and their pupils working into the 1980s and beyond – and often teaching in a similar style and with similar questions. Jebb's Victorian commentaries are still used as authoritative by classicists, with some justification, but few are willing to bring Jebb's philology into critical tension with his broader intellectual positions on Sophocles, or even with his theoretical take on tragic language, as if philology, a subject with a fascinating history, was timeless.[113] Styles of thought, sets of questions, assumptions of critical discourse continue, and continue to be challenged, even when the social, political and intellectual contexts have shifted radically. Critics locate their work – more and less self-consciously – within a perceived trajectory, especially when a heightened sense of the agonistic nature of criticism is pressing. This allows for affiliations which are wilfully old-fashioned, or wilfully trendy – as modes of engagement with a narrative of change within the comprehension of tragedy (no critic, of course, however representative, is simply and only a reflection of his or her time, but always actively participates in a sense of historical self-placement). So when Albrecht Dihle, a scholar who fought in the Second World War, declares in 1994 in a handbook on the history of Greek literature that "the problem of matricide . . . is suppressed by Sophocles",[114] a view which echoes a string of critics back to the Schlegels, and ignores the moral crisis on which so much contemporary criticism has focused, it seems extremely hard to place such a view "within its time" or to imagine how it is to be read "within its historical context". Should we seek a motivation for Dihle's perspective on the play in Dihle's personal history or personality? Is it because a handbook may have set out to be deeply conservative (as if such a position would be reliable)? Is it because Dihle's most committed academic interests are not focused on tragedy and consequently what we see is a view from Dihle's own early education, unmediated by modern work? Is it because Dihle has evaluated and found unsatisfactory all those critics since Reinhardt who have adopted a countervailing view? Is it an aggressive attempt to turn back the clock and bring Sophocles back into the fold as an icon of the decencies of humanism, and the glories of Hellenism? A gesture against Hofmannsthal and all his heirs? It can

---

[112] Discussed in Goldhill (2002) 166–72.

[113] This is an especially marked problem with Jebb, whose most tendentious comments are to be found in the notes rather than the introduction. On the history of philology, see now e.g. Most ed (1999); Most ed (2002); Timpanaro (2002); which offer a different sense of the history of philology from Pfeiffer (1968); Gigante (1989), not to mention Wilamowitz (1982).

[114] Dihle (1994) 112.

be really quite hard to fit a scholar into his or her historical moment – and to see how – with what self-consciousness and what blindness – a scholar works to fit himself or herself into history.

IV

We have traced in broad outline a major shift in the critical language of tragedy – how Electra lost her piety and how violence lost its holiness. We have seen that the trite cliché of "pious Sophocles" conceals the significance of a broad consensus of nineteenth-century readings of Sophocles and his *Electra*, a consensus which depends on a Christianizing teleology of the history of ethics, which finds roots both in Grotean liberal historiography and in German idealist criticism. Sophocles stands not just for a particular image of Hellenism but also for the place of such a classical heritage within the institutions of the state and in the cultural fabric of society. This image of Sophocles was challenged first from within a performance tradition (itself informed by German-speaking modernist thought), gradually by a few scholars who were often stridently criticized as exaggerated, eccentric, or unreliable because of their heterodox views, and then, after the Second World War, by a handful of classicists in positions of institutional and intellectual authority. By the end of the twentieth century, a new consensus had formed around the genre of tragedy as a democratic form which explored the tensions and ambiguities within Athenian civic discourse, and in *Electra* had discovered a play which provoked passionate and difficult questions about the psychological damage of revenge and the corrupting desire for violence (and those few who maintained the Victorian comprehension of the play were marginalized). Where Victorian critics had sought and found moral certainty and intense commitment, instantiated in a silence about the god-ordered matricide, modern critics sought and found the horror of undoubting violence and the distortions of extremism, instantiated in the screaming silence that can express no hesitation before brutal murder.

In broadest brush strokes, one could argue, then, that the history of criticism of Sophocles and the *Electra* in particular follows a tri-partite structure, first with a nineteenth-century consensus about Electra as long-suffering noble heroine, then with a period of transition where critical disagreement is a sign of the active shift in thinking about tragedy – a recognition that a lack of consensus is the status quo, then with a slowly formed new *status quo* which draws the disturbing psychological and moral portrait of an extremist Electra. Yet, there is far less clarity than such a schema proposes, even if such an overall picture is heuristically helpful. There are different velocities of change in different communities, as performance tradition, literary criticism, classical philology and popular culture seem to be moving at different rates and on different trajectories, interacting with each other on some occasions and, on others, fiercely protecting their own domains, and looking neither to left nor right. What is more, while scholars are self-conscious about the trajectory of criticism, and articulate their place within its history, elements of the history are also silently discarded – so that the role of Grotean historiography or arguments about a rise in human ethics towards Christianity are forgotten even when the bare judgements of nineteenth-century scholars are approvingly repeated many years later. Scholars such as Winnington-Ingram are embraced as "ahead of his time", other scholars seem "out of date", "backward looking". The motivation or effect of scholars who seem to stand out so markedly from the norms of their own time is hard to fit into any schema satisfactorily.

Indeed, although the contrast between the treatment of Sophocles at the end of the nineteenth century and his treatment at the end of the twentieth was described above as a "sea-change", it would be wrong, I think, to regard this transition as a paradigm shift, as Kuhn developed the idea, or as a conceptual rupture in Foucauldian terms. Rather, it would be better to see the process as one of appropriation, assimilation and recuperation. So, although no linguist in the twenty-first century would sensibly commit to a full-blown nineteenth-century theory of language, the philology of Jebb has continued to be assimilated as an authority into the scholarly tradition, often shorn of its bearings within such theorizing. So, too, literary critics continue to recognize the power and status of earlier readings, even as they position themselves in vehement denial of them. The critical debate remains sedimented with its history, layered with its oppositions. As Electra in Sophocles' play is locked into a repeated and repetitive argument with her mother, so modern criticism is still fighting its parents, still arguing with and through its Victorian forebears. The language of tragedy is in this way constantly burdened by its inheritance: reading Sophocles remains a historically-laden activity.

{ 9 }

Antigone and the Politics of Sisterhood

THE TRAGIC LANGUAGE OF SHARING

Sputiamo su Hegel*

—CARLA LONZI

Since Hegel . . .

In chapter 6, I discussed how nineteenth-century generalizing about the tragic tended to downplay the politics of Greek tragedy either by undervaluing plays which related directly to specific and localized political issues, or, in the case of a play such as *Antigone* in Hegel's hands, by treating politics at its most abstract and generalized level. In chapter 7 the Mendelssohn/Tieck *Antigone* emerged as a key production linking the philosophical arguments of the German Idealists with the practice of staging drama (and music), as well as providing the nineteenth century with a paradigmatic image of Antigone as a noble heroine, who was easy to fit into Christian-tinged models of (female) self-sacrifice and familial duty. In chapter 8, the performance tradition of *Electra* constructed a model of Sophocles' female heroine through contemporary models of femininity, ethics and religion, where Electra was repeatedly seen parallel to Antigone. This last chapter will pick up elements of each of these preceding discussions. Now I want to broach the politics of *Antigone* through its modern feminist appropriations, which have used the play as a springboard to redraft the politics of the family, gender and social engagement. Here we will see how the inheritance of Hegel has been most explicitly negotiated – in conflict, and by redefinition of where the force of Sophocles' drama is to be located. What is more, in chapter 3, the aggressive debates of the *Antigone* were instrumental

---

* For Teresa Brennan: *in memoriam*

in describing the dynamics of violent exchange in Sophocles, just as in chapter 2, Creon's observation of Antigone's lamenting exit was a test-case for the audience on stage – as this *kommos* was a paradigm of the dramatic power of Sophocles' choral dialogues in chapter 5. Now we will be focusing on how Sophocles' language of community and intra-communal dissent and violence – the claims and breakdown of exchange, the failures of sharing – contribute to the politics of post-Hegelian feminist debate. This final chapter, then, combines in an especially fitting way the two senses of the language of tragedy with which I have been working.

Antigone's history, as an icon for feminist thinking about the family and the state, is long, ongoing and passionate. But let's stall this history at the very first line of Sophocles' foundational play. To go back to the beginning, in order to trace how this verse's extraordinary act of address has paradoxically resulted in a misrecognition, a silencing that in turn poses a troubling question for the myths of kinship. There is no metaphor more potent in modern feminism than sisterhood. It is the problematic *invention* of that bond which Antigone encourages us to explore.

The language of this opening line has opened a critical debate about belonging and exclusion that has not stopped having purchase in contemporary political self-positioning.

$$\mathring{\omega} \; \kappa οι ν ὸν \; α \mathring{v} τ ά δ ε λ \phi ο ν \; \text{'}Ι σ μ ή ν η ς \; κ ά ρ α$$

Of common kin, my very sister, dear Ismene.

Antigone calls Ismene forth; and will dismiss her. And she remains a silenced, despised figure in the critical tradition. "Ismene is set aside", as Irigaray states – and herself performs.[1] For in the grand clash of ruler and resistance, male and female, blood and state, what place is there for poor Ismene? "Ismene seems indisputably a 'woman' in her weakness, her fear, her submissive obedience, her tears, madness, hysteria – all of which are met with condescending scorn on the part of the king. Ismene is subsequently shut up . . . with the other women."[2] As merely a '"woman"', Ismene is indeed scorned not merely by Creon, but also by Antigone and by critics. She becomes at best a foil for her sister, who "does not yield to the law of the city, of its sovereign, of the man of the family."[3] Or as Zizek puts it: "In Sophocles' *Antigone*, the figure with which we can identify is her sister Ismene – kind, considerate, sensitive, prepared to give way and compromise, pathetic, 'human' in contrast to Antigone, who goes to the limits . . ."[4] There is no

---

This chapter is dedicated in fondest memory to Teresa Brennan for whom feminist theory was always political activity.

[1] Irigaray (1985) 219.

[2] Irigaray (1985) 217–8.

[3] Irigaray (1985) 218.

[4] Zizek (1989) 116. Robert (2010) is typical, regrettably, in discussing Antigone "as a sister" (421), a sister "thanks to a blood relation that flows through sexual difference", without once even mentioning Ismene in his article.

doubt who the heroine is here, who provides feminist inspiration, who transcends being a '"woman"': *the woman*, with whom Irigaray identifies in her resistance to Lacan, *her* maître.[5] For Irigaray, reading *Antigone* is paradigmatic of a necessary engagement with antiquity in contemporary politics. Myth matters hugely to her feminist agenda: her project is to dismantle the symbolic furniture of the mind, the struts of patriarchy. That is where myth does its work, especially the intellectual myths of Plato's heirs.[6] It is this alone that could justify her intellectual hooliganism when she declares *Antigone* to "mark the historical bridge between matriarchy and patriarchy."[7] If this sentence is not a crass recapitulation of the myth of matriarchy, articulated by Bachofen and Engels (and more weakly echoed in modern myths of the Goddess)[8], it must be an ironic and provocative comment on how "history", from Irigaray's perspective, is the self-authorizing narrative of patriarchal society. Antigone is to become a weapon to set against that "history". Yet why, then, shut up Ismene with the other women? In a play which makes so much of kinship, can a sister be just one of the other women? A "woman"?

Since Hegel . . .

Kinship has been central to feminist responses to Hegel – the Hegel who is not only the author of the most pervasive reading of the conflict of the *Antigone* as a gendered opposition centred on the ties of the family and the state, but who is also the father of the most influential modelling of the teleological history of civilization against which Irigaray sets herself. Hegel's reading of *Antigone* depends on an opposition of family kinship and state authority, and it is precisely on his valuation of kinship and on his construction of the family, that feminist criticism has focused.[9] There have been two main lines of engagement. First, it has been emphasized that Hegel's analysis denies to Antigone an ethical consciousness. Because of her gender, she cannot achieve the full moral agency that would allow her accession to the political – the *Sittlichkeit* that we saw in chapters 7 and 8 to be central to the evaluation of tragedy's imaginative power. With considerable rhetorical potency, Irigaray puts as an epigraph to her discussion a lengthy quotation from Hegel on the physical, bodily difference between males

---

[5] See Leonard (2005) and for further on Lacan and *Antigone*, see also Miller (2008) 61–99, Zupancic (1998); Sjöholm (1998); Phelan (1997) 13–16; Eagleton (2010); Griffith (2010) Kahane, Ah. (2010). Irigaray (2010) 198–9 writes a section called tellingly "Sharing Antigone's Tragic Fate".

[6] See Leonard (1999) 152–68; Chanter (1995); Whitford (1991).

[7] Irigaray (1985) 217.

[8] A tradition I have discussed briefly in Goldhill (1986) 51–4. See Bachofen (1967); Engels (1972); Bamberger (1975); Pembroke (1965) 217–47; Pembroke (1967) 1–35. On Bachofen's background, see the riveting Gossman (2000).

[9] See Mills, P.J. ed (1996), especially Benhabib (1996); Mills (1987); Elshtain (1982) 46–59; Zerilli (1991) 252–75; Chanter (1995). I have a soft spot too for Lonzi (1970), whose title provides the epigraph to this chapter. Wilmer and Zukkauskaite eds (2010) and Hutchings and Pulkkinen eds (2010) give the current state of play, with full bibliographies.

and females, which concludes: "Thus, the simple retention of the conception in the uterus is differentiated in the male into productive cerebrality and the external vital. On account of this difference therefore, the male is the active principle; as the female remains in her undeveloped unity, she constitutes the principle of conception." For Plato's Socrates, real men have soul babies – thoughts – and only those men most tied to the bodily rather than the spiritual realm long for immortality through children with women; for Aristotle, men provide the guiding spirit that forms the (mere) matter provided by the mother. Hegel is in a long tradition when he makes bodily difference the ground and proof of the moral and political hierarchies of gender. The denial to Antigone of moral agency because of her gender provides the first point of criticism of his analysis.

Second, however, the very construction of the family and of kin by Hegel has been scrutinized. Antigone, as Judith Butler notes, both for Hegel and for those who work with his analysis, "articulates a prepolitical opposition to politics, representing *kinship as the sphere that conditions the possibility of politics without ever entering into it*".[10] This is strikingly evidenced by Irigaray whose critique, for Butler, thereby shows the deep influence of Hegel. "Woman is the guardian of the blood", she writes, "But as both she and it have had to use their substance to nourish the universal consciousness of self, it is in the form of *bloodless shadows* – of unconscious fantasies – that they maintain an underground subsistence."[11] This repressed existence can, however, erupt: "But at times the forces of the world below become hostile because they have been denied the right to live in daylight. These forces rise up and threaten to lay waste the community. To turn it upside down."[12] The hope is that "womanhood would then demand the right to pleasure, to jouissance, even to effective action."[13] The aim is to find a place to think from, where "blood's autonomous flow will never re-unite again".[14] Antigone, for Irigaray, can help us revalue the place of blood in politics, to rethink what blood means for patriarchal thought.

Butler's response to the Hegelian opposition, however, is differently aligned. She sets out to question whether kinship can exist "without the support and mediation of the state, and whether there can be the state without the family as its support and mediation."[15] She analyzes the impure, interwoven mutual interdependence of the discourse of family and state, and she emphasizes both the impure sexual origin of Antigone herself in the incestuous family, and the familial origin of the legitimacy of Creon's rule. Consequently, for Butler, Antigone's act of resistance produces "the social deformation of both idealised kinship and

---

[10] Butler (2000) 2.
[11] Irigaray (1985) 225. See Burian (2010); Chanter (2010); and in general Hutchings and Pulkinnnen eds (2010).
[12] Irigaray (1985) 225.
[13] Irigaray (1985) 226.
[14] Irigaray (1985) 226.
[15] Butler (2000) 5.

political sovereignty."[16] Most tellingly, the idealising readings of critics reproduce the blindnesses of the idealised rhetoric on stage. Butler aims to uncover
the messy political performativity of Antigone, in order to question the relation
between kinship and the reigning systems of cultural intelligibility:

> Antigone represents not kinship in its ideal form but its deformation
> and deplacement, one that puts the reigning regimes of representation
> into crisis and raises the question of what the conditions of intelligibility
> could have been that would have made her life possible, indeed, what
> sustaining web of relations makes our lives possible, those of us who
> confound kinship in the rearticulation of its terms?[17]

Butler's agenda – to see how a re-articulation of kinship terms can become
a politics which is acted out – takes her cue and inspiration from Antigone. As
the nineteenth-century critics found in Electra models of femininity to inspire
and confirm a sense of proper social behaviour, so for contemporary feminist
thinking, trying to undo the bonds of such ideological placements, the turn to
Antigone is intended to uncover a paradigm of engaged action, a *Sittlichkeit*. I
want to follow the logic of Butler's analysis, but to take her enquiry back to the
language of the opening line of Sophocles' play in order to question not merely
why Butler, like so many critics, avoids discussing Ismene, but also to interrogate what Antigone's address calls into being – and why silencing Ismene is
itself a revealing and worrying political gesture.

ὦ κοινὸν αὐτάδελφον Ἰσμήνης κάρα

Of common kin, my very sister, dear Ismene.

George Steiner in *Antigones* is particularly eloquent about the "fertile duplicity"
of these opening words.[18] *Koinon* means "common" or "shared". It can mean "kin",
as "sharing common blood", but it is also a key political term: "commonwealth",
"the common good" (though Steiner does not pursue this semantic level).[19] It can
imply a normative bond both at the civic and at the familial level, and an object or
aim of the community. Democracy's special commitment to the collective makes
it always a pointed term. But it is also a charged and troubling word for members
of an incestuous family, where what is common marks the confusion of incest.
What is it that Antigone and Ismene share? *Autadelphon* "very sister", a rare word,
insists that the mere appellation "sister" is not enough. Juxtaposed to *koinon* it
renders the relation between the two sisters "concretely hyperbolic".[20] It gives and

---

[16] Butler (2000) 6.
[17] Butler (2000) 24.
[18] Steiner (1984) 208. See also Miller (2008) 87–91; Dunn (2006) 183–5.
[19] See e.g. 162, where the chorus describes itself as "summoned by this common mandate", *koinôi
kêrugmati* – not only "shared" but "of common interest", and "of importance to the state".
[20] Steiner (1984) 209.

asks for a special form of recognition. The periphrasis *Ismenes kara*, lterally (as it were) "head of Ismene", normally implies respect, affection or both. Hence my translation "dear". (Only Hölderlin tries to transfer this idiom into a modern language: "O Ismenes Haupt", he translates, straining against the norms of language, almost to the point of parody, in his attempt to maintain the language's oddity.)[21] Every act of naming is an act of categorization, and the persuasive definition of this recognition is a powerful pleading. Hölderlin, again, strains to catch the pull of the address with his single, craggy opening word "Gemeinsamschwesterliches". Antigone is calling a charged and normative relationship into being.

Antigone's claim of sisterhood is, of course, fundamental to her action of burying her brother. It motivates her behaviour. She acts "as a sister", and there has been much critical commentary on how she relates to her brother (a relationship made doubly difficult by her Oedipal inheritance).[22] Yet the relationship of sisterhood is not simply or necessarily symmetrical, nor can it be taken for granted. In Homer, the foundational text of Greek culture, there is no relationship of sisterhood that demands such recognition. Brothers are a privileged connection, for sure. When Odysseus returns in disguise, he questions his son about the difficult state of the household. "Is it that the people hate you?", he asks, "Or do you find fault with your brothers, on whom a man trusts in a fight, even when the quarrel is huge" (*Od.* 16. 95–8). Telemachus rejects these ideas: not only do the people not hate him, but also he has no brothers to find fault with. For "Zeus has made my race single. Arkesias had a single son, Laertes; Laertes was father to Odysseus, single son; Odysseus gave birth to me, single son" (*Od.* 16. 117–20).[23] Brotherhood has two conflicting drives within it, which go to the heart of the patriarchal, patrilineal household. On the one hand, brothers indicate strength. A set of men to work the land and protect the property. To rely on one son to continue the family line is extremely risky in a society where family continuity is dangerously precarious at the best of times. But on the other hand, inheritance also makes plural brothers a source of dissension. How can the paternal property be split and remain viable? So Hesiod's *Works and Days*, no less a foundational text for the Greek family than the *Odyssey*, is predicated on the dramatic situation of two brothers, Hesiod and Perses, in conflict over the patrimony. Indeed, a string of brothers, from Eteocles and Polyneices to Atreus and Thyestes, find brotherhood to be the source of dissent, violence, and intrafamilial conflict. Brotherhood is a relationship that most fully articulates the tensions within the hierarchies of the family in the patriarchal, patrilineal household. To call on a brother is to open the normative, power-laden ties of such a relationship.

---

[21] On Hölderlin's *Antigone* see Steiner (1984) 66–106 (with further bibliography). My reference to parody should cue Houseman's famous parody of tragic diction: "O suitably attired in leather boots head of a traveller", cited in chapter 3 p56.

[22] Since Hegel. . . . See Derrida (1974); Irigaray (1985) (both originally published in 1974); Segal (1981) 184–90; Whitlock Blundell (1989) 106–48.

[23] On these lines see Goldhill (2010).

But in Homer, Hesiod, and indeed all our extant texts before the fifth century, sisterhood is not so charged. Even on the rare occasions when sisters are named as such, the act of naming brings none of the associations of power, precedence and threat from within or without. None of the rhetoric of family loyalty. It is not possible to call on a sister – either for a male or for a female. Even when sisters are made parallel because of their similar traits – Helen and Clytemnestra, say (*Od.* 11. 436–9) – it is a (rhetorical) example of "the plots of the race of women", not a family sign. Groups of sisters normally appear as "daughters of so-and-so" with no mention of their ties as sisters. Since a daughter/sister has such a different relationship to the household from the son/brother – there is no issue of precedence or, most importantly, of inheritance – the rhetoric of kinship is quite different. "Sister" is not a normative term of address: it is not an appeal. The system of power determines the scene of naming.[24]

Yet in the fifth century and in Athens in particular there immediately seems to be a telling difference in the rhetoric of affiliation. The general frame of the city-state, on the one hand, and the specific frame of Athenian democracy, on the other, change the structuring of the politics of the personal. The city-state redefines the nature of collective activity. Democracy, Athens' constitution, restructures the commitments of the individual to the collective in a particularly heightened manner. While the household depends on hierarchy, precedence, and the authority of the *kurios* [the master], democracy privileges horizontal relationships of citizenship: equality before the law. The rhetoric of family terms shifts in a fundamental way, as the political system changes. In democracy key institutions of the family, like burial, and key terms of family affiliation are taken over by the state ("the laws are my father and mother . . .", as Socrates famously puts it in the *Crito*, with whatever rhetorical ironies). What is more, brothers can become a civic, political symbol, rather than a token of family strength. "Fraternity", as Derrida has discussed at length, has remained central to the ideology of modern Western politics and its relation to ancient political theory. "All men are brothers under one universal father who wills the happiness of all" is a banner of Enlightenment revolutionary politics – its phallocracy, as Derrida puts it – which always puts fraternity next to liberty.[25] In this all-embracing shift in political rhetoric, and against the claim of fraternity, sisterhood also changes as a normative term. Sisterhood learns to speak.

In Homer, Agamemnon has three daughters (*Il.* 9. 144–5/286–7): Iphianassa, Laodike and Chrysothemis. Iphianassa is often taken to be the same name as Iphigeneia, though in another poem of the Homeric cycle, the *Cypria* (fr 13),

---

[24] There is surprisingly little mention in ancient Greece of "honour killing" or equivalent revenge based on the dishonour of a sister – of the sort familiar elsewhere from the response of Jacob's children to the rape of Dinah in Genesis 34 through to horrific current Islamic violence. Electra's humiliation is never explicitly a motivation for Orestes.

[25] Derrida (1974).

both Iphianassa and Iphigeneia appear (giving Agamemnon four daughters). In Hesiod (fr 23a16–7 [West]), however, Agamemnon has two daughters, Iphimede and Electra. Iphimede is sacrificed for the fleet, but saved miraculously by Artemis (as is Iphigeneia in most later tellings of this family history). But Electra has no story in Hesiod or Homer. Iphigeneia's (or Iphimede's) sacrifice is a terrible act of a father to a daughter, which leads to no narrative possibilities for Orestes, let alone Electra. Orestes – his story is told more than a dozen times by Homer – returns and takes revenge for his father's death as a sole agent, a man with a mission. There is no mention of any sister in this tale. But in Aeschylus' *Oresteia* (458 BCE) there is a pivotal shift of expressability. Now Electra is a character, a figure who speaks and who has a narrative.

In Aeschylus' *Choephoroi*, unlike Sophocles' *Electra* or Euripides' *Electra*, Electra is a conventionally proper girl. She speaks in the play primarily during acts of religious observance, such as the opening scene of pouring offerings, and the great mourning song: religious ritual is the privileged scene of public female utterance. She is sent inside by her brother as the moment of revenge approaches in order to wait in silence for marriage, which is the privileged role of a woman in the patriarchal family. Paradigmatically, she prays to be more pious than her mother (*Cho.* 140–41). Yet when Electra and Orestes meet in the most extraordinary recognition scene of all Greek tragedy, sisterhood becomes bizarrely highlighted. Electra approaches the tomb of her father, and finds on it a lock of hair. She holds the lock to her own head, and sees a similarity to her own. She finds a footprint by the tomb, places her own foot in it, and from these two signs of likeness recognizes that her brother has returned. This leap of faith was brilliantly mocked already by Euripides in his *Electra*, but its very strangeness raises a set of highly pertinent questions. What is it for a brother and sister to recognize each other? And like this? What is at stake in this act, which is a gesture not just of perception but also of authorization?

This recognition scene needs to be viewed within two frames. First, the *Oresteia* re-tells a Homeric story for the new political world of democratic Athens. The play finds closure, its answers, in the justice of the city. It provides a charter myth for the city's law courts, and celebrates the city as the condition of possibility for social order. It moves away from the hierarchical family towards the ties of citizens within the state. Second, the *Oresteia* is a play which redefines kinship. It sets matricide centre stage, and has the god of truth, Apollo, defend Orestes' act of kin-killing on the grounds that a mother is not a true parent of a child, but a mere guest-house for sperm: "the parent is he who mounts" (*Eum.* 660). This is a response precisely to a question of blood. "Am I of my mother in blood?", asks Orestes (*Eum.* 606). "Is not the blood of a mother most dear?", demands the chorus of Furies, asserting the integral, intimate and necessary tie of child to mother's womb (*Eum.* 607–8). "Judge this blood", begs Orestes of Apollo, his defender in the courtroom (*Eum.* 613). Apollo's judgement is that the mother's blood means nothing to the son. The

Oresteia works to devalue the role of the mother. (As Irigaray would note, blood underlies patriarchal politics.) Hence, before Clytemnestra bares her breast and demands respect for the place where he was nourished, Orestes' nurse has been brought on stage to lament his loss, as the woman who actually did suckle him. The mother's plea has already been dramatically undermined. Neither mother's milk nor mother's blood tie her to her child. These two frames of the democratic city and the re-evaluation of kinship are intimately interconnected (as gender and politics inevitably are). They provide the matrix in which the *Oresteia* articulates its sense of the subject of tragedy.

In the recognition scene, the tie between Electra and Orestes is asserted both as a physical link – same hair, same feet – and as a shared project of revenge. This recognition is also a way of rejecting – refusing to recognize – Clytemnestra. Both daughter and son have to undo the tie to the mother. Electra declares her mother "in no way lives up to the name mother" (*Cho.* 190–1), is "hated with all justice" – and declares that any affection for a mother now belongs to Orestes (*Cho.* 240–1). The recognition constructs a horizontal bond between brother and sister, which, in rejecting the mother, is part of the trilogy's move away from family blood to the ties of citizenship in the city. The threat that a daughter will or must be like her mother is fully enacted in Sophocles' *Electra*, as we have seen – which helps us appreciate the force of Electra's prayer in the *Choephoroi* to be different from her mother. But the city, in the *Oresteia*, is still patriarchal (and made up also of households), and the daughter must be returned to the house, her proper place. Electra can be like her brother, but by virtue of her gender must also remain quite different. In the way that brother and sister do and do not make a pair, this strange recognition of Electra and Orestes is formed within the tensions of this trilogy's dynamic movement between the power of the household and the power of the state. The shifting articulation of kinship and gender roles takes place within the shifting systems of power. The sheer strangeness of the recognition demands reflection on what is being recognized: How alike, how linked are brother and sister? The recognition scene constructs – performs – a new, non-Homeric tie between brother and sister. It is within the new democratic ideological frame of the city and citizenship that Electra and Orestes recognize the (family) tie which links them.

Antigone's relation to her brother is no less tied up with politics, as she establishes the ties of blood and kinship as a motivation above and beyond the edict of the state; and the problematic nature of Antigone's claim to be her brother's sister above all else has been extensively discussed.[26] But Antigone also has a sister. It is not just with sisterhood that the play opens, but with sisterhood articulated as sister to sister. And Antigone's relationship to her sister poses a particular difficulty for her paraded relationship to her brother, a difficulty that questions both Hegel's construction of family values and Butler's critique of them.

---

[26] See fn 21 above.

Let us look first at how Antigone rejects Ismene.[27] Ismene's response to Antigone's initial declaration that she will bury her brother is shock and despair at her sister's willingness to ignore the ruler's edict. She reminds Antigone of her family's terrible history (*Ant.* 49–57):

> Ah! Reflect how our father, sister,
> Died, hated and infamous:
> He himself with his own murdering hand
> Destroyed his double eyes because of his self-detected crimes.
> Then the mother wife, double word,
> Destroyed her life in a twisted noose.
> Third, two brothers on one single day
> In self-slaughter, wretches both, wrought
> Shared doom by each other's hands.

Her language strains to capture her family's incestuous and violent history. The address, "sister" (*o kasignêtê*) is strikingly juxtaposed to the bare noun, "father", who, she asserts, died as an "object of hate" (*apechthês*), rather than as the object of love (*philos*), which is how Antigone has described her brother as an expression of her passionate sense of family duty. Oedipus struck out his "double" eyes (and all words of doubling are inevitably significant in this family history, and much played with by Sophocles[28]), an act which led Jocasta, the mother/wife, "*double*" word, to hang herself. In turn, the *two* brothers killed each other. Here too the language of slaughter is uncannily mixed with the language of suicide and incest, their parents' sins. Nouns, verbs and adjectives are all in the dual form, an archaic linguistic usage used only for pairs of objects: it makes the brothers a natural pair, like hands or eyes. The participle I have translated "in self-slaughter" is *autoktonounte*: in Greek, "suicide", and "kin-murder" are both expressed by the term *autoktonein* and its cognates (the etymology of which is "self" [*auto*] and "killing" [*ktenein*]). It is not as easy a term as such lexical diagnosis suggests, and when two brothers willingly fight each other to the death, the confusion of "self" and "slaughter", "suicide" and "kin-murder" is apparent and significant.[29] But Ismene summarizes this fratricidal act tellingly as "shared doom", *koinon moron* (a term immediately reinforced by the chorus in their opening lyric, who also echo her enumerations of two and one (145–6): "born both of one mother and one father . . . they are sharers in a common (*koinou*) death.") As with the first word of the play, so here too *koinon* is a freighted term.[30] It implies a death that is shared, for sure,

---

[27] "Why is Antigone so quick to cease her relation to her sister, Ismene?" Phelan (1997) 15: she finds an answer through Lacan (13–16). . . .

[28] On incestuous word play in Sophocles, see Goldhill (1984) 177–220.

[29] I have learnt a great deal here from the fine PhD thesis of Matthew Hiscock (2007) which has shown how *autocheir* in particular is used by Sophocles and how complex a sense of transgression it encodes.

[30] See the sensible comments in Winnington-Ingram (1980) 134–6.

and a death that is of common kin, too. But the question it raises is whether this doom will be shared by the next pair in the family line. As Ismene goes on: "But now we two, left all alone – think how we will perish miserably if. . .". Ismene's recognition that she and her sister are a pair – the dual again – is part of an ominous narrative of paired destruction. What is *koinon*? Does the recognition of their familial tie, their sisterhood, bind them both together in a self-destructive descent into tragedy?

Antigone, however, hears nothing persuasive in Ismene's speech, and promises that she will complete the act on her own if necessary. Ismene tries at least to get Antigone to tell no one of her plan and promises silence on her part. Antigone, however, wants her acts to be broadcast (*Ant.* 86–7):

> Oh, denounce it! You will be much more hated
> For your silence if you do not announce it to the world.

Antigone's demand of loving duty (*philia*) for her brother is matched now by her willingness to see her sister as hated (*echthros*). So when Ismene warns her not to attempt the impossible, Antigone hisses (93–4): "If you say that, you will be hated (*echtharêi*) by me, and you will always be hated (*echthra*) by the dead man, and rightly so". Antigone's sense of *philia* is as polarised as Creon's and as impossible: if you disagree with her you are hated, even if you are a sister. If you are a brother you are loved, even when you attack the state.

When Ismene is brought in after the arrest of Antigone, crying, as the chorus comments, "tears of sisterly love (*philadelpha*)" (527), she willingly accepts responsibility for the burial. But Antigone denies her (538–9):

> Justice will not allow you this, since
> You did not will the act, nor did I share it with you.

Koinôsamên: "I did not make common [*koin-*]", "did not share" . . . Antigone rejects the pairing of sisters: they, unlike the brothers, will not have a *koinon moron*, "a common fate". So when Ismene begs (544–5) "Do not reject me, sister, let me die with you and honour the dead", Antigone replies (546): "Do not die a common death (*koina*)". The first line of the play asserted a common bond (*koinon*) between sisters. Now it is clear that this commonality is rejected in the same terms by Antigone. The two sisters will not then be parallel to the two brothers, and the implications of the series of duals in Ismene's telling of the family history will not be lived out. Ismene will not be destroyed, but, like Electra in the *Oresteia*, will go back inside the house to silence. This language of communality claimed and denied gives an even sharper edge to the irony we discussed in chapter 1 that Antigone's language systematically avoids the first-person plural, avoids constructing a verbal bond of the "we". At all levels, the language of tragedy poses the question of what is shared. The first word of the play, *koinon*, is a programmatic crisis of address that will fragment as it proclaims the ties of sisterhood.

II

Could two sisters be like two brothers? Could symmetry be maintained? Sophocles' *Electra* asks that question in a different but pointed way. Like Antigone, Electra has a sister, Chrysothemis, who does not wish to continue her family's line into self-destructive violence. Electra, like Antigone, is un- married, is wholly committed to her family ("Do not teach me to be bad to my *philoi*", she says [*El.* 395], in words Antigone would care to echo): she mourns her dead father incessantly, as Antigone dies to honour her dead brother. Electra, too, tries to persuade her sister to join her in a bold act against the authorities. When she hears the false tale of her brother's death, Electra decides that now she and Chrysothemis themselves must take on the act of revenge. She tries to bring Chrysothemis round to this idea by imag- ining their reception if they succeed in killing Clytemnestra and Aegisthus (*El.* 973–85):

> Do you not see what great glory you will win
> For yourself and for me, if you follow what I say.
> What citizen or stranger when he sees us
> Will not receive us with praise like this:
> "See these two sisters, friends,
> Who saved their paternal home,
> Who when their enemies were firmly established
> Risked their lives to be ministers of bloodshed!
> We must love these twain; we must all revere them.
> In festivals for the whole assembled city
> We must all honour them because of their manly virtue."
> Thus will everyone speak of us,
> So that in life and death our glory will not fail.

Electra imagines winning glory (*eukleian* 973; *kleos* 985), the standard aim of a Homeric hero or Athenian warrior. While Odysseus can praise his wife, Penel- ope, for having "*kleos* like a king" (*Od.* 19. 108–9), it is rare indeed for any woman even to be said to have won *kleos* let alone to act in order to win it. As Pericles famously states in Thucydides (2. 45), "a woman's *kleos* is not to be talked of for praise or blame by men". Electra however imagines Chrysothemis and herself fully celebrated in the public arena by citizens and foreigners alike. They will be lauded as saviours, and honoured in festivals by the city as a collective. The civic language here is strongly marked. They are revered by "citizen or stranger", "revered by the whole assembled city". Indeed, they are honoured (*timân*) in festivals as if they were heroes of the state, greeted or received (*dexiôsetai* 976) with cultic honour (*heortais* 981). In an Athenian context, there can be no doubt which cult is the model for Electra's remarks here. She is depicting herself and

Chrysothemis as if they were the tyrannicides.[31] Aristogeiton and Harmodius were two lovers who were honoured with cult because they killed the tyrant of Athens and thus freed the people. They are heroes of democracy, who were celebrated in the most popular drinking songs of the day as well as by state cult. Their statues were prominently displayed in the agora, the main public space of Athens. They are the archetypal pair of men as political role models. The phrase I have translated "Behold these two sisters" is in Greek *idesthe tôde tô kasignêtô*. These words are in the dual (hence "two"), and the whole passage of praise stays in this rare form. She is imagining the sisters as naturally paired. But the term *kasignêtô* can mean "brothers" as well as "sisters": it is ungendered. It certainly helps the slide between the two sisters and the model of the tyrannicides. This may seem like noble rhetoric in the pursuit of a noble act (and for many Victorian scholars, led by Jebb, so it has been standardly read). But the final word of praise should give us pause. Electra imagines the sisters being celebrated because of their *andreia*. Although *andreia* is often translated "bravery", or "prowess", it is a noun formed from the word *anêr*, "male adult", "man", and indicates the quality of manliness (hence my translation "manly virtue"). Can a woman be praised for *andreia*? Not without pause.[32] The problem of evaluating Electra as a figure and especially as an agent is no less heatedly debated than the problem of evaluating Antigone's action. As we saw in chapter 8, since Hofmannsthal and Strauss, and their reading of *Electra* through Rohde, Freud and Nietzsche, modern criticism has emphasized Electra's violence, her psychological disturbance, her diseased pursuit of glorious revenge.[33] She will not finally be able to act out the murder she imagines in this speech to Chrysothemis, as her brother returns to complete the killing. But her self-image as the object of praise for "manly virtue" not only draws the sisters closer still to the tyrannicides but also raises a question. Can the sisters be like the tyrannicides? Can they live out the role of the two men? Can they lift a sword and commit an act of political revolution to free the paternal property? The image of the armed woman is not a comfortable one for the Athenian imagination, nor is the female political revolutionary. Chrysothemis' response to Electra's speech in its dismissiveness mirrors this ideological frame. She rejects the plan as foolishly incautious and destined to fail miserably. But the terms she uses are telling (995–7):

> Where on earth have you turned your gaze that you have armed
> Yourself with such rashness and call me to help?
> Do you not see? You are a woman not a man.

Electra called on Chrysothemis to "see" her future glory, and to imagine the citizens and strangers declaring "See!"; now Chrysothemis turns this language against her: where was she turning her gaze when she came up with such a

---

[31] On the tyrannicides, see Taylor (1981).
[32] See Goldhill (1995) 137–42; and in general Rosen and Sluiter eds (2003).
[33] See Goldhill (2002) 108–77.

plan? Can she not *see* the basic fact of her gender? Electra's vision looks like a willed blindness to Chrysothemis. She rejects Electra's call to arms as "armed with rashness". Electra's appeal to *andreia* is marked as impossible because she is not an *anêr*, but a woman. For Chrysothemis, the two sisters can never live out the role of the two brothers. Women cannot be men. Sisters cannot be symmetrical with brothers. Indeed, when Orestes returns, he comes with Pylades, a comrade, an older man, a *philos*. It will be these two men, linked by *philia* but not by blood, who will kill the tyrants, under the instruction of a Tutor. Like Aristogeiton and Harmodius, Orestes and Pylades will become for the Greek rhetorical imagination an archetypal pair, a model. Electra, outside the house still, is separated from the male work of killing. "Women", she tells the chorus, "the men (*handres*) are on the point of fulfilling their task" (*El.* 1398). Electra and Chrysothemis cannot make a duo for heroic action.

Antigone's relationship to Ismene is not, then, in direct parallel to her relationship with Polyneices; nor is the relationship of the two sisters parallel to the relationship of the two brothers. Essential to the story of Eteocles and Polyneices (in whatever form the tale takes) is that Eteocles has control of Thebes and Polyneices attacks his own homeland in order to wrest it away from him. Theirs is a story of precedence and power, and the failure of *to koinon*. From Jacob and Joseph in the Bible to Shakespeare and beyond, the younger brother plays a particular role in narratives of family succession. It is unclear if such ideas have any purchase on Ismene and Antigone. Can one ask if Antigone is older than Ismene? In normal Greek terms, from the fact that Antigone in the play is certainly and emphatically on the point of marriage to Haimon (a man whose name echoes with "blood" [*haima*] in this play of blood), and from the fact that there is no mention of any such prospects for Ismene, one could assume that Antigone is the older sister. Not everyone has so read the dynamics, however. Kierkegaard, for example, in his ironic and very personal rewriting of the Antigone story does not include Ismene (yet another silencing), but when he imagines putting his Antigone on stage, he gives his heroine a bit more of a context: "She has a sister living, who is, I assume, older than herself and married".[34] (Few modern writers like to consider the implications that if Antigone is imagined as the average age for a *parthenos*, say, 14 or 15, then Ismene cannot be older than 13 or 14: and thereby not easily to be "shut up with the other women".) Sophocles' play has no indication that I can see to encourage us to think that comparative age or precedence has any significant role in sisterly interactions (where, again, modern readings are likely to make much of a dynamic of older and younger with sisters). Being first is everything to Polyneices and Eteocles; it does not enter the rhetoric of the sisters. Power relations determine the expressivity of kinship terms.

What happens to Ismene, then? The play follows Antigone's dismissiveness. On the one hand, she does not reappear after she is taken inside by the attendants

---

[34] Kierkegaard (1971) 160.

at the end of the second scene (577–81). She is not allowed even to be a spectator of the unfolding events, and no word is made of her as the tragedy progresses to its horrible conclusion. On the other hand, the discourse of the play through Antigone's language seems to kill her off. As Antigone processes to her death, she sings, "Behold me, princes of Thebes, the last remnant of the house of your kings" (940–1)[35]. Ismene is treated as if she were indeed no longer alive or no longer kin, no longer of common blood. Ismene is written – spoken – out of the family line. This silencing is all too often repeated, rather than analysed, by the critics.

Antigone's treatment of Ismene, then, moves from a passionate appeal to the normativity of sisterhood to an equally total rejection of her sister. From intense recognition to no recognition at all, from common blood to refusing the claim of the common. This may shed some light, finally, on the play's most notorious crux. As she is led to her death, Antigone explains that she would not have undertaken the forbidden burial for a husband or a child, since a husband or a child could be replaced, but since her mother and father are dead, her brother is irreplaceable (904–20). Goethe found her argument here "quite awful" ("ganz schlecht"), and it prompted him to hope that scholars would find reasons to declare it spurious, and many scholars have been duly encouraged to give reasons for deletion. Here is not the place to review centuries of debate. I have one simple point to make. Critics who want to delete these lines rely primarily on the assertion that these lines are incomprehensible and especially so in the mouth of Antigone. Those who defend the lines claim that they are comprehensible (and usually quote Herodotus 3. 119, where a similar argument appears), and thereby try to domesticate their oddness (though it should be noted that in Herodotus the argument is specifically to save the life of a still living brother, and even so is thought extraordinary by the king to whom it is made). But it is not clear to me that the lines must be either simply comprehensible or simply incomprehensible. Rather, they provide a moment of what Richard Buxton would call 'bafflement', a node of opacity in the text.[36] And this opacity is significant. It provokes a question to the audience's comprehension: what kinship ties do count and under what circumstances? What kinship ties are worth fighting for or dying for? How does a woman calibrate the potentially competing roles of sister, daughter, wife? Or, perhaps most pertinently, can Antigone's rhetoric of sisterhood make sense?

III

There is a double conclusion to this argument. First, while feminist readings of *Antigone* have been hugely and rightly influential in exploring the difficulties of Hegel's dominant model of approaching the play, within the ongoing work of

---

[35] The text has been thought difficult here. I have translated with Jebb. There is no reason to delete it, as Dindorf does.

[36] Buxton (1988) 41–51.

critical exchange between feminist writers it is fascinating to see how Ismene can be written out of the story. Hegel's obsession with the brother-sister relationship ignores the sister-sister bond "in his search for the ideal relationship as a male-female relationship of identity-in-difference".[37] "Pourquoi frère/soeur et non pas frères ou soeurs?", as Derrida asks, "Why brother/sister and not brothers/sisters?", a question he goes on to explore at length.[38] Yet the same strategy is followed by the feminist writers who work expressly in this Hegelian tradition. For Irigaray it means denying Ismene the name of woman, and "shutting her up". Irigaray finds it easy to associate herself with the revolutionary resistance of Antigone, and thus repeats the gesture of making Ismene the "other woman", the '"woman"' who must be excluded. Perhaps any political movement needs to invent and make an anathema of its other, but excluding one of the sisters might need particularly special theoretical care, which Irigaray does not seem to offer here. For Butler it involves ignoring her (as do so many critics, of all political colours). The attraction of Antigone's resistance leads, it seems, to a re-enactment of Antigone's dismissive attitude towards her sister, rather than an analysis of it. This is particularly odd for Butler, who wishes to interrogate how normative heterosexuality might be threatened by Antigone's version of kinship: "Although not quite a queer heroine, Antigone does emblematize a certain heterosexual fatality that remains to the end. . . . Her example, as it were, gives rise to a contrary form of critical intervention: What in her act is fatal for heterosexuality in its normative sense? And to what other ways of organizing sexuality might a consideration of that fatality give rise?".[39] Butler (who has herself been hailed as quite the queer heroine) wants to use Antigone to challenge the common sense of cultural intelligibility. Yet the asymmetries between brother and sister in Antigone's rhetoric of kinship are central to the problematic and fissured construction of *to koinon*, 'the common', in this play, and understanding *to koinon* is the most pressing imperative of its interrogation of family and politics. How much does Butler's story of the "not quite queer" Antigone rely on repressing her relation to her sister? On not wondering why Antigone is made to reject her sister in order to bury her brother? For Butler, as for Hegel, Antigone has a relationship solely with the male, and not with the female, Ismene. If blood and irreplaceability motivate Antigone's resistance to Creon, should not her claim to be the only sister left, when Ismene "remains to the end", be more worrying for the feminist myth of Antigone? The figuring of Ismene is integral to articulating the distortions of Antigone's self-positioning. In short, both Irigaray's and Butler's readings of *Antigone* show how the myth of the heroine is constructed with all the inspirational force and selective blindness of hero worship. Is that not both the value and the danger of myth for feminism?

---

[37] Mills (1996) 76.

[38] Derrida (1974) 169. Derrida analyses in great detail how Hegel's privileging of the brother/sister relationship causes immense difficulties for Hegel's own construction of the idea(l) of the family.

[39] Butler (2000) 72.

Is it possible to bypass this mythical thinking? Most recently, Bonnie Honig, from a sophisticated perspective of feminist political theory, has attempted to reclaim not merely Ismene but the bond between Antigone and Ismene as a model of sorority.[40] What is at stake for Honig is the potential of discovering a sense of agency that can escape from the binarism and aggression of Creon – and Hegel: "as they [Ismene and Antigone] act in agonistic concert, they hint at an alternative politics, and an alternative to Hegel's dialectic".[41] By agonistic concert, Honig means (and praises) "agonistic mutuality, pleasure, care, rage, cooperation and rivalry", as opposed to "a 'speedy abandonment' of one sister by the other".[42] Yet this pleasing description of "agonistic concert" requires an extraordinary act of wilful reading against the grain. For Honig, the first burial of Polyneices is actually completed by Ismene (although she has strongly denied this course of action in the prologue just as Antigone has strongly indicated she will do it)[43]; consequently, when Ismene tearfully claims to have buried the body – something denied by Antigone and dismissed by Creon – she was, for Honig, telling the truth, and Antigone in denying her sister's involvement is actually protecting her sister. There is between the two girls, argues Honig, a coded exchange that exceeds the comprehension of Creon (and generations of readers in thrall to Creon's view of things). Antigone saves her sister. The drastic redrafting of Sophocles' play offers a new image of sisters who despite their bitter arguments really love each other and would always be there for each other – which is a familiar enough cliché from Hollywood's family politics. Bypassing the myth of Antigone turns out to do no more than replace it with another myth, one that draws on and confirms a modern bourgeois theatre of desire. Can we – should we – avoid finding such self-confirmation in the estrangements of the *Antigone*?

The second strand of conclusion concerns not Sophocles' play and its role in the construction of an image of Antigone in one particular strand of post-Hegelian feminist theory, but the metaphor of sisterhood itself, which has been so important to a much broader feminist political activity. (It is perhaps not without irony that the feminist theory whose very level of theorizing has led it to be rejected by American feminist activists in particular, should be the figures who sideline Ismene . . . Feminism v feminisms, feminism for women v feminism for feminists are unresolved debates cued by this discussion in the

---

[40] Honig (2011); see also Honig (2010), Honig (2009). I have enjoyed debating this with Bonnie Honig and also with Miriam Leonard . . . a model of productive (sisterly) disagreements.

[41] Honig (2011) 63.

[42] Honig (2011) 64.

[43] The guard's account of the second burial (407–40) is particularly difficult for Honig. He describes how they uncovered the corpse, and when Antigone saw this had been done, she screamed and cursed those who had done the deed, and started to bury it again. If she did not do the first burial, she would not know to curse those who had unburied it. Honig's suggestion ([2011] 36) that Antigone is cursing only those who decreed the non-burial, strains deeply against the sense of *tourgon*, "the deed" in context.

current political context.) The hazard of this chapter is that it is worth our while to look carefully at how sisterhood learns to speak. And to see how a sister's relation to a brother is not the same as a sister's relation to a sister, and how two sisters cannot be the same as two brothers. What it means to call on a sister, or to speak as a sister, are normative ideals that develop within specific systems of social authority, and in the case of ancient Greece the shifting systems between the Homeric household and the (democratic) city-state change the condition of possibility for such rhetoric of kinship. The political construction of citizenship as fraternity frames the counter-construction of sisterhood. Sisterhood has proved a grounding metaphor of modern feminism, but its necessary implication with the broadest power structures of society is less commonly questioned. While black feminists or feminists from the Third World have questioned whether they are or want to be included in appeals to a universal sisterhood, the political and psychological conceptualisation of sisterhood itself remain largely uncontested: and hence replete with all the danger and value of myth. From the beginning, Sophocles' staging of the sisters Antigone and Ismene demands that we listen with great attention and self-consciousness to the normative and persuasive claim that "this is what we have in common; you are a very sister; you are dear". It recognizes that in the personal conflicts of the tragic narrative to come there is a difficult and unresolved claim of sisterhood. The tragic myth of Antigone also offers a profound way of thinking about myth and feminism productively through a critical gaze at the politics of sisterhood.

There is no more basic question in political thinking than what is shared, what is "common", the "common good", the ties that bind us. The continuing power of *Antigone*, since Hegel, to stimulate political responses stems from the drama's explorative and explosive tragic language of sharing, doubling, fissure, and autonomy. What we share, since Hegel, is the question of *where* the conflict in the *Antigone* is, the political question of what is shared. From the first word of the play . . . a passionate and overdetermined appeal . . . *ô koinon.*

{ Coda }

Reading, With or Without Hegel

FROM TEXT TO SCRIPT

This coda is forked in two directions. The first route it takes is to look back at the distinctiveness of Sophocles and his language of tragedy. The second direction leads forward to some of the broader theoretical implications of the structure of the book. The historical criticism of the second section of the book has posed a question to the philology of the first section. It is time to hazard some final words on this tension.

Let us begin with the distinctiveness of Sophocles. Each of the topics I have discussed in the first section of the book – irony, the staging of silence as a dramatic and moral question, the use of *stichomythia*, the expressiveness of choral metre and the narrative role of the chorus – are common to all our extant fifth-century tragedies. Indeed, it would be hard to find a discussion of Euripides that did not discuss his prevalent ironies; the silence of Aeschylus' dramatic characters was striking enough to be made into a joke by Aristophanes;[1] the use of shifting metres is brilliantly utilized by Aeschylus in the Cassandra scene of the *Agamemnon*, and the interplay of singing characters and a chorus is a Euripidean trademark.[2] So where is the distinctiveness of Sophocles?

Any answer to this question will inevitably be something of a hostage to fortune, when our extant dramas are such a small selection of the plays that were written, and when there are such evident continuities in tragic diction. Nor has this book entered into any extensive discussion of some familiar elements of what have often been taken as particularly Sophoclean in his dramaturgy: the Sophoclean hero, for example, the gods in Sophocles, and so forth.[3] Nonetheless, it is, I think, possible to offer some productive, summary general

---

[1] Best discussed by Taplin (1972).
[2] Hall (2006) 288–320.
[3] See Knox (1964); Winnington-Ingram (1980) 304–29.

remarks about Sophocles' language of tragedy. Now, it would be easy enough to point to many an apparently trivial uniqueness. Sophocles' extraordinarily free use of enjambment, for example, is unparalleled (though I have tried to argue that this is part of a particular perspective on the potential for metrical expressiveness in Sophocles).[4] So, too, one could no doubt offer statistical accounts of vocabulary and word forms, which would itemize Sophocles' linguistic mannerisms.[5] The Sophoclean hero takes shape within a particular vocabulary.[6] But this book has argued that Sophocles is most distinctive in the most central areas of tragic form, and experiments in uniquely exciting ways with the potential of such formal elements of the language of tragedy.

So, the phrase "Sophoclean irony" has been a commonplace of criticism to indicate the broad structural ironies of a play such as *Oedipus Tyrannus* as well as its more local linguistic ironies, where an audience knows what the characters on stage cannot.[7] As a development and critique of that model, I have suggested that the repeated use of "flickering irony", a doubtfully heard meaning which destabilizes the secure knowingness of the audience, combined with the precarious ironization of everyday words within a temporality of gradual and fragile recognition of the buried life of ordinary language, creates a peculiarly Sophoclean world of discomforted exchange, a world that contrasts both with the fierce, self-implicating metaphoricity of Aeschylus and with the pathetic interplay of cliché, reversal, and rhetorical self-awareness in Euripides. A more nuanced and more worrying Sophoclean irony, if you will. Sophocles' use of the audience on stage to create a mirror for the audience's reflectiveness, a node of ethical questioning, finds few parallels in Euripides, and, by virtue of its triangulation with the dialogues enacted by the other actors at the same time on stage, is different from the silence of Cassandra (or Niobe) in Aeschylus. A Sophoclean ethical triangulation. Similarly, in contrast to Aeschylus' more formally restricted and briefer exchanges, Sophocles' *stichomythia* has a remarkable density and dramatic movement. Euripides can certainly match such skill on occasion, though he is willing also to experiment with forms of political and rhetorical posturing which ancient critics found "frigid" (judgements with which modern critics have often too quickly concurred). Euripides less commonly constructs *agônes* where the *stichomythia* articulates contrasting and competing positions at a point of breakdown, and

---

[4] Figures usefully in Dik (2007) especially 168–224.

[5] So Long (1968). This approach has an extended tradition: see e.g. Campbell (1871) 4–98. My approach is closer to Budelmann (2000).

[6] Descibed in a seminal way by Knox (1964).

[7] "There is a thing called 'Sophoclean Irony'". Thomson (1926): cf Sedgewick (1935) 26: "The spectator knows the facts, the people in the play do not". Pfister (1991) 56 "This definition of dramatic irony largely coincides with the concept of 'Sophoclean Irony'". Ousby (1988) 475: "Tragic (or Sophoclean) irony lies in the distance between what the protagonists expect and the disastrous way things turn out". And many other such examples.

less commonly constructs three-handed or even four-handed dialogues of the intricacy of tone and dramatic manipulation that we see in *Philoctetes*, say, or *Electra*, where the three actors and chorus interrelate with the complexity of a string-quartet. So, too, I have emphasized how much each of the three tragedians experimented with choral form. But I have also been at pains to stress the extraordinary fluidity in the construction of the lyric voice in Sophocles – and, following on from Aristotle's praise, the flexibility by which the chorus becomes an actor within the narrative. There is no chorus in extant ancient tragedy that engages in the dramatic action with the variety and intensity of participation demonstrated by the chorus of the *Philoctetes*.

My discussions of these issues have been linked by a consistent focus not just on the language of tragedy, but also what could be called the rhetoric and politics of tragedy – that is, by the ways in which we can see Sophocles' theatre engaging with the democracy which is the system in which the plays were conceived, funded and performed. The flickering ironies are significant in part because of how they speak to the subject of democracy as a viewing, judging, knowing agent. The creation of an audience on stage similarly shows to the audience of the theatre the anguish and perils of the evaluative, ethical life, as *stichomythia* stages the potential for intellectual, personal and ideological dissension within the exchanges of public life. The chorus as collective articulates the voices of the community, and provides a frame and contrast for the often fierce commitment to self that the Sophoclean heroes uphold. My interest in the formal aspects of Sophoclean language is fully integrated with a wider picture of how tragedy functions in and contributes to a political, public life of the city. Yet Sophocles here too is distinctive. His plays do not end up, as Aeschylus' *Oresteia* does, with a spectacular celebration of the city as such; nor does he parade the cynicism and posturing of the politics of the assembly or law court with the relish of Euripides. It has even been suggested that politics and the *polis* are remarkably absent from Sophocles in comparison with Aeschylus and Euripides.[8] I would prefer to say that Sophocles' profound concern with the political is expressed in a more disseminated and abstract manner. But in this too we can see something of his particular dramatic voice.

The proof of these claims of distinctiveness is in the chapters of the first section. But there can be no doubt that for nineteenth-century critics Sophocles was not just distinctive but the apex of the privileged genre of tragedy. In handbook after handbook, critical discussion after discussion, a comparison of the three tragedians (often conducted through the three versions of Electra's story), proclaimed the supremacy of Sophocles. It is against such a broadly ascribed status that Nietzsche's championing of Aeschylus, or, from a very different

---

[8] I am thinking here of Griffin (1999) in particular. See in general Carter ed (2011).

perspective, Cardinal Newman's and John Keble's taste for Aeschylus' godli-ness,[9] or Verrall's or Mahaffy's love of Euripides, sounds out.

So, in an extension of Aristotle's praise, Oedipus in the *Oedipus Tyrannus* was the model of the suffering hero's *Sittlichkeit* for the German Idealist critics and their heirs, just as Antigone and Electra were paradigms of how such values were transformed by ideals of gender (in a way which has rightly stoked feminist criticism ever since). Sophocles too spoke to ideals of nationalism in an age of nationalism, as the *vaterländisch* bard of the glory that was Greece. And Sophocles embodied ideals of duty, piety and ethical growth within a Christian moral teleology: Sophocles was, in a fully religious sense, "pious", in a manner which contrasts with both Aeschylus and Euripides as poets of public morality. When Matthew Arnold wrote that Sophocles "saw life steadily and saw it whole" he summed up a Victorian Sophocles who exemplified a Winckelmannian sublimity and serenity in contrast with an Aeschylean cragginess and majesty, and a Euripidean self-consciousness and formal dis-ruptiveness.

The connections between my discussion of the critical language of tragedy in this second section of the book and my discussion of Sophocles' language in the first section are manifold. My focus on the lyric voice of the chorus and its role as an actor is in part at least a response to a set of questions which chapter 7 shows to have been put in place by nineteenth-century theorizing about the chorus. Similarly, my discussion of how ethical participation is constructed by the use of the audience on stage responds to the nineteenth-century concern with the *Sittlichkeit* of tragic heroes and the ethical growth of the audience – an essential strand of my historical account of the tragic and the chorus in chap-ters 6 and 7 (even if my discussion is not indebted to a Christian moral tele-ology in the same way as the nineteenth-century critical discourse). Each of my analyses of *Electra* and *Antigone* in the first five chapters is also a product of and a contribution to the history of criticism outlined in chapters 8 and 9, particularly in my modern understanding of gender and the role of ritual and violence in drama. But perhaps the most surprising connection, and the one which has been least explicitly articulated, concerns my first chapter and its attempt to refocus the discussion of Sophoclean irony.

For most critics and readers of tragedy these days, irony is a thoroughly familiar and expected frame of reference, and, indeed, "Sophoclean irony", as I suggested above, is something of a standard critical term. Yet although the word "irony" goes back to ancient Greek, of course, and has a long history in the tradition of rhetorical theory, the prevalence and force of the term changes drastically in the Romantic period.[10] "Romantic irony" – as an idea that goes

---

[9] Dowgun (1982) discusses the taste for Aeschylus in Oxford circles in the mid-century.

[10] Muecke (1969); Furst (1984); Booth (1974); de Man (1984); Hutcheon (1994); for pre-Romantic period see e.g. Knox (1961); Swearingen (1991); each with further extensive bibliography.

beyond a narrow rhetorical definition, and expresses a notion of what I called above "a world of discomforted exchange"– has been subjected to a detailed and sophisticated exposition.[11] As Handwerk epitomizes its modern history, "As nearly as any idea can be, Romantic irony was the progeny of a single person, Friedrich Schlegel, whose work has been a touchstone for almost every recent theoretical discussion of irony".[12] From Schlegel, through the dissenting voice of Hegel, and the interplay of novels, plays and poetry as much as philosophical theorizing, irony became something of a master trope (which proved the growing soil for modernist critical discourse after the Second World War with the work of D.C. Muecke, Wayne Booth, Peter Szondi, and, in particular, Paul de Man).[13] But the association of irony and drama, and, in particular, tragedy and dramatic irony, and, above all for the purposes of this book, the recognition of Sophocles as a privileged example of dramatic irony, can be located with remarkable precision in the foundational work of one man, Connop Thirlwall, whose article, "On the Irony of Sophocles", was recognized as breathtakingly original both at the time of its publication in 1833, and later by critics constructing the history of the critical discourse of irony.[14] "Some readers", begins Thirlwall, "may be a little surprised to see *irony* attributed to a tragic poet".[15] This litotes would be a baffling and even crazy way to start an article today, and it is a striking indication of the dangerously new territory Thirlwall was embarking on – and how much the horizon of expectation has changed since his foundational contribution.

Thirlwall is a fascinating figure, the liberal churchman *par excellence* of the Victorian era. He first came to public notoriety as the co-translator of Niebuhr's history of Rome, the work which introduced the threatening new critical history of antiquity into England – a critical, scientific model which had long-lasting and damaging implications for the institutions of the Anglican church, as well as for the authority of classics as a subject.[16] He had been at school with his long-term collaborator, George Grote, who wrote the best-selling liberal

---

[11] Good brief overview in Handwerk (2000). See Simpson (1979); Dane (1991); Garber (1988); Handwerk (1984), each with further extensive bibliography.

[12] Handwerk (2000) 207. Szondi (1986) 57–74 shows how Schlegel's discussion is part of his concern with the difference between antiquity and modernity, which was also important to theories of the chorus from Schiller onwards, as we saw in chapter 7.

[13] Muecke (1969); Szondi (1986) 57–74; de Man (1983); Booth (1974).

[14] Thirlwall (1833). The originating importance of Thirlwall has often been noticed in histories of irony, which are rarely interested in tragedy (see e.g. especially Dane [1991] 106–36; also Behler [1988] 76; Muecke [1970] 28; Sedgewick [1935]); but only in passing by historians of tragedy and its criticism. The first attested use of "tragische Ironie" may be Adrian Muller in 1806: see Lowe (1996) 522, though, unlike Thirlwall's, this usage has barely been noticed in any later sources. The *Révue Encyclopédique* (Paris, 1826) 683 notes that "tragic irony" is now applied to modern drama but dismisses such language as one of those "expressions étranges qu'on trouve trop frequement dans les ouvrages didactiques des allemandes".

[15] Thirlwall (1833): 483.

[16] See Goldhill (2011) ch 5 for discussion and bibliography.

history of Greece, which was taken as a political statement in support of democratic reform.[17] (He is buried in the same grave as Grote in Westminster
Abbey.) Thirlwall resigned from his fellowship at Trinity College, Cambridge,
because of his involvement in controversies over compulsory attendance at
Chapel and the failure of proper theological education for students. He rose
subsequently to become bishop of St David's in Wales under the patronage of
the Whig government, despite having translated Schleiermacher's shocking
commentary of St Luke, a publication which established his radical credentials
and dogged his progress in the church hierarchy for several years. As a bishop,
he stood out against preventing Archbishop Colenso from preaching during
the so-called Colenso scandal; he was the only bishop to vote for the disestab-
lishment of the Irish Church, and supported the admission of Jews to parliament, and he took a radical Liberal position on the Gorham case, which few
distinguished, and no high or even conservative churchmen could do. He was
also great friends with the Prussian diplomat, Bunsen, and actively supportive
in the establishment of the joint Prussian–English bishopric in Jerusalem,
which so annoyed the evangelical Christians. Thirlwall is a wonderful example
of the interconnections of liberal values in the institutions of church, classics
and social life in Victorian Britain. Despite or perhaps in line with this extraordinary career, he seems to have been an unpleasantly self-assertive and much
disliked man.[18]

Thirlwall is a key conduit for the dissemination of contemporary German
thinking in England through his translations of Niebuhr and Schleiermacher
(and in politics through his connections with Bunsen). His essay on irony in
Sophocles brought a new idea of irony to Greek tragedy, an idea heavily influenced by his reading of German critical thinking. He categorized different
forms of irony, concentrating on the recognition that an audience knew what
the characters on stage could not. His argument also shows the deep influence
of Hegel, especially in his analysis of *Antigone*. There is an irony, he writes, that
is like the "calm, grave, respectful" attention of a judge, observing two parties
arguing. "What makes the contrast interesting is, that the right and the truth
lie on neither side exclusively: that there is no fraudulent purpose, no gross
imbecility of intellect, on either; but both have plausible claims and specious
reasons to alledge [sic]; though each is too much blinded by prejudice or passion to do justice to the views of his adversary".[19] The irony is not in the

---

[17] See Turner (1981) for fine discussion of the political importance of Grote's work – and Thirlwall's
history of Greece, too.

[18] See Thirlwall (1936), a less hagiographic biography than many. "The repellent picture of Thirlwall
conceived by most of his clergy and by casual acquaintances is true – but incomplete", summarizes
Thirlwall (1936) 170.

[19] Thirlwall (1833) 489–90.

demeanor of the judge, however, but is structural: it "is deeply seated in the case itself".[20] Hegel would have resisted seeing irony in the clash of right and right in *Antigone*, but for Thirlwall, the struggle between Antigone and Creon, which, like Hegel, he sees as balanced in mutually defining exclusivities and affiliations, is now to be viewed through the perspective of Romantic irony.

There were a few voices raised in criticism of Thirlwall over the next seventy-five years, perhaps most notably that of Lewis Campbell in 1871 (whose extensive contribution to the popular and scholarly appreciation of Sophocles we traced in chapter 8). Campbell found Thirlwall's categories confused, and he rejected the image of irony as "the poet's face behind the mask, surveying his own creations with a sardonic smile" – an image he beefed up in 1904 into "the smile of conscious superiority, the dissembled laugh, the secret mocking of the unfortunate" which "impairs fullness of emotional sympathy".[21] For Campbell, high-minded friend of Jowett, Sophocles should not be tainted with any suggestion of snideness, which would prevent the engagement of the audience's proper feelings – and hence he tried to reject or qualify the language of irony for Sophoclean tragedy. Irony is, he writes tellingly, "inconsistent with the highest reverence".[22] But Thirlwall's influence was pervasive. It quickly became fully part of academic discussion.[23] In 1855 it was taken as a standard reference in a prize speech at Harrow School.[24] By 1904, Bradley's great book on Shakespeare's tragedies, influenced by Hegel through and through, took "Sophoclean Irony" as a state-of-the-art term of criticism. Plumptre, who we met in chapter 8 as a typical example of the Christianizing reading of a pious Sophocles as a route towards Jesus, in his school edition of *Ecclesiastes* (the sort of volume that would struggle for a market today), in turn uses Thirlwall's idea of Sophoclean irony to cast light on the biblical text.[25] Tellingly, Thirlwall appears in the bibliography of Horton-Smith's undergraduate essay which we

---

[20] Thirlwall (1833) 490.

[21] Campbell (1871) 112–8 for the full expression, reprised in Campbell (1904) 170.

[22] Campbell (1871) 117.

[23] See, for only one of many examples, [Lewes] (1845a): 62: "Those who have perused that essay, will at once comprehend us when we say that the Sophoclean chorus seems to us the favourite exponent of Sophoclean irony. We believe, with Hegel, that it represents the masses. . . ." (62). Dyer (1846a) vehemently criticizes Lewes, revealing some of the tension over the reception of Hegel on tragedy in England, in his sniffy disregard for "a metaphysician, shut up in his closet in Germany" (177). They also clashed over whether dancing took place in Greek choruses, with Lewes arguing surprisingly and vehemently against the proposition: Lewes (1845b); Dyer (1846b).

[24] William Trevor Kenyon "A Criticism of the Oedipus Tyrannus, noticing any points in which it may be compared to King Lear", in Prolusiones praemiis anniversariis dignatae et in auditorio recitatae Scholae Harroviensis, prid. Non. Jul. (Harrow, 1855) 48–70: "The Sophoclean irony consists in the contrasts between the view the characters on stage take of events and the view which the spectators know beforehand is the true one" (53) – citing Thirlwall.

[25] Plumptre (1881) 231–2.

also discussed in chapter 8 – standard reading for the smart student, 60 years on. "Sophoclean irony" had become part of the received image of tragedy – and so it has remained.

My first chapter, it turns out, then, is a reflective and critical gloss on the categories established by Thirlwall in the 1830s, developed as they were from his reading in contemporary German philosophy and literary criticism, now passed through a modernist redrafting of the pervasiveness and disruptiveness of irony. As this book has been at pains to demonstrate, our comprehension of the language of Sophocles is fundamentally informed, articulated, moulded by the language of the critical discourse of tragedy. The apparently unadorned normality for us of a term such as irony, as part of our critical understanding of tragedy, conceals its history, and the implications of that history.

Sophocles is distinctive in his tragic language, then, and distinctively appropriated in the nineteenth-century comprehension of the language of tragedy, a comprehension which remains foundational for contemporary critical discourse. But the point of bringing the two sections of this book into juxtaposition is to raise the vexing question of how such a philological understanding of the language of tragedy and such an awareness of the historical grounding of the critical language of tragedy can be assimilated with each other. How historical, how *self-consciously* historical, is our reading of Sophocles to be?

Now, my discussion of *Electra* ended, ringingly, with "Reading Sophocles remains a historically laden activity." And yet at one level, at least, this conclusion is completely self-evident. How could one disagree with the proposition that readers are historically located individuals? *Of course* responses to *Electra* take place within specific institutional frameworks – academia, opera, theatre, school, and so forth. We could easily describe these institutional frameworks as interpretive communities, as Stanley Fish has done, with their own structures of authority, evaluation, idealism, and their own protocols.[26] These interpretive communities are historically located and bring historically specific expectations with them. We can see how interpretive communities change over time and how different communities can interact with each other. Change within such frameworks can be drastic and abrupt – as imagined by Kuhn's paradigm shift or Foucault's notion of rupture – or, in the usual run of things, more gradual. Within any such narrative of change there are, even so, stragglers and outliers, the revolutionaries and the Luddites, those ahead of their time and the old-fashioned: the rashly conservative and the rashly radical.[27] For readers participate in communities in different ways – with varying degrees of self-awareness and with varying strategies of alienation and assimilation.

---

[26] Fish (1980), (1989).

[27] Foucault (1972), (1974); Kuhn (1962): both have been criticized from multiple angles, of course. We should note the importance of e.g. Bruno Latour (see e.g. Latour (1997)) for the continuation of this debate in history of science and e.g. Fritzsche (2004) in historiography.

Criteria of judgement shift over time and culture. At one level, that is, to describe reading as a historically laden activity is to say no more than people live and write in historically and culturally contingent environments. Which is self-evidently true and, as such, neither particularly instructive nor especially insightful.

So why bother to stress the historicity of reading? There are two immediately relevant answers to this question. First, we should see such an emphasis as an invitation to explore *how* this historicity is enacted or instantiated. That is, it is critically instructive and potentially insightful to try to understand the specific lineaments of the intellectual formation of scholars as it is embodied in their work. This helps produce a nuanced cultural history of a field of enquiry; it encourages us to see why scholars have framed questions and answers in the particular way they have; it is an integral element in answering Momigliano's insistent problem of how a scholar's biography relates to his or her intellectual activity.[28] One strategy of the previous chapters, consequently, was to attempt to uncover not the fact that readings *were* historically laden, but *how* they were and *how* such historicity had an impact on the organization of the criticism of Sophocles – the *regimes of knowledge* within which Sophocles has been read.

The second answer is that this emphasis on the historicity of reading also encourages us as critics to be more aware of the complex interactions between our own work and its historical placement. If, as Cicero suggests, not to know where one comes from is to remain forever a child, exploring one's place within a history of criticism is also part of the maturity of critical judgement.[29] Why such self-scrutiny – such suspicion of the self – should seem to me now a critical value no doubt has complex historical roots, connected to genealogies of modern criticism in Plato and Augustine as well as in the celebrated and highly confident modern masters of self-doubt from Nietzsche to Freud or Derrida. What Hegel called "the labour of the negative" – a willingness to enter into the endless and possibly crippling *mise-en-abîme* of historical self-consciousness – has become a sign of the self-presentation of modernity (with all the potential for smugness, blindness, and conceit that any act of self-presentation brings). Exploring historicity as the condition of criticism is a pressing challenge of modern scholarship. How our language of tragic criticism has been formed should be of concern to us.

And yet . . . and yet this recognition of the historicity of reading is not the whole story, not by any means. We need more, and above all we need to take account also of the *idealism* that drives criticism. This idealism takes different forms, and could be called by different names, but for the moment and with a great deal of diffidence I will call it "the scientific model". Much modern

---

[28] Momigliano (1966); Momigliano (1970).
[29] Cic. Orat. 120.13.

criticism has appropriated the language of science or *Wissenschaft* – an appropriation which motivates my choice of terminology – and it often implies a commitment to certain rules of evidence, to shared standards of objectivity, to shared criteria of argumentation. But I talk of the *idealism* of such a model because of its apparent commitment to the notion of a direct or even unmediated engagement with the object of study. In this scientific model, it is possible, indeed essential that the historicity of reading be acknowledged, but this contingency is acknowledged as the failure of the principles of scholarship. So it is right and necessary to point out that the medical treatment of pregnant women during the nineteenth and twentieth century was profoundly affected by social or ideological commitments with regard to the perceived status of women, especially in relation to the wounded soldiers of war, but this is understood within the scientific model as a failure of proper medical science where the accurate and objective evaluation of the health of the patient alone should be the determining principle of treatment.[30] Or, to take a more strident example, Nazi medical experimentation was fundamentally immoral because of its ideological agenda. In the ideal world, the argument goes, the scholar (scientist, medical practitioner) would not be distracted or informed by ideology, prejudice, or other historical contingencies.

This idealism is familiar in all forms of classical scholarship. Now, I am not particularly fussed by the naïvety of the scholar who, in full denial of the historicity of reading and the anxieties of epistemology, merely asserts an objective, pure and accurate knowledge of the past. (This antiquarian purist is a stereotype – sometimes lived up to – but it is not an intellectually defensible position.) What is far more interesting is how the idealism of the scientific model is so often written into the most sophisticated and historically aware criticism. So, at the most general level, historians have profoundly criticized Ranke's principle of recovering "wie es eigentlich gewesenist", "how it actually happened", and have blurred the boundaries between fiction and history both in the theory and in the practice of historiography. And yet the lure of the good source, the power of the claim of accuracy, the commitment to the value of capturing the past more closely remains strong and even essential in historical analysis. To show how historical contingency – ideological bias, moral qualms, racial prejudice – has informed a historical argument is a decisive criticism, even when the historicity of all writing is acknowledged. The idealism of what I have been calling the scientific model continues notwithstanding the recognition of the historicity of reading.[31]

---

[30] The work of Oakley (1980), (1984) has given rise to a string of further studies; similar figures for the USA in Temkin (1999).

[31] See for representative samples of work: Evans (2001); Jenkins (1991); Collis and Lukes eds (1982); Cannadine (2000); Burke (2007); Soffer (2008); Goldstein ed (1994); White (1973), (1978); Burke ed (1991) – and many others back to Collingwood and Carr and beyond!

I have just offered the most general form of argument from an arena where such debates about methodology are frequent and heated, and where claims and counter-claims have been well staked out. But we could also give a single highly localized example of the point I am trying to make. Eduard Fraenkel notoriously explained Agamemnon's decision in Aeschylus' *Agamemnon* to cede to his wife and to step on the tapestries on the grounds that Agamemnon was a "true gentleman".[32] This explanation has been leapt on by critics – with varying degrees of pain or understanding – as a *locus classicus* for an academic judgement affected by historical and cultural contingency. Yet the implied opposite to this – usually – is that we – the new, modern critics – can do better, can get closer to the ideal of how the fifth-century audience would have viewed this scene, or even, with whatever provisos, closer to what Aeschylus might have meant. Recognizing historical contingency, it seems, doesn't always lead, as one might think, to a *mise-en-abîme* of historical self-consciousness – but can also return somehow to the ideal of getting it right.

So in this book too, despite the arguments of this second section, which have been focused on the historicity of critical judgements about Sophocles, the opening five chapters looked at Sophocles' language without constantly reverting to a historically informed self-conscious self-critique of the questions I was posing or the answers I was expressing. This division between my two sections has been made not just for stylistic clarity, nor is it, I hope, merely heuristic opportunism. When I read Sophocles and revel in his language, I recognize that I share in the idealism of a direct, if not unmediated interaction with a text. Even though I know that I am a historically contingent reader, I take pleasure in Sophocles' plays – I find value in Sophocles' plays – *as if* I were not historically contingent. This "*as if*" is, I think, the grounding problem of the self-aware critic. Only a fundamentalist, religious or scholarly, could fail to be anxious about the challenges that have been mounted in the last two hundred years to the authority and value of the texts of the past, and our beliefs about them; but who could not recognize that such anxiety exists precisely because of the recognition of the authority and value invested in the texts of the past?

We are thus now in a position to outline what is perhaps the most pressing and vexing tension in contemporary criticism – namely, the tension between the drive towards historical self-consciousness and the drive towards the value invested in particular works of the past, or in particular pasts.

There have been several attempts by distinguished critics to negotiate this tension, but, even though I recognize the attractiveness of the impulse behind them, I have not found any of these strategies ultimately satisfying. It has, for example, become a commonplace to question the value of the classical

---

[32] Fraenkel (1950) *ad* 944ff.

texts: the role of antiquity's texts within the canon of Western culture has been sternly challenged – usually in the name of opposing the exclusionary and unpleasant values of imperialism, nationalism, sexism, elitism, racism and so forth, and often with a general suspicion of value judgements *per se*.[33] There are three main reasons why this strategy will not do – none of which, needless to say, involves arguing *for* the exclusionary and unpleasant values of imperialism, nationalism, sexism, elitism, racism, and none of which involves denying the place of privilege which classics has held within institutions of power and authority . . . First, and most simply, there is no integral or inherent link between studying the texts of antiquity and those negative values, or any general conservatism. Classics has been urgently associated with revolutionary thinking since the Renaissance, and has often been at the heart of radical political, religious, and social agendas. It is sloppy – ignorant – history to associate the study of classical antiquity *necessarily* with any particular set of values.[34] Second, to cut oneself off from such canonical material is to guarantee an insufficient understanding of generations of readers, who have themselves been formative for Western thinking, and, what's more, to fail to appreciate the importance of the ancient thinkers for the very categories of thought that still dominate Western thinking. Plato's contribution to our world-view still needs exploration, as does Nietzsche's obsession with Plato (say), because of their continuing influence on our patterns of thought. Whether or not Sophocles can be approached without Hegel, it would be an etiolated and distorting comprehension of Hegel that attempted to ignore the importance of Sophocles for his thinking. Part of understanding the value of Sophocles is exploring the value that generations of writers and artists have found in his works. Third, while it is necessary to interrogate the values with which criticism does its work, it is simply false to suggest that criticism can proceed without investing value and making value judgements. What, for example, would feminism look like without a passionate sense of value, and the judgements that come with it? What would be the value of criticism without values? So, while it is necessary to reflect seriously on how value is invested in particular texts and what the consequences of such investments are, I am quite unconvinced by arguments that attempt in this way to deny value to classical texts and their study.

From the other side, there is a more coherent argument, led by Kantian principles, which ascribes value to artworks, but which locates the value precisely within the individual reader's perception. That is, it is the reader's ascription of value to a text that gives the text its value. It is (only) my recognition of

---

[33] See e.g. both for polemics and the less polemical: Dubois (2001); (2010); Goff ed (2005); Goff and Simpson eds (2007); Hardwick and Gillespie eds (2007); Bernal (1987–1991) with Lefkowitz (1996); (2008); Lefkowitz and Rogers (1996).

[34] See Goldhill (2011).

the value of Nietzsche and of Nietzsche's Plato and of Plato that constructs the genealogy of influence used in the previous paragraph: the labour of the negative, the *mise-en-abîme* of historical self-consciousness, is fully embraced as the defining condition of criticism. The critic, expert in judgement, stands alone before the artwork. His writings in response trace "fragments from an *aesthetic* education".[35] While such arguments have been made with considerable sophistication, I remain anxious about the difficulty such a stance has with politics, history and community. It is extremely hard from such an intellectual position to aim for political purchase on the world, or to maintain a committed sense of a community. Especially with an arena such as Greek tragedy, to lose such purchase, to lose such a sense of community, is to disengage from the very work of the genre: a disengagement we may trace to Aristotle, and for which German Idealism, as we have seen, remains a central force, but which seems misplaced to me.

It may indeed be better to embrace the tension between historical self-consciousness and the value of particular texts as a defining condition of contemporary criticism – rather than attempt to resolve it. After all, drama itself is committed to dialogue, to a play or contest of different voices, and the tension between locatedness and generality is integral to Greek tragedy. As we have seen throughout this book, exemplarity is a recurrent problem within the dramas and the criticism of them: how Oedipus is or is not a paradigm for all humankind is a question which has not yet stopped being pertinent. It is important for me that the temporalities of this last sentence are observed. At one level, I am referring to a specific moment in an ancient text: "With you as paradigm, Oedipus, I count nothing mortal as happy", sing the chorus after Oedipus' horror is revealed (*Oedipus Tyrannus* 1193–6). Yet how the paradigm of Oedipus has been construed has changed radically over time and place: Freud's account of how we are all Oedipus is not the same as Hegel's or Aristotle's. What's more, the phrase "has not yet stopped" marks the continuity of this process rather than a fixed vantage point on a finished history. As we might say – using the structure of exemplarity again – just as Oedipus is *both* an especially specific person in that he kills his father and sleeps with his mother and blinds himself, *and* explicitly a paradigm for all humans, so the *Oedipus Tyrannus* as a play is *both* open to the historical contingencies of a series of specific and different understandings, *and* an object of value across time and communities. I want to keep both trajectories – the trajectory of value and the trajectory of historical self-consciousness, the trajectory of the general and the trajectory of the specific – in play, not least because I think it represents most accurately the state of contemporary criticism, as well as

---

[35] de Bolla (2001) 129; see also Martindale (2005), (2006), and the brief discussion in Hall and Harrop eds (2010).

speaking to the structuring of drama's exemplarity. I want to have my cake and eat it – or, less contentiously, to recognize the play of the "as if". The "as if" may be how we always engage with such works of the imagination . . .

One way we might rethink this perplexing problem is to move away from the vocabulary that has dominated the discussion in recent years and which has now tended towards the ossification of critical positions – namely, the language of the text. For the haute philologist, the text is the privileged term for the fixed object of a writer's production – or the object that needs fixing through textual criticism: the very words of the author. For the haute post-modernist the text or textuality marks the fluid state of historically contingent engagement with words and things – something there is no outside to, no end to: it has become an equally sacred critical term. I wonder – now, after so many years of thinking with the term "text" – whether the category "script" wouldn't lead into a more profitable discussion.

A script is a written or oral template which has the strange ability of main-taining itself through innumerable re-incarnations – and which only comes into voice in and through performance.[36] Now, *Hamlet* is almost never per-formed whole; the clown scene in *Othello* is so often cut that few know it exists; a Victorian *King Lear* could end with Lear and Kent alive, and Cordelia mar-ried to Edgar. In Serban's hands, a bare outline of *Trojan Women* was acted in a made-up language of grunts and shrieks and randomized syllables – with *no* words of the script, as it were, but it was still *Trojan Women*, just as was Gilbert Murray's English version for an audience scarred by the First World War, as was the Cambridge Greek play of the 1990s, where the language of Euripides was recited in Erasmian pronunciation. Any reading of the script performs it, and does so partially, dramatically, with an eye to imagined and real audiences, and with a knowledge that the definitive or full performance is no more than a claim of rhetoric. This is true even – especially – of the first or a single per-formance. A script may have a physical existence but it has no original. It has only performances (or silence). Yet it exists as a script. The more a script is performed, the greater its influence, value, and power to speak to audiences. And – the corollary – there can be boring, wacky, incompetent performances, however marvelous the script; performances which illuminate the script for a generation; performances which seem so far from the script that audiences resist the very performance as such. One way that literature and society inter-relate is as mutually informing scripts: the scripts of social ritual are embedded in literary narratives; literary narratives provide scripts through which social life is experienced.

---

[36] My use of the term *script* is influenced by the discussions of performance theory – see e.g. Worthen (2010), Worthen (2005) – with a background in a more developed history of the book e.g. McGann (1991).

I would suggest that "the script" is a useful model for thinking about the reading of Sophocles. The understanding of *Electra* as a pious play of ethical Christianity, and the understanding of *Electra* as the exploration of the violent psychological disruption of revenge are different "performances" or "enactments" of the "script" of *Electra*. They emerge as performances within culturally produced horizons of expectation, and speak most strongly to particular audiences. Like all performances, each of these readings is partial, distorting, illuminating . . . A performance has its historical contingency, while a script exceeds the process of its performance, without, however, ever attaining the status of an originary and fixed object.

It is easiest to see how the language of "the script" works with dramatic compositions such as the works of Sophocles, but I see no reason why such a conceptualization would not help us with even a work which proclaims itself as a "possession for all time" and which emphasizes the values of representing reality with as much accuracy as possible. The history of the reception – the reading – of Thucydides, both in antiquity and in modern historiography and political thought, reveals a series of engagements – partialities, claims and counter-claims, appropriations and insights – for which the idea of script and performance or enactment can provide a model. Again, there is no "first" and no "total" reading of Thucydides, no originary moment, only multiple and continuing engagements with a script which exceeds each of its (historically contingent) readings.

In short, I find readings of Sophocles' extraordinary works which are not aware of how regimes of knowledge and a history of criticism and a political positioning and a sense of community are necessary frames of engagement, will inevitably seem thin, childlike, as Cicero would say, in the ignorance of where they come from. But I also find discussions of the history of reading Sophocles which do not recognize the value of the works of Sophocles and do not contribute to my pleasure in and understanding of those works – which do not feed back into the reading of Sophocles – also of limited interest. The tension I have been describing between historical self-consciousness and critical discrimination becomes dynamic when both trajectories temper and inform each other. We set the historical contingency of reading against the assertion of value, as we set value against the assertion of historical contingency. The movement between these positionalities creates the space of contemporary critical debate. That is what this book has attempted to do, and what this programmatic conclusion aims to encourage for the future: to search for the critical space where we can bring history and philology together, creatively, dynamically: to find, indeed, that elusive place where history and philology rhyme.

{ GLOSSARY }

Most of these technical terms are defined when they first appear in the text, but are included in a glossary here for the ease of the non-classicist reader.

anapaest a metrical unit: anapaests are commonly used either as a sung form, "melic anapaests", or chanted, a form sometimes called "marching anapaests".

antilabe a verse that is divided between two or more speakers.

antistrophe a stanza in a *stasimon*, which has the same metrical pattern as the *strophe*.

bacchiac a metrical unit.

dimeter a verse of two metrical sequences (metra) – a shortened form of a trimeter.

dithyramb a form of choral song, often associated with highly excited singing. There was a competition for dithyrambic performances at the Great Dionysia in Athens, the same festival at which tragedy and comedy were performed, where each tribe entered a chorus.

dochmiac a metrical unit. Dochmiacs are often highly emotional.

ekkuklema a rolling platform which could bring out tableaux onto the stage from inside the house.

embolima a term Aristotle uses to describe choral odes that were added as musical interludes into plays but which were not thematically integral to the drama.

epode a free-standing stanza in a *stasimon* that comes after a *strophe* and an *antistrophe*.

hapax a grammatical term to indicate a word that occurs only once in our extant sources.

hemichorus a half chorus – where the full-body of the chorus is divided into two groups.

iambic the basic metre of tragic exchanges and speeches, the metre closest to human speech, according to Aristotle.

kommos a mourning song, usually antiphonal between a lead mourner or mourners and a group of condolers.

koruphaios the chorus leader.

lyric a term used for any verse form that was sung.

melic a term used for sung verse, to distinguish between sung and chanted forms.

parodos an entrance song, the opening song of a play, usually sung by the chorus or by the chorus with a solo actor.

particle a supplementary word indicating semantic emphasis, syntactic connection or tonal force.

polyptoton a grammatical term for the juxtaposition of the same word with different case endings.

scholia the comments written in the margin of a manuscript by ancient scholars.

stasimon (plural **stasima**) An ode in a drama, made up of *strophai* and *antistrophai*, which correspond in metrical form, and *epodes*, free-standing stanzas.

stichomythia the exchange of usually single lines between characters in dialogue.

strophe (plural strophai) A *strophe* is a stanza in a *stasimon*. It has the same metrical pattern as the *antistrophe*: the *strophe* and the *antistrophe* are said thus to "correspond".

strophic a term used to indicate that the choral song is made up of corresponding *strophe* and *antistrophe*.

theologeion the "god walk" – a raised platform above the stage house where gods can make an appearance.

tmesis a grammatical term to indicate the splitting the prefix and stem of a compound word.

trimeter the basic verse form of speeches and stichomythia in tragedy: a line made up of three metrical sequences (metra), which, in tragedy, are iambic: hence "iambic trimeter".

trochaic tetrameter a verse form of four metrical sequences (metra) which occurs occasionally in tragic dialogue – a lengthened trimeter.

{ BIBLIOGRAPHY }

This bibilography includes only works referrred to directly in the footnotes.

Abbott, E. ed (1880) *Hellenica: A Collection of Essays on Greek Poetry, Philosophy, History and Religion*, London.

Ackerman, R. (2002) *Myth and Ritual School: J.G. Frazer and the Cambridge Ritualists*, New York and London.

Alexiou, M. (2002) *Ritual Lament in Greek Tradition* 2nd ed, revised by D. Yatromanlakis and P. Roilus, Cambridge.

Allegre, F. (1905) *Sophocle: Étude sur les ressorts dramatiques de son theatre et la composition de ses tragedies*, Lyon and Paris.

Allen, R. (2006) "Sophocles' Voice: Active, Middle and Passive in the Plays of Sophocles", in de Jong and Rijksbaron eds (2006): 111–26.

Allison, H. (2001) *Kant's Theory of Taste: A Reading of the "Critique of Aesthetic Judgement"*, Cambridge.

Anderson, W.D. (1965) *Matthew Arnold and the Classical Tradition*, Ann Arbor.

Andraschke, P. (1997) "Felix Mendelssohn's *Antigone*", in Schmidt ed (1997): 141–66.

Anthon, C. (1853) *A Manual of Greek Literature*, New York.

Appia, A. (1962) *Music and the Art of the Theatre*, trans R. Corrigan and M. Dirks, Coral Gables, Florida.

Armstrong, R. (2005) *A Compulsion for Antiquity: Freud and the Ancient World*, Ithaca, NY.

Arnold, M. (1853) *Poems*, London.

Asmis, E. (1992) "Plato on Poetic Creativity", in R. Kraut ed (1992): 338–64.

Bachofen, J. (1967) *Myth, Religion and Mother-Right*, ed and trans by R. Mannheim, London.

Bamberger, J. (1975) 'The Myth of Matriarchy: why men rule in primitive society', in Rosaldo and Lamphere eds (1975).

Barker, E. (2009) *Entering the Agon: Dissent and Authority on Homer, Historiography and Tragedy*, Oxford.

Barner, W. (1971) "Die Monodie", in Jens ed (1971): 277–320.

Barnett, S. (2001) "Introduction", to Schlegel (2001): 1–16.

Barrett, W. (1964) *Euripides' Hippolytus*, Oxford.

Batchelder, A. (1995) *The Seal of Orestes: Self-Reference and Authority in Sophocles' Electra*, Lanham and London.

Beckman, W. (1999) *Marx, the Young Hegelians and the Origins of Radical Social Theory: Dethroning the Self*, Cambridge.

Beer, J. (2004) *Sophocles and the Tragedy of Athenian Democracy*, Westport.

Behler, E. (1986) "A.W. Schlegel and the Nineteenth-Century *Damnatio* of Euripides", *GRBS* 27:335–367.

Behler, E. (1988) "The Theory of Irony in German Romanticism", in Garber ed (1988): 43–81.

Belfiore, E. (1992) *Tragic Pleasures: Aristotle on Plot and Emotion*, Princeton.

Benhabib, S. (1996) 'On Hegel, Women and Irony', in Mills ed (1996): 25–44.

Benjamin, W. (1928) *Der Ursprung des deutschen Trauerspiels*, Berlin.

Benson, E.F. (1989) *David Blaize*, London.

Bernal, M. (1987–1991) *Black Athena: The Afro-Asiatic Roots of Classical Culture*, 2 vols, London.

Bers, V. (1985) "Dikastic *thorubos*" in Cartledge, P. and Harvey, D. (eds) (1985): 1–15.

Billings, J. (forthcoming) "Choral Dialectics: Hölderlin and Hegel" in Gagné and Hopman eds (forthcoming).

Blake Tyrrell, W. and Bennett, L. (1998) *Recapturing Sophocles' Antigone*, Lanham.

Boegehold, A. (1999) *When a Gesture Was Expected*, Princeton.

Boegehold, A. and Scafuro, A. eds (1994) *Athenian Identity and Civic Ideology*, Baltimore.

Boetius, S. (2005) *Die Wiedergeburt der griechischen Tragödie auf der Bühne des 19. Jahrhunderts: Bühnenfassungen mit Schauspielmusik*, Tübingen.

Bollack, J. (1991) *L'Oedipe Roi de Sophocle. Le Texte et ses interpretations*, III vols, Lille.

Bond, G. (1981) *Euripides' Heracles*, Oxford.

Booth, W. (1974) *A Rhetoric of Irony*, Chicago.

Bowie, A. (1993) *Schelling and Modern European Philosophy*, London and New York.

Bowie, A. (2003) *Music, Philosophy and Modernity*, Cambridge.

Bowra, M. (1944) *Sophoclean Tragedy*, Oxford.

Branham, B. (1989) *Unruly Eloquence: Lucian and the Comedy of Traditions*, Cambridge, MA.

Braulich, H. (1969) *Max Reinhardt: Theater zwischen Traum und Wirklichkeit*, Berlin.

Brecht, B. (1965) *The Messingkauf Dialogues*, trans J. Willett, London.

Brown, M. ed (2000) *The Cambridge History of Literary Criticism: Vol V: Romanticism*, Cambridge.

Brown, P. and Ograjensek, S. eds (2010) *Ancient Drama in Music for the Modern Stage*, Oxford.

Browne, R. (1853) *A History of Classical Literature*, London.

Browning, R. (1875) *Aristophanes' Apology*, London.

Browning, R. (1871) *Balaustion's Adventure*, London.

Budd, M. (1985) *Music and the Emotions: The Philosophical Theory*, London and New York.

Budelmann, F. (2000) *The Language of Sophocles: Communality, Communication and Involvement*, Cambridge.

Bulwer-Lytton, E. (1837) *Athens, its rise and fall: with views of the literature, philosophy, and social life of the Athenian people*, 2 vols, London.

Burian, P. (2010) "Gender and the City: Antigone from Hegel to Butler and Back", in J. Euben and K. Bassi eds (2010): 255–99.

Burke, P. (2007) *What Is Cultural History?*, Cambridge.

Burke, P. ed (1991) *New Perspectives on Historical Writing*, Cambridge.

Burton, R. (1980) *The Chorus in Sophocles' Tragedies*, Oxford.

Bushnell. R. (1988) *Prophesying Tragedy: Sign and Voice in Sophocles' Theban Plays*, Ithaca, NY.

Butler, E. (1935) *The Tyranny of Greece over the German Imagination*, Cambridge.

Butler, J. (2000) *Antigone's Claim: Kinship Between Life and Death*, New York.

Butler, M. (1981) *Romantics, Rebels and Reactionaries*, Oxford.

Buxton, R. (1982) *Persuasion in Greek Tragedy: A Study of Peitho*, Cambridge.

Buxton, R. (1988) "Bafflement in Greek Tragedy", *Métis* 3: 41–51.

Cairns, D. and Liapis, V. (1997) eds *Dionysalexandros: Essays on Aeschylus and his Fellow Tragedians in honour of Alexander F. Garvie*, Swansea.

Calder, W.M. III (2005)" 'The End of Sophocles' *Electra" GRBS* 4: 213–6.

Calder, W.M. III and Schlesier, R. eds (1998) *Zwischen Rationalismus und Romantik: Karl Ottfried Müller und die antike Kultur*, Hildesheim.

Cameron, A., and Kuhrt, A. eds (1983) *Images of Women in Antiquity*, London.

Campbell, L (1871) *Sophocles: The Plays and Fragments Vol I*, Oxford.

Campbell, L. (1879) *Sophocles (J.R. Green's Classical Writers)*, London.

Campbell, L. (1881) *Sophocles: The Plays and Fragments Vol II*, Oxford.

Campbell, L. (1891) *A Guide to Greek Tragedy for English Readers*, London.

Campbell, L. (1904) *Tragic Drama in Aeschylus, Sophocles and Shakespeare*, London.

Campbell, L. and Abbott, E. (1886) *Sophocles for the Use of Schools*, 2 vols, Oxford.

Cannadine, D. (2000) *What Is History Now?*, Basingstoke.

Carroll, J. (1982) *The Cultural Theory of Matthew Arnold*, Berkeley.

Carson, A. (1996) "Screaming in Translation: the *Elektra* of Sophocles" in Dunn ed (1996): 5–11.

Carter, D. (2011) ed *Why Athens? A Reappraisal of Tragic Politics*, Oxford.

Carter, H. (1914) *The Theatre of Max Reinhardt*, London.

Cartledge, P. and Harvey, D. (eds) (1985) *Crux: Essays in Greek History Presented to G.E.M. de Ste. Croix*, London.

Cartledge, P., Millett, P. and Todd, S. eds (1990) *Nomos: Essays on Athenian Law, Politics and Society*, Cambridge.

Cave, T. (1988) *Recognitions. A Study in Poetics*, Oxford.

Caygill, J. (1988) *Art of Judgement*, Oxford.

Chanter, T. (1995) *Ethics of Eros: Irigaray's Rewriting of the Philosophers*, New York and London.

Chanter, T. (2010) "Antigone's Political Legacies: Abjection in Defiance of Mourning" in Wilmer and Zukauskaite eds (2010): 19–47.

Clarke, G. ed (1989) *Rediscovering Hellenism: The Hellenic Inheritance and the English Imagination*, Cambridge.

Cogan, M. (1981) *The Human Thing: The Speeches and Principles of Thucydides' Histories*, Chicago.

Cohen, T. and Guyer, P. eds (1982) *Essays in Kant's Aesthetics*, Chicago.

Collini, S. (1991) *Public Moralists: Political Thought and Intellectual Life in Britain 1850–1930*, Oxford.

Collini, S. (1994) *Matthew Arnold: A Critical Portrait*, Oxford.

Collins, C. (1871) *Sophocles*, Edinburgh and London.

Collis, M. and Lukes, S. eds (1982) *Rationality and Relativism*, London.

Colson, P. (1935) *Life of the Bishop of London*, London.

Crane, G. (1996) *The Blinded Eye: Thucydides and the New Written Word*, London.

Cropp, M., Fantham, E. and Scully, S. eds (1986) *Greek Tragedy and Its Legacy: Essays Presented to D.J. Conacher*, Calgary.

Crowther, H. (1989) *The Kantian Sublime: From Morality to Art*, Oxford.

Csapo, E. and Slater, W. (1995) *The Context of Ancient Drama*, Michigan.

Dahlhaus, C. (1989) *The Idea of Absolute Music*, trans R. Lustig, Chicago.

Dale, M. (1967) *Euripides' Helen*, Oxford.

Dale, M. (1968) *The Lyric Metres of Greek Tragedy*, Cambridge.

Dane, J. (1991) *The Critical Mythology of Irony*, Athens, GA.

Davidson, J. (1995) "Homer and Sophocles' *Philoctetes*", in Griffiths ed (1995): 25–35.

Davies, M. (1999) "'Leaving out the Erinyes': the History of a Misconception", *Prometheus* 25: 117–128.

Davidson, J. (2006) "Sophocles and Homer: Some Issues of Vocabulary", in de Jong and Rijksbaron eds (2006): 25–38.

Davies, M. (1991) *Sophocles Trachiniae*, Oxford.

Dawe, R. (1978) *Studies in the Text of Sophocles III*, Leiden.

de Bolla, P. (2001) *Art Matters*, Cambridge, MA.

Deckinger, H. (1911) *Die Darstellung der persönlichen Motive bei Aischylos und Sophokles: Ein Beitrag zur Technik der griechische Tragödie*, Leipzig.

de Jong, I. and Rijksbaron, A. eds (2006) *Sophocles and the Greek Language: Aspects of Diction, Syntax and Pragmatics*, Leiden.

de Laura, D. (1969) *Hebrew and Hellene in Victorian Britain*, Austin.

de Man, P. (1983) *Blindness and Insight: Essays in the Rhetoric of Contemporary Criticism*, Minneapolis, MN.

de Man, P. (1996) "The Concept of Irony", in *The Aesthetic Ideology*, Minneapolis, MN.

Denniston, J. (1934) *Greek Particles*, Oxford.

Derrida, J. (1974) *Glas*, Paris.

Derrida, J. (1997) *Politics of Friendship*, trans G. Collins, London and New York.

Détienne, M. (1981) *L'Invention de la mythologie*, Paris.

Dieteren, F. and Kloeck, E. eds (1990) *Writing Women into History*, Amsterdam.

Dihle, A. (1994) *A History of Greek Literature, From Homer to the Hellenistic Period*, trans C. Krojzl, London and New York.

Dik, H (2006) *Word Order in Greek Tragic Dialogue*, Oxford.

Ditmars, E. van nes (1992) *Sophocles' Antigone: Lyric Shape and Meaning*, Pisa.

Dobrov, G. (2001) *Figures of Play: Greek Drama and Metafictional Poetics*, Oxford.

Donaldson, J. (1860) *Theatre of the Greeks: a Treatise on the History and the Exhibition of the Greek Drama*, Cambridge.

Dowgun, R. (1982) "Some Victorian Perceptions of Greek Tragedy", *Browning Institute Studies* 10: 71–90.

Droysen, G. (1959) *Ein tief gegründet Herz: Der Briechwechsel Felix Mendelssohn-Bartholdys mit Johann Gustav Droysen* ed C. Wehmer, Heidelberg.

Dubois, P. (2001) *Trojan Horses: Saving Classics from the Conservatives*, New York.

Dubois, P. (2010) *Out of Athens: The New Ancient Greeks*, Cambridge, MA.

Dué, C. (2003) *The Captive Woman's Lament in Greek Tragedy*, Austin, TX.

Duncan, I. (1968) *My Life*, London.

Dunn, F. (2006) "Trope and Setting in Sophocles' *Electra*", in de Jong and Rijksbaron eds (2006): 183–200.

Dunn, F. ed (1996) *Sophocles' Electra in Performance*, Stuttgart.

DuQuesnil, F. (1901) "Mounet-Sully de la Comédie-Française", *Le Théâtre* 67: 5–17.

Dyer, T. (1846a) "The *Antigone* of Sophocles and the *Foreign Quarterly Review*", *Classical Museum* 3: 176–89.

Dyer, T. (1846b) "On the Choral Dancing of the Greeks", *Classical Museum* 3: 229–45.

Eagleton, T. (1990) *The Ideology of the Aesthetic*, Oxford.

Eagleton, T. (2003) *Sweet Violence: the Idea of the Tragic*, Oxford.

Eagelton, T. (2010) "Lacan's Antigone", in Wilmer and Zukauskaite eds (2010): 101–09.

Easterling, P. (1973) "Presentation of Character in Aeschylus", *G&R* 20: 3–19.

Easterling, P. (1977) "Character in Sophocles", *G&R* 24: 121–9.

Easterling, P. (1978) "*Philoctetes* and Modern Criticism", *ICS* 3: 27–39.

Easterling, P. (1982) *Sophocles. Trachiniae*, Cambridge.

Easterling, P. (1990) "Constructing Character in Greek Tragedy", in Pelling ed (1990): 83–99.

Easterling, P. (1997) "Form and Performance", in Easterling ed (1997a): 151–77.

Easterling, P. (1997) "From Repertoire to Canon," in Easterling ed (1997b): 211–27.

Easterling, P. (1997c) "The Death Of Oedipus: What Happened Next", in Cairns and Liapis eds (1997): 133–50.

Easterling, P. (1999) "Plain Words in Sophocles", in Griffin ed (1999): 95–107.

Easterling, P. ed (1997) *The Cambridge Companion to Greek Tragedy*, Cambridge.

Eatock, C. (2009) *Mendelssohn and Victorian England*, Farnham.

Eliot, G. (1963) "The *Antigone* and its Moral", in *The Essays of George Eliot* ed T. Pinney, New York.

Ellis, C. (1897) *Shakespeare and the Bible*, London and Plymouth.

Ellis, C. (1902) *Christ in Shakespeare*, London and Bath.

Ellman, M. (1982) "Polytropic Man: patern ity, identity, and naming in *The Odyssey* and *A Portrait of the Artist as a Young Man*", MacCabe ed (1982): 72–104.

Else, G. (1986) *Plato and Aristotle on Poetry*, Chapel Hill, NC, and London.

Elshtain, J. (1982) "Antigone's Daughters", *Democracy* 2: 46–59.

Engels, F. (1972) *Origins of the Family, Private Property and the State*, trans E. Leacock, London.

Euben, J. and Bassi, K. eds (2010) *When Worlds Collide*, Lanham, MD.

Evans, R. (2001) *In Defence of History*, London.

Ewans, M. (1982) *Wagner and Aeschylus: The Ring and the Oresteia*, London.

Ewans, M. (2007) *Opera from the Greek: Studies in the Poetics of Appropriation*, Aldershot.

Falkner, T. (1998) "Containing Tragedy: Rhetoric and Self-Representation in Sophocles' *Philoctetes*", *ClAnt* 17: 25–58.

Faverty, F. (1951) *Mathew Arnold, The Ethnologist*, Illinois.

Ferrari, G. (1989) "Plato and Poetry", in Kennedy ed (1989): 92–148.

Ferris, D. (2000) *Silent Urns: Romanticism, Hellenism, Modernity*, Cambridge.

Field, G.G. (1981) *Evangelist of Race: the Germanic Vision of Houston Stewart Chamberlain*, New York.

Finglass, P. (2007) *Sophocles' Electra*, Cambridge.

Finley, M. (1983) *Politics in the Ancient World*, Cambridge.

Fish, S. (1980) *Is There a Text in This Class: The Authority of Interpretive Communities*, Cambridge, MA.

Fish, S. (1989) *Doing What Comes Naturally: Change, Rhetoric, and the Practice of Theory in Literary and Legal Studies*, Oxford.

Flashar, H. (1991) *Inszenierung der Antike: das griechische Drama auf der Bühne der Neuzeit 1585–1990*, Munich.

Flashar, H. (2001) "Felix Mendelssohn-Bartholdy und die griechiscge Tragödie. Bühnemusik im Kontext von Politik, Kultur und Bildung", *Abhandlungen der Sächsischen Akademie der Wissenschaft zu Leipzig, Philologisch-historische Klasse 78.1*, Stuttgart.

Foley, H. (1982) "The 'Female Intruder' Reconsidered: Women in Aristophanes' *Lysistrata* and *Ecclesiazusae*", *CP* 71: 1–21.

Foley, H. (1995) "Tragedy and democratic ideology: the case of Sophocles' *Antigone*", in B. Goff ed (1995).

Foley, H. (1996) "Antigone as a Moral Agent", in Silk ed (1996): 49–73.

Foley, H. (2001) *Female Acts in Greek Tragedy*, Princeton, NJ.

Ford, A. (2002) *The Origins of Criticism: Literary Culture and Poetic Theory in Classical Greece*, Princeton, NJ.

Foster, D. (2010) *Wagner's Ring Cycle and the Greeks*, Cambridge.

Foucault, M. (1972) *The Archaeology of Knowledge*, trans A. Sheridan, London.

Foucault, M. (1974) *The Order of Things: An Archaeology of the Human Sciences*, London.

Fraenkel, E. (1950) *Aeschylus Agamemnon*, 3 vols, Oxford.

Freeman, E. (1856) "Grote's *History of Greece*", *North British Review* 25: 141–72.

Friis Johansen, H. (1964) "Die *Elektra* des Sophokles: Versuch einer neuen Deutung", *C&M* 25: 8–32.

Fritzsche, P. (2004) *Stranded in the Present: Modern Times and the Melancholy of History*, Cambridge, MA.

Frontisi-Ducroux, F. (1995) *Du Masque au visage: aspects de l'identité en Grèce ancienne*, Paris.

Furley, D. and Nehemas, A. eds (1994) *Aristotle's Rhetoric: Philosophical Essays*, Princeton.

Furst, L. (1984) *Fictions of Romantic Irony*, Cambridge, MA.

Gagné, R and Hopman, M. (forthcoming) *Choral Mediation in Greek Drama*, Cambridge.

Gange, D. (2009) "Odysseus in Eden: Gladstone's Homer and the idea of universal epic, 1850–1880", *Journal of Victorian Studies* 14: 190–206.

Garber, F. ed (1988) *Romantic Irony*, Budapest.

Gardiner, C. (1987) *The Sophoclean Chorus: A Study of Character and Function*, Iowa City.

Garvie, A. (1972) "Deceit, Violence and Persuasion in the *Philoctetes*" in *Studi classici in onore di Quintino Cataudella* I, Catania: 213–26.

Garvie, A. (1998) *Sophocles. Ajax*, Warminster.

Geary, J. (2006) "Re-inventing the Past: Mendelssohn's *Antigone* and the Creation of an Ancient Greek Musical Language", *Journal of Musicology* 23.1: 187–226.

Geary, J. (2010) "Incidental Music and the Revival of Greek Tragedy from the Italian Renaissance to German Romanticism", in Brown and Ograjensek eds (2010): 47–66.

Geck, M. (1967) *Die Wiederentdeckung der 'Mathäuspassion' im 19. Jahhundert: die zeitgenössischen Dokumente und ihre ideengeschichte Deutung*, Regensburg.

Gellie, G. (1972) *Sophocles. A Reading*, Melbourne.

Gellrich, M. (1988) *Tragedy and Theory: the Problem of Conflict since Aristotle*, Princeton, NJ.

Gigante, M. (1989) *Classico e mediazione: contributi alla storia della filologia antica*, Rome.

Gildenhard, I. and Ruehl, M. eds (2003) *Out of Arcadia*, BICS Supplement 79, London.

Gilkes, A. H. (1880) *School Lectures on the Electra of Sophocles and Macbeth*, London.

Gilkes, A. (1894) *The Thing That Hath Been, or, A Young Man's Mistakes*, London.

Gilkes, A. (1905) *A Day at Dulwich*, London.

Gill, C. (1980) "Bow, Oracle and Epiphany in Sophocles' *Philoctetes*", *G&R* 27: 137–46.

Goehr, L. (1992) *Imaginary Museum of Musical Works: an Essay in the Philosophy of Music*, Oxford.

Goehr, L. (1998) *The Quest for Voice: on Music, Politics and the Limits of Philosophy*, Oxford.

Goehr, L. (2008) *Elective Affinities: Musical Essays on the History of Aesthetic Theory*, New York.

Goff, B. ed (1995) *History, Tragedy and Theory*, Austin.

Goff, B. ed (2005) *Classics and Colonialism*, London.

Goff, B. and Simpson, M. eds (2007) *Crossroads in the Black Aegean: Oedipus, Antigone, and Dramas of the African Diaspora*, Oxford.

Goheen, R. (1951) *The Imagery of Sophocles' Antigone*, Princeton, NJ.

Goldhill, S. (1984a) "Exegeisis: Oedipus (R)ex", *Arethusa* 17:177–220.

Goldhill, S. (1984b) "Two notes on τέλος and related words in the *Oresteia*", *JHS* 104: 169–76.

Goldhill, S. (1986) *Reading Greek Tragedy*, Cambridge.

Goldhill, S. (1990a) "The Great Dionysia and Civic Ideology", in Winkler and Zeitlin eds (1990): 97–129.

Goldhill, S. (1990b) "Character and Action: representation and Reading" in Pelling ed (1990): 100–27.

Goldhill, S. (1991) *The Poet's Voice: Essays on Poetics and Greek Literature*, Cambridge.

Goldhill, S. (1994) "Representing democracy: women at the Great Dionysia" in Osborne and Hornblower eds (1994): 347–70.

Goldhill, S. (1995) *Foucault's Virginity: Ancient Erotic Fiction and the History of Sexuality*, Cambridge.

Goldhill, S. (1996) "Collectivity and Otherness – The Authority of the tragic Chorus", in Silk ed (1996): 244–56.

Goldhill, S. (1997) "The audience of Athenian tragedy" in Easterling ed (1997): 54–68.

Goldhill, S. (2000a) "Whose Antiquity? Whose Modernity? The Rainbow Bridges of Exile", *Antike und Abendland* 46: 1–20.

Goldhill, S. (2000b) "Civic Ideology and the Problem of Difference: the Politics of Aeschylean Tragedy, Once Again", *Journal of Hellenic Studies* 120: 34–56.

Goldhill, S. (2000c) "Placing Theatre in the History of Vision", in Rutter and Sparks eds (2000): 161–82.

Goldhill, S. (2002) *Who Needs Greek? Contests in the Cultural History of Hellenism*, Cambridge.

Goldhill, S. (2003) "Tragic Emotions: the Pettiness of Envy and the Politics of Pitilessness" in Konstan and Rutter eds (2003): 165–180.

Goldhill, S. (2006) "Der Ort der Gewalt: Was sehen wir auf der Bühne?" in Seidensticker and Vöhler eds (2006): 140–68.

Goldhill, S. (2010) "Idealism in the *Odyssey* and the Meaning of *mounos* in *Odyssey* 16", in Mitzis and Tsagalis eds (2010): 115–28.

Goldhill, S. (2011) *Victorian Culture and Classical Antiquity: Art, Opera, Fiction and the Proclamation of Modernity*, Princeton, NJ.

Goldhill, S. and Hall, E. (2009) "The State of Play", in Goldhill and Hall eds (2009): 1–24.

Goldhill, S. and Hall, E. eds (2009) *Sophocles and the Greek Tragic Tradition*, Cambridge.

Goldhill, S. and Osborne, R. (1999) *Performance Culture and Athenian Democracy*, Cambridge.

Goldstein, J. ed (1994) *Foucault and the Writing of History*, Oxford.

Goodell, T. (1920) *Athenian Tragedy: a Study in Popular Art*, New Haven, CT.

Goodman, N. (1968) *Languages of Art: an Approach to a Theory of Symbols*, Indianapolis.

Gossman, L. (1994) "Philhellenism and Anti-Semitism: Matthew Arnold and his German Models", *Comparative Literature* 46: 1–39.

Gossman, L. (2000) *Basel in the Age of Burckhardt: a Study in Unseasonable Ideas*, Chicago.

Gould, J. (1978) "Dramatic character and 'human intelligibility'", *PCPS* 24: 43–67.

Gould, J. (1996) "Tragedy and Collective Experience", in Silk ed (1996): 217–43.

Gould, T. (1990) *The Ancient Quarrel between Poetry and Philosophy*, Princeton.

Gow, A.S.F. (1945) *Letters from Cambridge, 1939–1944*, London.

Gow, J. (1888) *A Companion to School Classics*, London and New York.

Goward, B. (1999) *Telling Tragedy: Narrative Technique in Aeschylus, Sophocles and Euripides*, London.

Grene, D. and Lattimore, R. eds (1954) *The Complete Greek Tragedies*, Chicago.

Griffin, J. (1999) "Sophocles and the Democratic City" in Griffin ed (1999): 73–94.

Griffin, J. ed (1999) *Sophocles Revisited. Essays Presented to Sir Hugh Lloyd-Jones*, Oxford.

Griffith, M. (1977) *The Authenticity of the "Prometheus Bound"*, Cambridge.

Griffith, M. (1999) *Sophocles. Antigone*, Cambridge.

Griffith, M. (2005) "The Subject of Desire in Sophocles' *Antigone*", in Pedrick and Oberhelman eds (2005): 90–135.

Griffith, M. (2010) "Psychoanalysing *Antigone*", in Wilmer and Zukauskaite eds (2010): 110–34.

Griffiths, A. ed (1995) *Stage Directions: Essays in Ancient Drama in Honour of E.W. Handley*, *BICS Suppl* 66, London: 25–35.

Gross, A. (1905) *Die Stichomythie in der griechischen Tragödie und Komödie: ihre Anwendung und ihr Ursprung*, Berlin.

Grote, G. (1846) *History of Greece*, 12 vols, London.

Hadas, M. (1950) *A History of Greek Literature*, New York.

Haigh, A. E. (1906) *Attic Theatre: a Description of the Stage and Theatre of the Athenians and of the Dramatic Performances at Athens*, Oxford.

Haldane, J. (1963) "A Paean in the *Philoctetes*", *CQ* 13: 53-.

Hall, E. (1996) "Is there a *polis* in Aristotle's *Poetics*?", in Silk ed (1996): 295–309.

Hall, E. (1999a) "Sophocles' *Electra* in Britain", in Griffin ed (1999): 261–306.

Hall, E. (1999b) "Actor's Song in Tragedy", in Goldhill and Osborne eds (1999): 96–122.

Hall, E. (2006) *The Theatrical Cast of Athens: Interactions Between Ancient Greek Drama and Society*, Oxford.

Hall, E, Alston, R. and McConnell, J. eds (2011) *Ancient Slavery and Abolition: From Hobbes to Hollywood*, Oxford.

Hall, E. and Harrop, S. eds (2010) *Theorizing Performance: Greek Drama, Cultural History and Critical Practice*, London.

Hall, E. and Macintosh, F. (2005) *Greek Tragedy and the British Theatre 1660–1914*, Oxford.

Hall, E., Macintosh, F. and Taplin, O. eds (2000) *Medea in Performance 1500–2000*, Oxford.

Hall, E., Macintosh, F. and Wrigley, A. eds (2004) *Dionysus Since 69: Greek Tragedy at the Dawn of the Third Millennium*, Oxford.

Hall, J. (1997) *Ethnic Identity in Greek Identity*, Cambridge.

Halliwell, S. (1986) *Aristotle's Poetics*, Chapel Hill, NC.

Halliwell, S. (1987) *The Poetics of Aristotle. Translation and Commentary*, London.

Halliwell, S. (1996) "Plato's Repudiation of the Tragic" in Silk ed (1996): 332–50.

Hamilton, R. T. (2008) *Music, Madness and the Unworking of Language*, New York.

Handwerk, G. (1984) *Irony and Ethics in Narrative*, New Haven.

Handwerk, G. (2000) "Romantic Irony" in Brown ed. (2000): 203–25.

Hansen, M. (1991) *The Athenian Democracy in the Age of Demosthenes*, Oxford.

Hardwick, L. and Gillespie, C. eds (2007) *Classics in Post-Colonial Worlds*, Oxford.

Haubold, J. (2000) *Homer's People: epic Poetry and Social Formation*, Cambridge.

Heath, M. (1987) *The Poetics of Greek Tragedy*, London.

Heiden, B. (1989) *Tragic Rhetoric: an Interpretation of Sophocles' Trachiniae*, New York.

Henderson, J. (1991) "Women and the Athenian Dramatic Festivals", *TAPA* 121: 133–47.

Henderson, L. (1976) "Sophocles' *Trachiniae* 878–92 and a Principle of Paul Maas", *Maia* 28: 19–24.

Henrichs, A. (1986) "The Last of the Detractors: Friedrich Nietzsche's Condemnation of Euripides", *GRBS* 27: 369–97.

Herald, H. (1915) *Max Reinhardt*, Berlin.

Hesk, J. (2000) *Deception and Democracy in Classical Athens*, Cambridge.

Heuner, U. (2006) "Killing Words: Speech Acts and Non-Verbal Actions in Sophocles' Tragedies" in de Jong and Rijksbaron eds (2006): 201–212.

Hinds, A.E. (1967) "The Prophecy of Helenus in Sophocles' *Philoctetes*", *CQ* 17: 169–80.

Hiscock, M. (2007) "Classical Suicide: Autocheiria and Ambivalent Autonomy", PhD Cambridge.

Hofmannsthal, H. von. (1952) *Selected Prose*, trans M. Holtinger, J. and T. Stern, New York.

Hofmannsthal, H. von (1953) *Gesammelte Werke* ed H. Steiner, Frankfurt.

Hölderlin, F. (1946–85) *Sämtliche Werke* 8 vols in 15, eds F. Beissner and A. Beck, Stuttgart.

Holst-Wahrhaft, G. (1992) *Dangerous Voices: Women's Lament and Greek Literature*, London.

Honig, B. (2009) "Antigone's Laments, Creon's Grief: Mourning, Membership and the Politics of Exception", *Political Theory* 37.1: 5–43

Honig, B. (2010) "Antigone's Two Laws: Greek Tragedy and the Politics of Humanism", *New Literary History* 41: 1–38.

Honig, B. (2011) "Ismene's Forced Choice: Sacrifice and Sorority in Sophocles' *Antigone*", *Arethusa* 44: 29–68.

Horton-Smith, L. (1896) *Ars Tragica Sophoclea cum Shakesperiana Comparata*, London.

Horton-Smith, L. (1915) *Family and College: Some Interesting Records and a Golden Wedding*, Cambridge.

Hostetter, A. (2003) *Max Reinhardt's Großes Schauspielhaus – Its Artistic Goals, Planning and Operation 1910–1933*, Lewiston.

Howald, E. (1930) *Die griechische Tragödie*, Munich and Berlin.

Hughes, D. (2007) *Culture and Sacrifice: Ritual Death in Literature and Opera*, Cambridge.

Hunt, L. ed (1989) *The New Cultural History*, Berkeley.

Hutcheon, L. (1994) *Irony's Edge: the Theory and Politics of Irony*, New York.

Hutchings, K. and Pulkkinen, T. eds (2010) *Hegel's Philosophy and Feminist Thought: Beyond Antigone*, New York.

Hutchinson, G. (1999) "Sophocles and Time" in Griffin ed (1999): 47–72.

Ihering, H. (1929) *Reinhardt, Jessner, Piscator oder Klassikertod*, Berlin.

Immerwahr, R. (1988) "The Practice of Irony in Early German Romanticism", in Garber ed (1988): 82–96.

Irigaray, L. (1985) *Speculum of the Other Woman*, trans G. Gill, Ithaca, NY.

Irigaray, L. (2010) "Between Myth and History: The Tragedy of Antigone", in Wilmer and Zukkauskaite eds (2010): 197–212.

Jacobs, M. and Warren, J. eds (1986) *Max Reinhardt: the Oxford Symposium*, Oxford.

Janvier, T. (1895) "The Comédie-Française at Orange", *The Century Magazine* 50.2: 165–81.

Jarratt, S. (1991) *Rereading the Sophists: Classical Rhetoric Refigured*, Carbondale and Edwardsville.

Jebb, C. (1907) *Life and letters of Sir Richard Claverhouse Jebb, O. M., LITT. D*, Cambridge.

Jebb, R. (1890) *Sophocles: The Philoctetes*, Cambridge.

Jebb, R. (1894) *Sophocles: The Electra*, Cambridge.

Jebb, R. (1896) *Sophocles: The Ajax*, Cambridge.

Jebb, R. (1898) *Sophocles: The Philoctetes*, Cambridge.

Jebb, R. (1900) *Sophocles: The Antigone*, Cambridge.

Jenkins, K. (1991) *Rethinking History*, London.

Jens, W. (1955) *Die Stichomythie in der frühen griechischen Tragödie*, Munich.

Jens, W. (1955b) *Hofmannsthal und die Griechen*, Tübingen.

Jens, W. ed (1971) *Die Bauformen der griechischern Tragödie*, Munich.

Johnson, J. (1991) "Music in Hegel's *Aesthetics*: a re-evaluation:", *British Journal of Aesthetics* 31.2: 152–62.

Kahane, A. (1928) *Tagebuch der Dramaturgen*, Berlin.

Kahane, Ah. (2010) "*Antigone*, Antigone: Lacan and the Structure of the Law", in Wilmer and Zukauskaite eds (2010): 147–67.

Kaibel, G. (1896) *Sophokles Elektra*, Leipzig.

Kaimio, M. (1988) *Physical Contact in Greek Tragedy: A Study of Stage Convention*, Helsinki.

Kavoulakis, S. (2003) *Philosophy and Revolution: from Kant to Marx*, London and New York.

Kain, P. (1982) *Schiller, Hegel and Marx: State, Society and the Aesthetic ideal of Ancient Greece*, Kingston and Montreal.

Kells, J. (1973) *Sophocles. Electra*, Cambridge.

Kennedy, G. ed (1989) *The Cambridge History of Literary Criticism* vol 1, Cambridge.

Kierkegaard, S. (1971) *Either/Or*, trans D. Swenson, Princeton, NJ.

King. H. (1983) "Bound to Bleed: Artemis and Greek Women", in A. Cameron and A. Kuhrt eds (1983): 117–25.

King, H. (1998) *Hippocrates' Woman: Reading the Female Body in Ancient Greece*, London.

Kirkwood, G. (1954) "The Dramatic Role of the Chorus in Sophocles", *Phoenix* 8: 1–22.

Kittmer, J. (1995) "Sophoclean Sophistics: a Reading of *Philoctetes*", *MD* 34: 9–35.

Kitto, H. (1961) *Greek Tragedy*, 3rd edition, London and New York.

Kitzinger, R. (2008) *Choruses of Sophokles' Antigone and Philoktetes: A Dance of Words*, Leiden.

Knox, B. (1957) *Oedipus at Thebes,* London and New Haven, CT.

Knox, B. (1964) *The Heroic Temper: Studies in Sophoclean Tragedy*, Berkeley.

Knox, N. (1961) *The Word "Irony" and its Contexts, 1500–1755*, Durham, NC.

Konstan, D. (2001) *Pity Transformed*, London.

Konstan, D. and Rutter, K. eds (2003) *Envy, Spite and Jealousy: the Rivalrous Emotions in Ancient Greece*, Edinburgh.

Kosak, J. (1999) "Therapeutic Touch and Sophocles *Philoktetes*", *HSCP* 99: 93–134.

Koven, S. (2004) *Slumming: Sexual and Social Politics in Victorian London*, Princeton.

Kraus, C. (1991) "ΛΟΓΟΣ ΜΕΝ ΕΣΤ' ΑΡΧΑΙΟΣ: Stories and Story-Telling in Sophocles' Trachiniae", *TAPA* 121:75–98.

Krausz, M. ed (1993) *The Interpretation of Music: Philosophical Essays*, Oxford.

Kraut, R. ed (1992) *The Cambridge Companion to Plato*, Cambridge.

Kuhn, T. (1962) *The Structure of Scientific Revolutions*, Chicago.

Lanni, A. (1997) "Spectator sport or serious politics: οἱ περιεστηκότες and the Athenian lawcourts", *JHS* 117: 183–9.

Lanni, A. (2006) *Law and Justice in the Courts of Classical Athens*, Cambridge.

Latour, B. (1997) *Nous n'avons jamais été modernes: essai d'anthropolgie symétrique*, Paris.

Leake, W. (1938) *Gilkes and Dulwich 18856–1914: a Study of a Great Headmaster*, London.

Lebeck, A. (1971) *The Oresteia*, Washington.

Leclerc, J-B. (1796/Year 4) *Essai sur la propagation de la musique en France: sa conservation et ses rapports avec le gouvernement*, Paris.

Lefkowitz, M. (1996) *Not Out of Africa: How Afrocentrism Became an Excuse to Teach Myth as History*, New York.

Lefkowitz, M. (2008) *History Lesson. A Race Odyssey*, New Haven, CT.

Lefkowitz, M. and Rogers, G. (1996) *Black Athena Revisited*, Chapel Hill, NC.

Leineks, V. (1982) *The Plays of Sophocles*, Leiden.

Leonard, M. (1999) "Irigaray's Cave: Feminist Theory and the Politics of French Classicism", *Ramus* 28: 152–68.

Leonard, M. (2005) *Athens in Paris: Ancient Greece and the Political in Post-War Paris*, Oxford.

Leonard, M. (forthcoming) *Socrates and the Jews: Hellenism and Hebraism from Moses Mendelssohn to Sigmund Freud*, Chicago.

Lesky, A. (1966a) *Gesammelte Schriften*, Berne.

Lesky, A. (1966b) *A History of Greek Literature*, trans J. Willis and C. de Heer, London.

Lessing, G.E. (1769) *Hamburgische Dramaturgie*, Halle.

Lesure, F. (1984) *Querelles des Gluckistes et des Picinistes*, 2 vols, Geneva.

Letters, F. (1953) *The Life and Work of Sophocles*, London and New York.

Levine, D. (2003) "Sophocles *Philoctetes* and *Odyssey* 9: Odysseus vs. the Cave Man", *Scholia* 12: 3–26.

[Lewes, G.H.] (1845a) "Antigone and its critics", *Foreign Quarterly Review* 35: 56–74.

Lewes, G.H. (1845b) "Was Dancing an Element of the Greek Chorus", *Classical Museum* 2: 344–67.

Lincoln, B. (1999) *Theorizing Myth: Narrative, Ideology and Scholarship*, Chicago.

Lloyd-Jones, H. and Wilson, N. (1990) *Sophoclea: Studies on the Text of Sophocles*, Oxford.

Long, A. (1968) *Language and Thought in Sophocles*, London.

Lonzi, C. (1970) *Sputiamo su Hegel*, Milan.

Loraux, N. (1981) *L'Invention d'Athènes*, Paris.

Lowe, N. (1996) "Tragic and Homeric Ironies", in Sile ed (1996): 521–33.

Lupner, D. and Vandiver, E. (2011) "Yankee She-Men and Octaroon Electra: Basil Lanneau Gildersleeve on Slavery, Race and Abolition", in Hall, Alston and McConnell eds (2011): 319–52.

Lurje, M. (2004) *Die Suche nach der Schuld: Sophokles' Oedipus Rex, Aristotles' Poetik und das Tragödienverständnis der Neuzeit*, Leipzig.

Maas, P. (1962) *Greek Metre*, trans H. Lloyd-Jones, Oxford.

MacCabe, C. ed (1982) *James Joyce: New Perspectives*, Brighton and Bloomington.

McCarthy, L. (1933) *Myself and Friends*, London.

McDonald, M. (2001) *Sing Sorrow: Classics, History and Heroines in Opera*, Westport.

McGann, J. (1991) *The Textual Condition*, Princeton, NJ.

McGlew, J. (2002) *Citizens on Stage: Comedy and Political Culture in the Athenian Democracy*, Ann Arbor, MI.

MacGregor, M. (1926) *Leaves of Hellas: Essays on Some Aspects of Greek Literature*, London.

Macintosh, F. (2009) *Oedipus Tyrannus*, Cambridge.

Macintosh, F., Michelakis, P. Hall, E. and Taplin, O. eds (2005) *Agamemnon in Performance 458 BC to AD 2004*, Oxford.

McLellan, D. (1969) *The Young Hegelians and Karl Marx*, London.

Macleod, L. (2001) *Dolos and Dike in Sophokles' Elektra*, Leiden.

Mahaffy, J. (1874) *Social Life in Greece from Homer to Menander*, London.

Mahaffy, J. (1883) *A History of Classical Greek Literature*, 2nd ed., 2 vols, London.

Mantziou, M. (1985) "The Palace Door in Sophocles' *Electra*", in Rybowska and Witczak eds. (1985): 189–95.

March, J. (1996) "The Chorus in Sophocles' *Electra*", in Dunn ed (1996): 65–81.

March, J. (2001) *Sophocles. Electra*, Warminster.

Marchand, S. (1996) *Down from Olympus: Archaeology and Philhellenism in Germany, 1750–1070*, Princeton, NJ.

Markantonatos, A. (2007) *Oedipus at Colonus: Sophocles, Athens and the World*, Berlin and New York.

Martindale, C. (1993) *Latin Poetry and the Hermeneutics of Reception*, Cambridge.

Martindale, C. (2005) *Latin Poetry and the Judgement of Taste*, Cambridge.

Martindale, C. (2006) "Thinking Through Reception", in Martindale and Thomas eds (2006): 1–13.

Martindale, C. and Taylor, A.B. eds (2004) *Shakespeare and the Classics*, Cambridge.

Martindale, C. and Thomas, R. eds (2006) *Classics and the Uses of Reception*, Oxford.

Marx, K. (1926) *The Eighteenth Brumaire of Louis Bonaparte*, trans E. and C. Paul, London.

Marx, P. (2006) *Max Reinhardt: vom bürgerlichen Theater zur metropolitanen Kultur*, Tübingen.

Massin, B. (1996) "From Virchow to Fischer: Physical Anthropology and "Modern Race Theories" in Wilhelmine Germany", in Stocking, G. ed (1996): 79–154.

Mastronarde, D. (1979) *Contact and Discontinuity: Some Conventions of Speech and Action on the Greek Tragic Stage*, Berkeley.

Méautis, G. (1957) *Sophocle: Essai sur le héros tragique*, Paris.

Meier, C. (1988) *Die politische Kunst der griechischen Tragödie*, Munich.

Meier, C. (1990) *The Greek Discovery of Politics*, trans D McLintock, Cambridge, MA.

Mendelssohn Bartholdy, K. (1872) *Mendelssohn and Goethe*, trans M.E. von Glehn, London.

Miller, P.A. (2008) *Post-Modern Spiritual Practices: the Construction of the Subject and the Reception of Plato in Lacan, Derrida and Foucault*, Columbia, OH.

Mills, P.J. (1987) *Women, Nature and Psyche*, New Haven, CT.

Mills, P.J. (1996) "Hegel's *Antigone*", in Mills ed (1996).

Mills, P.J. ed (1996) *Feminist Interpretations of G.W.F. Hegel*, University Park, PA.

Mitzis, P. and Tsagalis, C. eds (2010) *Allusion, Authority and Truth: Critical Perspectives on Greek Poetic and Rhetorical Praxis*, Berlin and New York.

Moggrath, D. ed (2006) *The New Hegelians: Politics and Philosophy in the Hegelian School*, Cambridge.

Momigliano, A. (1966) *Studies in Historiography*, London.

Momigliano, A. (1970) *Studies on Modern Scholarship*, ed G. Bowersock and T. Cornell, Berkeley and London.

Montiglio, S. (2000) *Silence in the Land of Logos*, Princeton, NJ.

Morshead, E. (1895) *The Ajax and Electra of Sophocles*, London.

Morrison, J. (1986) *Winckelmann and the Notion of Aesthetic Education*, Oxford.

Morrison, J. (2006) *Reading Thucydides*, Columbus, OH.

Most, G. (1998) "Karl Otfried Müller's Edition of Aeschylus' *Eumenides*", in Calder and Schlesier eds (1998): 349–73.

Most, G. ed (1999) *Commentaries=Kommentare*, Göttingen.

Most, G. ed (2002) *Disciplining Classics=Altertumswissemschaft als Beruf*, Göttingen.

Moulton, R. (1890) *The Ancient Classical Drama: A Study in Literary Evolution*, Oxford.

Muecke, D. (1969) *The Compass of Irony*, London.

Murray, G. (1905) *The Electra of Euripides*, London.

Murray, P. (1996) *Plato on Poetry*, Cambridge.

Musurillo, H. (1967) *The Light and the Darkness: Studies in the Dramatic Poetry of Sophocles*, Leiden.

Napolitano, M. (2010) "Greek Tragedy and Opera: Notes on a Marriage Manqué", in Brown and Ograjensek eds (2010): 31–46.

Nietzsche, F. (1956) *The Birth of Tragedy and the Genealogy of Morals*, trans. F. Golffing, New York.

Nietzsche, F. (1988) *Werke. Kritische Gesamtausgabe* eds, G. Colli and M. Montinari, Berlin.

Nauen, F. (1971) *Revolution, Idealism and Human Freedom: Schelling, Hölderlin and Hegel and the Crisis of Early German Idealism*, The Hague.

Nightingale, A. (1995) *Genres in Dialogue: Plato and the Construct of Philosophy*, Cambridge.

Nightingale, A. (2004) *Spectacles of Truth in Classical Greek Philosophy: Theoria in Its Cultural Context*, Cambridge.

Nooter, S. (forthcoming) *When Heroes Sing*, Cambridge.

Norwood, G. (1948) *Greek Tragedy*, 4th ed., London.

Nussbaum, M. (1986) *The Fragility of Goodness: Luck and Ethics in Greek Tragedy and Philosophy*, Cambridge.

Oakley, A. (1980) *Women Confined: Towards a Sociology of Childbirth*, Oxford.

Oakley, A. (1984) *The Captured Womb: A History of the Medical Care of Pregnant Women*, Oxford.

Ober, J. (1989) *Mass and Elite in Democratic Athens: Rhetoric, Ideology and the Power of the People*, Princeton, NJ.

Ober, J. (1999) *Political Dissent and Democratic Athens: Intellectual Critics of Popular Rule*, Princeton, NJ.

Ober, J. and Hedrick, C. eds (1996) *DEMOKRATIA: A Conversation on Democracies, Ancient and Modern*, Princeton, NJ.

Orgel, S. (1975) *The Illusion of Power: Political Theatre in the English Renaissance*. Berkeley.

Osborne, R. and Hornblower, S. eds (1994) *Ritual, Finance, Politics*, Oxford.

Ousby, I. (1988) *The Cambridge Guide to Literature in English*, Cambridge.

Paolucci, A. and Paolucci, H. (1962) *Hegel on Tragedy*, New York.

Parret, H. (1998) "Kant on Music and the Hierarchy of the Arts:": *Journal of Aesthetics and Art Criticism* 56.3: 251–64.

Patin, M. (1841–3) *Études sur les tragiques grecs, Sophocle*, Paris.

Patten, A. (1999) *Hegel on Freedom*, Oxford.

Paulin, R. (1985) *Ludwig Tieck: A Literary Biography*, Oxford.

Paulo, de C., Messina, P. and Stier, M. eds (1995) *Ambiguity in the Western Mind*, New York.

Pedrick, V. and Oberhelman, S. eds (2005) *The Soul of Tragedy: Essays on Athenian Drama*, Chicago.

Pelling, C. ed (1990) *Characterization and Individuality in Greek Literature*, Oxford.

Pembroke, S. (1965) "The Last of the Matriarchs': A study in the inscriptions of Lycia", *Journal of Economic and Social History of the Orient* 8: 217–47.

Pembroke, S. (1967) "Women in Charge: The function of alternatives in early Greek tradition and the ancient idea of matriarchy", *Journal of Warburg and Courtauld* 30: 1–35.

Peradotto, J. (1969) "Cledonomancy in the *Oresteia*", *AJP* 90: 1–21.

Pfeiffer, R. (1968) *History of Classical Scholarship*, Oxford.

Pfeiffer-Petersen, S. (1996) *Konfliktstichomyythien bei Sophokles: Funktion und Gestaltung*, Wiesbaden.

Phelan, P. (1997) *Mourning Sex: Performing Public Memories*, New York.

Pickard-Cambridge, A. (1968) *The Dramatic Festivals of Athens*, 2nd ed revised by Gould, J. and Lewis, D., Oxford.

Pillau, H. (1981) *Die fortgedachte Dissonanz: Hegels Tragödietheorie und Schillers Tragödie: Deutsche Antworten auf die französische Revolution*, Munich.

Pinkard, T. (1994) *Hegel's Phenomenology: The Sociality of Reason*, Cambridge.

Pinkard, T. (2000) *Hegel: A Biography*, Cambridge.

Pinkard, T. (2002) *German Philosophy 1760–1860: The Legacy of Idealism*, Cambridge.

Pippin, R. (1988) *Hegel's Idealism: The Satisfactions of Self-Consciousness*, Cambridge.

Pfister, M. (1991) *The Theory and Analysis of Drama*, Cambridge.

Plumptre, E. (1865) *The Tragedies of Sophocles*, London.

Plumptre, E.(1881) *Ecclesiastes, or the Preacher*, Cambridge.

Podlecki, A. (1990) "Could Women Attend the Theatre in Ancient Athens?" *AncWorld* 21: 27–43.

Poole, A. (1994) *Shakespeare and the Victorians*, London.

Potts, A. (1994) *Flesh and the Ideal: Winckelmann and the Origins of Art History*, New Haven, CT.

Prader, F. (1954) *Schiller und Sophokles*, Zurich.

Price, J. (2001) *Thucydides and Internal War*, Cambridge.

Prins, Y. (forthcoming) *Ladies' Greek*.

Pucci, P. (1982) "The *proem* of the *Odyssey*", *Arethusa* 15: 39–62.

Pucci, P. (1987) *Odysseus Polutropos*, Ithaca and London.

Pucci, P. (2003) *Sofocle. Philottete*, Milan.

Reinhardt, K. (1979) *Sophocles*, trans H. Harvey and D. Harvey, Oxford.

Renner, U. and Schmid, G.B. eds (1991) *Hugo von Hofmannsthal. Freundschaft und Begegnugen mit deutschen Zeitgenossen*, Würzburg.

Revermann, M. (2006) "The competence of audiences in fifth- and fourth-century Athens", *JHS* 126: 99–124.

Richardson, E. (2003) ' "A Conjugal Lesson" ': Robert Brough's Medea and the Discourses of Mid-Victorian Britain", *Ramus* 32: 57–84.

Riemer, P. and Zimmermann, B. eds (1998) *Der Chor im antiken und modernen Drama*, Stuttgart.

Rilke, Rainer Maria (1948) *Letters*, trans J. Greene and M. Herter Norton, New York.

Ringer, M. (1998) *Electra and the Empty Urn: Metatheater and Role Playing in Sophocles*, Chapel Hill, NC.

Ritter, J. (1982) *Hegel and the French Revolution: Essays on the* Philosophy of Right, Cambridge, MA.

Robert, W. (2010) "Antigone's Nature", *Hypatia* 25.2: 412–35.

Roberts, D. (1989) "Different Stories: Sophoclean Narrative(s) in the *Philoctetes*", *TAPA* 119: 161–76.

Robinson, D. (1969) "Topics in Sophocles' *Philoctetes*", *CQ* 19: 34–56.

Rood, T. (2004) *Thucydides: Narrative and Explanation*, New York.

Rosaldo, M. and Lamphere, L. eds (1975) *Women, Culture and Society*, Stanford.

Rose, H.J. (1934) *A Handbook of Greek Literature, From Homer to the Age of Lucian*, London and New York.

Rose, P. (1976) "Sophocles' *Philoctetes* and the teaching of the Sophists", *HSCP* 80: 49–105.

Rosen, R. and Sluiter, I. eds (2003) *Andreia: Studies in Manliness and Courage in Classical Antiquity*, Leiden.

Rousseau, J.-J. (1969) *Dictionaire de Musique*, Hildesheim.

Rudnytsky, P. (1987) *Freud and Oedipus*, New York.

Rutter, K. and Sparkes, B. eds (2000) *Word and Image in Ancient Greece*, Edinburgh.

Rybowska, J. and Witczak, K eds. (1985) *In Honorem Annae Mariae Komorincka* (Collectanea Philologica 2), Lodz.

Sandys, J. (1880) *The Bacchae of Euripides*, Cambridge.

Savage, R. (2010) "Precursors, Precedents, Pretexts: The Institution of Greco-Roman Theatre and the Development of European Opera" in Brown and Ograjensek eds (2010): 1–30.

Schelling, F. (1989) *The Philosophy of Art*, trans D. Stott, Minneapolis, MN.

Schiller, F. (1841) *The Bride of Messina: A tragedy with choruses*, trans by A. Lodge, London.

Schlegel, A. (1846) *A Course of Lectures on Dramatic Art and Literature* trans John Black, London.

Schlegel, F. (2001) *On the Study of Greek Poetry*, trans S. Barnett, Albany, NY.

Schmidt, C. ed (1997) *Felix Mendelssohn-Bartholdy Kongreß-Bericht*, Berlin.

Schmidt, D. (2001) *On Germans and Other Greeks: Tragedy and the Ethical Life*, Bloomington, IN.

Schmidt, J-U. (1973) *Sophokles. Philoktet*, Heidelberg.

Schopenhauer, A. (1958) *The World as Will and Representation*, 2 vols trans E. Payne, New York.

Schorske, C. (1980) *Fin-de-Siecle Vienna: Politics and Culture*, New York.

Schwinge, E.-R. (1968) *Die Verwendung der Stichomythie in den Dramen des Euripides*, Heidelberg.

Scott, W. (1984) *Musical Design in Aeschylean Theater*, Hanover and London.

Scott, W. (1996) *Musical Design in Sophoclean Theater*, Hanover and London.

Seaford, R. (1985) "The Destruction of Limits in Sophokles' *Elektra*", *CQ* 35: 315–23.

Seaford, R. (1987) "The Tragic Wedding", *JHS* 107: 106–30.

Seale, D. (1982) *Vision and Stagecraft in Sophocles*, Chicago.

Seaton, D. (2001) "Mendelssohn's Dramatic Music", in Seaton ed (2001): 192–204.

Seaton, D. ed (2001) *The Mendelssohn Companion*, Westport.

Sedgewick, G.G. (1935) *On Irony: Especially in Drama*, London.

Segal, C. (1966) "The *Electra* of Sophocles", *TAPA* 97: 473–545.

Segal, C. (1981) *Tragedy and Civilization: An Interpretation of Sophocles*, Cambridge, MA.

Segal, C. (1995) *Sophocles' Tragic World: Divinity, Nature, Society*, Cambridge, MA.

Seidensticker, B. (1991) "Die Stichomythie", in Jens ed (1991): 183–220.

Seidensticker, B. and Vöhler, M. eds (2006) *Gewalt und Ästhetik: Zur Gewalt und ihrer Darstellung in der griechischen Klassik*, Berlin.

Shaw, B. (1937) *London Music in 1888–1889 as Heard by Corno di Bassetto (Later Known as George Bernard Shaw) with Some Further Autobiographical Particulars*, London.

Shaw, M. (1975) "The Female Intruder: Women in Fifth-Century Drama", *CP* 70: 255–66.

Sheppard, J. (1918) "The Tragedy of Electra – According to Sophocles", *CQ* 12: 80–8.

Sheppard, J. (1920) *The Oedipus Tyrannus of Sophocles*, Cambridge.

Sheppard, J. (1927a) *The 'Electra' of Sophocles together with the first part of the 'Peace' of Aristophanes: The Greek texts, as performed at Cambridge by members of the University, 22nd-26th February 1927, together with English Verse Translations*, Cambridge.

Sheppard, J. (1927b) "*Electra* – a defence of Sophocles", *CR* 41: 2–9.

Siep, L. (1979) *Anmerkennung als Prinzip der praktischen Philosophie*, Freiburg and Munich.

Silk, M. (1996) "General Introduction", in Silk ed (1996): 1–11.

Silk, M. (1998) "'Das Urproblem der Tragödie': Notions of the Chorus in the Nineteenth Century", in Riemer and Zimmermann eds (1998): 195–226.

Silk, M. ed (1996) *Tragedy and the Tragic: Greek Tragedy and Beyond*, Oxford.

Silk, M. and Stern, J. (1981) *Nietzsche on Tragedy*, Cambridge.

Simpson, D. (1979) *Irony and Authority in Romantic Poetry*, London.

Sinclair, R. (1988) *Democracy and Participation in Athens*, Cambridge.

Sjöholm, C. (1998) "The Até of Antigone: Lacan, Heidegger and Sexual Difference", *New Formations* 35: 122–33.

Smither, H. (1977–2000) *A History of the Oratorio*, 4 vols, Chapel Hill, NC, and London.

Smither, H. (1985) "*Messiah* and Progress in Victorian England", *Early Music* 13: 339–48.

Soffer, R. (2008) *History, Historians and Conservatism in Britain and America: From the Great War to Thatcher and Reagan*, Oxford.

Sourvinou-Inwood, C. (1989) "Assumptions and the Creation of Meaning: Reading Sophocles' *Antigone*" *JHS* 109: 134–48.

Sourvinou-Inwood, C. (1990) "Sophocles' Antigone as a bad woman" in Dieteren and Kloeck eds (1990):11–38.

Stanford, W. (1963) *Sophocles Ajax*, London.

Stanford, W. and McDowell R.B. (1971) *Mahaffy: A Biography of an Anglo-Irishman*, London.

Steinberg. M. (1991) "The Incidental Politics to Mendelssohn's *Antigone*", in Todd ed (1991): 137–57.

Steiner, G. (1961) *The Death of Tragedy*, London.

Steiner, G. (1984) *Antigones*, London.

Steiner, G. (1996) "Tragedy, Pure and Simple", in Silk ed (1996): 534–46.

Stinton. T. (1976) "Notes on Greek Tragedy I", *JHS* 96: 121–45.

Stocking, G. (1987) *Victorian Anthropology*, London.

Stocking, G. ed (1996)*Volksgeist as Method and Ethic: Essays on Boasian Ethnography and the German Anthropological Tradition*, Madison,WI.

Strauss, B. (1993) *Fathers and Sons in Athens: Ideology and Society in the Era of the Peloponnesian War*, London and New York.

Stray, C. (1998) *Classics Transformed: Schools, Universities and Society in England, 1830–1960*, Oxford.

Stray, C. ed (2008) *An American in Victorian Cambridge: Charles Astor Bristed's "Five Years in an English University"*, Exeter.

Styan, J. (1982) *Max Reinhardt*, Cambridge.

Swearingen, C. Jan. (1991) *Rhetoric and Irony: Western Literacy and Western Lies*, Oxford.

Swift, L. (2010) *The Hidden Chorus: Echoes of Genre in Tragic Lyric*, Oxford.

Symonds, J.A. (1879) *Studies of the Greek Poets*, 2nd Series, London.

Szondi, P. (1961) *Versuch über das Tragische*, Frankfurt am Mein.

Szondi, P. (1986) *On Textual Understanding and Other Essays*, trans H. Mendelsohn, Manchester.

Szondi, P. (2002) *An Essay on the Tragic*, trans P. Fleming, Stanford.

Taplin, O. (1971) "Significant Actions in Sophocles' *Philoctetes*", *GRBS* 12: 25–44.

Taplin, O. (1972) "Aeschylean Silences and Silences in Aeschylus", *HSCP* 76: 57–97.

Taplin, O. (1978) *Greek Tragedy in Action*, London.

Taplin, O. (1987) "The Mapping of Sophocles' *Philoctetes*", *BICS* 34: 69–77.

Taplin, O. (1997) "Spreading the Word through Performance" in Goldhill and Osborne eds (1999): 33–57.

Tarrant, D. (1955) "Plato as Dramatist", *Journal of Hellenic Studies* 75: 82–9.

Tarrant, R. (1986) "Sophocles' *Philoctetes* 676–729", in Cropp, Fantham and Scully eds (1986): 121–134.

Taylor, M.W. (1981) *The Tyrant Slayers: The Heroic Image in Fifth-Century B.C. Athenian Art and Politics*, New York.

Temkin, E. (1999) "Driving Through: Postpartum Care During World War II", *American Journal of Public Health* 89: 587–95.

Thirlwall, C. (1833) "On the Irony of Sophocles", *Philological Museum* 2: 483–537.

Thomas, D. (2002) *Aesthetics of Opera in the Ancien Régime 1646–1785*, Cambridge.

Thomson, G. (1935) "Mystical Allusion in the *Oresteia*", *JHS* 55: 20–34.

Thomson, J.A.K. (1926) *Irony: An Historical Introduction*, London.

Tierney, M. (1937) "The Mysteries and the *Oresteia*", *JHS* 37: 11–24.

Timpanaro, S. (2002) *The Genesis of Lachmann's Method*, ed and trans G. Most, Chicago.

Todd, R. Larry, ed (1991) *Mendelssohn and His World*, Princeton.

Torrance, I. (2010) "Antigone and her Brother – What Sort of a Relationship?", in Wilmer and Zukauskaite eds (2010): 240–53.

Trubotchkin, D. (2005) "Agamemnon in Russia", in Macintosh, Michelakis, Hall, and Taplin eds (2005): 255–72.

Turner, F. (1981) *The Greek Heritage in Victorian Britain*, New Haven, CT.

Tyrrell, R. Y. (1909) *Essays on Greek Literature*, London.

Ussher, R. (1990) *Sophocles. Philoctetes*, Warminster.

van Erp Taalman Kip, A. (2006) "Words in the Context of Blindness", in de Jong and Rijksbaron eds (2006): 39–50.

Vaughan, C. (1908) *Types of Tragic Drama*, London.

Vernant, J.-P. and Vidal-Naquet, P. (1972) *Mythe et tragédie en Grèce ancienne*, Paris.

Vernant, J.-P. and Vidal-Naquet, P. (1981) *Myth and Tragedy in Ancient Greece*, trans J. Lloyd. Brighton.

Verrall, A.W. (1891) *The Student's Manual of Greek Tragedy*, London and New York.

Visser, T. (1998) *Untersuchungen zum Sophokleischen Philoktet*, Stuttgart and Leipzig.

Wagner, R. (1911) *My Life*, London.

Waldock, A. (1951) *Sophocles the Dramatist*, Cambridge.

Wardy, R. (1996) *The Birth of Rhetoric: Gorgias, Plato and their Successors*, London.

Wassmuth, C. (1868) *In Sophoclis de natura hominum doctrina multa inesse, quibus addu-camur ad doctrinam Christianam*, Kreuznach.

Webb, T. ed (1982) *English Romantic Hellenism 1700–1824*, Manchester.

Webster, T. (1970) *Sophocles. Philoctetes*, Cambridge.

Wenzel, C. (2005) *An Introduction to Kant's Aesthetics: Core Concepts and Problems*, Oxford.

West, M.L. (1982) *Greek Metre*, Oxford.

West, M.L. (1994) "Reginald Pepys Winnington-Ingram 1904–1993", *PBA* 84: 579–97.

Westcott, B.F. (1891) *Essays on the Religious Thought in the West*, London and New York.

White, H. (1973) *Metahistory: The Historical Imagination in Nineteenth-Century France*, Baltimore.

White, H. (1978) *Tropics of Discourse: Essays in Cultural Criticism*, Baltimore, MD.

Whitford, M. (1991) *Luce Irigaray: Philosopher in the Feminine*, London and New York.

Whitlock Blundell, M. (1989) *Helping Friends and Harming Enemies: A Study in Sophocles and Greek Ethics*, Cambridge.

Whitman, C. (1951) *Sophocles*, Cambridge, MA.

Wilamowitz-Moellendorff, U. von (1921) *Griechische Verskunst*, Berlin.

Wilamowitz-Moellendorff, U. von (1982) *History of Philology*, trans A. Harris, ed H. Lloyd-Jones, Baltimore, MD.

Wiles, D. (1997) *Tragedy in Athens*, Cambridge.

Wilkinson, A. (1978) *The Church of England and the First World War*, London.

Wilmer, S. and Zukkauskaite, A. eds (2010) *Interrogating Antigone in Postmodern Philosophy and Criticism*, Oxford.

Wilson, J. (1997) *The Hero and the City: An Interpretation of Sophocles' Oedipus at Colonus*, Ann Arbor, MI.

Wilson, P. (2000) *The Athenian Institution of the Khoregia: The Chorus, the City and the State*, Cambridge.

Winkler, J and Zeitlin, F. eds (1990) *Nothing to Do with Dionysus?*, Princeton, NJ.

Winnington-Ingram, A. (1940) *Fifty Years' Work in London*, London.

Winnington-Ingram, R. (1954–5) "The 'Electra' of Sophocles. Prolegomenon to an Interpretation", *PCPS* 183: 20–6.

Winnington-Ingram, R. (1980) *Sophocles: An Interpretation*, Cambridge.

Woodward, T. (1964) "*Electra* by Sophocles: The Dialectical Design I" HSCP 68: 163–205.

Woodward, T. (1965) "*Electra* by Sophocles: The Dialectical Design II" HSCP 70: 195–233.

Worman, N. (2000) "Infection in the Sentence: The Discourse of Disease in Sophocles' *Philoctetes*", *Arethusa* 33: 1–36.

Worman, N. (2002) *The Cast of Character: Style in Greek Literature*, Austin, TX.

Worthen, W. (2005) *Print and the Poetics of Modern Drama*, Cambridge.

Worthen, W. (2010) *Drama: Between Poetry and Performance*, Oxford.

Wunberg, G. (1972) *Hofmannsthal im Urteil seiner Kritiker*, Frankfurt.

Zajko, W. and Leonard, M. eds (2006) *Laughing with Medusa: Classical Myth and Feminist Thought*, Oxford.

Zeitlin, F. (1965) "The motif of the corrupted sacrifice in Aeschylus' *Oresteia*", *TAPA* 101: 645–69.

Zeitlin, F. (1997) *Playing the Other*, Chicago.

Zerilli, L. (1991) 'Machiavelli's sisters: women and the "conversation" of political theory', *Political Theory* 19: 252–75.

Zimmermann, B. (1992) *Dithyrambos: Geschichte einer Gattung*, Göttingen.

Zimmerman, A. (2001) *Anthropology and Antihumanism in Imperial Germany*, Chicago.

Zizek, S. (1989) *The Sublime Object of Ideology*, New York.

Zupancic, A. (1998) "Lacan's Heroines: Antigone and Sygne de Coufontaine", *New Formations* 35: 108–21.

{INDEX LOCORUM}

{GENERAL INDEX}